WERE YOU THERE?

POPULAR MUSIC AT MANCHESTER'S FREE TRADE HALL 1951 TO 1996

BY RICHARD LYSONS

First published in 2020

EMPIRE PUBLICATIONS

1 Newton Street, Manchester M1 1HW

ISBN: 978-1-909360-81-5

CONTENTS

FOREWORD MARCH

LEAFING THROUGH RICHARD LYSONS' THOROUGH HISTORY of popular music at the Free Trade Hall, I find it chock full of profound truths, just not ones readily apparent to its target audience. F'rinstance, it seems I saw Nana 'Bloody' Mouskouri - having been dragged there by my parents - before I saw my first pukka, parent-less rock concert, age 12, on November 15th 1972 - Slade, *Shades of Blue Orphanage*-era Thin Lizzy (the only time I saw them with Eric Bell in their Proggy pomp) and Suzi Quatro, pre-'Can The Can'?

And it seems exactly eleven weeks separate the end of one era-defining gig - *Jailbreak*-era Thin Lizzy (for a third time) and an astonishingly good Graham Parker & The Rumour - from a certain show at the Lesser Free Trade Hall: the Sex Pistols' Manchester debut, the most important gig in rock's tangled trajectory (spare me your contenders). No, I wasn't there for that one. On the other hand, my account of it (in *Anarchy In The Year Zero*) remains easily the most reliable. All others print the legend.

Nor was I at the Free Trade Hall for the second most important rock gig of 'em all (and I mean them all), even though I've lost count of the number of times I've been asked whether I was at the Dylan 'Judas' gig. I was six, for anti-Christ's sake!

However, that's another gig I've researched and written about ad infinitum (or is that nauseam?). Still, it took dear Richard to explain to me that this was the first rock gig at the FTH in six years (after the 1960 one ended in a riot, too), or that three days before His Bobness the equally challenging Ornette Coleman Trio played the hallowed hall (and to a Home Service radio audience), and no-one booed or heckled.

Of course, there are gaps in Richard's meticulously researched tome. I can find no mention anywhere of my own historic appearance on the main stage, singing Ralph Vaughan Williams' *Towards The Unknown Region*, for the rather churlish reason that I was accompanied by (okay, I was a constituent part of, if you insist) ninety-odd fellow members of the Manchester Grammar School choir. If Victoria Wood can make a film-length drama out of a bunch of school kids singing there, whither mine, I ask?

The actual performance may not have been memorable enough to warrant even a footnote to the Free Trade Hall's musical odyssey, but I still remember the excitement of being backstage at the fabled FTH, wandering its corridors. My one time behind the curtain. It wasn't the only time I was onstage, though. Like numerous others, I occasionally found that the seat I'd purchased for a show was behind the band, on the steps where the Hallé Orchestra sometimes sat. For years, I was unable to confirm these very seats were sold for that fabled Dylan '66 show, until finally Barry Feinstein, the late great photographer, showed me some of his shots of the show. Sure enough, you can see the feet of fans who had the best seats in the house for the end of the world (as we know it).

What no-one can seem to agree on was whether the sound on the evening of May 17th, 1966 was so-so or superb. Some clearly had problems with their hearing that night because one attendee wrote to the *Manchester Evening News* suggesting Dylan at one point apologised to the audience for the volume. In fact, he was telling his backing band (later, The Band) to, quote, 'play FUCKING loud!'

I don't know for sure if the sound that night was, as eye-witness Rick Sanders suggests, 'something that I'd never heard before... It was physical, rather than just listening to music.' But I do know that the sound at the FTH in the 70s, when Rock and its Mancunian headquarters were one synergetic unit, was as good as it got. And the louder the bands played - and Rainbow at the FTH still hold the award for the loudest effin' band I ever heard - the clearer the sound. It was like the venue was part of one visceral whole. Perhaps because it was.

Of the performances I saw there, many are a blur. Not because I wasn't blown away or was just wasted, but because I was spoilt by serendipity, blessed by circumstance, to have come of age when the biggest bands in the world - who were almost all British, incidentally - still played concert halls, and specifically the home of the Hallé Orchestra.

What was the best show I ever saw there? Probably Bowie with The Spiders in May 1973, the Aladdin Sane tour - the early show. After what I saw, I know not how Bowie got up and did another show. But he did. An 8 p.m. show, barely giving himself cause to pause after he left the stage and I left the building, slightly dazed, at 7.30.

In those days you could - as I did - blag one's way to the front of the queue, without a ticket. I'd spotted some fellow MGS pupils by the front door, and when the doors opened I raced up to the ticket office and said, Any returns? Fifth row, dead centre - not that I stayed there. Half way through the show two schoolgirls behind me ran to the front and I followed in their teeny-boppin' wake. From the lip of the stage, I could see David's testicles swinging in the breeze (so much for Japanese kimonos), but I mostly remember Ronson's guitar-sound and Bowie's stage presence. It was a profound experience, but it was merely one of many, in the twenty years - almost to the day - I frequented the hallowed hall. My last FTH show? Richard Thompson in 1992, when he performed the barely finished 'Bee's Wing'. I taped that one, documenting the FTH in free fall.

For four decades or more, it was a rare thing. As a venue, it was everything you would ever want - even down to its proximity to Oxford Road station, which allowed me to stay out late and get home safe when just a kid. It deserves to be memorialised, and Richard has done so by opening the door of history on Manchester's finest concert hall, then or now, reminding us that back in the day we were the many, but now are the few. Lest we forget.

Clinton Heylin

September 2020.

Anarchy In The Year Zero and *Judas: From Forest Hills To The Free Trade Hall* are both available from Route Books.

INTRODUCTION

EVEN BEFORE I ATTENDED A CONCERT AT THE FREE TRADE Hall in Manchester, I was aware of the venue from gig guides in *NME* and *Melody Maker*. It was part of the major city venue circuit imprinted upon the minds of 1970's music fans: Birmingham Town Hall; Bristol Colston Hall; Leicester De Montford Hall; Liverpool Empire; Newcastle City Hall; Sheffield City Hall; Southampton Guildhall. I must have also walked past the building on Peter Street as it was near to Manchester Central Library where my father often took me.

The first pop concert I ever attended was at the Free Trade Hall. The date was Saturday 12th February 1972. I still have the programme but not the ticket. The Strawbs headlined on their *Grave New World Tour* supported by Jonathan Kelly, a singer-songwriter, of course! A mime artist, Tony Crerar, was also on the bill. The train from my home town of Chester had been delayed and my friends and I ran from Manchester's Oxford Road Station, along Oxford Road and Peter Street to the Free Trade Hall. The support act, Jonathan Kelly, had started but we still could catch a few of his songs. Newly signed to the RCA label, Kelly had established himself as a powerful performer and, unlike so many singer-songwriters, he stood up.

During the interval I was able to purchase the official programme and wrote the Strawbs' set list on the back page during their set. Little did I know that this had been something of a Free Trade Hall tradition over the years where quite often there was even space in the official programmes to note down set lists. This is why there is such accurate documentation of many folk and jazz performers' concerts, such as Bob Dylan's 1965 solo tour, because people literally wrote down on their programmes each song title as it was performed.

This was The Strawbs' first tour after the departure of Rick Wakeman and fans were curious to see how Wakeman's replacement, Blue Weaver, would fit into the role of keyboard player. It was a brilliant concert with the band on the cusp of major success. Their acoustic guitars blended well with the Hudson-Ford rhythm section and Weaver's collection of keyboards: organ, piano and Mellotron. I am not sure if he had a Moog synthesiser with him! We sat very near the front and the sound system was clear but very loud.

Paul Morley, who is just two months older than me, also has a strong connection with the venue: "The Free Trade Hall played a big part in my past. I saw my first pop concerts there: Bolan, Bowie, Stewart, Floyd. Then I got avid and stupid and went to see everything – Fanny, Steeleye Span, Sabbath, Purple, Mott The Hoople, Wings, Quo, Nugent, Rush, Trower, Gallagher... It was the home of heavy metal, and I vividly remember the riot scenes, the carnage, the relentless stupidity of response, the enveloping Flash bang Gallop..."

Liz Naylor told John Robb about her Free Trade Hall experiences: "I saw Captain

Beefheart on my own in 1975; my mum came to pick me up after the gig! I was really young. I would feel slightly edgy at the gigs. It was great; there were all these people that you didn't see on the street. If you see footage from the time there are no freaks on the street. At the gigs I had this kind of sense of another world."

I agree with Naylor; gigs (and record shops) were the only places where one could enter the world described in the music press. Going to one's first gig was a rite of passage, absorbing oneself in an adult world of greatcoats, Newcastle Brown, cigarettes, loud music and flashing lights. This was the John Peel radio programme, *NME* and *Melody Maker* made real.

I did not realise in 1972 that most of the present Free Trade Hall building was just over twenty years old; I assumed that it had been built in the 19th century supporting the Anti-Corn Law campaign run by Richard Cobden and John Bright. Over the years I have realised the importance of the Free Trade Hall, not only in Manchester's political and social history, but also as a venue for the much-discussed Bob Dylan "Judas" gig.

I regret to say that I did not actively join the protests when the hall was threatened with closure in the 1990's. I remember being angry about its destruction but unfortunately did not visit the venue for one last time.

I wanted to discover what really happened at the Free Trade Hall over the years. Several people, even in local history circles, assumed that my main interest was either the 1966 Bob Dylan gig or the two Sex Pistols appearances at the Lesser Free Trade Hall. I have met music writers who attended these events and refer you to the specialist books available on both these artists. Terry Wyke's book *A Hall For All Seasons* is the first book to read if you want to know about the original building and the subsequent rebuilding. John H.G. Archer writes about the architecture of the Free Trade Hall in both Clare Hartwell's *Manchester* volume in the Pevsner Architectural Guides series (2001) and in *The Buildings Of England: Lancashire, Manchester And The South-East.* (2004). In the former book, there is a sad photograph of this magnificent building with a "Sold" sign on the front.

I am making no attempt to emulate the extraordinary quality and detail of *Keeper Of The Flame*, Bill Birch's book on modern jazz in Manchester. However I must single out this volume as it was both an inspiration to me at the beginning of my research and also an invaluable reference guide to a genre of music that was mostly unknown to me. I ended up triple-checking most of my information using the Free Trade Hall archives which were then in the Greater Manchester Record Office. As well as handwritten entries in a series of year by year diaries (that abruptly stop in 1988), there are tickets, programmes, posters, flyers and an exhaustive collection of financial records and contracts. Well done to the bright spark who saved all of these when the Free Trade Hall closed down. We are lucky that the hall was a civic venue and thus had a continuity that so many commercial venues lack. Is there an Odeon or Hardrock archive?

Next I ploughed through the *Manchester Evening News* from 1951 to 1996 on microfilm in the Manchester Room at Manchester City Library's temporary home on Deansgate. I also consulted the *NME* archive in the Music Library and back issues of *New Manchester Review*; *Mole Express* and *City Life* in the Local History section. Finally, I had access to a *Melody Maker* microfilm archive at the Sydney Jones Library at Liverpool University. While I was doing all this I was "distracted" by gigs at other Manchester venues – the Hardrock Concert Theatre, ABC Ardwick (later the Apollo), Palace Theatre, Opera House, Belle Vue's Kings Hall and the Odeon and started compiling lists of all those venues' events, too! Much later I was able to access the bound copies of *NME* at the wonderful British Library Reading Room at Boston Spa.

When is a gig not a gig? The *Manchester Evening News* had a full entertainment guide on Fridays, but Free Trade Hall concerts were also advertised on other days of the week. Some gigs were cancelled at very short notice, sometimes in the *Manchester Evening News* on the actual day of the concert. A Wizzard concert was allegedly stopped at the interval when singer Roy Wood lost his voice. Power cuts; lack of sales and other reasons forced some concerts to be cancelled. I have a huge list of cancelled gigs at the Free Trade Hall!

Before anyone else asks (thanks, C!), I have not attempted to list events at the Lesser Free Trade Hall. Many of these were minority events - small theatre productions and folk artists. The two Sex Pistols gigs in 1976 were very much the exception. I have omitted nearly all the classical concerts that took place at the Free Trade Hall, the exception being ones when the hall opened and when it closed, and a few events that involved celebrities such as Danny Kaye. The Hallé have their own archives.

I have also listed a sample of other events which took place at the Free Trade Hall over the years. There were regular boxing and wrestling nights, but I have included other sporting events, religious and political meetings and rallies and some trade and corporate events. As my editor says, 'Manchester is often described as a village so on that basis the Free Trade Hall was a very grand village hall'. It hosted everything from world renowned musicians and 'stars' to school speech days, degree ceremonies and children's concerts. The latter are not events you would associate with the modern day rock and pop venues in Manchester.

In order to place the Free Trade Hall in its context with the city's other major venues, I have listed the headline acts who appeared at ABC/Apollo Ardwick, Belle Vue's Kings Hall, Ardwick Hippodrome, Odeon, Opera House, Palace Theatre, G-Mex (now Manchester Central) and the Arena. These commercial venues are harder to chronicle as accurately as a civic venue such as the Free Trade Hall. I have omitted gigs at The Magic Village, Stoneground, Electric Circus, The Ritz, Internationals 1 & 2; The Royal Exchange, New Century Hall, Houldsworth Hall, Hacienda or clubs, universities or colleges (including all Academy venues).

Cities such as Manchester have to change, but readers need to remember that the Free Trade Hall was in walking (running?) distance of all central Manchester railway stations and surrounded by interesting and affordable places to eat and drink. Everything was conveniently close to each other: the Library Theatre, Odeon, Palace

Theatre, Opera House, Theatre Royal, Cornerhouse, Gallery, nightclubs and, of course, the Free Trade Hall, were all along the same spine of Quay Street, Peter Street and Oxford Road. The Opera House and Palace Theatre are happily still here, joined by the Albert Hall, which is just across the road from the Free Trade Hall in Peter Street. Live music has returned to this part of Manchester.

It is hard to overstate the importance of the Free Trade Hall in Manchester's popular music history. Sometimes, it is easier to list the biggest names who didn't appear there: Frank Sinatra; The Beatles (but Wings did!), Jimi Hendrix, Cream (although Baker, Bruce and Clapton all appeared separately) and The Clash, than those who did. A separate tome could be written just about the importance of the Free Trade Hall in civil rights and racial equality focussing on Paul Robeson, Billie Holiday, Nina Simone, Ray Charles and the scores of black blues and jazz acts and gospel singers and soul artists who appeared there over the years.

Between 1951 and 1996 pretty much every important phase of popular music was represented at the Free Trade Hall. The following will give the reader the most important names in the listings. This is by no means exhaustive and the categories are just guides. Some bands are a mix of American and British musicians (e.g. Crosby & Nash, Derek & the Dominoes; West, Bruce & Laing).

All Round British Entertainers

Shirley Bassey, Chas & Dave, Petula Clark, Russ Conway, Barbara Dickson, Gracie Fields, Rolf Harris, Mantovani, Kenneth McKellar, Andy Stewart, Frankie Vaughan, Roger Whittaker

American Blues

Eddie Boyd, Big Bill Broonzy, Rev Gary Davis, Willie Dixon, Champion Jack Dupree, Sleepy John Estes, Buddy Guy, Howlin' Wolf, Albert King, BB King, John Lee Hooker, Lightnin' Hopkins, Mississippi John Hurt, J.B.Lenoir, Otis Rush, Memphis Slim, Taj Mahal, Sonny Terry & Brownie McGhee, Big Joe Turner, T-Bone Walker, Muddy Waters, Junior Wells, Bukka White, Sonny Boy Williamson II.

American Folk

Joan Baez, Judy Collins, Rambling Jack Elliott, Julie Felix, Burl Ives, The Kingston Trio, New Lost City Ramblers, Phil Ochs, Peter, Paul & Mary, Buffy Sainte-Marie, Peggy Seeger, Pete Seeger, The Weavers.

American and Canadian Rock

Black Oak Arkansas, The Byrds, Canned Heat, Captain Beefheart, Creedence Clearwater Revival, The Doobie Brothers, J. Geils Band, Kiss, Little Feat, Love, Lynyrd Skynyrd, Mahogany Rush, Mountain, Ted Nugent, Rush, Spirit, The Tubes, Johnny Winter, Frank Zappa

American and Canadian Singer-Songwriters

Tori Amos, Leonard Cohen, Bob Dylan, Randy Edelman, Jose Feliciano, Rickie Lee Jones, Carole King, Kris Kristofferson, Rod McKuen, Don McLean, Holly Near, Tom Paxton, Dory Previn, Neil Sedaka, James Taylor

American Country

Johnny Cash, Emmylou Harris, Dr Hook, Hank Locklin, Buck Owens, Marty Robbins, Slim Whitman, Don Williams, Faron Young,

American Pop

The Beach Boys, Carpenters, The Four Freshmen, The Hi-Lo's, The KalinTwins; The Osmonds, Johnny Ray, Paul Revere & The Raiders, Frankie Valli & The Four Seasons .

American Punk & New Wave

Blondie, Mink DeVille, Devo, The Ramones, Jonathan Richman, The Runaways, Talking Heads, Television.

American Song Stylists

Tony Bennett, Harry Connick Jr, Ella Fitzgerald, Judy Garland, Billie Holiday, Johnny Mathis, Carmen McRae, Lou Rawls, Jeri Southern, Sarah Vaughan, Nancy Wilson, Andy Williams.

American Soul And Funk

Booker T. & The MGs, The Commodores, The Drifters, Roberta Flack, Isaac Hayes, Kool & The Gang, George McCrae, The Miracles, Johnny Nash, Diana Ross & The Supremes, Nina Simone, Percy Sledge, The Stylistics, The Temptations, The Three Degrees, Junior Walker And The All-Stars

British Blues

Duster Bennett, Long John Baldry, Paul Jones, John Mayall, Fleetwood Mac, Groundhogs, Ten Years After.

British Folk

Harry Boardman, The Bothy Band, Anne Briggs, Alex Campbell, Ian Campbell Folk Group, Martin Carthy & Dave Swarbrick, Clan Alba, The Corries, Donovan, Five Hand Reel, The Fivepenny Piece, Robin Hall and Jimmie McGregor, The High Level Ranters, The Oldham Tinkers, Leon Rosselson, The Spinners, Isla St Clair, Cyril Tawney, Three City Four, The Watersons, Bernard Wrigley, The Young Tradition.

British Folk Rock

Fairport Convention, Fotheringay, Incredible String Band, Jack The Lad, Lindisfarne, Magna Carta, Pentangle, Steeleye Span, The Strawbs. Richard and Linda Thompson..

British Jazz

Kenny Ball, Chris Barber, Acker Bilk, Ken Colyer, Johnny Dankworth, Tubby Hayes, Dill Jones, Cleo Laine, Humphrey Lyttleton, George Melly, Mick Mulligan, Ottilie Patterson, Ronnie Scott, Alex Welsh, Mike Westbrook, Yana.

British Pop

The Bootleg Beatles, Darts, Kiki Dee, The Dooleys, Sheena Easton, David Essex, Adam Faith, Emile Ford, Billy Fury, Gerry & The Pacemakers, The Hollies, Hot Chocolate, It Bites, The Kinks, Paul McCartney & Wings, M People, Mud, The New Seekers, The Nolans, Pilot, Cliff Richard, The Searchers, The Shadows, Showaddywaddy, Slade, Marty Wilde, Mari Wilson

British Rock

Argent, Audience, Baker Gurvitz Army, Barclay James Harvest, Black Sabbath, Edgar Broughton Band, Arthur Brown's Kingdom Come, Camel, Caravan, Curved Air, Deep Purple, Diamond Head, Dr Feelgood, East Of Eden, ELO, ELP, The Enid, The Faces, Family, Rory Gallagher, Genesis, Gentle Giant, Gong, Greenslade, Keef Hartley Band, Hawkwind, Head, Hands & Feet, Humble Pie, Jackson Heights, Jethro Tull, Judas Priest, King Crimson, Led Zeppelin, The Moody Blues, Motorhead, Nazareth, The Nice, Pink Floyd, Procol Harum, Queen, Quintessence, Rockpile, The Rolling Stones, Sensational Alex Harvey Band, Status Quo, Stone The Crows, Thin Lizzy, Traffic, Robin Trower, Uriah Heep, Van Der Graaf Generator, Darryl Way's Wolf, The Who, Yes.

British Punk & New Wave

Alternative T.V, Buzzcocks, Elvis Costello & The Attractions, Ian Dury & The Blockheads, The Police, The Sex Pistols, The Undertones.

British Singer Songwriters

Tasmin Archer, Joan Armatrading, Colin Blunstone, Roy Harper, Elton John, John Martyn, Ralph McTell, Al Stewart, Peter Sarsedt, Mike Scott, Labi Siffre, Cat Stevens, Judie Tzuke.

European Jazz – Dutch Swing

Dutch Swing College, Jan Garbarek, Stephane Grappelli, Jacques Loussier.

European Rock

Kraftwerk, Faust, Magma, Golden Earring, PFM, Scorpions. Tangerine Dream.

Glam Rock

David Bowie, The Glitter Band, Mott The Hoople, Mick Ronson, Roxy Music, Alvin Stardust, The Sweet, T.Rex, Wizzard.

Gospel And Spirituals

Marian Anderson, Andrae Crouch And The Disciples, Edwin Hawkins Singers, Larry Norman, Paul Robeson, Sister Rosetta Tharpe, Clara Ward, Sheila Walsh.

Humorists

Jack Benny, Blaster Bates, The Bonzo Dog Band, Victor Borge, Max Boyce, Jasper Carrott, Julian Clary, Billy Connolly, Jack Dee, Ken Dodd, Ben Elton, Dick Gregory, Joyce Grenfell, Lenny Henry, Sean Hughes, Eddie Izzard, Danny Kaye, Tom Lehrer, Paddy Roberts, Anna Russell, Scaffold, Alberto Y Los Trios Paranoias, Bob Williamson, Norman Wisdom, Victoria Wood.

Indian and Pakistani Music

Noor Jehan, Babla Kanchan, Nusrat Fateh Ali Khan, Ustad Imrat Khan, Ustad Vilyayat Khan, Ravi Shankar.

Irish Folk

Dominic Behan, Mary Black, The Chieftains, The Clancy Brothers, De Danaan, The Dubliners, Foster & Allan, The Fureys, The Johnstons, The McPeake Family, Christy Moore, Noel Murphy, Mary O'Hara, Planxty, The Wolfetones.

Jazz Rock

Jack Bruce, Chicago, Colosseum, If, The Mahavishnu Orchestra, Manfred Mann Chapter Three, Soft Machine.

Manchester Bands

A Certain Ratio, The Chameleons, Distant Cousins, The Fall, Happy Mondays, James, Joy Division, The Membranes, Simply Red, The Smiths.

Modern American Jazz

Count Basie, Dave Brubeck, Chick Corea, Ornette Coleman, Miles Davis, Duke Ellington, Erroll Garner, Dizzy Gillespie, Lionel Hampton, Herbie Hancock, Woody Herman, Keith Jarrett, Stan Kenton, Roland Kirk, Branford Marsalis, Thelonious Monk, The Modern Jazz Quartet, Oscar Peterson, Buddy Rich.

New Orleans Jazz

Louis Armstrong, George Lewis, Kid Ory.

Rock 'n' Roll

Freddie Bell & The Bell Boys, Chuck Berry, Gary "US" Bonds, Freddy Cannon, The Everly Brothers, Jerry Lee Lewis.

Skiffle

Dickie Bishop, Beryl Brydon, Lonnie Donegan, Shirley Douglas, Chas McDevitt, Nancy Whiskey.

Swing And Dance Bands

Tommy Dorsey, Ted Heath, Harry James, Syd Lawrence, Glenn Miller Orchestras.

World Music Artists

Alaap, The Bhundu Boys, The Burundi Drummers, Inti Illimani, Jo'burg Hawk, Kodo Drummers, Miriam Makeba, Nana Mouskouri, Nina & Frederick, Paco Pena, Los Paraguayos, Manitas de Plata, Esther & Abi Ofarim, Osibisa, El Sali and His Spanish Dance Company, The Swingle Singers, Stomu Yamashta,

1980's And 1990's Bands

10,000 Maniacs, Aztec Camera, The Beautiful South, The Blue Nile, The Charlatans, Cowboy Junkies, Echo & the Bunnymen, Jesus And Mary Chain, Martin Stephenson and the Daintees, Suede, The Sugarcubes.

Compiling these listings has convinced me that no venue in Britain, including the Royal Albert Hall, Hammersmith Odeon and Royal Festival Hall in London can rival the Free Trade Hall for such an extraordinary range and quality of artistes. The names speak for themselves.

It has sometimes been hard to pin down the length of many tours; quite often those traditional rivals, *Melody Maker* and *NME* give different gig details. Often the record company advertisements contradict news items or gig listings. I have tried to be as accurate as possible so apologies if I have not counted a crucial gig by Steeleye Span at West Runton Pavilion in my overall totals!

I hope that this book helps to jog readers' memories about the Free Trade Hall. I want it to be a celebration of the heyday of the venue rather than a requiem for yet another historic building in central Manchester that has been destroyed. While I was writing this book, the Odeon at the top of Oxford Road was demolished. Even the Luftwaffe did not manage that!

Richard Lysons
October 2020

The Fifties

Jazz, Skiffle and early Rock 'n'Roll

1951	
Nov 16th	HALLÉ ORCHESTRA AND HALLÉ CHORUS; conductor: Sir John Barbirolli. Kathleen Ferrier (contralto).
INAUGURAL FESTIVAL OF CONCERTS	
Nov 17th	HALLÉ ORCHESTRA; conductor: Sir John Barbirolli.
Nov 18th	HALLÉ ORCHESTRA conductor: Sir John Barbirolli.
Nov 19th	HAMBURG RADIO SYMPHONY ORCHESTRA; conductor : Dr Hans Schmidt-Isserstedt
Nov 20th	HAMBURG RADIO SYMPHONY ORCHESTRA; conductor : Dr Hans Schmidt-Issersted
Nov 21st	CONCERTGEBOUW ORCHESTRA; conductor: Eduard Van Beinum
Nov 22nd	BBC SYMPHONY ORCHESTRA; conductor: Sir Malcolm Sargent. BBC Women's Chorus
Nov 23rd	CONCERTGEBOUW ORCHESTRA; conductor: Eduard Van Beinum
Nov 24th	HALLÉ ORCHESTRA; conductor: Sir John Barbirolli.
Nov 25th	HALLÉ ORCHESTRA; conductor: Sir John Barbirolli.
Dec 8th	GRAEME BELL & HIS AUSTRALIAN JAZZ BAND SUPPORT: Christie Brothers Stompers; Saints Jazz Band
Dec 12th	ART STUDENTS BALL
Dec 24th	AMBASSADORS DANCE ORCHESTRA
Dec 26th	WILF RIGBY & HIS ORCHESTRA

ON NOVEMBER 16, QUEEN ELIZABETH (LATER THE QUEEN Mother) officially opened the new Free Trade Hall, as her husband King George VI was too ill to attend. A 60-page commemorative brochure was produced for the occasion which is a fascinating record of the hall's history and rebuilding. 5000 copies of the brochure were printed. There are beautiful illustrations by John Cunliffe throughout the brochure including artists' impressions of the large hall and the rear foyer. The whole publication is detailed, optimistic and proud with descriptions of the building, its heating, lighting and sound systems. Advertisements (described as "trade announcements"!) from many Manchester institutions such as Kendals, The House Of Forsyth and *The Manchester Guardian* all contribute to the importance of this event.

The Foreword in the brochure was written by The Lord Mayor, Councillor Collingson, JP. :

"The Manchester Free Trade Hall has for decades symbolised the traditional independence of Manchester people, their loss of liberty, their tolerance and their fearless loyalty to great ideals. From the platform of the Free Trade Hall has flowed the inspiration of philosophical wisdom in the realms of political and economic theory, music, scholarship, and all those subjects stimulating and testifying to the cultural and intellectual progress of the people.

"The physical resurrection of the Free Trade Hall, after its destruction by enemy action, is, to us in Manchester, the rededication of our efforts towards the promotion of all that is good in human relationship. That spirit of Manchester which has quickened so many noble causes still burns brightly in her people . The name of Manchester shines in the realms of culture, of music and of scholarship. Her name is great in the fields of religion, politics, industry, commerce and sport. These things go together to build up a healthy and well-balanced community and all have their part in the Free Trade Hall that belongs to them all.

"We are deeply grateful to all who have helped to carry through the physical restoration of the Free Trade Hall, to the Committee of the Corporation who conceived the project, to the architect, to the engineers, and to the builders and craftsmen. All have contributed to the great work with splendid loyalty and energy.

"To mark the historic re-opening of the Hall in this Festival Year 1951, we are holding a Festival of Music. It is fitting that it should be so marked since the voice of music knows no international boundaries and bestirs no enmity. As the prestige of the Manchester Free Trade Hall stood high in the past, so in the future may its fame be undiminished. May its rich and worthy traditions be for ever upheld and the name of the Manchester Free Trade Hall be for all time associated with the peaceful advancement of life's most noble projects."

The City Architect, Leonard C. Howitt – who was also the architect for the new building - described the interior.

"In the Large Hall the total seating capacity is 2,860 for public meetings and 2,534 for orchestral concerts. The ground floor contains 1,194 designed so that they can be dissembled and stacked in chair store or re-arranged to suit any particular function. All seats are of the tip-up variety, with Dunlopillo upholstery and acoustically absorbent surfaces underneath to avoid sound reflections when unoccupied. The raking Grand Circle and Side Circles contain 880 fixed seats and above the Grand Circle is the Balcony, seating 460. The floor is of English beech, polished for dancing and normally protected by a canvas covering. The platform is arranged

in tiers to accommodate a hundred instrumentalists or seating for 300, and incorporates a piano lift from an air-conditioned store which also houses the console of the Compton Electrone organ. Provision has been made for the attachment of a fore-stage when extra platform space is needed."

The whole brochure is full of optimism and fascinating detail. Howitt's article concludes with: *"All concerned have taken pride in their association with the restoration of the great public building which has played such a prominent part in Manchester life for almost a hundred years, and which can now look forward to another century of service to the city."* The new Free Trade Hall actually lasted less than half a century.

In the last two months of 1951 Mancunians got accustomed to having "their" venue back in operation after so many years of closure and uncertainty. I have listed the first ten days with its series of classical concerts by British, Dutch and German orchestras.

Kathleen Ferrier was born in Higher Walton in Lancashire and grew up in Blackburn. She showed an early talent as a pianist, winning several amateur competitions. Ferrier did not take up singing seriously until 1937. She made her stage debut in 1946 in *The Rape of Lucretia* at Glyndebourne. Ferrier's contralto voice was very popular; her renditions of 'The Keel Row' and 'Blow The Wind Southerly' are still played and enjoyed. Sadly, Ferrier was diagnosed with cancer in March 1951 but continued performing. She died in 1953 aged only 43.

Graeme Bell was an Australian band leader, pianist and composer whose band played Dixieland jazz. They arrived in Britain in early 1948 and Bell started the Leicester Square Jazz club in London playing music specifically for dancing. This very popular club tended to divide the jazz community, some of whom thought that dancing to jazz was rather frivolous. Bell's Free Trade Hall appearance was the penultimate date on a British tour of many one-nighters.

Wilf Rigby was a band leader who hailed from Warrington. His orchestra won a *Melody Maker* Big Band Competition and regularly played in the north west at such venues as the Parr Hall, Warrington. Rigby married the orchestra's singer, Joan Plant in 1959.

At Belle Vue, Josh White's two appearances were some of the first major concerts by a solo blues/folk performer in Britain. White had moved to London at the start of the decade and was later given his own TV series by Granada. The Hippodrome in Ardwick Green featured a variety of jazz and dance bands.

Other events at the Free Trade Hall

December 2nd – British Soviet Friendship Society

Elsewhere (Headliners Only)

Belle Vue (Kings Hall) – Josh White.

Hippodrome – Graeme Bell's Australian Jazz Band, Billy Cotton & His Band, Dr Crock and His Crackpots, Deep River Boys, Ted Heath and His Music, Joe Loss, Ivor Mairants with Jazz Academy, Sid Philips & His Band, The Squadronaires, Hedley Ward Trio, Eric Winstone Orchestra.

1952		
Feb 5th	DON COSSACK CHORUS AND DANCERS	
Feb 8th	*OLD TYME BALL* - Harry Davidson's Band	
March 22nd	MICK MULLIGAN AND HIS MAGNOLIA JAZZ BAND AND THE GEORGE MELLY TRIO	*Kae Allan And His Orchestra; Eric Silk And His Southern Jazz Band; The Saints Jazz Band; John Harper (compère)*
March 25th	*DANCE AND FLOOR SHOW* – Larry Gordon Girls; Bob Grey; Gladys Church; The Master Singers; Billy Butler's Orchestra	
April 8th	*'BEHIND THE LINES IN OCCUPIED FRANCE'* with Captain Peter Churchill & Mrs Peter Churchill GC (Odette)	
April 19th	*THE 1952 JAZZ CAVALCADE STAR PARADE* Charles Galbraith And His Jazz Stompers; The Gallion Jazz Band; Cy Laurie And His Jazz Four; Bryan Burn's Boogie Bouncers; Michael Black (compère)	
May 3rd	HUMPHREY LYTTELTON AND HIS BAND	*The Saints Jazz Band; Merseysippi Jazz Band*
Sept 23rd	THE JUBILEE SINGERS - Negro spirituals	
Oct 10th	BILLY BUTLER BAND; John Forde; Rita Williams; Daisy May and Saveen; Henry Locke; Edward Clifford (piano)	
Oct 11th	MARIAN ANDERSON – Negro Spirituals	
Oct 25th	*JAZZ BAND BALL* with Jay Leslie's Broadcasting Band	*The Pete Fenton Orchestra*
Nov 25th	*JAZZ BAND BALL* with Jay Leslie's Broadcasting Band; The Pete Fenton Orchestra; Jolson Sings Again - Finalists	
Dec 24th	*CHRISTMAS EVE CARNIVAL* with Nat Temple And His Orchestra	
Dec 26th	*BOXING NIGHT CARNIVAL* with Vic Lewis And His Orchestra	

This was the first full year that the new Free Trade Hall was open. There were a few variety shows and jazz concerts with first appearances by Humphrey Lyttelton, George Melly and Mick Mulligan. All these would become Free Trade Hall regulars over the years.

The Don Cossack Chorus was a men's chorus of exiled Cossacks who were founded by Serge Jaroff in 1921. In 1930 they travelled to the USA where they were granted US citizenship six years later. Jaroff conducted the choir for sixty years.

Harry Davidson was an orchestra leader who played piano, violin and cello. His *Those Were The Days* BBC radio programme ran for almost 30 years.

Mick Mulligan was an Armstrong-style trumpeter who had led a band since 1947. He and his band would appear eleven times at the Free Trade Hall over the next decade. Mulligan's band featured Ian Christie on clarinet and Frank Parr on trombone.

George Melly would appear sixteen times at the Free Trade Hall, first with Mick Mulligan's Band and later, in the 1970's, with John Chilton's Footwarmers. In the 1950's Melly was a keen young jazz singer and his book, *Owning Up* describes this time in hilarious and often obscene detail. In the 1960's Melly developed a new career as a journalist, writing for *The Observer* about the arts. Another book of his, *Revolt Into Style,* was written at this time and was one of the first books to treat pop both seriously and unpretentiously.

Larry Gordon's (Empire) Girls had appeared in a show in 1951 called *Do You Remember? - Eight Music Hall Names That Will Live Forever* starring George Robey. **Gladys Church** was known as 'The Whistling Songstress', otherwise known as a "siffleur", and had performed in British music halls. She was a big influence on a younger soon-to-be famous whistler, Ronnie Ronalde.

The charity lecture entitled *Behind The Lines In Occupied France* given by **Captain Peter Churchill** and his wife **Odette** must have been a fascinating evening. Mrs Churchill was awarded the George Cross for her bravery during the war and was memorably portrayed by Anna Neagle in the film *Odette.*

The 1952 Jazz Cavalcade Star Parade promised 'Four bands in a Festival of Jazz, New Orleans & Dixieland Music.' Both **Charles Galbraith** and **The Gallion Jazz Band** would also appear in the *Big Jazz Show* at the Royal Albert Hall in June of this year alongside fifteen other jazz bands, as part of a series of shows called *Mammoth Concerts*. **Bryan Burns Boogie Bouncers** were led by 'keyboard wizard' Bryan Burns. The tour consisted of six dates covering the north of England and Scotland.

Cy Laurie & His Jazz Band would appear four times at the Free Trade Hall. Clarinettist Laurie was a leading figure in post-war trad jazz in Britain and had led his own band since the late 1940's. He organised "all night raves" and enjoyed great success at his Windmill Street club in London.

Humphrey Lyttelton was a fine trumpet player and his musical career started after the war with George Webb's Dixielanders. He soon led his own band and became

Britian's leading jazz revivalist. Later, Lyttelton broadened his repertoire and included saxophonists in his line-up. He appeared seven times at the Free Trade Hall between 1952 and 1963 and popped up again nearly a quarter of a century later in 1987.

The Jubilee Singers were a long running African-American gospel singing group who popularised the Negro spiritual tradition, especially amongst white audiences. They were based at Fisk University in Nashville and their repertoire included 'Swing Low, Sweet Chariot'. The group had first toured Britain in 1873!

Marian Anderson was an American contralto singer who was an important figure in the struggle against racial prejudice. In 1939 the Daughters of the American Revolution refused permission for Anderson to sing to an integrated audience at Constitution Hall. This led to her performing for President Roosevelt on Easter Sunday in the same year on the steps of the Lincoln Memorial in Washington in front of 75,000 people. Anderson had toured Europe since the early 1930's, singing arias from opera, spirituals and popular songs. She later sang at President Kennedy's Inauguration.

Rita Williams led her own group who recorded extensively as backing singers for such names as Geoff Love, Shirley Bassey, Billy Cotton and Victor Silvester.

Saveen (born Albert Edward Langford) was an extraordinary ventriloquist who used both a live dog and puppets as part of his act. **Daisy May** was his most popular character, a tiny schoolgirl doll. Saveen appeared on television in the 1950's and 1960's, always immaculately dressed in top hat and tails. There are clips on YouTube of him, including a comeback appearance on Paul Daniels' television show shortly before Saveen's death in 1994.

Jay Leslie's Broadcasting Band - as the name suggests- were one of dozens of dance bands who would play on the BBC's Light Programme (the forerunner of Radio 2).

Nat Temple was from East London and had formed his own band in 1944, after playing with the likes of Ambrose, Geraldo and Lew Stone. By 1950 Temple's orchestra was broadcasting regularly and was a regular on "Music While You Work" into the mid-1960's.

Vic Lewis was a British jazz guitarist and bandleader. He had worked with George Shearing, Stephane Grappelli, Ted Heath and Jack Parnell. Lewis later formed his own ensemble in 1946 initially playing swing but subsequently followed the style of Stan Kenton.

Across the city, the Hippodrome in Ardwick Green was the main live music venue, while the King's Hall in Belle Vue hosted a small number of concerts. Yma Sumac was a Peruvian soprano with a four-octave range who had a very successful career. Laurel & Hardy appeared for a week at the Palace Theatre, staying nearby at the Midland Hotel.

Other events at the Free Trade Hall

February 9th – Vienna Boys Choir
March 15th – Boxing Finals
October 18th – Luton Girls Choir and the Irish Guards Band

Elsewhere (Headliners Only):

Belle Vue (Kings Hall)- Cab Calloway, Gracie Fields, Lena Horne, Burl Ives, Radio Jazz Carnival, Yma Sumac.

Hippodrome- Kenny Baker & His Rhythm Group, Big Bill Broonzy, Tito Burns Sextet, Christy Boys Stompers, Johnny Dankworth Seven, Kenny Graham's Afro-Cubists, Ted Heath And His Music, Bill Johnson, Pat Kirkwood, Vic Lewis Orchestra, Tessie O'Shea, Jack Parnell's Music Makers, Donald Peers, Ralph Sharon Sextet, Anne Shelton, Max Wall, Jimmy Young.

Palace Theatre - Laurel & Hardy.

1953		
March 16th to April 5th	*MANCHESTER CENTENARY FESTIVAL*	
March 16th	LARRY ADLER with the Hallé Orchestra and Sir John Barbirolli	
August 22nd	NATIONAL BAND OF NEW ZEALAND with Maori Songs led by Frederick Renata Heketoro	
October 9th	BILLY BUTLER ORCHESTRA	*Jon Pertwee; John McHugh; Ross and Howitt; Billy Maynard*
December 24th	NAT TEMPLE AND HIS ORCHESTRA	*Dean Raymond and Roy Garnett featuring Ronnie Chamberlain and Tubby Hayes*
December 26th	VIC LEWIS AND HIS ORCHESTRA	
December 31st	JACK PARNELL AND HIS ORCHESTRA	

THERE WERE FEW POPULAR MUSIC EVENTS THIS YEAR. **Larry Adler,** the virtuoso harmonica player, guested with the Hallé Orchestra. Adler, a victim of McCarthyism, moved to Europe in the early 1950's escaping his blacklisting in the U.S.A. He had appeared at the Proms in London in 1952 performing a piece specially written by Ralph Vaughan Williams. Adler was largely responsible for making the chromatic harmonica a respected musical instrument. His clever score for the film *Genevieve* was to follow.

The National Band of New Zealand was formed in 1953 and played at Coronation events in London, including a Royal Garden Party at Buckingham Palace.

Jack Parnell was a drummer and musical director. He was co-leader of the Vic Lewis- Jack Parnell Jazzmen and worked with Ted Heath for seven years. Parnell later worked at ATV for a quarter of a century leading the staff orchestra and provided the music for such programmes as *The Benny Hill Show* and *The Muppets*.

Over at the Hippodrome in Ardwick there were orchestras, comedians, solo singers and seven nights of Laurel & Hardy on their final British tour. At the Palace Theatre Frank Sinatra played for six nights in July; Sinatra never appeared at the Free Trade Hall - his loss!

Other Events at the Free Trade Hall:

March 14th – Holiday Fellowship Reunion Dance
April 13th – Table Tennis Tournament
June 13th – Assemblies of God Youth Rally
September 26th – Everest Expedition Climbers Lecture
December 12th – Weight Lifting Display

Elsewhere (Headliners Only) :

Belle Vue (Kings Hall) – Bob Hope, Frankie Laine, Mantovani, Jack Parnell, Johnny Ray, Sarah Vaughan.

Hippodrome – Tito Burns And His Band, Billy Daniels, Leslie Ferguson, Laurel & Hardy, Vic Lewis & His Orchestra, Humphrey Lyttleton Orchestra, The Merry Macs, Tessie O'Shea, Jack Parnell Orchestra, Frank Randle, Ronnie Ronalde, Ronnie Scott Orchestra, Harry Secombe, David Whitfield, Teddy Wilson.

Palace Theatre- Billy Cotton Band, Burl Ives, Guy Mitchell, Frank Sinatra.

1954		
Feb 12th	BILLIE HOLIDAY with Carl Drinkard (piano)	*Don Rendell Jazz Six; Jasper Livesey And His Band; Bobby Micklebrough's Bobcats; Tony Kinsey Trio; Tommy Whittle; Ronnie Ross and Dick Hawdon*
March 16th	GAELIC LEAGUE CONCERT	
April 16th	OBERKIRCHEN CHILDREN'S CHOIR	
October 9th	YUGOSLAV NATIONAL DANCERS AND SINGERS	
October 15th	DILL JONES; CHRIS BARBER'S JAZZ BAND with Monty Sunshine; Lonnie Donegan & The Skiffle Group; Alex Welsh's Dixielanders; George Melly; Cy Laurie Band with Al Fairweather	

THIS YEAR SAW THE BRITISH DEBUT OF THE LEGENDARY **Billie Holiday** in February as she started her short UK tour in Manchester. Tickets were priced from 3/6 to 8/6 and were available from Forsyths music shop or "hall on night." Bill Birch's *Keeper Of The Flame* includes some wonderful photographs. Billie stayed at the Midland Hotel, a few yards down Peter Street, accompanied by her husband and manager Louis McKay.

Max Jones, jazz correspondent of *Melody Maker* was there: *"At Manchester she was very happy until the microphone gave way after 'Blue Moon', her eighth number. She then gave us 'My Man' unaided by electricity (most wonderful it sounded from the front rows) then retired without doing the encores - 'I Only Have Eyes For You' and 'Strange Fruit.'*

"All the same it had been a fine concert. (Carl) Drinkard, Tony Kinsey, Sammy Stokes and - for certain numbers - trumpeter Dickie Hawdon and tenormen Don Rendell, Tommy Whittle and Ronnie Ross, gave Billie what I thought was the best support she got on her short tour.

"And Billie's own performance moved me more than any of her others- perhaps because it was my first Billie Holiday concert,perhaps because the hall was good, the crowd dead silent, and I was positioned to catch every vocal inflection and every gesture of face, hand and shoulder.."

Bill Birch's account is slightly different: *"Unexpected circumstances however turned the evening into a disaster when the stage amplification system cut out twice when (Billie) was singing... the lead microphone crackled and fizzed out completely soon into her third song and, visibly shaken, (she) left the stage..*

"Hopes were raised fifteen or so minutes later when the Rendell Six reappeared to play a fourth number that went off without a hitch. By all accounts, Ms Holiday needed considerable persuasion to return on stage and then, soon into her second song the system failed a second time...

"Perplexed and bewildered she refused to reappear a third time though the fault had been

detected and repaired. The building's main lift had been creating an electric crackle that radiated throughout the wiring in the main auditorium."

Billie Holiday played just two other concert dates on this British tour : Nottingham Astoria and the Royal Albert Hall. After the London concert, Holiday appeared at the Flamingo Club in Leicester Square. She had already played all over Europe - Scandanavia, Germany, the Low Countries, Switzerland and France.

The Oberkirchen Children's Choir from Germany had an international hit with 'The Happy Wanderer' which had stayed in the UK singles charts for 26 weeks! They had toured extensively and performed the previous year at the Eisteddfod in Llangollen, winning a prize.

October 15th saw a packed line-up of British jazz and skiffle acts. **Dill Jones** was a Welsh pianist who specialised in the jazz stride style. He appeared nine times at the Free Trade Hall in the next five years. Later, Jones worked on the Queen Mary liner and moved to New York in the early 1960's.

Chris Barber had studied trombone and double bass at the Guildhall School Of Music and worked with Ken Colyer before starting his own band. In July of this year Barber and his band recorded an album called *New Orleans Joy* (Decca 1954). The album contained two skiffle songs - 'Rock Island Line' and 'John Henry' alongside the jazz numbers. Banjo player **Lonnie Donegan** sang and played guitar on the skiffle songs, accompanied by Barber on double bass and Beryl Bryden on washboard.

Alex Welsh was a Scottish jazz singer, cornet and trumpet player who had moved down to London. His Chicago style jazz band played clubs and concerts, as well as broadcasting on the radio and recording several British jazz classics. Welsh would return to the Free Trade Hall nearly twenty years later supporting George Melly.

Other Events at the Free Trade Hall:

January 30th – Co-op Holiday Association Dance
March 26th – Manchester Ship Canal Company Dinner Dance
April 14th – Parade Of British Cotton Fashion
October 30th & November 1st – Vienna Boys Choir
December 3rd to 4th – Daily Worker Bazaar

Elsewhere (Headliners Only):

Belle Vue (Kings Hall) – Nat "King" Cole and the Johnny Dankworth Orchestra, Frankie Laine, Humphrey Lyttleton, Yma Sumac.

Hippodrome – Kenny Baker Quartet, Chris Barber Band, Billy Cotton And His Band, Johnny Dankworth Orchestra, Jazz Unlimited, Teddy Johnson & Pearl Carr, Joe Loss Orchestra, Al Martino, Guy Mitchell, Jack Parnell Orchestra, Sid Phillips And His Band, Lita Roza, Ronnie Scott Orchestra, Dickie Valentine, Frankie Vaughan.

Palace Theatre – Max Bygraves, Billy Daniels, Billy Eckstine, Betty Garrett, Lena Horne, Ken MacKintosh Orchestra, Al Martino, Guy Mitchell, Larry Parks.

1955	
Jan 21st	TED HEATH AND HIS MUSIC
March 14th	GAELIC CONCERT
April 5th	OBERKIRCHEN CHILDREN'S CHOIR
May 7th	TED HEATH AND HIS MUSIC
October 15th	*SIXTH INTERNATIONAL FESTIVAL OF UNITED NATIONS FOLK DANCE*

THIS WAS ANOTHER QUIET YEAR FOR POPULAR MUSIC BUT the Free Trade Hall was busy with lectures; dances; darts matches, wrestling, school speech days, choirs and numerous other events. In December alone there were no less than eight dances booked for organisations from Kelloggs to the Royal Technical College.

Ted Heath and his orchestra went on to play several times at the Free Trade Hall over the next decade. After working with such names as Firman, Hylton, Ambrose and Geraldo, Heath started his own band in 1944 and later played Sunday concerts at the London Palladium for eight years. He was Britain's most famous bandleader and toured the USA regularly.

At Belle Vue, Ella Fitzgerald and Oscar Peterson attracted large crowds; both later often appeared at the Free Trade Hall. The British Musicians Union ban on foreign musicians still prevented audiences seeing American bands and orchestras and was not lifted until October. This move would have a huge positive effect on the Free Trade Hall's reputation as a popular music venue.

Other Events at the Free Trade Hall:

January 18th – Faraday Lecture
March 5th – Rag Show – Manchester University Union
April 16th – Sons Of Temperance Friendly Society Dinner Dance
April 30th – Wrestling Contest
May 11th – Evening Chronicle Cookery Forum
August 22nd – Salt Lake Mormon Tabernacle Choir
October 31st – Hairdressing Demonstration – all day

Elsewhere (Headliners Only):

Belle Vue (Kings Hall) -Ella Fitzgerald, Oscar Peterson.

Hippodrome – Kenny Baker's Dozen, Chris Barber Band, Ivy Benson Band, Big Bill Broonzy, Tito Burns Sextet, Tony Crombie Orchestra, Johnny Dankworth Orchestra, Ray Ellington Quartet, Ronnie Hilton, Tubby Hayes Orchestra, Vic Lewis Orchestra, Humphrey Lyttleton, Al Martino, George Melly, Mick Mulligan and British Modern All Stars, Ronnie Scott Orchestra, David Whitfield, Tommy Whittle Quintet.

Palace Theatre - The Crew Cuts, Johnnie Ray.

1956		
March 12th	*DAILY EXPRESS 'RHYTHM WITH THE STARS'* Eddie Calvert; George Melly; Ronnie Scott And His New Orchestra; Dill Jones; Hedley Ward Trio; Chris Barber And His Band; Ottilie Patterson; Lonnie Donegan Skiffle Group; Marie Benson.	
March 16th	*GAELIC LEAGUE CONCERT*	
May 31st	Norman George; Alan Clive; The Kentones; Bob Monkhouse; Eve Boswell; Mickey Keirby And His Kosher Jammers	
June 17th	The Saints; The Zenith Six; Martin Boland's Skiffle; Mick Mulligan And His Band with George Melly; Ronnie Scott; Hector Gedall Trio; Karen Hagen Trio	
Sept 16th	HUMPHREY LYTTELTON AND HIS BAND	*Bruce Turner; Johnny Picard*
Oct 13th	SEVENTH FOLK DANCE INTERNATIONAL FESTIVAL	
Oct 20th	*DAILY EXPRESS 'RHYTHM WITH THE STARS'* Jill Day; Hedley Ward Trio; Mick Mulligan Band; Kenny Baker; Dill Jones; The Kirchin Band; Keith Christie; Janie Marden; Ronnie Scott	
Nov 11th	ALL STAR TRADITIONAL GROUP	*The Saints; White Eagle Jazz Band; Martin Boland's Skiffle with Mary Downer; All Star Modern & Mainstream Session with Joe Harriott; Trond Svennevig and his New Band*
Nov 17th	SOVIET TV STARS Dancers; Acrobats; Singers; Instrumentalists	
Nov 26th	The Nixa Label presents *CAVALCADE OF JAZZ* with Chris Barber's Jazz Band with Ottilie Patterson	*The Dick Bishop Skiffle Group; The Bertie King/ Dill Jones Trio; Jimmy Skidmore*

RETURN VISITS BY CHRIS BARBER, GEORGE MELLY, LONNIE Donegan and Ronnie Scott marked 1956 while The *Daily Express* sponsored two *Rhythm With The Stars* events in March and October with star-studded bills. October's tour went to six northern venues.

George Melly: *"I myself began, as the years went by, to appear quite frequently outside the band, not only on the radio, but as a solo compère and performer. One of the most profitable and enjoyable of these extra-Mulligan jobs was for Paddy McKiernan who organised for three years a show called 'Rhythm Of The Stars', designed to expand the sales of the Daily Express in the north. The first year I compèred and sang a spot with Chris Barber. The second I just sang with Mick, but in my own spot and billed as a solo artist; the third year I compèred again and sang with Mick, but what seemed to me absolutely fabulous was what I got paid. A hundred pounds ! I had never earned so much in my life in such a short period.*

"The show consisted of a mixed bill, part jazz, part pop. The first year the star was Eddie Calvert. We opened in Manchester, the hall was packed with Chris Barber fans, and Eddie got the bird. he came down to the dressing room in a very bad temper and began to bawl out Paddy (McKiernan) while he changed. Every time he swore, his father, who was sitting there in a cap, said 'Now, now, Eddie,' in a mild voice.

In the middle of his diatribe he suddenly turned on me. 'It's all right for you,' he shouted, 'you're only an amateur.' After so long on the road I took exception to this, and told him I had been singing 'Frankie and Johnny' - the number had gone down particularly well - for over eight years almost every night.

'Was that you falling down?' snapped Eddie. I said it was.

'You'll get cancer, you know,' he spat out, and returned to the attack."

Chris Barber and his Band, with **Ottilie Patterson** on vocals, appeared at the March concert. Patterson had made her debut with Barber's band on January 9th in 1955 at London's Royal Festival Hall. She eventually married Barber and sang with him for many years. Patterson was a white blues singer with a rare power and authenticity. By November Barber was headlining his own concert and became an established performer, easily outlasting his trad jazz peers with his skilful adaptation of his sound. He was a regular at the Free Trade Hall over the next 40 years. In the meantime 'Rock Island Line' had been released as a single in November 1955 and entered the singles charts in January 1956, eventually reaching No. 11. This kickstarted the skiffle boom and Lonnie Donegan's career. He was signed to a solo contract with the Nixa label and visited the USA twice.

Preston born **Eddie Calvert** was known as 'The Man With The Golden Trumpet' and had had two No. 1 hit singles with 'Oh Mein Papa' and 'Cherry Pink And Apple Blossom White' - the first British instrumentalist to do so.

Marie Benson was an Australian singer who came to Britain in 1948. She was one of the original members of The Stargazers, a vocal group formed by Cliff Adams and Ronnie Milne.

The event on May 31st was organised by the New Manchester Jewish Sportsmen's Committee. Standing out alongside the less familiar names is one **Bob Monkhouse**.

Monkhouse was at the beginning of his career, although he had been writing for such children's comics as *The Beano* and *Dandy*. In 1958 he would appear in *Carry On Sergeant*, the first film in the long-running series.

Karen Hagen (born Hannelore Wienberg) was a German pianist who had played around Manchester with Ronnie Scott. She later formed a twelve-piece dance band and played at the Regional Finals of the *Melody Maker* 1957 National Championship at Belle Vue.

Jill Day became the main vocalist in the Geraldo Orchestra in 1954 when they topped the bill at the London Palladium. She co-starred in the West End production of *The Talk Of The Town* and appeared in British films.

Kenny Baker was a trumpet player with few equals; his "faultless technique" gave him a fifty year career. He had played lead trumpet for Ted Heath and then led his own Baker's Dozen band. Baker played the trumpet in the film *Genevieve* when actress Kay Kendall was miming. Three decades later, Baker provided the music for ITV's *The Beiderbeck Trilogy*.

The Cavalcade Of Jazz concert in November was described in *Melody Maker:* "For the first time, a recording company is to sponsor a jazz package tour to showcase its own artists." The Free Trade Hall concert was the second night of an eight day tour.

Over at Belle Vue, the Stan Kenton Orchestra made two appearances, benefiting from the lifting of the Musicians Union ban on American bands. The second date was added because of demand for tickets. Lionel Hampton also played Belle Vue in November where there was stage invasion by some fans! After this incident, the Free Trade Hall became the favoured Manchester venue for jazz artists for the next fifteen years. The London based promoter, Harold Davison made the Free Trade Hall a regular venue for the tours he organised.

Other Events at the Free Trade Hall:

January 9th – Hallé Ball – Bert Hornby And His Orchestra
February 4th – Ramblers Association Dance
March 26th – Public Meeting with Malcolm Muggeridge
July 1st –Young Christian Workers Rally
Nov 18th - Mosley Speaks!
November 25th – Printers Pension, Almhouse, Orphan Asylum Corporation Brass Band Concert

Elsewhere (Headliners Only)

Belle Vue (Kings Hall): Louis Armstrong, Lionel Hampton, Stan Kenton, Slim Whitman.

Hippodrome: Kenny Baker, Chris Barber Band, Art Baxter's Rock 'N' RollSinners, Eddie Calvert, Ken Colyer, Billy Cotton And His Band, Johnny Dankworth Orchestra, Ray Ellington Quartet, Tony Hall's Hall Stars, The Ink Spots, Tony Kinsey Quartet, Ken Mackintosh And His Band , George Melly , Mick Mulligan And His Band, Ruby Murray, Jack Parnell Orchestra, The Saints, Ronnie Scott Quintet, Mel Torme, Alex Welsh And His Dixielanders.

Palace Theatre: Billy Daniels, Lonnie Donegan, Billy Eckstine, Al Martino, Jimmy Young.

1957		
Date	HEADLINERS	*Support*
Jan 4th	THE PAT BOONE SHOW (two houses)	*Alma Cogan; Jack Parnell And His Orchestra*
Jan 19th	TED HEATH AND HIS MUSIC (two houses)	
Feb 1st	EDDIE CONDON AND HIS ALL-STAR JAZZMEN	*Humphrey Lyttelton And His Band*
Feb 5th	LONNIE DONEGAN AND HIS SKIFFLE GROUP	*First House: The Bluenote Jazzmen; Second House: The Saints; Eddie Manson; The International Trond Svennevig Trio*
Feb 17th	GEORGE MELLY; Mick Mulligan And His Band White Eagle Jazz Band	*Beryl Bryden; Tommy Whittle; Trond Svennevig Trio; Paul Beattie Skiffle; Dave Usden*
Feb 22nd	BIG BILL BROONZY; 'BROTHER' JOHN SELLERS	*The Trond Svennevig Group; The Alpha New Orleans Brass Marching Band; Bob Barcley; The Zenith Six; Eric Batty's Jazz Aces; The Ceramic City Jazzmen*
March 16th	GAELIC LEAGUE CONCERT	
April 6th	JAZZ MATINEE: Humphrey Lyttelton And His Band	*The Saints*
April 24th	*DAILY EXPRESS* 'RHYTHM WITH THE STARS' Yana	*Mick Mulligan Band; Dill Jones Trio; Frank Holden; Jazz Couriers; Hedley Ward Trio; Chas McDevitt Skiffle Group; Beryl Bryden; George Melly*
April 27th	GEORGE LEWIS NEW ORLEANS JAZZ BAND	*Ken Colyer And His Band; The Skiffle; Bob Kelly Blues*
May 11th	GERRY MULLIGAN QUARTET (two houses)	*The Jazz Today Unit*
June 6th	FREDDIE BELL AND THE BELL BOYS (two houses)	*Chas McDevitt Skiffle Group with Nancy Whiskey; Terry Lightfoot Jazzmen; Yolanda*

June 16th	MIDSUMMER SPECIAL with Kenny Baker, Mick Mulligan And His Band; George Melly	*Jimmy Jackson; Eric Batty's Jazz Aces; Paul Beattie Shuffle*
Sept 28th	JIMMY RUSHING; HUMPHREY LYTTELTON AND HIS BAND	
Oct 5th	JACK TEAGARDEN, EARL HINES ALL STARS	*Cozy Cole*
Oct 14th	DAILY EXPRESS RHYTHM WITH THE STARS with Yana and Ronnie Scott/ Tubby Hayes Jazz Couriers	*Hedley Ward Trio; Frank Holder with the Dill Jones Trio; Chas McDevitt*
Nov 17th	TONY KINSEY QUARTET	*George Melly with Mick Mulligan And His Band; Dill Jones Trio;, Beryl Bryden; Zenith Six; Malcolm Gracie; Sheila Poyser; Jerry Dawson (compère)*
Nov 26th	DON RENDELL JAZZ SIX	*The Saints; David Ellis Orchestra; Jerry Dawson (compère)*
Nov 30th	TED HEATH AND HIS MUSIC	
Dec 9th	SISTER ROSETTA THARPE with Chris Barber's Jazz Band with Ottilie Patterson	
Dec 14th	MODERN JAZZ QUARTET (two houses)	*Don Rendell Jazz Six*

RESTRICTIONS ON AMERICAN PERFORMERS WERE NOW relaxed and both pop names and modern jazz groups were allowed to cross the Atlantic and perform in Britain.

Pat Boone was a clean cut American singer who had hits with pale cover versions of rock 'n' roll songs by Fats Domino and Little Richard. He also sang ballads, rivalling Elvis Presley's popularity. Boone had four Top 10 singles this year. He was the first major rock 'n' roll artist to appear in Britain. Boone was undertaking a short, seven-date tour.

Eddie Condon was a guitarist/ banjoist who was based in Chicago and later moved to New York City. He encouraged racially integrated sessions, playing a sophisticated version of Dixieland jazz. Condon's name spread through his own American television programme, a best selling autobiography and his many recordings.

Lonnie Donegan "The King Of Skiffle" was at the height of his success this year. Donegan's later drift into comedy and novelty material should not obscure his importance as the inspiration for most British pop groups in the 1960's. His strongest material (such as his shamanistic version of 'Frankie And Johnny') still sounds extraordinary. Other skiffle acts such as Ken Colyer, Nancy Whiskey and Chas McDevitt also appeared at the Free Trade Hall as support acts to jazz bands.

The White Eagle Jazz Band had played at Liverpool's Cavern Club before it was officially opened. They went on to become Sunday night regulars at the Cavern. The band's leader was clarinettist Martin Boland.

Big Bill Broonzy was in his fifties when he appeared at the Free Trade Hall; he had toured Europe in 1951 to wide acclaim. This was the first solo performance by a black artist at the Free Trade Hall, paving the way for so many more in years to come. The tour started in London and went to thirteen other venues. Sadly, Broonzy suffered from throat cancer and on March 9th 1958 a benefit concert was held for him at the Coliseum Theatre in London. Broonzy died the following year.

Yana (born Pamela Guard) was from Essex and had been a hairdresser's assistant and fashion model before becoming a singer. She sang at the Pigalle restaurant in London and even had her own BBC television show in 1956. Yana later appeared on *Sunday Night At The London Palladium*. A tour with Bob Hope of American military bases also raised her profile. Inevitably, an attractive female singer such as Yana was compared to Marilyn Monroe. But, like many 1950's singing stars, she faded from view in the next decade.

Clarinettist **George Lewis's** band were probably the first American ensemble to play the Free Trade Hall; he was a big influence on such British clarinet players as Acker Bilk and Monty Sunshine. Lewis was born in New Orleans at the turn of the century and had played in a variety of bands since he was a teenager. He would return to the Free Trade Hall two years later. This concert was recorded and is still available on CD.

Gerry Mulligan was an American saxophonist, playing both baritone and soprano. He had worked as an arranger, as well as playing with Gene Krupa and Miles Davis. Mulligan's 1957 Free Trade Hall debut featured Bob Brookmeyer on trombone and piano. He would return to the venue six years later. As was often the case, the Free Trade Hall was the penultimate night of the tour, the thirteenth of fourteen dates.

In June **Freddie Bell And The Bell Boys** played the Free Trade Hall. The group had appeared in the film *Rock Around The Clock* alongside Bill Haley And The Comets. Bell was one of the first American rock 'n' roll acts to play Britain. He had already played on a package tour with Tommy Steele in May. Later in the year Bell had his only British hit, 'Giddy-Up-A Ding Dong' which reached No. 4.

Jimmy Rushing was an American blues "shouter" and pianist who had worked for Count Basie for thirteen years before going solo. He toured Britain with Humphrey Lyttleton and his powerful and versatile voice was widely admired. Dave Brubeck called Rushing "the daddy of them all " among blues singers.

Trombonist **Jack Teagarden** had played with the Paul Whiteman Orchestra in the 1930's and then started his own big band. After a few years working with Louis Armstrong, Teagarden teamed up with pianist **Earl "Fatha" Hines** for a European tour. Hines was from Pennsylvania and moved to Chicago, working with Louis Armstrong, before forming his own band. He later returned to work with Armstrong for a short time. Hines would return to the Free Trade Hall ten years later. This appearance featured former members of Louis Armstrong's All Stars band.

Tubby Hayes was a supremely talented tenor saxophone player who also excelled at the flute and vibraphone. He had played professionally since the age of fifteen and had worked with Kenny Baker, Ambrose, Vic Lewis and Jack Parnell. In 1957 Hayes formed the Jazz Couriers with Ronnie Scott. He died tragically young at the age of 37.

Tony Kinsey was a British jazz drummer and composer and a founder member of the Johnny Dankworth Seven, staying with them for two years. He later led his own small groups featuring many of Britain's best jazz musicians. Kinsey later accompanied such American visitors as Ella Fitzgerald, Oscar Peterson, Lena Horne and Sarah Vaughan.

Chris Barber introduced **Sister Rosetta Tharpe,** an American gospel singer on a twenty-date British tour. She was a unique act; playing an electric Gibson guitar and dressed in a ballgown! Luckily, blues and folk singers from America were not classified by the American Federation of Musicians as "musicians" and could join the American Guild of Variety Artists. The British Variety Artists' Federation had no problems with its American counterpart and therefore, such artists could come over to perform in Britain. An advertisement in *Melody Maker* informs us of *The Sister Rosetta Tharpe Book Of Negro Spirituals* (eighteen songs) for just three shillings and sixpence.

Chris Barber: "*Sister Rosetta had brought sheet music with her from when she worked with the sixteen-piece Lucky Millinder band in the USA, but not all the Barber band could read music. I said, 'Sister, would you play a number and we'll join in.' And she played 'Every Time I Feel The Spirit.' It was absolutely, mind-bogglingly wonderful. The best, most immediate, unexpected experience ever. She acted as if she'd found a band she'd never heard before, but which she'd needed to have all her life. You can hear the fire of her performance and the incredible reaction of the audience on the recording of the concert we played with her at the Free Trade Hall in Manchester a few days later on 9th December 1957.*"

Fortunately for us, this recording is available on CD: *The Blues Legacy: Lost & Found Vol. 1* (Classic Studio T 2008). The Barber Band were on terrific form by themselves; the front line of Barber on trombone, Monty Sunshine on clarinet and Pat Wilcox on trumpet was pretty faultless, on both fast and slower numbers. Barber introduces Sister Rosetta and she launches into 'Every Time I Feel The Spirit.' Over sixty years later, the performance still sounds fresh and exciting. Tharpe sings three solo numbers, accompanying herself on electric guitar. Then the Barber band join her for the rest of the concert. The interplay between this British jazz band and Tharpe's gospel singing is extraordinary. Ottilie Patterson joins in for 'When The Saints Go Marching In' and a reprise of 'Old Time Religion.'

Don Rendell was a British saxophonist who worked with American musicians on US bases during the war. He was a founder member of the Johnny Dankworth Seven, also working with Stan Kenton and Woody Herman. Rendell led his own group and later collaborated with the likes of Graham Bond, Michael Garrick and Barbara Thompson.

The Modern Jazz Quartet made their first appearance at the Free Trade Hall in December. This was part of a sixteen-date tour. They proved to be extremely popular and made six return appearances. Formed by pianist John Lewis, the MJQ had started out as the rhythm section for Dizzy Gillespie but became one of the most admired and longest running small jazz groups. The quartet featured Milt Jackson on vibraphone. They were together for twenty years with Lewis also acting as musical director, composer and arranger. The quartet even released two albums on the Beatles' Apple label.

Other Events at the Free Trade Hall:

January 1st – Hallé Ball
March 4th – Affleck & Brown Dinner Dance
March 27th – Evening Chronicle Darts Final
November 24th – Fairey Aviation Band; CWS (Manchester) Band

Elsewhere (Headliners Only):

Belle Vue (Kings Hall): Count Basie, Frankie Laine

Hippodrome: Tony Crombie And His Rockets, Johnny Dankworth Orchestra, Terry Dene, Lonnie Donegan, Billy Eckstine, Ronnie Hilton, Chas McDevitt Skiffle Group, Jack Parnell's Music Makers, Tex Ritter, Marion Ryan, Frankie Vaughan, Jimmy Young.

Odeon: Paul Anka, Bill Haley And The Comets.

Palace Theatre: Shirley Bassey, Petula Clark, Ken Dodd, Charlie Gracie, Guy Mitchell, Harry Secombe, Dickie Valentine.

1958		
Jan 10th	DUTCH SWING COLLEGE	*Johnny Duncan and His Blue Grass Boys; Neva Raphaello*
Feb 1st	GLENN MILLER ORCHESTRA with Ray McKinley featuring the Lenny Hambro Quintet	*Lorry Peters and Ronnie Craig*
Feb 14th	DAVE BRUBECK QUARTET featuring Paul Desmond	*Ronnie Scott with Zenith Six; Tubby Hayes; The Jazz Couriers*
March 7th	*NORTHERN JAZZ FESTIVAL* with Chris Barber's Band and Ottilie Patterson	*Dill Jones*
March 29th	*THE DISC STAR SHOW* with Laurie London; Chas McDevitt Skiffle with Shirley Douglas; Nancy Whiskey And Her Skiffle	*Paul Beattie Quintet; Joe Palin Quintet; The Saints*
April 5th	*EASTER SATURDAY JAZZ SHOW* with Sister Rosetta Tharpe	*Alex Welsh And His Band; Merseysippi Jazz Band; Beryl Bryden; Alan Hare Orchestra*
April 12th	JOHNNIE RAY with Ken Mackintosh and his Orchestra	
April 26th	CHRIS BARBER AND HIS BAND with Ottilie Patterson	*Sonny Terry and Brownie McGhee*
May 11th	HUMPHREY LYTTELTON AND HIS BAND; Marie Knight	*Mick Mulligan And His Band with George Melly*
May 17th	*JAZZ AT THE PHILHARMONIC* with Ella Fitzgerald and The Oscar Peterson Trio (two houses)	*Dizzy Gillespie; Roy Eldridge; Stan Getz; Coleman Hawkins; Sonny Stitt; Lou Levy; Herb Ellis; Max Bennett; Gus Johnson; Ray Brown; Dill Jones Trio*

Sept 13th	THE HI-LO'S AND TED HEATH AND HIS MUSIC	*Bobby Britton; Shelley Marshall*
Sept 20th	*JAZZ FROM CARNEGIE HALL* with JJ Johnson; Kai Winding; Red Garland; Kenny Clarke; Oscar Pettiford; Zoot Sims; Lee Konitz; Phineas Newborn; Jack Fallon; Don Lawson (two houses)	
Oct 4th	PAUL ROBESON -– Negro Spirituals, Popular Ballads and Folk Songs	*Lawrence Brown; Bruno Rankin (piano)*
Oct 10th	KALIN TWINS (two houses)	*Eddie Calvert; Cliff Richard And The Drifters; The Most Brothers; The Londonaires: Tony Marsh*
Oct 18th	ANNA RUSSELL with Eugene Rankin (piano)	
Oct 26th	CHRIS BARBER'S JAZZ BAND with Monty Sunshine Trio; Ottilie Patterson; Muddy Waters with Otis Spann	
Nov 24th	*ARTS FESTIVAL OF JAZZ* with Cy Laurie And His Jazz Band; Yana, Ronnie Scott, Tubby Hayes and The Jazz Couriers	*The Jazz Traders*
Dec 5th	CHRIS BARBER AND HIS BAND with Ottilie Patterson and Monty Sunshine	

IN 1958 MANY BIG AMERICAN JAZZ NAMES MADE THEIR Free Trade Hall debut – Dave Brubeck, Ella Fitzgerald, Oscar Peterson - all were to return to the venue again and again.

The Dutch Swing College was Europe's longest playing jazz band, performing traditional Dixieland jazz to a huge international following. It was formed in 1945 under the leadership of Peter Schilperoot who played clarinet and saxophones. He led the band for 45 years up to his death in 1990.

Various **Glenn Miller** tributes appeared throughout the five decades of the post-war Free Trade Hall. Miller had disappeared in December 1944 while flying over the English Channel, but his music really did live on. A successful biopic in 1954 starring James Stewart even had an Oscar-nominated soundtrack album (directed by Henry Mancini) and there was a steady demand to hear Miller's arrangements live. Later, Syd Lawrence recreated the Glenn Miller sound with great accuracy.

Dave Brubeck's Quartet appeared on Valentine's Day at a concert presented by the National Jazz Federation; it sold out in advance. The concert was recorded and is available on the Solar label. This was Brubeck's first British tour which visited sixteen venues. The quartet played the Free Trade Hall eight times between 1958 and 1967 and reappeared a quarter of a century later for one concert in 1992.

Chris Barber appeared three times, once at a Northern Jazz festival, once introducing **Sonny Terry and Brownie McGhee** and, later in the year, introducing **Muddy Waters** and **Otis Spann**. Barber's crucial role in promoting American blues and gospel music in the UK is often underestimated. Without his genuine and generous patronage, these American acts would probably never have appeared on British concert stages.

Chris Barber: "*One reason we chose Sonny Terry and Brownie McGhee for our next such tour in April and May 1958 was that they had worked on Broadway shows including Finian's Rainbow and Cat on a Hot Tin Roof. That type of work had already taken them outside their normal black environment. In other words we felt they'd be familiar with working with people like us, and playing to concert audiences like the ones we had in England and Europe. Brownie was a very nice man, lovely to work with and a very good musician. He - and Sonny, his musical partner - really justified the choice that we made, now that we realised we could bring members of the Guild of Variety Artists over to Europe ourselves. Like Big Bill and Sister Rosetta, they were people with whom we wanted to work, in order to get closer to the music and to learn more about playing it right. We all worked very well together and they'd created a great sound.*"

Again, the guest artists performed their own set which included 'Midnight Special', 'John Henry' and 'Worried Life Blues' and the Barber band joined them for 'This Little Light Of Mine' and a medley of 'Glory' and 'I'm Going To Walk And Talk With Jesus' which also featured Ottilie Patterson. This can be heard on *The Blues Legacy : Lost & Found Vol. 1* (Classic Studio T 2008).

Laurie London had just one hit record, his up-tempo version of 'He's Got The Whole World In His Hands' which reached No. 12 at the end of 1957. London was a teenager from Bethnal Green who was backed on the record by the Geoff Love Orchestra. The single went on to sell over a million copies in the USA and was the most successful record by a British male artist in the 1950's in that country.

Chas McDevitt had played with the Crane River Jazz Band before forming his own skiffle group. The group covered Elizabeth Cotten's 'Freight Train' and manager Bill Varley suggested that a female singer might give them an edge over the many other skiffle groups. Folk singer **Nancy Whiskey** joined McDevitt's group at the end of 1956 and they re-recorded 'Freight Train'. It reached No. 5. The group appeared in the USA on the Ed Sullivan Show and the single became a million seller over there. Whiskey left the group at the end of the year and went on to form her own skiffle group. **Shirley Douglas** replaced Nancy Whiskey in McDevitt's group.

Sister Rosetta Tharpe performed at eight concerts in England during March and April, but this tour was reportedly less successful than the one with Chris Barber.

Johnnie Ray was an American singer, songwriter and pianist. Long before rock 'n' roll, Ray had an exciting stage act, falling on the floor and crying in order to create teenage hysteria. He had had three chart-toppers with 'Such A Night', 'Just Walking In The Rain' and 'Yes Tonight Josephine.' Ray's career in the USA was on the decline but he had a huge following in Britain.

The first **Jazz At The Philharmonic** package came to Britain in May with Manchester being the penultimate night of the fifteen-date tour. Reportedly, tickets were being offered at high black market prices. This was **Ella Fitzgerald's** first appearance at the Free Trade Hall. America's First Lady Of Song was still recording her Great American Songbook series. This year, Fitzgerald's album, *Ella Fitzgerald Sings The Irving Berlin Songbook* (HMV 1958) reached No. 5 - her highest chart position in Britain. Ella Fitzgerald returned to the Free Trade Hall every year between 1959 and 1969, except for 1968. She made one final appearance in 1977.

Oscar Peterson was a Canadian jazz pianist who made his debut at New York's Carnegie Hall in 1949. Peterson worked with such greats as Louis Armstrong, Billie Holiday and Count Basie. He accompanied Ella Fitzgerald on several British tours as well as appearing in his own right.

The Hi-Lo's were an American vocal quartet. Their name referred to their extreme range of both voices and physical height; the group originally had two tall singers and two short ones. The group formed in 1953 and have - with the inevitable line-up changes - stayed together ever since. The Hi-Lo's made their British debut at the Free Trade Hall, the first of a twenty-two-date tour.

The **Jazz From Carnegie Hall** concert in September featured seven great jazz names and featured a front line of Zoot Sims (saxophones), Lee Konitz (saxophones), J.J. Johnson (trombone) and Kai Winding (trombone). The Free Trade Hall concert was the final night of a fourteen-date tour.

Paul Robeson's association with Britain went back to the 1920's when he performed in *Voodoo* and *Showboat* on the London stage. Robeson later played the title role in *Othello* and starred in the 1940 film, *The Proud Valley,* about Welsh miners. He was always linked to politically radical causes and was blacklisted in the USA from 1950 to 1955. In 1958 Robeson's right to travel was restored after he had been denied a passport, a victim of Senator McCarthy and the House Un-American Activities Committee. Using London as a base, Robeson undertook a world tour in 1958 which included Manchester as the fourth of twenty British dates.

One of the first British pop package shows, starring **The Kalin Twins**, appeared in October, supported by a young **Cliff Richard**, Cliff's increasing popularity started to overshadow the headliners. The Kalins were from New York and had topped the British singles charts in September with 'When'. This was their only hit record. The Kalins only toured Britain once but reappeared in 1989 at Cliff Richard's *The Event* concerts at Wembley Stadium, perhaps this was Cliff's way of saying thank you.

Anna Russell was an English-Canadian singer, pianist and comedian who showed off her skill for parody in a one woman show. Her set piece was a humorous twenty-two minute synopsis ofWagner's Ring cycle! Russell also parodied Gilbert & Sullivan, Lieder, folk, music hall, blues and jazz. Her album, *Anna Russell Sings* (Philips 1953) was a best seller.

Muddy Waters and **Otis Spann** were introduced to British audiences by Chris Barber.

Chris Barber: "*By this time we weren't nervous about playing with legendary figures. We also felt confident about how to tackle playing with Muddy... His schedule was so tight that we had no time to rehearse with him before he joined us for the first concert at Newcastle upon Tyne, on a Sunday night.*

"So on the Sunday in Newcastle, he and Otis just turned up, not really knowing what to expect. After a hurried chat we told him that we would go on and do a set, and then he would join us after a number or two in the second half. He heard us playing New Orleans jazz in the first half, and didn't say much about it in the interval. He didn't say anything either way to indicate whether he liked or disliked what he was hearing; he just asked what we'd start with. I said, 'Hoochie Coochie Man.' He said, 'Yeah.' I sang him the opening riff and he asked, 'What key?' I said, 'A.' He just said, 'Okay.'

"So we went out to do a couple of songs, and then we called him on. In that theatre, there were windows in the door that led on to the stage, and as we played we could see him and the pianist Otis Spann peering through those little windows and watching as we played our traditional jazz numbers. Then I announced them and as they came on stage we played the opening riff. Their faces lit up like watermelon eaters! They knew at once we were on their wavelength, so we kept playing and they came out. We dropped the volume right down for them, and it was the most impressive, exciting feeling. They hadn't expected us to know or care about their music. We had a really good time with them both."

The recording of the Free Trade Hall concert starts in exactly the same way; Barber introduces Waters and Spann and the band launch into 'Hoochie Coochie Man.' This was, arguably, the start of the blues explosion in Britain and certainly the first time that an electric slide guitar was heard alongside a traditional jazz band. On 'Rollin' Stone' Muddy Waters has a solo performance, but the band return for three more songs, the final one, 'Walkin' Thru The Park,' is then reprised and Otillie Patterson joins in. Barber is exactly right; his band really do provide an effective and appropriate backing to Waters and Span. This can be heard on *The Blues Legacy: Lost & Found Vol. 2* (Classic Studio T 2008).

The Arts Festival of Jazz was organised by David Ellis, a local music teacher whose own band, The Jazz Traders, opened the bill. Yana made a return appearance to the Free Trade Hall along with Ronnie Scott, Tubby Hayes and The Jazz Couriers. Unfortunately, the concert was on a fog-bound Monday evening and attendance was low.

Over at Belle Vue, the Duke Ellington Orchestra made its first UK appearance since 1933. One can only imagine how frustrating it must have been for British jazz fans to be deprived of such a talent for a quarter of a century.

Other Events at the Free Trade Hall:

January 6th-7th – Physical Culture Display
March 18th – Evening Chronicle Darts Finals
April 5th – NCH Festival with Bob Arnold (Tom Forrest from 'The Archers')
December 27th – Jews Benevolent Fund Ball

Elsewhere (Headliners Only):

Belle Vue (Kings Hall): Paul Anka, Duke Ellington Orchestra, Mario Lanza, Frankie Vaughan.

Hippodrome: Jackie Dennis, Lonnie Donegan, Johnny Duncan And The Bluegrass Boys, Russ Hamilton, Marvin Rainwater.

Odeon: The Treniers, Sarah Vaughan.

Palace Theatre: Shirley Bassey, The Beverley Sisters, Vic Damone, Diana Dors, Dickie Henderson, Guy Mitchell, Sarah Vaughan.

1959		
Jan 1st	*HALLÉ BALL* with Lew Stone	
Jan 10th	*THE BIG TEENAGE SHOW* with Cliff Richard And The Drifters; Johnny Duncan And The Blue Grass Boys	*Mike Preston; Joy and Dave Adams; Johns and Kennedy; Betty Smith Quintet; Jimmy Tarbuck*
Jan 31st	GEORGE LEWIS NEW ORLEANS JAZZ BAND	*Ken Colyer's Jazzmen*
Feb 21st	COUNT BASIE ORCHESTRA featuring Joe Williams (two houses)	
March 24th	*1959 SPECTACULAR* with Diana Dors; Billy Fury	*The Mudlarks; Bill Maynard; Dickie Dawson; Paul Beattie;*
April 3rd	MARTY WILDE AND THE WILDCATS (two houses)	*Joe "Mr Piano" Henderson; Lorrae Desmond; The Avon Sisters*
April 11th	CLARA WARD AND THE WARD SINGERS (two houses)	*Humphrey Lyttleton And His Band*
April 12th	ACKER BILK AND HIS PARAMOUNT JAZZ BAND	
April 18th	WOODY HERMAN & HIS ALL-STARS	
April 20th	CHRIS BARBER AND HIS BAND with Ottilie Patterson and Monty Sunshine	
April 25th	JOHNNY DANKWORTH AND HIS ORCHESTRA	*The Seven & Bobby Breen; The Jazz Couriers with Ronnie Scott and Tubby Hayes;*
May 9th	*JAZZ AT THE PHILHARMONIC* with Ella Fitzgerald and the Oscar Peterson Trio (two houses)	*Gene Krupa Quartet; Lou Levy Quartet; Stan Getz and Roy Eldridge*

May 31st	SHIRLEY BASSEY	*Ronnie Aldrich And The Squadronaires with Peter Morton; Joan Baxter. Cliff Townsend: The Squadcats*
July 11th	CLIFF RICHARD AND THE DRIFTERS	*Wee Willie Harris; Peter Elliott; The Bachelor Brothers; The Rockets; Jackie Day; Alan Field (compère)*
July 19th	ACKER BILK AND HIS PARAMOUNT JAZZ BAND IN *SUNDAY NIGHT ON THE DELTA*	
August 28th	FRANKIE VAUGHAN with Frank Weir and his Orchestra	*Raymond Long (piano), Clive Allen and Bobby Joy; Lorne Lesley; David Fontaine*
Sept 7th	EMLYN WILLIAMS *A BOY GROWING UP* (Dylan Thomas stories)	
Sept 20th	THE WEAVERS	*Sonny Terry and Brownie McGhee; Johnny Duncan*
Sept 26th	*THE NEWPORT JAZZ FESTIVAL* with The Dave Brubeck Quartet; Dizzie Gillespie Quintet; Buck Clayton All-Stars (two houses)	*Vic Ash Quintet*
Oct 10th	*FOLK DANCE FESTIVAL*	
Oct 11th	*MANCHESTER JAZZ FAIR* with George Melly; Mick Mulligan And His Band; Kenny Baker; Micky Ashman And His Band; Ian Christie Trio	
Oct 18th	SHIRLEY BASSEY with Ken Mackintosh And His Orchestra	*Alan Black; Shirley Western; Kenny Bardell*
Oct 24th	KID ORY AND HIS CREOLE JAZZ BAND	*Terry Lightfoot And His New Orleans Jazzmen*

Nov 14th	CLIFF RICHARD AND THE SHADOWS	*Al Saxon; Peter Elliott; The Southlanders; The Landis Brothers; Roy Young; The Swinging Tommy Allen Group; Tony Marsh (compère)*
Nov 15th	ACKER BILK AND HIS PARAMOUNT JAZZ BAND	
Nov 21st	*AN ENTERTAINMENT OF RARE, COMIC AND CURIOUS MUSIC* - devised by Fritz Spiegl with The Liverpool Music Group and The Peter Mountain String Quartet	
Nov 23th	*JAZZ PANORAMA* with Tubby Hayes; Kenny Baker	*Keith Christie; Fairweather Brown All Stars; Bruce Turner; George Melly (compère)*
Dec 4th	MODERN JAZZ QUARTET (two houses)	*Ronnie Ross and Joe Harriott*
Dec 13th	SHIRLEY BASSEY with Frank Weir and his Orchestra	*Karl Denver Trio*
Dec 14th	CHRIS BARBER AND HIS BAND with Ottilie Patterson and Monty Sunshine	

LEW STONE WAS A BANDLEADER AND ARRANGER WHO HAD worked with Bert Ambrose, the BBC Dance Orchestra and Al Bowlly. His orchestra played at top hotels and restaurants and was broadcast on Radio Normandy and Radio Luxembourg. Stone provide the music for over forty British film soundtracks.

1959 saw many package tours; **The Big Teenage Show** now saw **Cliff Richard** headlining. **The Drifters** were his British backing group, renamed The Shadows by the autumn, because of pressure from the American vocal group of the same name. Cliff Richard appeared no less than three times in 1959 and returned to the venue five times up until the mid-1970's and made one more appearance for a gospel concert in 1991.

Johnny Duncan came from the American state of Tennessee and had come to Europe on military service. He replaced Lonnie Donegan for the skiffle part of the Chris Barber Band's set. Duncan left Barber in February 1957 and formed his own act with the Blue Grass Boys as his backing band. Duncan's second single was an updated version of a calypso song called 'Last Train To San Fernando' which reached No. 2.

Count Basie made his Free Trade Hall debut in February filling two houses, the last night on a fifteen-date tour. He would return to the Free Trade Hall ten more times and his orchestra even appeared at the venue after his death. Basie formed his own band in the 1930's and moved to New York where the line-up was expanded. Basie's singer was **Joe Williams** - not to be confused with Big Joe Williams, the blues artist- who appeared with the orchestra from 1954 to 1960 before going solo.

The 1959 Spectacular co-starred **Diana Dors** and **Billy Fury**. Diana Dors studied at the London Academy Of Music And Dramatic Art and appeared in films from 1947 onwards, joining the Rank 'Charm School'. After a mixed experience in Hollywood she returned to England. The following year Dors released her only solo album, *Swinging Dors* (Columbia 1960), accompanied by an orchestra directed by Wally Stott. Billy Fury was born Ronald Wycherley in Liverpool and was one of the many young male performers who were renamed by manager Larry Parnes. His album *The Sound Of Fury* (Decca 1960) was the first British rock 'n' roll album and featured Joe Brown on guitar. Fury wrote all the songs himself, sometimes under the pseudonym of Wilbur Wilberforce. Despite this, most of Fury's hits were to be ballads.

Marty Wilde was born Reginald Smith and, like Billy Fury and several others, was re-named by Larry Parnes. He had had four Top 5 hits with covers of American singles. Wilde, unlike his most of his contemporaries, was also a songwriter and wrote his fifth hit, 'Bad Boy' himself. He had sprung to national fame through appearances on *6.5 Special* on BBC1 and, later, *Oh Boy* where he was the resident star. However, Wilde was soon eclipsed by a slightly younger singer called Cliff Richard.

The Clara Ward Singers were an American gospel group who emerged from an earlier group, The Ward Singers. Both were led by Clara Ward who was born in Birmingham, Alabama. The group went on to perform in Las Vegas, night clubs and other secular venues. Ward was accompanied by Humphrey Lyttelton at the Free Trade Hall and on two other dates in Newcastle and Birmingham.

Clarinettist **Acker Bilk** had worked with Ken Colyer before forming his own band. His **Paramount Jazz Band** turned fully professional in 1957. Bilk would appear no less than fourteen times at the Free Trade Hall over the next five years. He proved to be the biggest star of the trad jazz boom in Britain with his trademark bowler hat and waistcoat. In 1961 Bilk's self-penned 'Stranger On The Shore ' reached No. 2 in Britain, going on to sell a million copies.

Woody Herman's Anglo-American Big Band included nine British jazz musicians. Herman played the clarinet and the alto and soprano saxophone and had been leading bands since the mid-1930's. These bands were called 'The Herds' and had included the likes of Stan Kenton, Stan Getz and Art Pepper in the past. At this concert Herman featured Charlie Byrd on guitar and no less than five trumpeters and three trombonists. This was the penultimate night of a nineteen-date tour.

In February of this year, the **Chris Barber Band** had a hit single with 'Petite Fleur' which reached No. 3 and stayed in the charts for nearly six months. This Sydney Bechet tune was a showcase for Barber's clarinettist Monty Sunshine.

Johnny Dankworth and his Orchestra played four times at the Free Trade Hall between 1959 and 1963. Dankworth had studied at the Royal Academy of Music and became interested in bebop. He formed the Johnny Dankworth Seven in 1950 and formed a big band in 1953. Dankworth had a hit single in 1961 with 'African Waltz' and went on to write many film and television scores. From 1971 onwards he was musical director for his wife Cleo Laine.

Shirley Bassey appeared at the Free Trade Hall three times this year and returned regularly over the next two decades. This Cardiff born singer had a No.1 single at the start of the year with 'As I Love You'. Bassey's chart career started in 1957 with her version of 'The Banana Boat Song' and has continued for six decades.

Frankie Vaughan was a singer, actor and all-round entertainer. He enjoyed an unbroken run of hit singles since 1954 including a No. 1 with 'The Garden Of Eden' in 1957. The album, *Frankie Vaughan At The London Palladium* (Philips 1959) reached No. 6.

Emlyn Williams was a Welsh writer, dramatist and actor. He was famous for his one man shows, especially when he played Charles Dickens and presented - as Dickens himself had done - excerpts from his novels. On this occasion Williams was performing an evening of fellow Welshman Dylan Thomas's writing.

The Weavers were a pioneering folk group featuring the vocal talents of Ronnie Gilbert, Lee Hays, Fred Hellerman and Pete Seeger. They formed in 1948 and had several chart hits, often orchestrated by Gordon Jenkins. The Weavers disbanded in the early 1950's during the McCarthy era but made a successful comeback in 1955 for a Christmas concert at Carnegie Hall. By 1959 the group had lost Pete Seeger who concentrated on his solo career. He was replaced, first of all, by Erik Darling, a member of The Tarriers. The Free Trade Hall concert was the third night of an eight-date tour.

The **Newport Jazz Festival** concert on September 26th was hosted by Voice Of America's Willis Conover. Conover presented a jazz programme on that radio station and was involved in producing the original festivals at Newport. He was more popular outside the USA so his broadcasting voice would have been familiar to British audiences. The two shows (at 6 00pm and 8 30 pm) were both opened by Buck Clayton's All Stars; the second half of each show featured a fifteen minute set by Britain's Vic Ash Quintet before Brubeck's quartet appeared. The Free Trade Hall date was the halfway point on a sixteen-date tour.

Trombonist **Kid Ory** was in his early seventies when he appeared at the Free Trade Hall. Ory was present at the very beginning of jazz, playing with King Oliver in the 1920's and, later, with Louis Armstrong. In the 1930's Ory retired as he could not compete with the big bands. But, thanks to radio programmes in 1944 hosted by Orson Welles and sponsored by Standard Oil, Ory enjoyed a career revival for the rest of his life. The Free Trade Hall concert was part of a fifteen-date tour.

Fritz Spiegl was principal flautist with the Royal Liverpool Philharmonic Orchestra and later famous for his arrangement of the folk song 'Johnny Todd ' for the *Z Cars* television series. Spiegl was also known as a humorist and writer, organising classical concerts with novelty items which drew young people into concert halls. His concert in November featured 'A County Wedding Symphony' (also known as 'Peasant Wedding') for bagpipes, hurdy-gurdy and orchestra by Leopold Mozart; 'Lambeth Walk Immortalised' by Franz Reizenstein (played by the composer) and 'Overture Semiramide' (Rossini-Czerny) arranged for eight pianos, sixteen pianists and thirty-two hands!

The Modern Jazz Quartet were on their second British tour and the Free Trade Hall concert was the penultimate night of fifteen dates.

Other Events at the Free Trade Hall

January 1st – Hallé Ball with Lew Stone
March 2nd – Trans-Antarctic Lecture
March 5th – NCH Festival Of Queens with Bobby Charlton,Harry Corbett and Sooty
March 22nd – Labour Party and Russian Visitors 2pm – 530pm; Unionist Movement – Oswald Mosley – 6.30pm – 10pm
May 1st – CND Public Meeting
September 25th – Evening Chronicle Fashion Show
November 2nd – Cookery Demonstration
December 19th – Kellogg's Staff Dance

Elsewhere (Headliners only)

Belle Vue (Kings Hall): Louis Armstrong And His All Stars, Cliff Richard And The Drifters.

Hippodrome: Paul Anka.

Odeon: The Big Beat Show starring Billy Fury.

Palace Theatre: Max Bygraves, Billy Eckstine, Bruce Forsyth, Cy Grant, David Whitfield. Royal Variety Performance (Liberace, Cliff Richard, Marty Wilde et al.).

The Sixties

Blues and Jazz legends perform and Dylan is called 'Judas'

1960		
Jan 16th	THE PLATTERS	*Cuddly Dudley with Carl Barriteau's Band; Vic Lewis (compère)*
Jan 24th	MICKEY ASHMAN AND HIS BAND	*Dick Charlesworth's City Gents*
Jan 30th	EMILE FORD AND THE CHECKMATES (two houses)	*Edna Savage; Johnny Le Roy; Paul Beattie and the Beats*
Feb 6th	SARAH VAUGHAN with The Johnny Dankworth Orchestra (two houses)	
Feb 19th	ADAM FAITH with The John Barry Seven	*Emile Ford And The Checkmates; The Avons; Mike Preston; Little Tony;*
Feb 21st	ACKER BILK AND HIS PARAMOUNT JAZZ BAND	
Feb 27th	JERI SOUTHERN	*Rose Murphy; Elaine Delmar; Slam Stewart; Matt Monroe; The Modern Jazz Six*
Feb 29th	EMLYN WILLIAMS AS CHARLES DICKENS	
March 4th	PAUL ROBESON	*Lawrence Brown (piano)*
March 12th	*JAZZ AT THE PHILHARMONIC* WITH ELLA FITZGERALD (two houses)	*Shelly Manne and his Men; Roy Eldridge; Jimmy Giuffre Trio; Paul Smith Quartet*
April 1st	RUSS CONWAY	*Bill Maynard; Eddie Falcon; Bert Weedon; The Barry Sisters; Derek Hilton Quartet*
April 3rd	CHRIS BARBER AND HIS JAZZ BAND; Ottilie Patterson; Sister Rosetta Tharpe	*Monty Sunshine Quartet*
April 8th	SHIRLEY BASSEY with Ken Mackintosh And His Orchestra	*Alan Black; Kenny Bardell; Shirley Western The Mackpies*
April 20th	MARTIN DEMMY - demonstration	

April 22nd	THE EVERLY BROTHERS	*The Dallas Boys; Lance Fortune; Freddy Lloyd Four; Danny Hunter; The Flee-Rekkers with Jimmy Barron; Cherry Wainer with Don Storer; Tony Marsh (compère)*
April 25th	COUNT BASIE AND HIS ORCHESTRA	*Joe Williams*
April 29th (midnight to 7am)	*ALL NIGHT SWINGER JAZZ BAND BALL* with Mick Mulligan And His Band with George Melly	*Paul Beattie and the Beats; The Collegians; Eggy Ley's Jazzmen; Kenny Baker; Shirley Vincent; Claude Powell; Brian Woolley's Jazzmen; The Saints; The Yorkshire Jazz Band; Pete Haslam's Collegians*
May 1st	ACKER BILK AND HIS PARAMOUNT JAZZ BAND	
May 10th	FREDDY CANNON and The Cannonballs	*Mike Preston; The Avons; The Four Jays; Bob Bain (compère)*
May 27th	KENNETH McKELLAR	*Lucille Graham*
May 28th	MICK MULLIGAN AND HIS BAND with George Melly; Simon Wheeler Vintage Jazz Band	*Cy Laurie & His Band (In aid of YWCA)*
June 8th	CHRIS BARBER AND HIS BAND with Ottilie Patterson and Monty Sunshine	
June 28th	TOM LEHRER	
August 21st	ACKER BILK AND HIS PARAMOUNT JAZZ BAND	
Sept 3rd	*JAZZ FROM THE RONNIE SCOTT CLUB* Victor Feldman; The Tubby Hayes Big Band; Ronnie Scott Quintet; Jimmy Deucher; Keith Christie; Johnny Scott	
Sept 12th	CHRIS BARBER BAND with Ottilie Patterson	*Muddy Waters with Otis Spann*
Sept 18th	BOB WALLIS AND HIS STORYVILLE JAZZMEN	*The Clyde Valley Stompers with Fiona Duncan*

Sept 22nd	DONALD WOLFIT with Rosalind Iden in *SCENES FROM SHAKESPEARE*	
Sept 27th	MILES DAVIS QUINTET FEATURING SONNY STITT (two houses)	*Vic Ash and Harry Klein; The Jazz Five*
Oct 2nd	ACKER BILK AND HIS PARAMOUNT JAZZ BAND	
Oct7th	*ROCK 'N' TRAD SPECTACULAR : THE NEW NOISE OF 1960* Billy Fury with Joe Brown billed to appear; replaced by Marty Wilde	*Vince Eager; Peter Wynne; Tommy Bruce; Davy Jones; Johnny Gentle; Duffy Power*
Oct 15th	FESTIVAL OF FOLK DANCING	
Oct 22th	PADDY ROBERTS	*Al Koran; Julie Jones; Dennis Newey And His Quintet*
Oct 28th	ANNA RUSSELL	
Oct 29th	CARMEN McRAE (two houses)	*The Jazz Five; Ronnie Scott Quintet; Tubby Hayes Quartet; The Jazz Couriers*
November 12th	*TOC H FESTIVAL OF MUSIC* with Reginald Leopold And The Palm Court Orchestra	*Elton Hayes; June Glynne; John Ogden*
December 4th	JUDY GARLAND with Norrie Paramour And His Orchestra	
December 9th	SHIRLEY BASSEY with Ted Heath And His Music	*Pat Brand (compère)*
December 10th	DIZZY GILLESPIE QUINTET	*Jimmy Smith Trio*
December 11th	ACKER BILK AND HIS PARAMOUNT JAZZ BAND	
December 12th	REGINALD LEOPOLD AND THE PALM COURT ORCHESTRA with Elton Hayes, John Ogdon and June Glynne	

THE START OF A NEW DECADE DEMONSTRATED THE SHEER variety and quality of the acts appearing at the Free Trade Hall. Top selling American pop acts such as The Platters and The Everly Brothers appeared there interspersed with such black icons as Paul Robeson, Ella Fitzgerald, Sarah Vaughan, Miles Davis and Carmen McRae. The Free Trade Hall did a great deal for supporting racial equality and awareness giving audiences the opportunity to see some of the most talented black American jazz, blues and gospel performers. British jazz was at the height of its popularity; Acker Bilk, for example, appeared four times. On two occasions this year Chris Barber again introduced American artists – Sister Rosetta Tharpe and Muddy Waters – giving them a major showcase and concert audience. American jazz continued to be well supported.

The Platters were an American vocal group who had appeared in the film *Rock Around The Clock* in 1956. They had reached No.1 in Britain with their version of 'Smoke Gets In Your Eyes' in 1959. The group had appeared for a week at the Palace Theatre in April 1957. This was their second British tour, visiting ten venues.

Mickey Ashman was a double bass player who had worked with Chris Barber and Humphrey Lyttelton. He left Barber in 1956 at the same time as Lonnie Donegan, joining the latter's band. Ashman then led his own band.

Emile Ford was born in Saint Lucia and had moved with his family to London in the mid-1950's. He studied sound engineering at Paddington Technical College and learned to play a number of musical instruments. In 1959 Ford formed the Checkmates and signed with the Pye label. The group reached No.1 in December 1959 with 'What Do You Want To Make Those Eyes At Me For?' which was self-produced.

Sarah Vaughan appeared with Johnny Dankworth and his sixteen-piece orchestra. Vaughan was making her Free Trade Hall debut, having appeared at Manchester Odeon in 1958. She had worked with Billy Eckstine and Earl Hines and made both popular records for Mercury and more jazz-orientated material for EmArcy. This concert was the penultimate night of a fourteen-date tour.

Adam Faith had had his second No. 1 hit single, 'Poor Me', earlier in the year. He had risen to fame on the television series, *Drumbeat*. Faith's records benefitted from the expert arrangements by film composer, John Barry.

Jeri Southern was an American jazz pianist and singer who specialised in torch songs. Her single 'Fire Down Below' had reached No. 22 in Britain in 1957. A shy person who suffered from performance anxiety, Southern gave up performing to teach and compose film themes.

Russ Conway's unique piano style apparently came from a shortened third finger on his right hand ! He had twenty hit singles between 1957 and 1963, including two No. 1's: 'Side Saddle' and 'Roulette'.

In 1960 **the Everly Brothers** had left the Cadence label and signed with Warner Brothers for a reported $1 million. Their first single for their new label was 'Cathy's Clown', written by Don Everly. It reached No.1 in both Britain and the USA. This was the Everlys' first British tour and consisted of twenty-two dates. They were backed by the Crickets who had stayed together after the death of Buddy Holly.

Graham Nash tells his story of the concert: *Sometime after the new year began I spotted an ad in the Manchester newspaper. The Everly Brothers live and in concert at the Free Trade Hall. Oh, you bet I was going to be there. Allan (Clarke), too. And we made up our minds that some way, somehow, we were going to meet our heroes. It was a dream of ours that wouldn't quit. Of course, we never thought it would happen but we talked out a plan that seemed logical at the time and determined to give it our best shot. The night of the show we were eight miles high – adrenaline pumping, heart beating outside my chest. We had great seats, maybe eight rows back. My sister Elaine was with us…and they were fucking fabulous. Did all their hits. Two acoustic gray Gibsons, strumming them like mad. They sounded incredible. They sang around one mike, perfect balance. And those voices! C'mon, who did anything like that? They were just stunning.*

Nash continues his story to describe how the two young future Hollies waited outside the Midland Hotel for over three hours to meet the Everly Brothers. He describes the evening as a "school night for a lot of the audience" (sic), but April 22nd was actually a Friday! Unfortunately, Nash is not always a reliable narrator. The account is littered with melodrama and inaccuracies. But, it seems that Don and Phil Everly were friendly to Nash and Clarke and – when the Americans heard about the latter's singing ambitions - they encouraged them to "keep doing it."

Freddy Cannon had reached Number Three earlier in the year with the frantic single, 'Way Down Yonder In New Orleans'. His album *The Explosive Freddy Cannon* (Top Rank 1960) did even better and topped the British charts. Cannon was in the middle of a short seven-date tour. Later in May he joined Johnny Preston and Conway Twitty for a longer series of concerts.

Kenneth McKellar trained as an opera singer at the Royal College of Music but later turned to singing traditional Scottish songs. He made regular appearances on such television programmes as *The White Heather Club.* McKellar would later represent the UK in the Eurovision Song Contest.

The American humorist **Tom Lehrer** appeared in June on his second British tour. Ticket prices started at 3/6 and went up to 10/6 and were available from Forsyths music shop. Lehrer had recently toured Australia and New Zealand and played just six dates in Britain. His two albums, *Songs By Tom Lehrer* (Decca 1958) and *An Evening Wasted With Tom Lehrer* (Decca 1960) were incredibly popular. Songs such as 'Poisoning Pigeons In The Park' and 'The Elements' – the latter using a tune from Gilbert and Sullivan's *The Pirates Of Penzance* – never seem to lose their appeal. An academic at Harvard, Lehrer retired at the peak of his success. He recorded some more songs for the American version of *That Was The Week That Was* in the mid-1960's including 'The Vatican Rag'. Lehrer, simply, was unique. No-one has combined satire and musicianship as cleverly as him.

The *Melody Maker* Jazz Weekend featured an **All Night Jazz Band Ball**. The ball on April 29th was advertised as having an "All Night Snack Buffet" with "egg and bacon breakfast included if required". The public were told: "The whole of the floor will be cleared for dancing and jiving. Sitting out in the Circle."

Melody Maker reported on the highlights of the weekend; "The fabulous trumpet playing of Kenny Baker. The enthusiasm of couples still jiving away when the All-Night Ball ended in bright sunshine. The spectacle of fans, having taken their fill of jazz, tucking into an egg-and-bacon breakfast in the lounge of the Free Trade Hall." On the Saturday evening there was a 'Meet The Critics' session at the Bodega Restaurant. Sunday night's Acker Bilk concert was sold out: "Hundreds had to be turned away from the final Acker Bilk concert. The storm of rapturous applause shook the roof of the Free Trade Hall."

Billy Fury was billed to appear on October 7th along with Joe Brown and other names in the Larry Parnes stable. This was advertised, in true Parnes hyperbole, as a *Rock 'n' Trad Spectacular*: The New Noise Of 1960 promising Billy and "his company of 50." But there were problems. The following day the *Manchester Evening News* had the headline, 'THEY'RE ALL WILD ABOUT FURY SHOW' with an article by an un-named reporter: *Rock star Billy Fury's fans were furious when they arrived at the Free Trade Hall, Manchester to see their idol top the bill in a one-night show. For show manager Mr Robert Holland-Ford told them that Billy Fury would not be appearing – taking his place would be Marty Wilde.*

Screaming teenagers besieged the booking office asking for their money back. 'We booked to see Billy. Marty is no compensation,' they yelled at the doorman.

'We could not refund the money as all the bookings for the show were made through an agency. It was chaos here for ages until they quietened down and agreed to watch the show.' said a Free Trade Hall spokesman today.

Billy Fury and two other rock singers, Peter Wynne and Joe Brown were unable to appear because of illness,' said Larry Parnes, the man behind the show.

By October 10th the *Manchester Evening News* had the headline, 'ROCK MAY BE BANNED' and stated: *Manchester Town Hall Committee will have a full report on Wednesday about disturbances at the Free Trade Hall rock 'n' roll concert last week when stink bombs were thrown on the stage and doors defaced with lipstick and messages carved with nail files. The report on the incidents, which followed the non-appearance of four 'pop' singers could mean a complete ban on rock 'n' roll concerts in the hall.*

Town Hall superintendent Mr Harold Lighter, who was at the hall during the performance, said today that there had been other incidents during previous rock 'n' roll concerts there, but this was the first time stink bombs had been thrown. Seats had also been loosened due to youngsters rocking about…

By mid-week the *Manchester Evening News* letters page began to print the public's reaction. Valerie Somers of Cheetham wanted to express her "disgust and amazement at the way teenagers were treated". She questioned "why should four leading stars of the show be all affected by the 'flu' at the same time?" A Mrs Ainsworth of Prestwich was similarly suspicious about the number of stars suffering from 'flu'. She thought that, "the show should have been cancelled, and held at some future date, the tickets still being valid". Three 'Angry Teenagers' from Chorlton-cum-Hardy wrote in to say, "Towards the end of the show we were informed that four of the stars, including the main ones (ie Fury and Brown) would not be appearing." They felt that they "should have had the apology in the programme earlier."

In *Stage & Television Today*, nearly a month later in its November 3rd issue, proclaimed 'Manchester Slams Shut The Door' with an angry comment piece: "*The easiest course for anyone in authority to take when up against a problem is to ban, to forbid, to censor, or to prohibit. This is the solution Manchester City Council have found to the question posed by the bad behaviour of a few youngsters of the thousands attending rock 'n' roll shows at their Free Trade Hall. It is, of course, a great deal easier than having on duty enough attendants to keep order- but it hits at innocent and guilty alike, and the many are deprived because the few offend. The Manchester ban follows a disturbance which arose when billed artistes failed, because of illness, to turn up. The places of the absentees were completely filled but a small section of the audience was not satisfied and took it out on the furnishings.*"

A cursory look at the listings for the next few years suggests that the ban on rock 'n' roll and pop persisted. There were no more pop concerts for the rest of the decade, with the sole exceptions of Diana Ross And The Supremes and The Beach Boys. For the next few years the Free Trade Hall featured jazz, blues and folk, while pop package tours came to the Odeon, Palace Theatre and ABC Ardwick. Apart from Dylan's 1966 "Judas" concert, there were no rock concerts until 1968.

Paddy Roberts was a songwriter, singer and humorist. He co-wrote Ruby Murray's 1955 No. 1 single 'Softly Softly' and wrote 'Lay Down Your Arms' for Anne Shelton, another No. 1 hit. Roberts' own E.P, *Strictly For Grown-Ups* (Decca 1959) was No. 1 for nineteen weeks and an album of the same name reached No. 8. One notable track was 'Ballad Of Bethnal Green'. Roberts' slightly risqué lyrics were clearly very popular. Roberts' performance was advertised as "Paddy's only British appearance prior to six weeks American T.V. Series."

Carmen McRae was born in Harlem in New York and became a much admired jazz singer and pianist. McRae was seventeen when she met Billie Holiday who became a friend and mentor. This led to a career which lasted over 50 years. She appeared at the Monterey Jazz Festival seven times over a period of twenty years. McRae collaborated with such names as Noel Coward, Sammy Davis Jr, Dave Brubeck and Louis Armstrong.

Donald Wolfit was an English actor-manager famous for his Shakespearean roles on stage, especially King Lear and Richard III. He also featured in over thirty films including *Room At The Top*, *Lawrence of Arabia* and *Becket*.

Trumpeter **Miles Davis** only appeared at the Free Trade Hall once; fortunately the concert was recorded. Davis brought his quintet to the venue and the second house was sold out in advance. This was the fourth night of a twelve-date tour. A contemporary review praised the technique and excitement of the musicans, but found fault with Davis's "couldn't care less attitude" to the audience. A letter in

Melody Maker from Alan Stevens stated: "Mean and moody, but magnificent- that was Miles in Manchester. Is it just an act? Or is he really contemptuous of his audience? Not a word did he say, no acknowledgement of applause, no announcements, no smiles- nothing to betray his emotions.

"But who cares? Why should he talk when his trumpet can speak so eloquently? The sheer artistry of his playing was well-nigh overwhelming. Backstage, he seemed friendly enough. That couldn't care less attitude could be one big publicity stunt."

Judy Garland had contracted hepatitis in November 1959 and had been dangerously ill. Happily she recovered and played the London Palladium the following August. After postponements earlier in the autumn of 1960, Garland played the Free Trade Hall in December accompanied by a British orchestra. Advertised as "Manchester's Greatest One Night Stand Together On One Bill," tickets were relatively expensive, starting at 10/- and going up to 30/-. Even this concert was nearly cancelled because Garland's seven-year-old daughter, Lorna (Luft) was seriously ill. The *Manchester Evening News* reported: "After only three hours sleep, Judy was up at 7 a.m. today visiting the Harley Street nursing home where Lorna was taken last night for an operation for acute appendicitis."

Sid Phillips was a British clarinettist, bandleader and arranger. He had worked with Ambrose and led his own Dixieland jazz band from 1949 onwards. Both Kenny Ball and George Shearing had been members of Phillips' band.

The Dizzy Gillespie Quintet appeared in December. Trumpeter Gillespie had previously appeared in May 1958, supporting Ella Fitzgerald and Oscar Peterson. He had played with Charlie Parker in the early days of bebop. Gillespie's trademark trumpet's bell was at an angle of 45 degrees so that he could hear the notes that he was playing sooner.

Other Events at the Free Trade Hall

February 12th – Film Lecture- Conquest Of Space- Madam Sputnik
April 4th – Boxing
May 13th – CND Public Meeting
May 19th – Unveiling of suffragette plaque
June 11th – New York Salvation Army Staff Band
November 19th – Methodist Youth Rally

Elsewhere (Headliners Only):

Hippodrome – Joe Brown, Eddie Cochran, Dutch Swing College, Adam Faith, Emile Ford And The Checkmates, Billy Fury, Gene Vincent.

Odeon –Bobby Darin, Duane Eddy, Jimmy Jones, Cliff Richard And The Shadows.

Palace Theatre – Adam Faith, Liberace, Anthony Newley, Johnny Preston, Conway Twitty, Marty Wilde.

1961		
Jan 27th	DAVE BRUBECK QUARTET	*Joe Harriott Quintet*
Jan 29th	CHRIS BARBER JAZZ BAND with Ottilie Patterson	*Diz Disley*
Feb 2nd	ACKER BILK AND HIS PARAMOUNT JAZZ BAND	
Feb 4th	FRANKIE VAUGHAN with Billy Ternent And His Orchestra	*Tony Fayre; Ted Lune*
Feb 18th	MANTOVANI AND HIS ORCHESTRA	
Feb 25th	JUNE CHRISTY; THE FOUR FRESHMEN (two houses)	*Bob Miller And The Millermen*
Feb 26th	BOB WALLIS AND HIS STORYVILLE JAZZ BAND	
March 11th	ELLA FITZGERALD with the Lou Levy Quartet	*Oscar Peterson Trio*
March 12th	MONTY SUNSHINE AND HIS BAND; BERYL BRYDEN	
April 1st	CHRIS BARBER JAZZ BAND with Ottilie Patterson	
April 9th	KENNY BALL AND HIS JAZZMEN	
May 6th	THE THELONIOUS MONK QUARTET (two houses)	*Art Blakey's Jazz Messengers*
May 13th	ACKER BILK AND HIS PARAMOUNT JAZZ BAND	
July 2nd	THE TEMPERANCE SEVEN	*Mike Cotton's Jazzmen*
July 9th	MONTY SUNSHINE AND HIS BAND WITH BERYL BRYDEN	
Aug 27th	SHIRLEY BASSEY with Ken MacKintosh And His Orchestra	
Sept 10th	KENNY BALL AND HIS JAZZMEN	
Oct 1st	ACKER BILK AND HIS PARAMOUNT JAZZ BAND	
Oct 7th	MODERN JAZZ QUARTET (two houses)	
Oct 14th	INTERNATIONAL FOLK DANCE FESTIVAL	

Nov 12th	CHRIS BARBER JAZZ BAND with Ottilie Patterson	
Nov25th	DAVE BRUBECK QUARTET (two houses)	*Vic Ash- Harry Klein "Jazz Five"*
Dec 2nd	NINA AND FREDERICK with Malcolm Mitchell And His Trio	*Bryan Burdon; The Three Sonnettes; Vic Perry; Mike and Bernie Winters; Salici Puppets*
Dec8th	HUGHIE GREEN SHOW with *Double Your Money*	*Malcolm Mitchell And His Trio*
Dec10th	THE MELBOURNE NEW ORLEANS JAZZ BAND	*Mike Cotton's Jazzmen; Jeanie Lamb*
Dec 24th	FRED SCHOFIELD AND HIS ALL STARS	
Dec 26th	JACK KIRKLAND AND HIS BROADCASTING BAND	

IT WAS ANOTHER BUSY YEAR FOR BOTH BRITISH AND American jazz acts; Britain tended to produce Trad jazz stars while American jazz was usually Modern. Between them, British bandleaders Kenny Ball, Chris Barber, Acker Bilk and Monty Sunshine appeared at ten concerts, exceeding the number of American performances. Dave Brubeck appeared twice and Thelonious Monk made his Free Trade Hall debut.

Mantovani was born in Venice and his family moved to Britain in 1912. His orchestras played a light sound of "cascading strings". Before The Beatles, Mantovani was Britain's most successful album seller. His albums were often used by shops to demonstrate hi-fi stereo equipment.

June Christy co-headlined with the Four Freshmen. Christy had replaced Anita O'Day as vocalist for Stan Kenton before pursuing a solo career. She reunited with Kenton for his *Innovations In Modern Music Orchestra* album. Christy's cool jazz style was popular for many years and she made over twenty albums including *June Christy Recalls Those Kenton Days* (Capitol 1959).

The Four Freshmen vocal group were founded in 1948 and were later helped by Stan Kenton to obtain a recording contract. The group's jazz-based four-part harmonies were extraordinary. The Four Freshmen's first album was *Voices In Modern* (Capitol 1955). One of their biggest hits was 'Their Hearts Were Full Of Spring' which was later covered by the Beach Boys. At the Free Trade Hall, the group would also play seven musical instruments between them; Ross Barbour played drums and trumpet; Ken Albers also played trumpet and doubled on the mellophonium; Don Barbour played the guitar and Bob Flanigan doubled on guitar and double bass!

Bob Wallis And His Storyville Jazz Band actually hailed from Bridlington in Yorkshire, but dressed as Mississippi gamblers on stage! Wallis had played trumpet with his local Salvation Army Band before discovering jazz and setting up his own band. After briefly playing with both Ken Colyer and Acker Bilk, he joined up with Hugh Rainey's All Stars and they shortly changed their name to the Storyville Jazz Band. The Band's first album, *Everybody Loves Saturday Night* (Top Rank 1960) reached No. 20 for one week.

Monty Sunshine left the Chris Barber Band at the end of 1960 and soon formed his own band. He appeared twice with his new band at the Free Trade Hall this year. 'Petite Fleur' sold millions of copies around the world, but Sunshine did not benefit financially from record sales. However, he sustained a career after leaving Barber and was especially popular in Germany.

Trumpeter **Kenny Ball** formed his own Dixieland jazz band in 1958 and soon had hit singles with 'Samantha', 'Midnight In Moscow' and 'March Of the Siamese Children'. Ball played the Free Trade Hall five times in total. Ball was, by far, the most popular trad jazz bandleader but was not admired by the critics. However, he had both a superb technique and the shrewd sense to stick to what the public wanted.

Thelonious Monk had studied piano from the age of ten and played in Baptist churches and with an evangelist. He later worked with Kenny Clarke, Coleman Hawkins and Dizzy Gillespie. Later Monk formed a quartet with John Coltrane. 1961 saw Monk's first tour of Europe and he came to the Free Trade Hall on the same bill as Art Blakey's Jazz Messengers. The Free Trade Hall concert was the sixth night in an eight-date tour. Monk was not only a brilliant performer, but one of jazz's most celebrated composers. His 'Round Midnight' tune is one of the most covered in the genre.

The Temperance Seven were a nine-piece jazz band (explained as "one over the eight"!) from London. They had two big hit singles in 1961, 'You're Driving Me Crazy' (No. 1) and 'Pasadena' (No. 4) which were produced by George Martin. The group's music was a deliberate re-creation of the jazz and dance bands of the 1920's and 1930's and the musicians dressed in Edwardian fashions. For a couple of years the Temperance Seven were seemingly everywhere; television; the London Palladium; a Royal Command Performance and films. Their influence on such bands as the Bonzos, New Vaudeville Band and Bob Kerr's Whoopee Band cannot be overstated.

The Dave Brubeck Quartet's November concert was timely as their hit single, 'Take Five' was in the British charts, peaking at No. 6. The quartet had already undertaken a seven-date tour in January and returned to Britain for thirteen more concerts at the end of the year.

Nina and Frederick were an incredibly popular - and photogenic – Danish-Dutch duo who performed a mix of folk music, calypso and standards. Their 'Little Donkey' single had been a Top 3 hit over the previous Christmas. A second album, *Nina And Frederick* (Columbia 1961) had reached No.11 earlier in the year. Their British television series, *Nina And Frederick At Home* was also screened this year.

Hughie Green's *Double Your Money* show started on Radio Luxembourg and then transferred to ITV where it ran for thirteen years. Green had served in the Canadian

Air Force and appeared in Hollywood films. Later he would host *Opportunity Knocks* and *The Sky's The Limit.*

The Melbourne New Orleans Jazz Band were formed in 1957 and won the best New Orleans jazz group in Australia prize. The band arrived in Britain in autumn 1961 led by clarinettist, Nick Polites. They had released records on the Swaggie label and in 1962 released their *Jazz Down Under* EP on EMI's Columbia label.

Jack Kirkland And His Broadcasting Band had won First Prize at the West Riding District Championship for best dance band, sponsored by *Melody Maker.*

Other Events at the Free Trade Hall

March 16th – Gaelic League Concert
April 13th – Fashion Show
November 8th – Vienna Boys Choir
December 15th – Royal Technical College Salford Student Union Dance

Elsewhere (Headliners Only)

ABC Ardwick: Adam Faith, Billy Fury, Robert Horton, Cliff Richard And The Shadows.

Hippodrome: Billy Fury.

Odeon: The Allisons, Johnny Mathis, Mike Preston.

Palace Theatre : Sammy Davis Junior, Karl Denver, Dickie Henderson, Anthony Newley, Johnnie Ray, Frankie Vaughan.

1962		
Jan 28th	ACKER BILK AND HIS PARAMOUNT JAZZ BAND	
Feb 3rd	BUDDY GRECO AND CLEO LAINE with The Johnny Dankworth Orchestra (two houses)	
Feb 11th	THE TEMPERANCE SEVEN	*Mike Cotton's Jazzmen*
Feb 17th	DIANA DORS WITH TED HEATH AND HIS MUSIC	
Feb 24th	*JAZZ AT THE PHIL* WITH ELLA FITZGERALD with the Paul Smith Trio	*Coleman Hawkins and Roy Eldridge Quintet*
March 4th	KENNY BALL AND HIS JAZZMEN	*Papa Bue's Viking Jazz Band; Clinton Ford*
March 24th	THE FOUR FRESHMEN (two houses)	*Jeri Southern; Kenny Baker's Band; Danny Williams; Matt Monro*
March 25th	CHRIS BARBER JAZZ BAND WITH CLINTON FORD AND OTTILIE PATTERSON	
March 26th	MANTOVANI	
March 30th	*WEST INDIAN CONCERT* STARRING THE MIGHTY SPARROW (presented by Melodisc Records)	*The Mighty Terror – Kentris Fagan; Laurel Aitken; Lord Kitchener; Horace James; Allistair Bain and his West Indian Dancers; George Edwards And His Seven Stars Steel Band*
April 7th	COUNT BASIE AND HIS ORCHESTRA WITH IRENE REID (two houses)	*Lambert, Hendricks and Ross*
April 16th	JOYCE GRENFELL –"MONOLOGUES AND SONGS"	
April 29th	ACKER BILK AND HIS PARAMOUNT JAZZ BAND	
May 12th	LOUIS ARMSTRONG AND HIS ALL STARS – (two houses)	*Gerry Brown's Jazzmen*
June 3rd	ERROLL GARNER	

June 9th	SHIRLEY BASSEY with The Nelson Riddle Orchestra	*The Hi-Los*
July 22nd	KENNY BALL AND HIS JAZZMEN	*The Saints Jazz Band; George Melly; Jerry Dawson (compère)*
Sept 9th	CHRIS BARBER AND HIS JAZZ BAND with Ottilie Patterson	
Sept 30th	PAPA BUE AND HIS VIKING JAZZ BAND	*Eric Krans' Dixieland Pipers*
Oct 6th	GEORGE SHEARING QUINTET (two houses)	*Joe Williams with The Junior Mance Trio*
Oct 21st	*AMERICAN FOLK BLUES FESTIVAL* Jump Jackson; Memphis Slim; T-Bone Walker; John Lee Hooker; Sonny Terry and Brownie McGhee (two houses)	*Willie Dixon; Helen Humes; Jimmy D "Shaky Jake" Harris; Joe Panin*
Oct 27th	THE BOB HOPE SHOW	
Nov 24th	DAVE BRUBECK QUARTET	*Ronnie Scott Quartet*
Nov 25th	ACKER BILK WITH HIS PARAMOUNT JAZZ BAND	
Dec 1st	JOHNNY MATHIS AND TED HEATH AND HIS MUSIC	*Don Rendell Four*
Dec 9th	CHRIS BARBER'S BAND with Ottilie Patterson; introducing Louis Jordan	
Dec 24th	PAUL BEATTIE AND HIS BAND	*Johnny Downes And The Dolphins*
Dec 26th	CLINTON FORD AND THE BANDLEADERS	*Paul Beattie And The Beats*

BUDDY GRECO WAS AN AMERICAN POP AND JAZZ SINGER and pianist who had worked with Benny Goodman. He had appeared at the London Palladium in 1949. Greco's version of 'The Lady Is A Tramp' was a Top 30 hit in 1960. His appearance at the Free Trade Hall was a one-off concert before Greco started a four week season at the Bal Tabarin in London's Mayfair.

Cleo Laine had worked with the Johnny Dankworth Seven and big band in the mid-1950's. After marrying Dankworth she made guest appearances with him, as well as starring in musicals and plays. Laine would later make successful collaborations with John Williams and James Galway. She performed more regularly with Dankworth and they would return to the Free Trade Hall.

Ella Fitzgerald's tour, under the umbrella of *Jazz At The Philharmonic*, consisted of seventeen dates, visiting ten provincial venues.

The Four Freshmen's tour lasted ten days and the Free Trade Hall concert was the penultimate night of the tour which finished in London.

At **Chris Barber's** March concert, Howlin' Wolf was unable to appear as he was hospitalised. He was replaced at the last minute by **Clinton Ford**. Ford was from Salford and had sung with the Merseysippi Jazz Band in Liverpool, as well as playing in skiffle goups. He had had a Top 30 hit with 'Old Shep' in 1959 and was in the singles charts with 'Fanlight Fanny' at the time of the Free Trade Hall concert. Ford headlined his own concert later in the year on Boxing Day.

The Mighty Sparrow was a calypso vocalist from Trinidad, having moved there from Grenada as a child. He won the Calypso Crown of 1956 for his song, 'Jean And Dinah.' Sparrow was also famous for his 'Cricket Lovely Cricket' tribute to Garfield Sobers. This Free Trade Hall calypso concert was culturally and historically very important, showing the impact of the growing West Indian community in Manchester. Several white performers had attempted to make calypso style songs, but this was the real thing.

Irene Reid was born in Savannah, Georgia and went on to win the amateur contest at the Apollo Theatre in Harlem, New York five weeks running. She then worked with Dick Vance for two years. Reid sang with Count Basie in the early 1960's, before becoming a solo artist.

Joyce Grenfell was a British actress, comedian and singer. Her humorous monologues showed an extraordinary eye and ear for detail, most famously as a teacher in 'George - Don't Do That.' Grenfell worked with William Blezard who both composed her songs and accompanied her on the piano.

Louis Armstrong was 61 years old when he made his sole appearance at the Free Trade Hall, the final night of a thirteen-date British tour. Armstrong's trumpet playing had started when he was a boy in the Colored Waifs' Home in New Orleans. Later he worked with Kid Ory and King Oliver before forming his Hot Five and Hot Seven groups. In the late 1940's Armstrong formed the six piece All Stars who toured relentlessly for most of the rest of his life.

Erroll Garner was a much loved and imitated jazz pianist. This was his first British tour which visited eight venues. Garner's album *Close Up In Swing* (Philips 1961), reached No. 20 in the charts. His composition, 'Misty' soon became a standard.

Papa Bue, born Arne Bue Jensen in Copenhagen, was a Danish trombonist and bandleader who founded and led the Viking Jazz Band. Their name was given to them by American writer and humorist, Shel Silverstein who had watched one of their concerts in Copenhagen and praised their playing ability. The band played Dixieland style jazz. The Danish band was on a three-week British tour in exchange for a tour of Denmark by Len Baldwin and His Dauphine Street Six.

London-born pianist **George Shearing** had been blind since birth. He played with The Ambrose Dance Band and went on to work with Harry Parry and Stephane Grappelli. In 1947 Shearing settled permanently in the USA and formed his very popular quintet. He played to near-full houses at the Free Trade Hall this year. Joe Williams appeared with him, replacing an indisposed Sarah Vaughan.

The American Folk Blues Festival was heralded in *Melody Maker* thus:

"Britain is going blues crazy! With nine days to go before Melody Maker's *giant Blues and Folk Festival, thousands of fans from all parts of Britain are preparing to invade Manchester. The date: October 21. Venue: Free Trade Hall. Attraction: the biggest ever concentration of world blues talent ever to be presented on one bill in this country. These nine internationally famous artists will be in Britain for one night only. Already coach-loads of fans are set to converge on Manchester from Scotland, Cardiff, Nottingham, Coventry, Norwich and other centres..."*

"Paddy McKiernan: 'The artists are flying in from the Continent for this one-night stand. The demand for tickets is proving tremendous.'

The concerts had a huge effect on young blues fans in the UK. Paul Jones (later of Manfred Mann) hitch-hiked from Oxford to Manchester to see the concert, while Mick Jagger, Keith Richards, Brian Jones and Jimmy Page travelled up from London with other blues fans in a rented panel truck! Tickets were priced from 3s 6d to 12s 6d. A nineteen-year-old photographer, Brian Smith, was able to take some extraordinary pictures, including one of T-Bone Walker playing his guitar at an almost horizontal angle. Behind him– on the stage seats – are rows of young men and women, with virtually all the males wearing jackets and ties.

Memphis Slim both sang and played boogie woogie piano. He had been a regular pianist for Big Bill Broonzy before forming his own band, House Rockers. Slim had made a live album, *At The Gate Of Horn* (Veejay 1959) and later appeared at the Carnegie Hall and the Newport Jazz Festival. He moved to Paris in 1962, following the tradition of so many American writers and performers. **T-Bone Walker** was essentially responsible for being the first to play electric guitar in the blues genre. He was a massive influence on the likes of BB King and John Lee Hooker. Walker amazed the Free Trade Hall audience with both his technique and when he played his guitar behind his head! He returned to the Free Trade Hall four years later as part of a *Jazz At The Philharmonic* package and again in 1968 for that year's American Folk Blues Festival.

John Lee Hooker was originally from Mississippi and moved to Detroit, working in a car factory by day and playing music at night. He started recording in 1948 and eventually had a big seller with 'Boogie Chillen'. Like many of his contemporaries, Hooker benefitted from the folk-blues revival, appearing at the Newport Folk Festival. 1962 was his first visit to Europe. Hooker returned to the Free Trade Hall several times over the next 30 years. **Armand 'Jump' Jackson** was a drummer and band leader who was born in New Orleans, but had moved up to Chicago. Jackson had founded his own record label, La Salle Records in 1959.

Paul Jones: *"I think that those shows were so important... because you didn't get the opportunity to see these guys live. There was something about having seen them live, you just thought, 'Oh man, I'm part of this immense tradition.' I had heard Memphis Slim live and obviously I'd heard jazz music live for years, but I'd heard very little live blues. It was hearing it live and so many of them all on the same evening that made me think, 'This is really it. There's nothing else for me.' That was a real kick to see all that on one evening. I was buzzing for weeks. That was very much a catalyst thing."*

John Lee Hooker: *"The first time I went to Europe was 1962. And boy it was just like the president or Jesus comin' in... Every night was a sell-out. Standing room only, no matter how big the place was."*

The story was told in *Mojo* magazine: *"When (Horst) Lippman and (Fritz) Ran inaugurated the package tours in 1962, the only UK date was at Manchester's Free Trade Hall. The Rolling Stones borrowed a van to attend; writer Neil Slaven took a "hell on wheels" trip by coach: "It rained incessantly and we spent a lot of time hanging around in doorways trying to get our clothes to dry out. But we were agog at seeing the guys for the first time. For me the big deal was seeing John Lee Hooker; at the time we thought T-Bone Walker was a bit Vegas, while Willie Dixon and Memphis Slim obviously had it down pat."*

In *The First Time We Met The Blues* David Williams gives a first-hand account of the build up to the concert, the journey there and back and the actual concerts. It is an entertaining read and includes several of Brian Smith's iconic photographs of T-Bone Walker, Willie Dixon and John Lee Hooker. The book's foreword is written by Jimmy Page, no less!

Unsurprisingly, over the next five decades the accounts of the evening begin to differ. Keith Richards (even more unsurprisingly!) has a different version, claiming that Mick Jagger borrowed his parents' Triumph Herald to drive up to Manchester! The sleeve notes to the Rhythm and Blues CD of the concert state that fathers of British blues, Alexis Korner and John Mayall, were also in the audience. It appears that ABC TV filmed the second show and broadcast it in two parts for its *Tempo* programme. The CD features an off-air recording that was made by "direct line into a Tandberg reel to reel recorder."

Johnny Mathis had been having hit records in Britain since 1958. He had switched from jazz to a more middle of the road "smooth" pop music and became incredibly popular. Mathis's version of 'Misty' reached No. 12 in 1960. This was an eight-date tour with the Free Trade Hall the penultimate night before a final concert in London. Mathis returned to the Free Trade Hall twice in the 1970's.

Louis Jordan was due to appear with Chris Barber at the end of the year. A singer, alto saxophonist and band leader, Jordan had been playing professionally since the 1930's. His most famous songs included 'Choo Choo Ch'Boogie', 'Saturday Night Fish Fry' and 'Caldonia'. Jordan was a big influence on rock 'n' roll music. His Free Trade Hall appearance would have been the third night of a nine-date tour. However, ticket-holders were told on the night that Jordan would not be appearing due to illness. Some of the audience declined to stay and asked for their money back.

Other Events at the Free Trade Hall

January 1st – Toc H Ball with stars of 'Coronation Street'
April 25th to 26th - North West Gas Board Cookery Competition
May 24th – Lebanese Dancing Display
September 12th -13th – Fashion Show
December 31st – British Sailors Society Dance

Elsewhere (Headliners Only)

ABC Ardwick: Chubby Checker, The Everly Brothers, Cliff Richard And The Shadows, Del Shannon, Helen Shapiro.

Odeon: Ronnie Carroll, The Crickets, Adam Faith, Billy Fury, Neil Sedaka, Bobby Vee.

Palace Theatre: Joe Brown, Sam Cooke, Adam Faith, Helen Shapiro, Sophie Tucker, The Tornados.

1963		
Jan 19th	DUKE ELLINGTON ORCHESTRA (two houses)	
Jan 27th	KENNY BALL AND HIS JAZZMEN	*Clinton Ford*
Feb 17th	ACKER BILK AND HIS PARAMOUNT JAZZ BAND	
March 2nd	ELLA FITZGERALD WITH THE OSCAR PETERSON TRIO (two houses)	
March 3rd	CHRIS BARBER BAND with Ottilie Patterson	
March 16th	SHIRLEY BASSEY with Woolf Philips and His Concert Orchestra	*Matt Monro*
March 30th	DAILY WORKER *CELEBRATION* with Ian Campbell Folk Group; Kay Molinari; Terry Whelan and Dave McAdam; Manchester Unity Theatre	
April 13th	THE KINGSTON TRIO	*The Temperance Seven*
April 27th	GERRY MULLIGAN QUARTET WITH BOB BROOKMEYER (two houses)	*Johnny Dankworth Orchestra*
May 18th	RAY CHARLES and his Orchestra and the Raelets	
July 28th	*ASIAN CULTURAL CONCERT* with Mohammed Rafi; Geeta Dutt; Jeeran Kala (two houses)	
Sept 26th	COUNT BASIE ORCHESTRA with Sarah Vaughan; Jimmy Rushing	*Kirk Stuart Trio*
Sept 27th	JOHNNY DANKWORTH AND HIS ORCHESTRA	*Terry Lightfoot's Jazzmen*
October 19th	ERROLL GARNER	
November 23rd	STAN KENTON ORCHESTRA (two houses)	
December 8th	ACKER BILK AND HIS PARAMOUNT JAZZ BAND	

December 24th	*XMAS EVE CARNIVAL* – Non-Stop Dancing Humphrey Lyttelton And His Band	*Syd Munson's Orchestra; Jack Kirkland And His Orchestra*

THIS WAS A YEAR DOMINATED BY JAZZ WITH BRITISH NAMES (Ball, Barber, Bilk, Dankworth and Lyttelton) and American visitors (Ellington, Peterson, Basie, Mulligan, Kenton and Ella).

This year saw **Duke Ellington's** debut at the Free Trade Hall; both houses were sold out. He had appeared at the King's Hall at Belle Vue in 1958 and was now in his early 60's. Ellington was a composer, arranger, pianist and, of course, bandleader. He had started playing at the Cotton Club in the 1920's and led his own orchestra for decades. Ellington toured Europe throughout the 1960's, returning to the Free Trade Hall in 1964, 1965, 1966, 1967 and finally, in 1969. Two days on the 1963 tour were spent filming at Granada Television's Chelsea Studios.

The Ian Campbell Folk Group had been performing since the late 1950's. Their E.P. *Ceilidh At The Crown* (Topic 1962) was the first live folk club recording to be released. The group signed this year to the Transatlantic label and would later appear at the Newport Folk Festival, Royal Albert Hall and on several television programmes. They would appear six times at the Free Trade Hall.

Terry Whelan had been a stalwart of the north-west folk scene since the late 1950's. He appeared at the Wayfarer's Folk Club in Manchester alongside Dave Hillary and Harry Boardman.

The Kingston Trio was a million-selling folk act in their native USA and had had several No.1 albums. Their only big hit single in Britain was their version of 'Tom Dooley' which reached No. 5 in 1958, two places below Lonnie Donegan's rendition. John Stewart had joined the group in 1961, replacing Dave Guard. The trio had just released their album, *New Frontier* (Capitol 1962) but they were coming to the end of their dominance in American folk music. This concert was one of only a four-date British tour.

Ray Charles made his first appearance at the Free Trade Hall this year. He had been recording since 1949 and brought the fervour of gospel music into rhythm and blues. Charles could perform both uptempo songs like 'What'd I Say' and slow ballads like 'Drown In My Own Tears'. He moved record labels in 1959 to ABC where he was able to have both artistic and financial freedom. His two *Modern Sounds In Country And Western Music* albums (HMV 1962/ 1963) were huge hits in Britain and a single taken from the first volume, 'I Can't Stop Loving You' reached No. 1 in July 1962. Charles would return to the Free Trade Hall on three more occasions.

The **Count Basie** and **Sarah Vaughan** concert was filmed by Granada Television.

Jimmy Rushing was a larger than life blues "shouter" and often called Mr 'Five By Five' referring to his similar height and width! Rushing had sung with Count Basie between 1935 and 1948, as well as with Ellington and Brubeck. He was back singing with Count Basie on the latter's 1963 tour.

Other events at the Free Trade Hall

January 5th to 11th – Pram Fair
February 15th to 16th - Leonard Bernstein And The New York Philharmonic Orchestra
March 8th – NCH Festival Of Queens with Pat Phoenix
September 6th – Cookery Demonstration
December 24th – Christmas Eve Carnival – Non-Stop Dancing
December 26th – Boxing Night Carnival – Non-Stop Dancing

Elsewhere (Headliners only)

ABC Ardwick: The Beatles, Billy Fury, Gerry And The Pacemakers, Cliff Richard And The Shadows, Bobby Rydell, Helen Shapiro.

Belle Vue (Kings Hall): *Daily Mail* International Jazz Festival.

Odeon: The Beatles, Brook Benton, Joe Brown, Dion, Duane Eddy, The Everly Brothers, Brenda Lee, John Leyton, Roy Orbison, Del Shannon, The Tornados.

Palace Theatre: John Barry Seven, Adam Faith, Tony Hancock, Jet Harris and Tony Meehan.

1964		
Jan 20th	TOMMY DORSEY ORCHESTRA WITH FRANK SINATRA JUNIOR	
Jan 24th	CHRIS BARBER'S JAZZ BAND WITH OTTILIE PATTERSON	
Feb 9th	KENNY BALL AND HIS JAZZ MEN	
Feb 22nd	PETE SEEGER	
Feb 29th	DUKE ELLINGTON AND HIS ORCHESTRA (two houses)	
April 4th	ABC TELEVISION'S *HULLABALOO* with Rory McEwen; Ian Campbell Folk Group; Isla Cameron; Bob Davenport; Malcolm Price Trio	
April 8th	ELLA FITZGERALD AND OSCAR PETERSON TRIO (two houses)	*Roy Eldridge Quartet*
April 25th	MODERN JAZZ QUARTET (two houses)	*Laurindo Almeida*
May 8th	*THE AMERICAN FOLK, BLUES AND GOSPEL CARAVAN* with Sonny Terry and Brownie McGhee; Muddy Waters; Sister Rosetta Tharpe	*Mississippi John Hurt; Rev Gary Davis; Cousin Joe Pleasants; Otis Spann*
May 24th	*HOOT'NANNY: A FOLK BLUES CONCERT* Dominic Behan; Alex Campbell;	*Malcolm Price Trio; Nigel Denver; The Haverim; North West 4*
May 31st	CHRIS BARBER AND HIS BAND with Ottilie Patterson	
June 6th	DAVE BRUBECK QUARTET (two houses)	*Ronnie Scott Quartet*
July 11th	RAY CHARLES, his Orchestra And The Raelettes	
Sept 9th	GRACIE FIELDS	
Sept 28th	NINA AND FREDERICK with The Keith Chalkley Trio and Ray Dempsey (guitar)	
Oct 17th	ERROLL GARNER	

Oct 22nd	*AMERICAN FOLK BLUES FESTIVAL* with Howlin' Wolf; Sonny Boy Williamson; Lightnin' Hopkins; Sleepy John Estes; Willie Dixon (two houses)	*Sugar Pie DeSanto*
December 4th	*FOLK/CND* with Ian Campbell Folk Group; Alex Campbell; Bob Davenport; Cyril Tawney; Hylda Sims and Roseanne Law	
December 6th	*BIG CITY BLUES* with Howlin' Wolf; Hubert Sumlin; Chris Barber's Blues Band with Ottilie Patterson; Long John Baldry and The Hoochie Coochie Men (two houses)	

BY NOW THE TRAD JAZZ BOOM WAS VIRTUALLY OVER WITH no appearances by Acker Bilk, just two by Chris Barber and only one by Kenny Ball. American jazz stars included Dave Brubeck; Duke Ellington; Ella Fitzgerald, Oscar Peterson and Erroll Garner. Folk music was clearly growing in popularity. One folk concert was promoted by CND, showing the importance of music in the peace movement.

The Tommy Dorsey Orchestra was still touring after their leader's death in 1956. Dorsey had employed a young Frank Sinatra in the 1940's. Sinatra's young son, **Frank Sinatra Jnr,** had a hard act to follow but appeared at the Free Trade Hall this year with the Dorsey Orchestra. Later, Frank Junior would work with his father as musical director. This concert was filmed by Granada Television with four cameras. The director was Philip Casson who had been responsible for the Little Richard show on Granada.

Pete Seeger had appeared at the Lesser Free Trade Hall in 1961, but this was his first - and only - appearance in the main hall. Seeger was a folk singer and social activist and his songs included 'Turn! Turn ! Turn!', 'Where Have All The Flowers Gone?' and 'If I Had A Hammer.' Luckily, this concert was recorded and shows Seeger's remarkable skill at performing. He also made two 'In Concert' programmes for BBC Television's *Tonight In Person*. Excerpts may be seen on YouTube.

Duke Ellington was on a six-date British tour and recorded a 45 minute programme for BBC-2 while he was in the country.

Eton-educated **Rory McEwen** hosted ATV's *Hullabaloo* folk music programme. He had visited the USA and learned to master Leadbelly's twelve-string guitar technique. McEwen also appeared on the BBC *Tonight* television programme singing topical calypsos and folk songs. **Isla Cameron** was a Scottish singer and had released a solo folk song album, *Through Bushes And Briars* (Tradition 1956). She also worked with Ewan MacColl and Peggy Seeger. Cameron provided the singing in the 1967 film *Far From The Madding Crowd* for Julie Christie.

Bob Davenport was a folk singer from the North East who moved down to London. He made two E.P's : *Geordie Songs* (Collector Records 1959) and *Wor Geordie* (Topic 1962). Davenport was invited by Pete Seeger to perform at the Newport Folk Festival in 1963.

The Malcolm Price Trio was a British group who played American songs. They recorded an EP *Pickin' On The Country Strings* (Oak 1963). The trio featured mandolin and autoharp and later made an album, *Way Down Town* (Decca 1965).

After the Ella Fitzgerald and Oscar Peterson concert in April, there were complaints about "poor acoustics". This situation had also been reported at the Sarah Vaughan/ Count Basie concert the previous September and at one of the blues packages. All of these concerts had been filmed by Granada TV. Similarly, in January the vocalists at the Tommy Dorsey gig had been reported as " inaudible" when it had been filmed by Granada. On April 9th the Town Hall Superintendent wrote to promoter Harold Davison to tell him that there would be "no more televised shows." This may have pleased concert-goers at the time but would leave very little filmed footage of popular music at the Free Trade Hall.

The American Folk, Blues And Gospel Caravan featured Sister Rosetta Tharpe, Sonny Terry, Brownie McGhee and Muddy Waters who had all been introduced to British audiences in the late 1950's by Chris Barber. Other artists on the bill - Rev Gary Davis, Cousin Joe Pleasants and Mississippi John Hurt - were less familiar to British audiences. A young Joe Boyd was tour manager and had assumed - and hoped - that the different artists would play together, but "resentments and objections came at me from all sides... What emerged, to my naive surprise, was that they were almost complete strangers to one another." Happily, as the tour went on, the different artists - from different parts of the USA and different traditions - began to play together.

Joe Boyd: "*Most halls were sold out, and little by little my notions were added to the show. Ransom (Knowling) played a number with Brownie and Sonny and accompanied Cousin Joe (Pleasants) and Sister Rosetta for their entire sets. Willie (Dixon) started joining Otis (Spann)*

for his song with Rosetta, then Brownie was persuaded to play some guitar behind Cousin Joe. The atmosphere began to feel like a friendly get-together rather than a formal concert."

Although the Free Trade Hall concert was not filmed for posterity, there was another, arguably more imaginative, showcase for these legendary performers. Granada Television, as well as producing *Coronation Street* and many other innovative programmes, often seized the opportunity to film American visitors to the Free Trade Hall and many jazz performances had been recorded.

Joe Boyd:"*In Manchester, producer Johnny Hamp ... set us up at a disused railway station with fake bales of cotton for Sonny and Brownie and a dolly to film Muddy walking down 'that lonesome railroad track.'... Towards the end, when Rosetta gets the audience clapping along... I glimpsed my twenty-one-year-old self in the background, clapping!*"

Fortunately, this footage is still available and is a treat for both blues fans and railway aficionados. It was filmed at Chorlton-cum-Hardy Station (now rebuilt as a Metrolink stop) and has Sister Rosetta Tharpe arriving in a carriage. The Manchester weather provides a literal accompaniment to Tharpe's rendition of 'Didn't It Rain?'

Dublin born **Dominic Behan** was a folk singer, songwriter, writer and active Irish Republican. He migrated to London and wrote well-received plays, poems, songs and books and worked with Ewan MacColl. Behan accused Bob Dylan of plagiarizing his song 'The Patriot Game' for 'With God On Our Side'. Both songs share the same tune. Dylan is heard being disparaging about Behan in the film, *Don't Look Back.*

Alex Campbell was a Scottish folk singer who was one of the biggest names on the scene. After busking in Paris, he returned to Britain and made a vast number of albums including *Alex Campbell Sings Folk* (Society 1964). Campbell had a huge influence on his fellow performers and was something of a mentor to Sandy Denny at the start of her career.

Gracie Fields had played at Belle Vue twice in the 1950's, but this was her only Free Trade Hall appearance. She was now in her mid-sixties and this year saw Fields' final

British tour, after five years of retirement at her home on the island of Capri. The Free Trade Hall concert was the second night of eleven dates. Two months later she played the Royal Variety Performance and footage on YouTube shows a flawless and powerful medley of 'September Song' and 'Scarlet Ribbons'.

Ray Charles began his 1964 British tour at the Free Trade Hall; his concert in Croydon was filmed by Rediffusion Television.

The American Folk Blues Festival was advertised as "A Documentary of the Authentic Blues" and visited four provincial cities, as well as two nights in Croydon. The Free Trade Hall concert was fortunately filmed and *The American Folk-Blues Festival – The British Tours 1963- 1966* DVD gives us priceless footage of not just the extraordinary blues performers, but also the inside of the Free Trade Hall and the audience! We first see **Sonny Boy Williamson** performing solo with his harmonica which he even plays with his left nostril at one point! On 'Getting Out Of Town' Williamson is joined by a rhythm section which includes **Willie Dixon** on double bass. Dressed in a bowler hat and tailored suit, Williamson gives a memorable performance with even more nostril playing and inserting the harmonica into his mouth! Guitarist Hubert Sumlin plays a brilliant, economical solo.

Lightnin' Hopkins appeared solo, sitting at the front of the Free Trade Hall stage with his amplifier next to him. Hopkins was a country bluesman from Texas who had been encouraged by Blind Lemon Jefferson. After a career playing for black audiences, Hopkins was rediscovered by Sam Charters, a blues fan, and this led to a comeback album, *The Roots Of Lightnin' Hopkins* (Folkways 1959). Later he played Carnegie Hall alongside Pete Seeger and Joan Baez. On the DVD Hopkins performs two songs: 'Come Go With Me' and a much slower 'Lightnin's Blues'.

Sleepy John Estes was born in Tennessee at the end of the nineteenth century and was blinded in one eye as a child. His singing and guitar playing were an influence on Big Bill Broonzy. Estes was totally blind by 1949. His career was revived in the 1950's by his appearance in a documentary film by David Blumenthal. He, unfortunately, is not seen in the DVD.

Sugar Pie DeSanto was more of a soul singer, having played with Johnny Otis who gave her that name. She sings a cover of Jimmy Reed's 'Baby What Do You Want Me To Do' and then, after a bit of comic on-stage banter with the musicians, 'Rock Me Baby'. DeSanto is definitely more "show-biz" than her fellow artistes, wearing a shortish ballgown, long black gloves and plenty of eye-liner. She seems to be about half the size of double-bass playing Willie Dixon!

Howlin' Wolf headlined the concert and had actually reached the singles charts in Britain in 1964 with 'Smokestack Lightning'. Wolf dominated the Chicago blues scene after the war and worked with Willie Dixon who provided him with an endless supply of memorable songs. The Wolf comes on to the stage to great applause. In the footage of the Free Trade Hall concert he performs 'Smokestack Lightning' and the audience clap along. On 'Don't Laugh At Me', he plays rhythm guitar. Wolf's guitarist Hubert Sumlin is wonderful to watch; a guitar hero who does not need to show off and who looks about half of his thirty-one years. The audience is incredibly well-behaved, especially the ones who are sitting behind the stage. Even the late-comers tiptoe in. The audience do not whoop or cheer during the songs or even applaud solos, but wait until the end of each song before showing their genuine appreciation. Some of them are smoking but none are drinking - the opposite of so many concerts nowadays! There is something inspirational about seeing this young all-white audience giving so much respect and recognition to a black American musician who is the same generation as their parents.

Soon after the tour, the Rolling Stones released their cover of Howlin' Wolf's 'Little Red Rooster' hit. The song - written by Willie Dixon - reached No.1, the second of two chart-toppers by the Stones in 1964. It was a brave move for a pop group at the time to release an authentic blues song as a single.

A **Folk/CND** concert in December included **Cyril Tawney**, an English singer-songwriter who sang songs from Devon and Cornwall. Tawney had served in the Royal Navy where he became interested in navy songs, he had appeared on radio and television and had been called the "Founding Father of the West Country folk revival." One of Tawney's songs, 'Sally Free And Easy' has been covered by many folk artists including Bob Dylan, The Pentangle and The Corries. **Hylda Sims** had been given a guitar as a teenager by Ivor Cutler. She started singing in 1950's Soho and joined the City Ramblers Skiffle Group.

Big City Blues saw **Howlin' Wolf** return to the Free Trade Hall just two months after his previous visit. By now, **Chris Barber** was leading a blues band. **Long John Baldry's** nickname was appropriate: he was six foot seven inches tall. Baldry was leading **The Hoochie Coochie Men** who had previously been the Cyril Davies All Stars. British harmonica player Davies had sadly died at the beginning of the year aged only 31.

Melody Maker offered a detailed review under the headline 'Wolf, Baldry, Barber Wow Manchester': *"The combined bands of Chris Barber's Blues Band and Long John Baldry's Hoochie Coochie Men played 'C Jam Blues' with a spot of 'Woodchoppers Ball' and 'One O'Clock Jump' thrown in. It nearly stopped the show, building up tremendous excitement. Long John, too, scored a big personal success despite being inaudible for two numbers due to a mystery breakdown in the hall's new £3000 amplification system and Ottilie Patterson's way-out version of 'St Louis Blues' was another big success.*

"Six numbers from Howlin' Wolf closed the show. Nothing could have followed his authoritative renditions of the blues in every mood. High spots were 'May I Have A Talk With You,' 'C'mon Baby,' 'Walk With Me,' 'Goin' Down Slow'- and his final number - 'Howlin' For My Baby' with its fantastic riff backing."

Chris Barber explained his band's subtle changes: "We already made a much more fundamental change to the band, by adding a blues guitarist to the line-up, alongside the banjo... I felt we needed the sound of a blues guitarist to broaden the range of what we could do in concert ourselves. So, in August 1964, I brought in a guitarist for our album *Good Morning Blues*, called John Slaughter."

Other events at the Free Trade Hall

February 8th – Judo Demonstration
March 9th – Boxing - In Aid Of The Jewish Blind Society
September 25th – Fashion Show
November 21st – Methodist Youth Rally

Elsewhere: (Headliners Only)

ABC Ardwick: The Beatles, Dave Clark Five, The Hollies, Cliff Richard And The Shadows.

Belle Vue (Kings Hall) - Jerry Lee Lewis.

Odeon : The Animals, Shirley Bassey, Chuck Berry, The Big Beat Scene, Adam Faith, Freddie And The Dreamers, Billy Fury, The Hollies, Manfred Mann, Roy Orbison, The Rolling Stones, The Searchers, Bobby Vee, Dionne Warwick.

Palace Theatre : Cannonball Adderley Sextet, Lonnie Donegan, Frank Ifield, The Rolling Stones, Mel Torme, Gene Vincent.

1965		
Jan 29th	*AMERICAN NEGRO GOSPEL FESTIVAL* with Bishop Samuel Kelsey; The Original Five Blind Boys Of Mississippi (two houses)	*Inez Andrews And The Andrewettes; The Congragation Of The Temple Church , Washington D.C. with Sister Lena Philips Jones; Rev. John I. Little*
Feb 20th	*SONG FESTIVAL '65* with Matt McGinn; Sandra Kerr; Anne Briggs; Sydney Carter; Three City Four; The Dubliners; Sandy and Jeanie	
Feb 27th	DUKE ELLINGTON AND HIS ORCHESTRA (two houses)	
March 20th	THELONIOUS MONK QUARTET	
April 13th	ELLA FITZGERALD AND THE OSCAR PETERSON TRIO (two houses)	*Tommy Flanagan Trio*
April 24th	TONY BENNETT with The Ralph Sharon Trio (two houses)	*Johnny Spence And His Orchestra; Morgan James Duo*
May 7th	BOB DYLAN	
May 28th	SHIRLEY BASSEY with Cyril Stapleton And His Show Band (two houses)	
June 1st	LOUIS ARMSTRONG AND HIS ALL STARS (two houses)	*Terry Lightfoot's Jazzmen*
June 4th	*AMERICAN FOLK SONG AND BLUES CONCERT* with Jack Elliott; Rev. Gary Davis; Buffy Sainte-Marie; Julie Felix; Derroll Adams	
Sept 24th	PETER, PAUL AND MARY	
Sept 25th	COUNT BASIE ORCHESTRA (two houses)	
October 1st	JOAN BAEZ	

Oct 15th	*AMERICAN FOLK BLUES FESTIVAL* With JB Lenoir; Buddy Guy; Eddie Boyd; John Lee Hooker; Roosevelt Sykes; Big Walter; Mississippi Fred McDowell; Doctor Ross; Big Mama Thornton (two houses)	*Freddie Below; Lonesome Jimmy Lee; Shakey Horton*
Oct 16th	*DAILY WORKER FOLK CONCERT* with Nigel Denver; Enoch Kent; Sandra Kerr and John Faulkner; The Watersons; Peter McGovern; Terry Whelan	
Oct 18th	THE CLANCY BROTHERS AND TOMMY MAKEM	
Oct 23rd	MODERN JAZZ QUARTET	
Nov 27th - morning	*MANCHESTER FOLK FESTIVAL –* The Spinners – children's concert	*Local Morris men*
Nov 27th - afternoon	*MANCHESTER FOLK FESTIVAL 'CONTEMPORARY AND AMERICAN'* Dominic Behan; Ralph Rinzler; Ian Campbell Folk Group; NW Folk Four; Phil Ochs; Cyril Tawney; Doc Watson	
Nov 27th - evening	*MANCHESTER FOLK FESTIVAL 'TRADITIONAL SONGS AND RITUAL DANCES'* A.L. Lloyd; Bob Davenport And The Rakes; Cyril Tawney; Felix Doran, Bob Roberts; Charlie Bate; Scan Tester; Fred Jordan; Phoebe Smith; Britannia Coconut Dancers	
Dec 3rd	THE CORRIE FOLK TRIO	*Paddy Bell*
Dec 4th	DIZZY GILLESPIE QUINTET (two houses)	*Jimmy Smith Trio*

A YEAR THAT SAW A BALANCE OF FOLK, BLUES AND AMERICAN jazz; American folk stars – Bob Dylan; Peter, Paul And Mary and Joan Baez all made their Free Trade Hall debut.

The American Negro Gospel Festival was jointly promoted by the National Jazz Federation. This was the first festival of its kind to play in Britain. The Free Trade Hall concert was the first of six dates around England, concluding at Croydon's Fairfield Halls. Bishop Kelsey was a singing minister who had moved to Washington D.C. in 1923. He set up a radio ministry which lasted for four decades. Kelsey also made records of traditional gospel songs but was cheated on his deserved royalties.

There was an album released featuring both singing and sermonising, *Bishop Samuel Kelsey And The Congregation Of The Temple Church Of God In Christ, Washington D.C.* (Polydor 1965). Vocalion released EP's by The Five Blind Boys Of Mississippi and Inez Andrews to coincide with the tour.

Matt McGinn was a Scottish folk singer and songwriter. Born in Glasgow, the eighth of nine children, he later met Pete Seeger and was invited to perform at the Carnegie Hall in New York, alongside Bob Dylan. McGinn appeared on *Broadside Ballads Volume 1.* **Sandra Kerr** was an English folk singer and a member of the Critics Group which was led by Ewan MacColl and Peggy Seeger. Later in the decade, Kerr and John Faulkner made a duet album on Argo. The couple later wrote the music for the *Bagpuss* children's television series.

Anne Briggs is best known for her definitive version of 'She Moves Through The Fair.' She appeared on the compilation *The Iron Muse* (Topic 1963) and released her own EP, *The Hazards Of Love* (Topic 1963). Later, Briggs moved to Ireland. **Sydney Carter** was a poet, songwriter and folk musician who had worked with Donald Swann and Sheila Hancock. He is most famous for writing the words to 'Lord Of The Dance', using an old Shaker tune, 'Simple Gifts.' Carter later recorded the song with Martin Carthy, The Johnny Scott Trio and the Mike Sammes Singers (Elektra 1966.)

The Three City Four were an English folk group comprising Martin Carthy, Marian Mackenzie, Leon Rosselson and Ralph Trainer. Their eponymous first album was released this year (Decca 1965). The group concentrated on contemporary songs written in the folk tradition, Rosselson being the main writer.

The Dubliners were an Irish folk band who formed in 1962 and were originally called The Ronnie Drew Ballad Group after their joint lead singer. Their new name really did come from the title of James Joyce's novel. After recording three live albums for Transatlantic, the Dubliners signed with Major Minor Records in 1965. The hit - 'Seven Drunken Nights' -came two years later, helped by relentless plugging on Radio Caroline and reached No. 7. The record label's owner, Phil Solomon, was also a co-director of the pirate radio station! The group's first studio album *A Drop Of The Hard Stuff* (Major Minor 1967) reached No. 5 and stayed in the charts for 41 weeks. Traditional folk music had never before had this sort of chart success and exposure. The Dubliners appeared nine times at the Free Trade Hall between 1965 and 1983.

Sandy & Jeanie Darlington were an American duo playing old-time country music, accompanying themselves on banjo, autoharp, fiddle and guitar. Their self-titled first album was released this year (XTRA 1965).

The **Duke Ellington** tour was twelve dates long and the Free Trade Hall concert was the penultimate night. Ellington also recorded two television programmes for BBC-2 while he was in Britain.

Tony Bennett made his first appearance at the Free Trade Hall this year; he would return five more times. Bennett had started singing while serving in the American

Army's entertainment unit at the end of World War Two. He topped the American charts at the beginning of the 1950's but his career faded towards the end of that decade. Bennett made a major comeback in the early 1960's and won a Grammy for 'I Left My Heart In San Francisco'. He appeared at the Free Trade Hall with long-time collaborators arranger-pianist Ralph Sharon and trumpet player Bobby Hackett.

Bob Dylan was on his first British tour and the Free Trade Hall was the last of six provincial gigs before he played two nights at the Royal Albert Hall in London. D.A. Pennebaker's *Don't Look Back* film of the tour is a fascinating historical document of Britain in 1965. We see Dylan's train arrive at Manchester Victoria Station on one of the outer platforms. The next scene is Dylan sound-checking in a dark, empty hall.

Dylan played two sets at the Free Trade Hall, mixing his older material with six songs from his new album, *Bringing It All Back Home* (CBS 1965). On the extra disc of the *Don't Look Back* DVD, entitled *Bob Dylan 65 Revisited*, we see Dylan in a Free Trade Hall dressing room playing blues on his guitar. A member of the Free Trade Hall staff makes conversation and asks Dylan if he had come down from Newcastle that day. There is then a discussion about Pennebaker's camera. A young female fan, "Carol", (who we have already seen outside Dylan's hotel in Liverpool) sits close to Dylan. Tom Wilson, Dylan's record producer, is standing in the room and smoking. The scene changes to Dylan singing 'If You Gotta Go, Go Now' a hit single later in the year for Manfred Mann. The camera is high up on the left Side Circle of the venue. At the end of the song, the camera pulls back to reveal the spartan nature of the stage. There are two microphone stands and a stool with a glass of water and Dylan's harmonicas. This was long before stage monitors became compulsory equipment at all live concerts!

The original *Don't Look Back* film then cuts to the Dylan entourage – Dylan himself, Bobby Neuwith, manager Albert Grossman and record producer Tom Wilson fleeing the Free Trade Hall while the National Anthem plays over the tannoy. They have problems leaving the building, getting lost in the maze of backstage corridors and trying to find an exit. Was this the inspiration for a similar scene in *This Is Spinal Tap*? The men eventually emerge in Southmill Street where the side of the Theatre Royal is clearly seen. We can also see Central Station in the background. Girls scream as Dylan appears and we hear a male voice: "Get a taxi, Pete!" The fans run after Dylan's car. It is worth remembering how young these people were: Dylan was about to celebrate his 24th birthday, Neuwith was 25 years old, Grossman was – amazingly – only 38 years old and Wilson, already a veteran record producer, was 34!

John Faulkner was born in London and met Ewan MacColl and Peggy Seeger who introduced him to British and Irish folk music.

In June a mixed group of folk and blues artists appeared. **'Rambling' Jack Elliott**

- despite being of Jewish parentage in Brooklyn- had the image of a cowboy and had met Woody Guthrie. Elliott was a big influence on Bob Dylan and used to introduce the latter as his "son" in American folk clubs. Elliott had made an album with **Derroll Adams** called *The Rambling Boys* (Topic 1958). Adams was born in Portland, Oregon and busked all over the world in the 1950's. He met Donovan and Paul Simon in England in 1965. Adams can be seen in the Savoy Hotel party scene of the film, *Don't Look Back* talking to Dylan who is clearly aware of Adams' work with Elliott.

Rev. Gary Davis returned to the Free Trade Hall after appearing on the American Blues, Folk And Gospel Caravan in 1964. Born in 1896, Davis was a virtuoso blues guitarist who was huge influence on younger players. He was ordained in 1937, adding 'Reverend' to his name. Later Davis moved to New York and preached and sang on the streets of Harlem. Like many veteran blues musicians, his career revived in the 1960's with appearances at folk festivals.

Buffy Sainte-Marie was a Canadian singer-songwriter who had been born on the Piapot Plains Cree First Nation Reserve in Saskatchewan. She was orphaned and adopted as an infant, and was raised in Massachusetts. After university, Sainte-Marie moved to Greenwich Village and performed at the Gaslight Cafe. Her first album *It's My Way* (Fontana 1964) included her composition, 'Universal Soldier' which was later successfully covered by Donovan and became a theme song for the anti-war movement.

Julie Felix was born in California and came to Britain in the early 1960's, signing to Decca. She was one of the first artists to cover songs by Bob Dylan, Leonard Cohen and Woody Guthrie. Felix went on to appear on David Frost's television show and have her own BBC series where she often duetted with her guests. She appeared at the Free Trade Hall every year between 1965 and 1971.

American folk trio **Peter, Paul and Mary** were incredibly successful in the USA, not least in bringing Dylan's songs to a wider audience. In Britain their version of 'Blowin' In The Wind' reached No. 13 in autumn 1963 and three albums reached the Top 20 in the next eighteen months. The Free Trade Hall concert was the third of a nine-date British tour. While in Britain, the trio recorded two *Tonight In Person* programmes for BBC1 which can be seen on YouTube.

Joan Baez travelled with Bob Dylan on some of his 1965 British tour but did not appear on stage as Dylan seemed to be deliberately putting the 'protest' era of his career behind him. Baez had already had reached the Top 10 in Britain with her album *In Concert Volume Two* (Fontana 1964). In 1965 she had great success in Britain, with three more albums reaching the Top 10. Baez's cover of Dylan's 'It's All Over Now, Baby Blue' reached No. 22 in the singles charts. Her sole Free Trade Hall appearance was part of an eleven-date British tour.

The American Folk Blues Festival visited seven venues and the opening night was at the Free Trade Hall. There were two houses, one at 6.30 pm and one at 8.40

pm. **JB Lenoir** moved from Missisippi to Chicago where he was encouraged by Big Bill Broonzy. Lenoir had a skill for political commentary in his songs. He worked twice with Willie Dixon. Sadly, Lenoir died in a car crash in 1967 aged only 37. **Buddy Guy** was something of a youngster on this tour; he had not reached his 30th birthday! Born in Louisiana, Guy moved north to Chicago and eventually signed to Chess Records. Here he worked as a session guitarist for Muddy Waters, Willie Dixon and others. Later, Guy worked with Junior Wells and recorded for Vanguard. **Eddie Boyd** moved from Mississippi to Chicago and played piano with Muddy Waters and Sonny Boy Williamson. His song, 'Five Long Years' was covered by many other blues artists. After this 1965 tour, Boyd settled in Europe, first in Paris and then in Helsinki. He went on to record with Peter Green.

Roosevelt Sykes was a blues pianist who grew up in St. Louis, applying his church organ experience to playing barrelhouse piano. He recorded for various labels and moved to Chicago and, subsequently, New Orleans. **Big Walter**, like his 'Little' namesake, was a harmonica player. Born in Mississippi, Walter 'Shakey' Horton moved between Memphis and Chicago and eventually joined Muddy Waters' band, briefly replacing Junior Wells. **Mississippi Fred McDowell** was yet another Delta bluesman rescued from obscurity by the 1960's revival. Despite his moniker, McDowell was from Tennessee originally, but later moved to Mississippi where he both farmed cotton and played the blues. Here he was 'discovered' by Alan Lomax and Shirley Collins in the late 1950's.

Doctor Ross was a one-man blues band whose nickname originated when he was a paramedic in the army. Ross worked on the General Motors assembly line in Michigan while performing at night! **Big Mama Thornton** is best known for singing the original versions of 'Hound Dog' and 'Ball And Chain' before the songs were successfully covered by Elvis Presley and Janis Joplin respectively. Thornton's career revived after this tour and she signed to Arhoolie. Her album, *Big Mama Thornton With The Chicago Blues Band* (Arhoolie 1966) featured both Muddy Waters and Otis Spann.

Nigel Denver was born in Glasgow and became a member of CND. His eponymous first album (Decca 1965) featured Martin Carthy on guitar. **Enoch Kent** was born in Scotland and his first single was 'The Ballad Of Johnny Ramensky' in 1959. He contributed to the *Irish Rebel Songs* album (Ace Of Clubs 1963), singing 'The Manchester Martyrs.' **Pete McGovern** was born in Liverpool of Irish parents and worked on the railway where he was an active trade unionist and campaigner. McGovern is most famous for writing 'In My Liverpool Home'.

The Watersons comprised sisters Lal and Norma, brother Mike and their cousin John Harrison. They had run a folk club in their native Hull and recorded for Topic. The Watersons' unaccompanied four-part harmony singing was an important part of the folk revival. Their first album was *Frost And Fire* (Topic 1965).

This year saw the first Free Trade Hall appearance for **The Spinners.** The group were formed in 1958 and associated with Liverpool where they ran a folk club, the

Triton, for many years. The Spinners mixed traditional songs with new songs written in the folk genre. In 1963 they had signed with Fontana and released two albums recorded at the Philharmonic Hall, Liverpool. The group went on to make the most appearances of any non-classical artists at the Free Trade Hall.

The Clancy Brothers consisted of Tom, Paddy and Liam. They soon teamed up with whistle player, **Tommy Makem**. The group were the founders of the New York folk revival in the late 1950's and gained a large following. Their ubiquitous Aran jumpers had originally been sent to the Clancys by their mother who had heard about the winter weather in New York. Soon these jumpers became the group's trademark, boosting sales of the product around the world. Signed to Columbia Records in the USA, the Clancys' most famous songs included 'Jug Of Punch' and 'The Leaving Of Liverpool.' Their album, *Isn't It Grand Boys* (CBS 1966) would reach No. 22 in Britain. The Clancys -without Makem - returned to the Free Trade Hall in 1970.

Phil Ochs was born in Texas but moved to Greenwich Village and became part of the New York folk scene, most notably as a protest singer. He had an uneasy relationship with Bob Dylan. His second album was *I Ain't Marching Anymore* (Elektra 1965). Ochs suffered from depression and this may have prevented him gaining greater popularity.

Ralph Rinzler was a singer and mandolin player. He was a member of the Greenbriar Boys who had played at Folk City in Greenwich Village. Rinzler was the co-founder of the Smithsonian Folklife Festival in Washington DC; he was working at the Smithsonian Museum at the time.

Doc Watson had been discovered by Ralph Rinzler and released records on the Vanguard label. He was something of a multi-instrumentalist, playing guitar, banjo, autoharp, harmonica and mandolin, despite being blind. Watson was a pioneer of the flat-picking technique on the guitar.

A.L. "Bert" Lloyd was also important in the folk song revival in Britain. He was a song collector and actually served on a whaling ship, collecting more songs. Lloyd also sang and made several albums on Topic Records. He worked with Vaughan Williams on *The Penguin Book Of Folk Songs*.'

The Corrie Folk Trio were a Scottish group featuring Ronnie Browne, Bill Smith and Roy Williamson who were the resident group on the BBC's 'Hoot'nanny' programme. They recorded an album with Paddie Bell in 1964 and a second album, *The Promise Of The Day* (Waverley 1965). Smith left the group in 1966 and Browne and Williamson became The Corries. The Corries returned to the Free Trade Hall in 1970.

Whereas American jazz was represented by the likes of Duke Ellington, Thelonius Monk, Ella Fitzgerald, Oscar Peterson, Count Basie and The Modern Jazz Quartet, by 1965 British jazz had totally disappeared!

Other events at the Free Trade Hall

February 22nd – Vienna Boys Choir
March 12th – NCH Festival Of Queens
May 1st – Kodak Film Show
October 8th - *Africa* film of The Ronald E. Shann Central African Expedition

Elsewhere (Headliners Only)

ABC Ardwick: The Bachelors, The Beatles, Cilla Black, Billy Fury, Roy Orbison, Peter and Gordon, Gene Pitney, Helen Shapiro, Nancy Wilson.

Belle Vue (Kings Hall): P.J. Proby.

Odeon : Chuck Berry, Victor Borge, Wayne Fontana And The Mindbenders, Herman's Hermits, Frank Ifield, Cliff Richard and The Shadows, The Rolling Stones, The Searchers, Del Shannon, Tamla Motown Tour.

Opera House : Marlene Dietrich.

1966		
Jan 14th	*AMERICAN NEGRO GOSPEL FESTIVAL* with Bishop Samuel Kelsey; The Gospelaires Of Dayton, Ohio; The Dorothy Norwood Singers Of Chicago; Rev. John I. Little; The Harmonizing Four Of Richmond, Virginia	
Feb 5th	THE SPINNERS	
Feb 14th	*FOLK SONG ANCIENT AND MODERN* with The Watersons; Tom Paxton	*Hedy West; Alex Campbell; Louis Killen ; Roy Guest (compère)*
Feb 19th	ELLA FITZGERALD; DUKE ELLINGTON ORCHESTRA (two houses)	
March 14th	WOODY HERMAN AND HIS ORCHESTRA	
April 2nd	OSCAR PETERSON TRIO	
April 25th	JULIE FELIX	*Mike Seeger; The McPeake Family*
April 29th	THELONIOUS MONK QUARTET	
May 14th	ORNETTE COLEMAN TRIO	*The Lehal Wind Ensemble playing "Forms And Sounds For Wind Quartet"*
May 17th	BOB DYLAN AND THE HAWKS	
May 28th	*GOSPEL RHYTHM FESTIVAL* The Folktellers; The Calvary Links; The Cobblers; The Crossbeats; The Gospel Four; The Persuaders; The Witnesses; Dave Eastwood (compère)	
June 3rd	THE SPINNERS	
June 4th	ERROLL GARNER TRIO	
Sept 3rd	THE SPINNERS	
Sept 24th	MODERN JAZZ QUARTET	

Sept 29th	*AMERICAN FOLK-BLUES FESTIVAL* with Big Joe Turner; Sleepy John Estes and Yank Rachell; Junior Wells; Robert Pete Williams; Otis Rush; Sippie Wallace; Jack Myers	*Freddie Below; Little Brother Montgomery; Roosevelt Sykes;*
Oct 8th	WHITE HEATHER CLUB CONCERT with Robin Hall and Jimmie McGregor; Anne and Laura Brand; Jimmy Shand	
Oct 21st	CHRIS BARBER BAND	*Zenith Six*
Oct 22nd	Manchester Peace Committee Presents *FOLK SONG '66* with The McPeakes; Three City Four; Matt McGinn; Jacqueline and Bridie; Sandra Kerr and John Faulkner; The Young Contemporaries; (compère – Karl Dallas)	
Oct 29th	THE DAVE BRUBECK QUARTET	
Nov 5th	TOM PAXTON; JUDY COLLINS	
Nov19th	*FOLK HOOTENANNY* with Alex Campbell; Matt McGinn; Paddie Bell;	*The Pennine Folk Group*
Nov 24th	JACQUES LOUSSIER TRIO	
Dec 3rd	*JAZZ AT THE PHILHARMONIC* with Dizzy Gillespie; Clark Terry; Coleman Hawkins; Zoot Sims; James Moody ; Teddy Watson; T-Bone Walker; Louis Bellson; Bob Cranshaw; Benny Carter (two houses)	
Dec 9th	THE SPINNERS	

THIS WAS A YEAR OF BLUES, FOLK AND JAZZ CONCERTS. THERE were several festivals/packages – a Folk Song Festival; a Hootenanny and a Peace concert.

The **American Negro Gospel Festival** was promoted by the National Jazz Federation. As well as the Free Trade Hall appearance, the singers appeared two days later at Croydon's Fairfield Halls.

This year had two appearances by American singer-songwriter **Tom Paxton**, and he would return no fewer than eleven times to the Free Trade Hall. In February Paxton was promoting his latest album, *Ain't That News* (Elektra 1965). He shared headlining in November with **Judy Collins**, a fellow Elektra recording artist. Collins had signed to the label in 1961, originally concentrating on the traditional repertoire.

She soon began to cover contemporary songwriters such as Bob Dylan and Gordon Lightfoot. Collins' sixth album, *In My Life* (Elektra 1966) featured songs by Leonard Cohen. Paxton and Collins appeared at just four British venues: the Royal Albert Hall, Birmingham Town Hall, Cardiff's Sophia Gardens and the Free Trade Hall.

Ella Fitzgerald undertook a short tour with **Duke Ellington's Orchestra**. Ellington's band would play the first half of the concert and then provide backing for Fitzgerald in the second half. Ella Fitzgerald's previous Free Trade Hall appearances had been with jazz trios, so it must have been a wonderful treat to have both these jazz legends on the same stage. The tour began and ended in London with just three provincial dates in between.

Ornette Coleman was a self-taught saxophonist who began playing professionally in the 1950's. He was a master of improvisation and influenced the free-jazz movement in both the USA and Europe. Coleman's trio featured bass player, David Izenzon and drummer, Charles Moffett. Later, he would lead a quartet and also work with a rock rhythm section. Supporting Ornette Coleman were The Lehal Wind Ensemble. Lehal is an anagram of the name 'Hallé'; the group were members of the orchestra! During the evening, Coleman's composition 'Forms And Sounds For Wind Quartet' was performed for only the second time. This concert was recorded and is available on CD.

Melody Maker (April 30th 1966) announced 'Dylan Brings Own Group', stating;

"Bob Dylan arrives in Britain for his second British tour on Monday (May 2nd) and is bringing his American backing group with him. The group- just called the Group- will play all Dylan's British dates with him. They will accompany the singer for half of each concert and he will do the other half alone."

The return appearance of **Bob Dylan** on May 17th was controversial because of this backing band, better known as **The Hawks**. This concert has been widely discussed by Heylin (2016), Lee (1998) and many, many others. As Greil Marcus said, "C.P. Lee was there, but the point is that he can put you there too." Lee's book is a riveting personal account of the gig and, indeed, "the road" to it. The inclusion of photographs by fifteen-year-old Paul Kelly are a fascinating addition.

This was, effectively, the first 'rock' gig at the Free Trade Hall. The combination of the group's gear and the recording equipment meant that ticket holders in the first three rows of the hall had to be moved. Recordings of the concert were bootlegged for many years and mistaken for the Royal Albert Hall date on the same tour. The recording was officially released over 30 years later and is a fascinating document of this extraordinary evening. In the first half of the concert Dylan played a solo acoustic set of seven songs; three songs were from *Bringing It All Back Home* (CBS 1965) and two were from *Highway 61 Revisited* (CBS 1965). But, most important, there were two brand new songs, 'Fourth Time Around' and 'Visions Of Johanna' that were unfamiliar to audiences. Both of these songs would appear on the *Blonde On Blonde* (CBS 1966) album that was released a month later.

After the interval Dylan brought on the band - all (except drummer Mickey Jones) who become known as 'The Band' two years later. They open with a new song, 'Tell Me Momma' and follow it with a song from *Another Side Of Bob Dylan* (CBS 1964) 'I Don't Believe You'. Dylan briefly blows his harmonica and states "This is called 'I Don't Believe You'. It used to go like that, now it goes like this." This is greeted by mild laughter from the audience.

Rick Saunders told Clinton Heylin, "The level of sound was something that I'd never heard before, especially being so close up to it. I was just blasted out of my skin. It was physical rather than just listening to the music. It took a long time before I could recognise what the tunes were."

While the band are tuning before the next song, slow handclaps start from some sections of the audience. Next we hear 'Baby Let Me Follow You Down', a song from Dylan's first album. This is followed by genuine applause. Dylan announces his next song and there is shouting and slow handclapping which speeds up. Between 'Leopard -Skin Pill-Box Hat' and 'One Too Many Mornings', there is more restlessness in the audience. Dylan mumbles incoherently into his microphone. Gradually, the audience quietens and we clearly hear him saying "..if only you just wouldn't clap so hard." Again, there is applause and even laughter. We hear shouting and more slow handclapping before 'Ballad Of A Thin Man', and, after the song finishes, things seem to get uglier. It was at this point that the infamous "Judas!" comment was heard from the audience. Dylan replies, "I don't believe you... You're a liar," and then says "play fucking loud!" to the drummer. The Hawks launch into the final song, 'Like A Rolling Stone' from *Highway 61 Revisited* (CBS 1965). There is warm applause, Dylan says "Thank you," and the band leaves the stage. The National Anthem fades in over the loudspeakers.

Since then there have been (apart from the two recommended books) radio documentaries, umpteen web discussions and articles about this incident. Film footage of the concert-goers and their reactions was included in *Eat The Document* and later in Martin Scorcese's film, *No Direction Home*. For those of us who were not there, the recordings are both an incredible delight and a priceless piece of history. Unlike so many live albums, *Live 1966* (Columbia 1998) stands up to repeated listening.

The day after the concert, the manager of the Free Trade Hall wrote to promoter Tito Burns complaining about the disruption caused by the recording equipment.

"Dear Mr Burns,

You will recall that 'phone calls to your office yesterday obtained your agreement to the recording by C.B.S. Recordings of the Bob Dylan Concert held at the Free Trade Hall last evening. You will also be aware that the conditions of letting permit recordings to be taken provided that the written consent of the Manager (myself) is given and that the hirer must inform me in writing not less than 21 days beforehand of such intention to record.

Yesterday, however, we received this request from C.B.S. who had been instructed by Bob Dylan's manager, and had no alternative but to agree and also to obtain your agreement as hirer of the Hall. In the event, the equipment which was brought was so much that seats (already sold) had to be taken out and the patrons found alternative places. Also patrons on the platform seats were put to disadvantage by reason of the equipment. This recording also caused my staff to be in attendance from 2 p.m. continuously through until 12 midnight and it was necessary for the Chief Fire Officer to be called to inspect the installation. To offset these extra charges caused by the recording I am enclosing an invoice for £65, I understand you will be able to recover this from Mr. Grossman, Bob Dylan's personal manager.

What causes me more concern however, is the damage to the reputation of the Free Trade Hall. The patrons attending paid to hear and see a Concert, not a recording session. If recording is to take place, the event should be so advertised, and the public not misled into paying good money for a Concert, only to be annoyed by all the extraneous ritual of recording. I was extremely annoyed myself by the arrogant and overbearing manner adopted by the persons employed on the recording. We were practically held to ransom:- if recording was not permitted then no concert - practically sums up the situation.

This will just not do, and for the sake of your reputation as well as ours, I ask you to ensure well in advance whether or not recordings are to be done at future bookings and to word your advertisements accordingly.

Yours faithfully "A.S."

The Erroll Garner Trio visited the Free Trade Hall halfway through an eight-date British tour.

The American Folk-Blues Festival featured over ten artists from the USA. **Big Joe Turner** was a blues shouter and known as 'the Boss of the Blues.' He recorded the original version of 'Shake, Rattle And Roll' which was covered and bowdlerised by Bill Haley. The festival tour rescued Turner from the jazz lounges of Los Angeles and started something of a revival of his career. **Junior Wells** had made his name playing harmonica for Muddy Waters and later worked with Buddy Guy. **Otis Rush's** guitar playing was a big influence on Eric Clapton, Peter Green and Jeff Beck. Rush had moved - like so many others - to Chicago and had been inspired by Muddy Waters. The festival only visited two British venues - the Royal Albert Hall and the Free Trade Hall.

Scottish folk duo, **Robin Hall and Jimmie MacGregor**, had a twenty-year partnership and frequently appeared on television, most notably on the BBC *Tonight* programme. The duo had extraordinary exposure for four years on this programme, appearing nightly from Monday to Friday. They recorded over twenty albums together, two of which featured songs from the television programme: *Tonight And Every Night* (HMV 1962) and *The Next Tonight Will Be...*(HMV 1963).

The McPeakes hailed from Belfast and three generations of the family played in the group. The group grew out of the McPeake Trio which featured Francie I and his sons, Francie II and James. They were joined by the third generation Francie, his sister Kathleen and cousin Tommy. The McPeakes played uilleann pipes and sang Irish folk songs. Their first album was *The McPeake Family* (Topic 1963), followed by *At Home With The McPeakes* (Fontana 1965).

The Jacques Loussier Trio appeared at the Free Trade Hall for the first time in November, the first of nine appearances in the next decade. Loussier had studied at the Conservatoire National Musique in Paris for six years before travelling around the world. In 1959 he formed the Jacques Loussier Trio and the group used Bach's compositions as a basis for jazz improvisation. The *Play Bach* albums ran to five volumes over the next few years. Loussier's recording of Bach's 'Air on the G String' was used for the Hamlet cigar advertisements for over 35 years in Britain.

The **Jazz At The Philharmonic** concert in December is described by Bill Birch as, "star-studded and tied with a gold braid... a marvellous array of stars, full of technical mastery and melodic improvisation befitting the Free Trade Hall's last jazz concert of the year." The Free Trade Hall was also the final venue on this seven-date British tour. Dizzy Gillespie made a return visit to the venue at this concert.

Other events at the Free Trade Hall

February 15th – Vienna Boys Choir
March 1st – Faraday Lecture
April 18th - 19th – Kodak Colour Show
November 12th – Judo Demonstration

Elsewhere (Headliners Only):

ABC Ardwick: The Rolling Stones

Odeon : The Beach Boys, Georgie Fame, Chris Farlowe And The Thunderbirds, The Hollies, Roy Orbison, Alan Price Set, Otis Redding, The Small Faces, Dusty Springfield, Walker Brothers,

Palace Theatre : Freddie And The Dreamers, Johnny Mathis, Gene Pitney, The Who

1967		
Jan 21st	WOODY HERMAN ORCHESTRA (two houses)	
Feb 10th	ELLA FITZGERALD WITH DUKE ELLINGTON AND HIS FAMOUS ORCHESTRA (two houses)	
Feb 13th	BERT JANSCH	
Feb 18th	THE SPINNERS	
Feb 25th	NEW LOST CITY RAMBLERS	*The Watersons; The Tinkers; The Four Folk; Roy Guest (compère)*
March 6th	THE SWINGLE SINGERS	
March 9th	RAVI SHANKAR with Alla Rakha (tabla)	
March 14th	*IRISH NATIONAL CONCERT* WITH JACK CRUISE	*The Johnstons; Edmund Browne; John McNally*
March 18th	*JAZZ FROM A SWINGING ERA* with Earl Hines; Buck Clayton; Bud Freeman; Roy Eldridge; Vic Dickenson; Budd Johnson; Sir Charles Thompson; Bill Pemberton; Oliver Jackson	
March 20th	SIMON AND GARFUNKEL	
March 31st	*SECOND MSG FOLK HOOTNANNY* with Ian Campbell Folk Group	*Nigel Denver; Barry Ogden*
April 7th	BUDDY RICH AND HIS ORCHESTRA	
April 8th	MSG FOLK PRESENT The Taverners; The Pennine Folk; The Grehan Sisters; Lyn Taylor	
April 14th	*FESTIVAL FLAMENCO GITARO 1967* Twelve Spanish Gypsy Dancers, Singers And Guitarists	
April 17th	*THE TENOR OF JAZZ* with Eddie 'Lockjaw' Davis, Ben Webster, Bud Freeman and Eddie Miller	*Alex Welsh Band; Lennie Felix Trio*
April 18th	DICK GREGORY; NINA SIMONE	*The Peddlers*
April 21st	RAY CHARLES And His Orchestra and The Raelets	

May 5th	THE McPEAKE FAMILY; IAN CAMPBELL FOLK GROUP	*Cyril Tawney; Isla Cameron; The Young Tradition; Manchester Morris Men*
May 12th	THE SPINNERS	
May 13th	COUNT BASIE ORCHESTRA WITH TONY BENNETT (two houses)	
June 4th	JULIE FELIX	
July 15th	*MANCHESTER'S FIRST COUNTRY AND WESTERN FESTIVAL* with Carl Belew And The Hillsiders	*The County Five*
Sept 22nd	*FOLK MEETS JAZZ* with The Four Folk; The Zenith Six with Marcia	*introduced by Peter Wheeler*
Oct 2nd	*WHITE HEATHER CLUB* featuring Robin Hall and Jimmy MacGregor; Jimmy Shand Junior And His Band	
Oct 7th	*TOP BRASS* with Maynard Ferguson And His Anglo-American Orchestra	*Bob Brookmeyer/ Clark Terry Quintet; Nat Pierce Trio; Doc Cheatham/ Benny Morton Quintet*
Oct 9th	TOM PAXTON	
Oct10th	JACQUES LOUSSIER TRIO	
Oct28th	DAVE BRUBECK QUARTET	
Nov 4th	NOEL MURPHY; THE BEGGARMEN; JACQUELINE AND BRIDIE; THE TAVERNERS	
Nov 11th	BERT JANSCH, INCREDIBLE STRING BAND, AL STEWART	*John Renbourn; Dorris Henderson*
Nov 25th	THE STAN GETZ QUARTET	*Kenny Graham*
Dec 2nd	THE SPINNERS	

Dec 3rd	LUIS ALBERTO DEL PARANA Y LOS PARAGUAYOS	*Carmen de Santana*
Dec 9th	MODERN JAZZ QUARTET	

THE SUMMER OF LOVE WAS BARELY VISIBLE AT THE FREE Trade Hall except perhaps for the appearances of Ravi Shankar and The Incredible String Band. The Magic Village in Cromford Court became the main "underground" venue in 1968 and such acts as Tyrannosaurus Rex, Jethro Tull, Edgar Broughton Band and Roy Harper would play there. See Sykes (2012) for a full gigography of this venue.

Ella Fitzgerald played only three concerts in Britain in 1967 with **Duke Ellington's Orchestra**. The first night was at the Free Trade Hall, followed by two London shows. Ellington, however, played several concerts without Fitzgerald before and after their shows together.

Bert Jansch was a gifted acoustic guitarist from Glasgow. He moved down to London in 1963 and later signed to Transatlantic Records. Jansch's fourth solo album, *Nicola* (Transatlantic 1966) would be released in July. He would return to the Free Trade Hall on nine more occasions, either with Pentangle or as a soloist.

The New Lost City Ramblers were Mike Seeger (half-brother to Pete), John Cohen and Tracy Schwarz. They played old-time string band music and were responsible for the revival of this rural Southern music of the Appalachian and Ozark areas. The Ramblers had researched their music from both Library of Congress field recordings and the repertoire of traditional performers. Their tour started at the Royal Albert Hall, before visiting eight provincial venues. The BBC *Tonight In Person* television programme filmed the group during the tour.

The Swingle Singers made their debut at the Free Trade Hall as they undertook their first full scale British tour. Formed in Paris in 1962, this eight-piece French vocal group started as session singers backing such stars as Charles Aznavour and Edith Piaf. The lead soprano was Christiane Legrand, sister of the composer Michel Legrand. Their first album, *Jazz Sebastien Bach* (Philips 1963) was only meant for family and friends but it was picked up by a radio station. In the late 1960's and early 1970's the group's wordless versions of classical music were a ubiquitous part of British culture. Frequent television and radio appearances made them a household name.

George Harrison's patronage of Indian classical music gave **Ravi Shankar** a worldwide profile and audience. Harrison had first met Shankar in 1965 at the Asian Music Circle in London. This led to the Beatle being given lessons in sitar technique by the Indian master and the featuring of the instrument on 'Norwegian Wood'. Shankar started his British tour at the Free Trade Hall, having already performed in Italy and Scandinavia. Shankar later performed at the Monterey Pop Festival in June of this year, showing how much the counter-culture had embraced him. Shankar appeared on four other occasions at the Free Trade Hall over the next decade.

Jazz From A Swinging Era featured several former members of Count Basie's Orchestra, as well as Bud Freeman and Earl Hines. The tour visited twelve concert halls and performed twice at Ronnie Scott's Club in London.

Simon and Garfunkel's appearance was clearly a highlight of the year. The Free Trade Hall diary states the duo's requirements: "2 grey stools" and "rehearsal 1 hour before doors open"; how simple things were in those days! Tickets for this concert started at five shillings (25p!) and went up to fifteen shillings (75p). The duo were on a three-date tour: their other appearances were at The Birmingham Theatre and London's Royal Albert Hall. Their second album, *Sounds Of Silence* (CBS 1966) was still in the British album charts a whole year after its entry. But their third album, *Parsley, Sage, Rosemary And Thyme* (CBS 1966) curiously failed to chart on its release. 1968 would see the huge success of the single 'Mrs Robinson' and no less than four of the duo's albums, including the original soundtrack album for *The Graduate* film.

Buddy Rich was an extraordinary drummer and made the first of five appearances at the Free Trade Hall in April. This was his Manchester debut and sold out in advance. Rich, something of a child prodigy, had played with Artie Shaw and Tommy Dorsey. He started his own big band in 1966 as very much a showcase for his incredible speed and dexterity.

On April 8th Manchester Sports Guild presented a folk concert at the Free Trade Hall with three local acts. **The Taverners** were from Blackpool. One of their members, Alan Bell, realised that the Fylde Coast area was lacking in traditional songs so started writing his own compositions in the folk idiom. Their album *A Round With The Taverners Folk Group* (Studio Republic 1968) was recorded live at the Guild's folk club. **The Grehan Sisters** - Marie, Francie and Bernie - had moved from County Roscommon in Ireland to Manchester in 1967. They later released an album, *On The Gallymore Mountains* (Transatlantic 1967). **Lyn Taylor** was another local folk singer who later appeared on the *Folk Session At The MSG* (MSG Folk 1967) alongside The Taverners, The Pennine Folk and Harry Boardman.

Festival Flamenco Gitaro 1967 visited five venues in Britain in April; their Free Trade Hall appearance was the third date with the tour finishing at the Royal Albert Hall.

Dick Gregory was born in St Louis, Missouri and started his career as a comedian while serving in the armed forces. In 1961 he was spotted by Hugh Hefner who hired Gregory to work at the Chicago Playboy Club. Gregory was the first black American comedian to cross over and perform to white audiences. He was very much identified with the civil rights movement. **Nina Simone** had recently moved record labels from Philips to RCA Victor. *Nina Simone Sings The Blues*, (RCA Victor 1967) was her twelfth studio album. The record included 'Backlash Blues', a joint composition with Langston Hughes about the plight of black people in the USA. Simone's subsequent releases saw her have Top 10 singles in Britain with songs from both the musical *Hair* and the Bee Gees. Her tour with Dick Gregory visited five concert halls and concluded with two club appearances in London.

The Count Basie Orchestra appeared in May with **Tony Bennett** at the start of a short tour. Basie also appeared without Bennett on five other British dates. This was Basie's sixth visit to the Free Trade Hall.

Carl Belew was an American country singer and songwriter from Oklahoma. His most famous song 'Am I That Easy To Forget' was covered by many other artists. Belew had also written songs for the likes of Eddie Arnold and Jim Reeves.

The Four Folk were a quartet who covered songs such as 'Dirty Old Town' and 'The Leaving Of Liverpool' on their only album *Hard Cases* (Reality 1966). Both songs were also in The Spinners' repertoire and would have been heard in most folk clubs around this time. **The Zenith Six** were a trad jazz band who had first appeared at the Free Trade Hall in 1956; they had an E.P. recorded at The Royal Festival Hall. Concerts that included both jazz and folk were not uncommon and harked back to the days, a decade earlier, when skiffle was a feature at trad jazz events.

Maynard Ferguson's 'Top Brass' show featured a mixture of British, American and Canadian jazz musicians. Ferguson had studied at the French Conservatory in Montreal and played with Stan Kenton in the early 1950's. Ferguson was a brilliant trumpet player with a particular skill in upper register work.

The Dave Brubeck Quartet concert in October was sold out. This was the quartet's eighth - and final - British tour as they were soon to disband. Brubeck visited just eight venues on this tour.

Irish folk musician and actor **Noel Murphy** was born in Killarney and moved to London in 1962, playing professionally from 1964 onwards. He made his first recordings with the E.P. *Irish Songs* (Columbia 1966) and *Nya-a-a-a-h* (Fontana 1967). Later Murphy was joined by Davey Johnstone to become the duo, Murf & Shaggis.

The Beggarmen had met at De La Salle College in Middleton and soon teamed up with two Irish singers to form a larger group. They performed in local folk clubs and on television. The group recorded their eponymous album (Studio Republic 1969) at Manchester Sports Guild and the Crown & Anchor in Hilton Street, Manchester.

Jacqueline and Bridie - Jacqueline McDonald (usually known as Jackie) and Bridie O'Donnell - were both teachers in Liverpool. In 1964 they gave up teaching to become the first full time British female folk song duo. Jackie and Bridie's Folk Club attracted an amazing range of guests and ran for many years. The duo released an album *Hold Back The Dawn* (Fontana 1964) and later signed with Major Minor. Like their label mates The Dubliners, Jackie and Bridie were plugged incessantly on Radio Caroline but, in their case, this did not lead to hit records.

The Incredible String Band were a unique Scottish duo, managed and produced by Joe Boyd. They were touring to promote their first hit album, *5000 Spirits* (Elektra 1967) and were already moving away from the folk and "underground" clubs to concert halls.

Al Stewart had performed at such London folk venues as Bunjies and Les Cousins. He released his debut album, *Bedsitter Images* (CBS 1967) this year. Stewart would appear five more times at the FTH over the next seven years.

The Stan Getz Quartet visited the Free Trade Hall on the last night of a five-date tour. Tenor player Getz had previously appeared at the Free Trade Hall in 1959 in a Jazz At The Philharmonic tour. In the eight years in between, Getz had become a household name with his bossa nova collaborations with Charlie Byrd and the Gilbertos. The piano player at this 1967 concert was a young Chick Corea.

Luis Alberto Del Parana Y Los Paraguayos were originally a trio formed by Parana who later led this larger group. The trio were paid by the Paraguayan government to spread the country's music in Europe through an 'Official Cultural Mission.' The Paraguayan group formed in the 1950's and toured Europe to great acclaim. Their popular blend of Latin American and Mexican music was often seen on television and sold millions of albums around the world.

The Modern Jazz Quartet played the last popular concert of the year. This was the first night of only four dates that the quartet played in Britain on this tour.

Other events at the Free Trade Hall

February 4th – The Ivor Novello Story – charity concert
April 28th – English Country Dance Society
May 2nd - 3rd – Kodak Colour Show
September 25th – Africa Wild Life – film

Elsewhere (Headliners Only):

Belle Vue (Kings Hall): The Dubliners, The Kinks, The Move, The Tremeloes.

Odeon: Charles Aznavour, The Beach Boys, Victor Borge, The Clancy Brothers And Tommy Makem, Arthur Conley, The Four Tops, Jimi Hendrix Experience, The Hollies, Engelbert Humperdinck, Tom Jones, Roy Orbison, Gene Pitney, Sam And Dave, Percy Sledge, The Small Faces, Spencer Davis Group, Cat Stevens, Walker Brothers.

Palace Theatre : Fats Domino, Jimi Hendrix Experience , The Move, Pink Floyd, Otis Redding.

1968		
Jan 20th	JULIE FELIX	
Feb 2nd	THE SPINNERS	
Feb 9th	*FOLK FESTIVAL '68* with The Watersons	*Bert Jansch; Hedy West; Harry Boardman*
Feb 10th	WOODY HERMAN AND HIS ORCHESTRA (two houses)	
Feb 27th	MANITAS de PLATA and supporting company	
March 2nd	INCREDIBLE STRING BAND	
March 18th	BUDDY RICH AND HIS ORCHESTRA WITH TONY BENNETT (two houses)	
March 19th	JACQUES LOUSSIER TRIO	
April 1st	ESTHER AND ABI OFARIM	
April 6th	MARTIN CARTHY AND DAVE SWARBRICK	*Anne Briggs; The Pennine Folk; Pete Rodger*
April 26th	THE SPINNERS	
April 27th	COUNT BASIE ORCHESTRA AND GEORGIE FAME (two houses)	
May 4th	THE JOHNNY CASH SHOW	*Carl Perkins; The Tennessee Three; June Carter; James Royal And The James Royal Set*
May 8th	FESTIVAL FLAMENCO GITARO 1968	
May 17th	LOU RAWLS WITH THE TED HEATH ORCHESTRA	*The Peddlers; The Keith Mansfield Strings*
May 24th	*FOLK SPECIAL* with Tom Rush, The Young Tradition and Diz Disley	
July 3rd	ESTHER AND ABI OFARIM	
July 14th	USTAD IMRAT KHAN	
Sept 21st	*BLUES OLD AND NEW* - FAMILY	*Jo-Ann Kelly ; Stefan Grossman*
Sept 28th	BUDDY RICH AND HIS ORCHESTRA	
Sept 30th	OSCAR PETERSON TRIO	

Oct 4th	THE SPINNERS (10TH ANNIVERSARY CONCERT)	
Oct 8th	JACQUES LOUSSIER TRIO	
Oct 18th	INCREDIBLE STRING BAND	
Oct 25th	THE DUBLINERS	
Oct 26th	*AMERICAN FOLK BLUES FESTIVAL 1968* John Lee Hooker; T-Bone Walker; Big Joe Williams (two houses)	*Jimmy Reed; Curtis Jones; The Eddie Taylor Blues Band; Al Smith (mc)*
Nov 5th	OXFAM FOLK CONCERT starring Julie Felix and Al Stewart	*Blonde On Blonde; The Pennine Folk; Orange Blossom Sound; Eamonn and Gerry*
Nov 9th	THE PENTANGLE (two houses)	
Nov 15th	TOM PAXTON	
Nov 16th	MANITAS de PLATA AND COMPANY	
Nov 23rd	DIANA ROSS AND THE SUPREMES	
Nov 26th	RAVI SHANKAR with Alla Rakhar (tabla)	
Nov 30th	ALEX CAMPBELL;	*Hamish Imlach; The Taverners*
Dec 6th	THE SPINNERS	
Dec 13th	JIMMY SMITH TRIO	
Dec 21st	*FOLK EXPLORATIONS* with Martin Carthy and Dave Swarbrick	*Johnny Silvo; The Pennine Folk; Randal Hurley (narrator)*

A MIX OF MODERN JAZZ AND FOLK MUSIC PERFORMANCES predominated in 1968 but there was little sign of the growing "underground" rock music scene developing beyond the walls of the Free Trade Hall.

A folk festival in February saw **The Watersons** making their farewell appearance. This tour included a concert at the Royal Albert Hall. Their fourth album, *A Yorkshire Garland* (Topic 1968) was their last for seven years. The group reformed in the early 1970's and Martin Carthy joined them soon after.

Manitas de Plata was born in southern France of gypsy heritage and became a brilliant and unconventional flamenco guitarist. He had played Carnegie Hall in New York in 1965 and appeared at the Royal Variety Performance this year. His spring tour visited eleven major venues and included two Royal Albert Hall appearances.

De Plata made two appearances at the Free Trade Hall this year.

The Incredible String Band returned to the Free Trade Hall for two appearances this year. By now, this Scottish duo had a Top 5 hit album, *The Hangman's Beautiful Daughter* (Elektra 1968) with a devoted following.

Joe Boyd :"*I persuaded Roy Guest to book the Royal Festival Hall, Birmingham Town Hall, Manchester Free Trade Hall and the Liverpool Philharmonic. He thought I was mad, but the tour began a few weeks after release of the LP and most of the halls sold out. Watching the audiences enter those staid bastions of classical music reminded me of the early UFO audiences coming down the stairs of the Blarney Club a year before. They were delighted with themselves: freaks in the provinces didn't realize they were so numerous.*"

Over the next eighteen months, the Incredibles would play the Royal Festival Hall, Royal Albert Hall, Fillmore East in New York and the Woodstock Festival! The group, later expanded to include other musicians, returned to the Free Trade Hall five times over the next few years.

Buddy Rich was on a short tour with **Tony Bennett** which only visited three venues outside London. The Free Trade Hall appearance was two concerts - 6.45pm and 9pm. According to Birch, "Few seats remained unsold for the first house, but the second was a sell-out." Rich appeared again in September, but without a vocalist.

Esther and Abi Ofarim appeared twice in 1968. They were an Israeli couple who had had a No. 1 hit single in March with 'Cinderella Rockefella', a 1920's ragtime pastiche which they had performed on *The Eamonn Andrews Show*. Like a lot of novelty hit singles, 'Cinderella Rockefeller' was not representative of the duo's usual repertoire - a mixture of American and Israeli folk songs. Their album, *2 In 3* (Philips 1968) reached No. 6 in the British charts. The Ofarims' spring tour visited ten venues including two nights at the Royal Albert Hall. These were their first British concerts.

Martin Carthy released *But Two Came By* (Fontana 1968), the fourth of five albums with fiddler **Dave Swarbrick**. Swarbrick had left the Ian Campbell Folk Group in 1966 and had released his own first solo album *Rags, Reels And Airs* (Fontana 1967) with Carthy as guest. Both musicians would join folk rock bands within the next two years: Swarbrick with Fairport Convention and Carthy with Steeleye Span. The duo would play together sporadically right up to Swarbrick's death in 2016.

Count Basie Orchestra were on their ninth British tour with **Georgie Fame** featured as guest vocalist. Fame had had several hit singles in Britain, including two chart-toppers, but it was the success of his album, *Sound Venture* (Columbia 1966) with Harry South's orchestra that led to his tour with Basie.

Johnny Cash performed for the first time in May at the Free Trade Hall on the first date of his British tour. He returned to Manchester in October, playing at the Odeon on his second British tour of the year. By this time, Cash had made his chart breakthrough in Britain with his album, *At Folsom Prison* (CBS 1968) which reached No. 8 and stayed in the charts for a whole year.

Lou Rawls was an American singer, songwriter and producer. He performed the counterpoint vocals on Sam Cooke's 'Bring It On Home To Me.' After making several jazz albums, Rawls moved into soul music and had his biggest hit in 1976 with 'You'll Never Find Another Love Like Mine' on the Philadelphia label. Rawls only played two concerts in Britain with the Ted Heath Orchestra - the Free Trade Hall and the Royal Albert Hall.

Tom Rush was a folk singer who tended to cover other people's songs. After two years with the Prestige label, he signed to Elektra. Rush's album *The Circle Game* (Elektra 1968) was the first time that songs by Joni Mitchell, James Taylor and Jackson Browne were brought to widespread public attention. The same album contained his most famous composition, 'No Regrets,' later covered by The Walker Brothers.

Family were the first rock band to appear at The Free Trade Hall since The Hawks supported Bob Dylan in 1966. Their first album *Music In A Doll's House* (Reprise 1968) had reached the Top 40. Vocalist Roger Chapman's singing style was an acquired taste, but the group had a solid following with hit singles and albums and went on to appear twice at the Isle Of Wight Festival. Family's Free Trade Hall appearance was advertised as *Blues Old And New* and they were supported by British blues singer Jo-Ann Kelly and American ragtime guitarist Stefan Grossman.

The Spinners appeared four times in 1968, celebrating their tenth anniversary as a group at their concert in October. Often, the Free Trade Hall diary merely stated "Folk Song Concert" when they were booked - a researcher's nightmare!

The American Folk Blues Festival returned to the Free Trade Hall after an absence of a year as part of an eight-date tour. **Jimmy Reed** made his Free Trade Hall debut. Reed's career took off in 1955 when he started on a string of hits such as 'Big Boss Man' and 'Bright Lights, Big City', both of which were covered by umpteen white groups. By the late 1960's, Reed's career was in decline with health and personal problems dominating his life. **Big Joe Williams** was a country blues singer born in Mississippi. He played a nine-string guitar and was much influenced by Charley Patton. Like so many other blues artists, Williams' career was rescued by the folk-blues revival.

The Pentangle comprised two folk guitarists, Bert Jansch and John Renbourn, a female singer, Jacqui McShee and a jazz rhythm section with Terry Cox on drums and Danny Thompson on double bass. The group had made their concert debut in June at the Royal Festival Hall in London. Their manager, Jo Lustig, cleverly guided their career which was initially very successful. The Free Trade Hall was the second night of a twelve-date tour of major venues. Their first album, *The Pentangle* (Transatlantic 1968) had reached No. 21 earlier in the year.

Diana Ross & The Supremes were one of the few Tamla Motown acts to appear at the Free Trade Hall. This was the group's second visit to Britain this year. Five days before the Free Trade Hall concert, Ross had made an impassioned speech about racism during the group's slot at the Royal Variety Performance. This was the year that both Martin Luther King and Robert Kennedy were assassinated, but Ross's speech may also have been prompted by the appearance of The Black And White Minstrel Show on the same bill. Initially, Diana Ross refused to perform on the same bill as these "black-face" performers.

Jimmy Smith popularized the sound of the Hammond organ in jazz. He often used the moniker 'The Incredible' on album covers and tour posters. Smith recorded over twenty albums on the Blue Note label and had hits with such tunes as 'Walk On The Wild Side' and 'Who's Afraid Of Virginia Woolf.' He became the most famous jazz organist of all time and his influence is unmistakeable on such British players as Steve Winwood, Graham Bond, Georgie Fame and John Mayall. His album, *Got My Mojo Workin'* (Verve 1966) had reached No. 19. This Free Trade Hall concert was one of five dates that the trio played in Britain in December.

Other events at the Free Trade Hall

March 16th – The Mario Lanza Story concert in aid of Imperial Cancer Research
July 27th – Bulgarian Army Ensemble
October 14th -15th – Marks & Spencer Fashion Show

Elsewhere (Headliners Only):

Belle Vue (Kings Hall)–Andy Williams.

Odeon – The Beach Boys, Victor Borge, Johnny Cash, Maurice Chevalier, The Clancy Brothers And Tommy Makem, The Herd, Tom Jones, The Kinks, Peter, Paul and Mary, Gene Pitney, The Seekers, Simon And Garfunkel, The Tremeloes, Scott Walker.

Palace Theatre - The Bee Gees, Cilla Black, The Dubliners, The Hollies, Solomon King.

1969		
Feb 1st	DONOVAN	
Feb 8th	THE SPINNERS	
Feb 15th	7.30PM - CLARKE/ BOLAND BIG BAND; ROLAND KIRK QUARTET	*Philly Joe Jones Group*
Feb 15th	9PM – *THE BLUES SCENE '69* JOHN LEE HOOKER	*Aynsley Dunbar Retaliation; Champion Jack Dupree; The Groundhogs; Jo-Ann Kelly*
Feb 21st	LOS PARAGUAYOS	*Carmen de Santana*
Feb 22nd	TYRANNOSAURUS REX	*Vytas Serelis (sitar);David Bowie (mime); John Peel –(compère)*
March 8th	JULIE FELIX	
March 15th	MODERN JAZZ QUARTET	
March 28th	SCAFFOLD; BONZO DOG BAND	
April 11th	*COUNTRY MEETS FOLK* with Tom and Smiley, Steve Benbow And The Taverners	
April 19th	NANA MOUSKOURI AND THE ATHENIANS	
April 25th	MARTIN CARTHY AND DAVE SWARBRICK	*Jeremy Taylor; The Oldham Tinkers*
April 26th	TONY BENNETT WITH COUNT BASIE AND HIS ORCHESTRA	
April 29th	BB KING; FLEETWOOD MAC (two houses)	*Sonny Terry and Brownie McGhee; Duster Bennett; Long John Baldry (compère)*
May 3rd	THE SPINNERS	
May 6th	TEN YEARS AFTER JETHRO TULL	*Clouds*
May 7th	BEST OF ISRAEL with Shoshana Damari, Hedva & David, Ran Eliran, Juki Arkin	
May 10th	*FOLK EXPLORATIONS no.2* with Peter Sarstedt	*Johnny Silvo; The Pennine Folk; Randal Herley (narrator)*

May 13th	JOHN MAYALL	
May 16th	WOODY HERMAN AND HIS ORCHESTRA	
May 21st	DON PARTRIDGE PRESENTS *THE BUSKERS* 'Paris' Nat Scaffer (compère); Jasper and Steve; Ike Greenwood and Freddie Winters; Johnny Eagle; Susan Keeley with Bobby Shaw; ' Bano and Spoons'; Mike Griggs; Dave Brock; The Road Stars; Gordon Giltrap; Megan Aitkman	
May 24th	ELLA FITZGERALD with her Trio and The Ronnie Scott Orchestra (two houses)	
May 31st	HOWLIN' WOLF; FREDDIE KING	*John Dummer Blues Band; Chris Trimming – (compère)*
June 8th	THE BEACH BOYS (two houses)	*Paul Revere And The Raiders; Joe Hicks; compère – Alan Field*
June 15th	LED ZEPPELIN	*Liverpool Scene; Blodwyn Pig*
June 22nd	PINK FLOYD	
July 5th	USTAD VILYAYAT KHAN (SITAR) with Sankha Kumar (tabla)	
August 16th	*FOLK CONCERT – PETERLOO ANNIVERSARY* with Harry Boardman and Leon Rosselson; Michael Foot MP	
Sept 26th	OSCAR PETERSON TRIO	
Sept 27th	THE SPINNERS	
Oct 2nd	JETHRO TULL	*Savoy Brown; Terry Reid*
Oct 17th	JACQUES LOUSSIER TRIO	
Oct 18th	PENTANGLE	
Oct 31st	INCREDIBLE STRING BAND	
Nov 8th	ROLF HARRIS SHOW	*Joe Benjamin and Tony Cawley; The Pattersons; Harry Bence Orchestra*
Nov 10th	JOHN MAYALL	
Nov 21st	TYRANNOSAURUS REX	*John Peel and Friends*
Nov 22nd	BUDDY RICH ORCHESTRA	
Nov 24th	THE BONZO DOG BAND	*Greasy Bear; Ron Geesin*
Nov 26th	DUKE ELLINGTON AND HIS ORCHESTRA (two houses)	

Nov 27th	MADRID FLAMENCO	
Dec 3rd	MANITAS de PLATA AND HIS COMPANY	
Dec 12th	SONNY LESTER'S JAZZ WAVE LIMITED with Thad Jones-Mel Lewis Big Band	*Jimmy McGriff Quintet; Freddie Hubbard Group; Jeremy Steig Group*
Dec 13th	THE SPINNERS	
Dec 15th	SYD LAWRENCE ORCHESTRA	*Kevin Kent; The Skylarks*
Dec 19th	TEN YEARS AFTER	*Blodwyn Pig; Stone The Crows*

THIS YEAR SAW ROCK BANDS PLAYING REGULARLY AT THE Free Trade Hall, as part of the British concert hall "circuit". Bands such as Led Zeppelin, Jethro Tull, Ten Years After and Pink Floyd were now playing these venues around the country.

Donovan's career had something of a stop-start theme; after his folk hits in Britain, he had beaten everyone by recording arguably the first psychedelic song, 'Sunshine Superman' in late 1965. Record company problems delayed its release on both sides of the Atlantic. Subsequently, British and American releases were often out of step with each other which must have been confusing and frustrating for his fans at home. Later in 1969, Donovan would work with the Jeff Beck Group on the 'Goo Goo Barabajagal' single, but his concert in February appears to be a solo performance.

The Clark-Boland Big Band was created in 1961 when American drummer Kenny Clarke teamed up with Belgian pianist, Francy Boland; they were joined by bass player, Jimmy Woode. For the February concert, the band had what Birch called," a star-studded international line-up" featuring four trumpeters, three trombonists and three tenor saxophonists. Birch continues, "This one-off concert, which began at 6.30pm, lasted for over three hours and is still talked about to this day." After six concerts, the band played a two-week residency at Ronnie Scott's where they broke house records.

John Lee Hooker had appeared as part of blues packages at the Free Trade Hall in 1962, 1965 and 1968, but this year he was headlining, the first of four such concerts at the venue over the next twenty years. The Groundhogs accompanied Hooker on this tour. This was the final night of a six-date tour, sponsored by *Melody Maker*.

Many rock bands started as white blues copyists and subsequently widened their repertoire by writing their own material. Nonetheless, the blues boom was at its height with black and white performers appearing throughout the year. They came together when **B.B. King** and **Fleetwood Mac** shared top billing in April. This tour was King's first time on a British stage. By now Fleetwood Mac were having hit singles and albums in Britain with their single 'Albatross' reaching No. 1 in January

1969. Manchester was the final night of the eight-date tour and B.B. King invited Fleetwood Mac and other musicians onstage for a jam very early on in his headlining set.

The diversity of the music scene showed the strong influence of Radio One DJ John Peel who had championed groups such as **Tyrannosaurus Rex** from the start. Peel acted as compère at the group's February concert, one of a six-date provincial tour. **David Bowie** made his first appearance at the Free Trade Hall as a mime artist on the same bill! By November Tyrannosaurus Rex had a new bongo player when Mickey Finn replaced Steve Peregrine Took. Took's final album with the group, *Unicorn* (Regal Zonophone 1969) had reached No. 12 in June of this year.

The Free Trade Hall diary for the March 28th joint **Scaffold/ Bonzo Dog Band** gig states, "warn them about using fireworks etc." This must be a reference to the Bonzos' Roger Ruskin Spear who was liable to make his robots explode and misbehave! Both groups had had recent big hit singles, Scaffold with 'Lily The Pink' and the Bonzos with 'I'm The Urban Spaceman.' Both Scaffold and the Bonzos were often seen on television, the latter in *Do Not Adjust Your Set* alongside some future Pythons. Later, members of both groups would form Grimms. The Bonzos returned in November on what was their final tour before splitting up, promoting their album, *Keynsham* (Liberty 1969).

There was a **Country Meets Folk** programme on BBC Radio from 1967 to 1969, presented by Wally Whyton. The programme encouraged an eclectic approach to the two genres. **Tom and Smiley** had released a bluegrass album (Saga 1968) and followed it up with *Country Style With Tom & Smiley* (Fidelity 1969). **Steve Benbow** was a British guitar player and singer who had worked with the likes of Ewan MacColl.

Nana Mouskouri was an unlikely star, with her Greek heritage and distinctive black rimmed spectacles. She had trained at the Conservatoire in Paris and sang in several languages. Her first album to chart in Britain was *Over And Over* (Fontana 1969) which reached the Top 10 and stayed in the charts for an amazing 97 weeks. Mouskouri's BBC television series ran from 1968 to the mid-1970's and featured her backing musicians, The Athenians.

John Mayall appeared at the Free Trade Hall for the first time in May. His lead guitarist (following Eric Clapton and Peter Green) was future Stones member Mick Taylor. This line-up had recorded the album, *Blues From Laurel Canyon* (Decca 1969). This was one of the last dates that Taylor played with Mayall. The band leader returned in November promoting his next album, *The Turning Point* (Polydor 1969) which was revolutionary in its lack of electric lead guitar or drums. Instead, the band featured saxophone, flute and acoustic guitar. Mayall would appear seven times in total at the Free Trade Hall, each time with a different line-up!

On May 6th **Ten Years After** were meant to share top billing with **Jethro Tull** but TYA's singer and guitarist, Alvin Lee, was ill and the group failed to appear. This concert was the first night of a six-date tour and Radio One D.J. Pete Drummond was compère. Ten Years After did appear at the end of the year, having dazzled the audience at the Woodstock Festival in August with Lee's ultra-fast guitar technique. TYA released two albums this year, *Stonedhenge* (Deram 1969) and *Ssssh* (Deram 1969) and both reached the Top 10 in Britain. But it was clear that Ten Years After's priority was conquering America, where they toured an amazing 28 times in six years.

Jethro Tull appeared twice this year. Like Fleetwood Mac, the group benefitted from having *Top Of The Pops* exposure. 'Living In The Past' - with its unusual 5/4 rhythm- had reached No. 3 in the spring. Their second album, *Stand Up* (Island 1969) had topped the charts in August.

Freddie King was perhaps the least famous of the so-called 'Three Kings' - Albert, B.B. and himself - but he had been admired by Eric Clapton who covered King's 'Have You Ever Loved A Woman' and 'Hideaway'. King came to the public's attention at the 1968 Texas Pop Festival, having already been signed to the Atlantic subsidiary, Cotillion, by King Curtis. Later, King was signed by Leon Russell to Shelter Records.

The Beach Boys made their only appearance at The Free Trade Hall, having previously appeared at the Odeon in 1966, 1967 and 1968. There were two performances: 6.00 pm and 8.30 pm. At this point the group were more popular in Britain than in the USA. Their album, *20/20* (Capitol 1969) reached No. 3 in the British charts and the group had two Top 10 singles with 'I Can Hear Music' and 'Break Away.' The Beach Boys' 1969 British tour was just seven dates long. Earlier in the day the band had performed at King Edward Nurses Home in Leeds General Infirmary. This was arranged by DJ Jimmy Savile who was a volunteer at the hospital at the time. The Beach Boys played a 75 minute long set with just three acoustic guitars and Dennis Wilson's drum sticks to an audience of about 150 nurses and doctors.

Keith Badman: "*The hospital event is taped privately by a doctor, and captured professionally on film, partly screened for the first (and only) time on BBC-1's* Top Of The Pops *on June 19th set to 'Break Away'. After the performance, Al (Jardine) ends up in casualty after he complains of feeling unwell; a doctor in the hospital says he is suffering from complications following a head cold.*"

Amazingly, the Beach Boys appeared to have travelled from Leeds to Manchester for the evening's performances without further hiccups. This was, of course, before the construction of the M62 motorway!

"Best Of Israel" was a ten-date British tour featuring Israel's leading folk singers. They included Shoshana Damari who was known as the "Queen of Hebrew Music ". Damari was born to Jewish parents in Yemen who emigrated to Israel. She toured the world during her career. Ran Eliran was known as "Israel's Ambassador Of Song" and appeared on the Ed Sullivan Show in the USA and performed in Las Vegas.

Peter Sarstedt was at No. 1 for four weeks with the name dropping single 'Where Do You Go To My Lovely?' Sarstedt won the 1969 Ivor Novello Award for Best Song

Musically and Lyrically for this. He was not strictly a "one hit wonder" as the follow-up, 'Frozen Orange Juice' reached the Top 10 later in the year. Sarstedt's eponymous first album (United Artists 1969) reached No. 8 but only stayed in the charts for four weeks.

One-man band **Don Partridge** had been a busker for many years before appearing on the Eamonn Andrews Show on television. This led to Partridge being signed to EMI and having two Top 5 hit singles with 'Rosie' and 'Blue Eyes'. Later in 1968 he appeared on a pop package tour and at the *NME* Pollwinners' Concert at Wembley Empire Pool. In January 1969 Partridge hired the Royal Albert Hall for a 'Buskers Concert' featuring many of his fellow street performers who would share the profits equally. This led to a ten-date Buskers' Tour where the same people travelled around the country in an old London Transport bus. This concert showcase included future leader of Hawkwind, Dave Brock and guitarist Gordon Giltrap. Both of these would return to the Free Trade Hall in the years to come. Partridge briefly worked with Giltrap but soon returned to travelling and busking.

Led Zeppelin made the first of two appearances at the Free Trade Hall as part of a short British tour. They were supported by Blodwyn Pig, led by former Jethro Tull guitarist, Mick Abrahams, and Liverpool Scene who combined humour, poetry, rock and jazz. Zeppelin had first appeared in Manchester at the College of Technology in November 1968 and played again for students at the University in March 1971. The Free Trade Hall diary states: "No trouble here - Lead (sic) Zeppelin, a problem elsewhere".

Pink Floyd made their first appearance at the Free Trade Hall this year. The tour, consisting of twelve dates, boasted the band's Azimuth Co-ordinator with "360 degree sound." Floyd were just about to release a third album, *More* (Harvest 1969), their soundtrack for the French film of the same name. Floyd had appeared in May at Manchester College of Commerce and recorded the concert. This became part of the live half of their next album *Ummagumma* (Harvest 1970).

Ustad Vilyayat Khan was an Indian classical sitar player. Born in East Bengal, Khan developed 'gayaki ang' which tries to replicate vocal music. He first performed on stage at the age of sixteen and had a recording career of over 65 years, as well as broadcasting on All India radio for almost as long.

Harry Boardman was a Lancashire-born folk singer who sang both unaccompanied and while playing his own banjo and concertina. He had appeared on the compilation album, *Deep Lancashire* (Topic 1968).

Leon Rosselson had been in The Galliards with Robin Hall and Jimmie McGregor and, later, in the Three City Four with Martin Carthy. His satirical style had led him to contributing songs to BBC-1's *That Was The Week That Was*. Rosselson's songs were often political and he would later write 'The World Turned Upside Down' which was covered by the likes of Billy Bragg and Chumbawamba.

Rolf Harris' recent notoriety should not obscure the fact that in 1969 he was at the heart of BBC Light Entertainment with shows on Saturday night television. Harris was also a gifted musician playing such unusual instruments as the wobble board, didgeridoo and Stylophone. Later in the year he would have the Christmas No.1 single, 'Two Little Boys'.

Syd Lawrence's Glenn Miller tribute made the first of many appearances at the Free Trade Hall. Lawrence was a British bandleader and trumpeter who joined the Northern Dance Orchestra in 1953. He used to team up with colleagues to play Glenn Miller tunes at the Mersey Hotel in Manchester. Eventually Lawrence set up his own orchestra to focus on the swing era music that he loved so much. This year he released his album *Syd Lawrence with the Glenn Miller Sound* (Fontana 1969).

Sonny Lester's 'Jazz Wave Limited' was a promotion by A & R man Lester to bring attention to artists on the Solid State label whose records he produced. The concert featured the Thad Jones/Mel Lewis Big Band. According to Birch, the concert was not a great success with a delayed and shortened programme and mix ups with instruments, band uniforms and equipment. The Free Trade Hall concert was the first night of this short British tour.

Other events at the Free Trade Hall

January 3rd-11th – Holex Exhibition
March 4th – Clairol Hair Show
March 17th – Affleck & Brown Fashion Show
April 8th -10th – Student Christian Congress
May 9th – Scottish Country Dancing

Elsewhere (Headliners Only)

Belle Vue (Kings Hall): Willie Nelson, Hank Snow.

Odeon – Chet Atkins, Vikki Carr, The Clancy Brothers And Tommy Makem, Val Doonican, George Hamilton IV, Humble Pie, Engelbert Humperdinck, Tom Jones, The Moody Blues, Gene Pitney, Cliff Richard And The Shadows, Nina Simone, Stevie Wonder.

Palace Theatre– Henry Mancini, Mothers Of Invention, Nina Simone, The Spinners, Scott Walker, The Who.

The Seventies

The Glory Years as a Rock venue and a revolution upstairs

1970		
Jan 5th	THE CLANCY BROTHERS	*Finbar and Eddie Furey*
Jan 6th	EL SALI AND HIS SPANISH DANCE COMPANY	
Jan 30th	JULIE FELIX	
Feb 3rd	THE NICE	
Feb 6th	FAIRPORT CONVENTION	
Feb 11th	*JAZZ MEETS FOLK* RAHSAAN ROLAND KIRK'S ALL-AMERICAN QUINTET	*Garry Farr*
Feb 13th	*FOLK FESTIVAL* with The High Level Ranters, Cyril Tawney, Harry Boardman, Tim Hart and Maddy Prior	
Feb 14th	DEEP PURPLE	*Ashton Gardner and Dyke*
Feb 21st	BOOKER T. & THE MG'S (two houses)	*Blue Mink; Jimmy Ruffin; Red River Band; Johnnie Walker*
Feb 23rd	THE DUBLINERS	*Noel V. Ginnity (compère)*
Feb 27th	THE CONSTRUCTION COMPANY	*Gravy Train; Grizzly Bear; Blind Eye; Julian Roach; Ian Maclean*
Feb 28th	THE SPINNERS	
March 14th	NOEL MURPHY AND SHAGGIS	*Jeremy Taylor; Diz Disley*
March 20th	FOTHERINGAY	*The Humblebums; Nick Drake*
April 11th	NANA MOUSKOURI AND THE ATHENIANS	
April 21st	COLOSSEUM	*Quintessence*
April 25th	GLENN MILLER BAND featuring Buddy De Franco	
April 29th	TAJ MAHAL	*Rare Bird*
May 2nd	THE CORRIES	
May 9th	TONY BENNETT with COUNT BASIE AND HIS ORCHESTRA (two houses)	
May 11th	JOHN MAYALL featuring Duster Bennett	

May 12th	ROBIN HALL AND JIMMIE MacGREGOR	*Jackie and Bridie*
May 15th	TASTE	*Beggar's Opera*
May 20th	TOM PAXTON	
May 22nd	VICTOR BORGE	
May 25th	TEN YEARS AFTER	*Matthew's Southern Comfort; Writing On The Wall*
June 11th	ROY HARPER	*The Strawbs*
June 13th	SOFT MACHINE	
June 20th	KEEF HARTLEY BIG BAND	
June 28th	BARCLAY JAMES HARVEST and the Barclay James Harvest Symphony Orchestra	
July 18th	INCREDIBLE STRING BAND	
Sept 6th	MANFRED MANN'S CHAPTER THREE	*East Of Eden*
Sept 9th	TASTE	*Stone The Crows; Jake Holmes*
Sept 13th	CANNED HEAT	*Groundhogs*
Sept 26th	THE SPINNERS	
Sept 28th	DEREK AND THE DOMINOES	*Brett Marvin and the Thunderbolts*
Oct 2nd	HARRY JAMES AND HIS ORCHESTRA	
Oct 3rd (midnight concert)	JETHRO TULL	*Procol Harum; Tir Na Nog*
Oct 7th	THE WHO	*The James Gang*
Oct 9th	PENTANGLE	
Oct 14th	THE DUBLINERS	
Oct 21st	JACQUES LOUSSIER TRIO	
Oct 24th	INCREDIBLE STRING BAND	
Oct 25th	LUIS ALBERTO DEL PARANA Y LOS PARAGUAYOS	

Date	Main act	Support
Oct 31st	*AMERICAN FOLK, BLUES AND GOSPEL FESTIVAL* Sonny Terry and Brownie McGhee; Sister Rosetta Tharpe; Bukka White; Champion Jack Dupree; Willie Dixon Chicago Blues All-Stars; Robert Patterson Singers	
Nov 6th	FAIRPORT CONVENTION	*Roger Ruskin Spear And His Giant Kinetic Wardrobe*
Nov 10th	GINGER BAKER'S AIRFORCE	
Nov 11th	BUDDY RICH BIG BAND (two houses)	
Nov 16th	FAMILY	
Nov 21st	FOTHERINGAY	*Stefan Grossman*
Nov 25th	EDWIN HAWKINS SINGERS	
Nov 27th (midnight concert)	FRANK ZAPPA AND THE MOTHERS OF INVENTION	
Dec 4th	WOODY HERMAN ORCHESTRA	
Dec 7th	EMERSON, LAKE AND PALMER	
Dec 19th	THE SPINNERS	
Dec 21st	PINK FLOYD	

BY NOW THE "PROGRESSIVE" ROCK SCENE WAS DOMINATING the Free Trade Hall gig list with the appearances of such big names as Deep Purple, Pink Floyd and Jethro Tull.

El Sali and his Spanish Dance Company featured flamenco dancing and music. An album, *Flamenco!* (Decca /Phase 4 1966) featured the very first recordings of guitarist Paco Pena.

The Nice had started as P.P. Arnold's backing band and were one of the very first progressive rock bands in Britain, before splitting up this year. Keith Emerson was known as an accomplished and exhibitionist keyboard player, doing all sorts of things to his Hammond organ! The Nice's second single was an instrumental version of Leonard Bernstein's 'America' and the group were banned from the Royal Albert Hall for burning the American flag while performing this tune. The Nice's album, *Five Bridges* (Charisma 1970) reached No. 2. Keith Emerson later appeared in December with his new "supergroup" Emerson, Lake & Palmer (ELP) with Greg Lake (ex-King Crimson) and Carl Palmer (ex-Atomic Rooster). The other members of The Nice also went on to form their own groups - Jackson Heights (Lee Jackson) and Every Which Way (Brian Davidson). Both groups would subsequently play the Free Trade Hall.

Fairport Convention were now without a female lead singer, but guitarist Richard Thompson and fiddle player Dave Swarbrick shared vocal duties. They appeared twice at the Free Trade Hall this year - in February and November. In between these appearances Fairport toured the USA and the album, *Live At The LA Troubadour* (Island 1977), shows what a formidable live act they were. The group's album *Full House* (Island 1970) was released in July and reached No.13. Thompson would leave at the beginning of 1971 to pursue a solo career.

Rahsaan Roland Kirk was blinded as a small child but took to playing a trumpet at the age of nine. He was famous for playing three wind instruments simultaneously. As well as the conventional tenor saxophone, Kirk played the manzello and stritch, two old versions of saxophones that had been used by Spanish military bands. He also played flute, clarinet and whistles. Kirk was a unique artist who saw jazz as 'black classical music' and was one of the genre's most gifted improvisers. He died tragically young in 1977 after suffering two strokes.

Tim Hart and Maddy Prior were still recording and touring as a duo even though they were members of folk rock band Steeleye Span. They had released two low budget albums, volumes one and two of *Folk Songs Of Olde England* (Tepee 1968). The duo recorded a third album, *Summer Solstice* (Mooncrest 1971).

Deep Purple had just released their album, *Concerto For Group And Orchestra,* (Harvest 1970) a partnership with Malcolm Arnold and the Royal Philharmonic Orchestra. This was their first appearance at the Free Trade Hall. Later in the year their album, *Deep Purple In Rock* (Harvest 1970) was hugely successful, establishing them in the very highest tier of progressive rock bands. The band played two college gigs in Manchester later in the year, one at John Dalton College and the second one at Manchester University.

Booker T. & The MG's had played in Britain on the legendary Hit The Road Stax tour in 1967 as the backing group for Otis Redding, Sam And Dave et al. Their own single 'Time Is Tight' had reached No. 4 in 1969. This year the group released *McLemore Avenue* (Stax 1970), their instrumental version of The Beatles' *Abbey Road* album. This tour was nine dates long.

The Construction Company gig was advertised in the *Manchester Evening News* : 'You've seen part of it on T.V. You've heard a lot about it. Now here it is the WHOLE thing LIVE in the flesh : The Construction Company.' This project included members of Gravy Train (from St. Helens) and Sleep who hailed from the Whalley Range area. Sleep and other local bands had appeared on *Octopus*, a music programme on Granada Television.

Fotheringay was Sandy Denny's group after she left Fairport Convention. She teamed up with her boyfriend (later husband), Trevor Lucas of Eclection. They appeared twice at the Free Trade Hall this year: March and November. The March concert was part of a short tour, while the autumn concert was one of twelve dates. Fotheringay's eponymous album (Island 1970) reached No. 18. These were the only times that Sandy Denny played at this venue.

Colosseum were led by drummer Jon Hiseman and featured two other former members of John Mayall's Bluesbreakers' *Bare Wires* line-up, saxophonist Dick Heckstall Smith and bassist Tony Reeves. At the time they were arguably the leading jazz-rock group in Britain. Their second album, *Valentyne Suite* (Vertigo 1969) had reached No. 15 the previous year.

Taj Mahal was a second generation American blues musician who benefitted from being part of the CBS Sounds Of The Seventies promotion. He had appeared alongside Santana and It's A Beautiful Day at the Royal Albert Hall earlier in April.

The Corries were now a duo and renowned for being versatile multi-instrumentalists. This created a problem in terms of swapping instruments at concerts so the solution was a combolin. These strange looking custom made stringed instruments combined guitar, mandolin, the Spanish bandurria and sympathetic strings. Their album, *Strings And Things* (Columbia 1970) showcased these instruments and had detailed descriptions of them on the sleeve's back cover. The Corries were extremely popular in both Scotland and England, performing their own brand of Scottish folk music.

John Mayall was enjoying a peak in his long career and his album, *Empty Rooms* (Polydor 1970) reached No. 9 this year. He invited one-man blues band Duster Bennett to tour with him, first in the USA and then in Britain on an eleven-date tour.

Duster Bennett told *Melody Maker:* "*The idea is that John (Mayall) wants to give me more exposure. He did several concerts with me in Ireland recently, and offered me the chance to stay with the band until such time that I wanted to leave. The edges are still a bit frayed; for example I shall still be doing my own spot, and will be sitting out on some of the band's numbers... The idea is for this opportunity to act as a stepping stone. John doesn't really see me as a band member, but I need the experience.*"

Mayall explained, "I would like to do something really good - and if I can help to establish a deserving artist to be seen by the audiences he warrants then I'll be pleased." As Bennett biographer, Martin Celmins stated, "these mainly concert halls afforded Duster audience numbers that would take literally years to match by playing the small blues clubs that were his bread and butter." Bennett had supported Fleetwood Mac and B.B. King on their joint British tour in 1969 and appeared at the Free Trade Hall with them.

Between **Taste's** May and September appearances at the Free Trade Hall, the band had played a storming set at the Isle of Wight Festival, earning no less than five encores. Some of this performance was featured on their album, *Live At The Isle Of Wight* (Polydor 1972) and, more recently, on a DVD and expanded CD. Taste's autumn tour was twelve dates long and their final one before the band split up at Christmas.

Victor Borge was a Danish-American comedian, pianist and conductor. He escaped from wartime Scandinavia and settled in the USA. Borge first appeared on Rudy

Vallee's radio show and later worked with Bing Crosby and Frank Sinatra. His skills as a pianist allowed him to make elaborate musical jokes which are timeless. In the 1970's Borge was often joined on stage by opera singer Marilyn Mulvey.

By 1970 **Soft Machine** had lost both its psychedelic edge and founder members Daevid Allen and Kevin Ayers and were now firmly a jazz rock band. The band's album *Third* (CBS 1970) reached No. 18, their highest chart placing. Their Free Trade Hall appearance was part of a five-date provincial tour. Later in the year, in August, Soft Machine were the first rock band invited to play at the BBC Proms at the Royal Albert Hall.

Keef Hartley was another former drummer with John Mayall and had formed his own band, recording for the Decca label. He appeared twice at the Free Trade Hall, firstly with his 'Big Band' which had an expanded horn section. The 'Big Band' tour consisted of half a dozen dates. The band's album, *The Time Is Near* (Deram 1970) reached the Top 50 in the autumn and was their only chart placing.

Barclay James Harvest hailed from Lancashire and played at the Free Trade Hall for the first time this year, accompanied by an orchestra led by Robert John Godfrey. The group were one of the first signings to EMI's progressive label, Harvest and their first album was released in June. Barclay James Harvest returned to the Free Trade Hall eight times.

Manfred Mann's Chapter Three was, as the name suggested, a third incarnation in that band's career. Only Mike Hugg remained alongside Manfred from previous line-ups. Chapter Three were signed to the progressive Vertigo label and had a jazz rock slant. They released their second album in October but it was not a success.

Canned Heat made just one appearance at the Free Trade Hall; they had played Manchester College of Commerce in January. Their key member, Al "Blind Owl" Wilson had been found dead on September 3rd this year and yet the remaining band members played the Free Trade Hall only ten days later! The band had been contracted to play a festival in Germany and perhaps were scared of litigation. Wilson had sung lead on 'On The Road Again' and 'Goin' Up The Country' as well as playing guitar and harmonica. Surviving co-lead singer, Bob "The Bear" Hite had sung on 'Let's Work Together', the group's biggest British hit and was a more extrovert presence on stage. There were just six British dates on this visit. Another guitarist, Joel Scott Hill joined the band during its European tour.

Eric Clapton - in his guise as leader of **Derek And The Dominoes** - also made his only appearance at the Free Trade Hall during the last leg of the band's UK concerts. They had made their debut at the Lyceum in London and then played club dates around the country in a deliberately low-key approach. There was a clause in the band's contracts stipulating that the bill did not over-emphasise Clapton's name as a crowd-puller. Derek And The Dominoes' sole studio album, *Layla And Assorted Love Songs*, (Polydor 1970) did not chart in Britain until 2011!

American trumpeter **Harry James** had played with Benny Goodman in the 1930's and briefly employed a young Frank Sinatra as his vocalist. From 1939 onwards James led his own band which included Buddy Rich at one point. By 1957 James had re-formed his big band and toured for the next two decades. This was James's first visit to Britain and the Free Trade Hall concert was part of a ten-date tour.

Jethro Tull were on a twelve-date British tour; there were three late night shows: the Free Trade Hall and Birmingham concerts started at midnight and at Glasgow there was a slightly earlier start at 11.30pm. Audiences were promised a three hour show.

In early October **The Who** made their only appearance at the Free Trade Hall. The band had recorded a gig at Leeds University earlier in the year and released it in June, *Live At Leeds* (Track 1970). The Who's astonishing appearance at the Isle Of Wight Festival in August of this year is luckily captured on film. The Free Trade Hall concert was part of an eleven-date tour this month.

Free Trade Hall Diary: "Two door glass panels kicked in by 'Dirty Filth'. Audience very good. Trouble from outside. Police sent for to eject advance party at 1.45pm. Concert 35 minutes late starting. Admin argument. Dirtiest group to have used the hall. Not again."

In Richard Houghton's useful *I Was There* series, the volume on The Who includes a first hand account of the gig from Colin Joy:

"A totally different Who played the Free Trade Hall in 1970- they were bloody loud! The main emphasis of the tour was to capitalise on their appearance at Woodstock and the Isle of Wight Festivals, and to bring their showpiece Tommy to the stage. The album when originally released was not to everyone's cup of tea, but, live it was a masterpiece mixed in with The Who's back catalogue of stage favourites.

"Townshend had his trademark hand swinging guitar playing down to a tee, Daltrey was throwing his microphone high in the air at every opportunity, Moon's drumming was over the top and Entwistle occasionally moved - not too much but he moved! The problem was the band got louder and louder, but the set seemed to go on forever as they played the full Tommy album, with all the instrumentals. It was a good night which took no prisoners. They did 34 songs in all. It was a long, long deafening night."

On a personal note, I saw The Who in Manchester three years later at Kings Hall, Belle Vue on the Quadrophenia tour. I remember both how small the musicians on stage looked from my 80p seat at the back of the venue, but also how distinctive the band were in their stage act and musicianship. If you went to see The Who live, it was unsurprising that they lived up to their reputation. I remember Townshend's guitar strap breaking and people were shouting at him, urging him to smash his instrument!

The American Folk, Blues and Gospel Festival brought a similar bill to the Free Trade Hall as 1964, giving the Manchester audience another opportunity to see these ageing - but extraordinary - performers. The Free Trade Hall was the second night of the tour. This was **Sister Rosetta Tharpe's** final appearance at the Free Trade Hall; she was now 55 years old and, sadly, had suffered a stroke in Geneva during the tour. The festival returned to Britain and played eight more shows.

Another gospel act, **The Edwin Hawkins Singers,** had had a huge hit in the UK in 1969 with 'Oh Happy Day'; tickets were priced from 8/- (40p) to 18/- (90p); the Free Trade Hall diary entry merely says "flop", but no financial records exist. Ten days later the group played the Royal Albert Hall. There were also concerts in Birmingham, Liverpool and Nottingham.

Ginger Baker's Airforce's gig was cancelled on the night because Baker had a stomach complaint. According to a press report, "an apology (was) made to (the) audience and their money refunded."

This year saw the final appearances of both **Woody Herman's Orchestra** and **Buddy Rich's Big Band.** We were seeing the decline in popularity of modern jazz. Both bands were now playing short British tours.

Frank Zappa and the Mothers Of Invention played a midnight concert in November as part of a European tour. This line-up of the band included former Turtles, Howard Kaylan and Mark Volman on vocals. Zappa had enjoyed four consecutive Top 50 albums in Britain this year, the most recent being *Chunga's Revenge* (Reprise 1970). This was to be his only appearance at the Free Trade Hall.

Pink Floyd appeared just four days before Christmas. They played two sets, the second half being a performance of their album, *Atom Heart Mother* (Harvest 1970) with a brass section and choir conducted by John Alldis.

Other events at the Free Trade Hall

January 3rd – Wrestling
April 17th -18th – Australian Wild Life Films
May 26th – June 6th – Photography At Work Exhibition
October 5th – Chris Bonington Lecture

Elsewhere (Headliners Only)

Belle Vue (Kings Hall) – Blood, Sweat And Tears.

Odeon: Charles Aznavour, Long John Baldry, Bobby Bennett & Alan Randall, Georgie Fame, Julie Felix, The Four Tops, Engelbert Humperdinck, Tom Jones, Alan Price, Cliff Richard, Sam And Dave, Joe Tex, Vyjayanthimala.

Palace Theatre - The Beach Boys, Lulu, Slim Whitman.

1971		
Jan 20th	BLACK SABBATH	*Freedom; Curved Air*
Jan 29th	KEEF HARTLEY BAND	*Third Ear Band*
Jan 30th	VAN DER GRAAF GENERATOR	*Lindisfarne; Genesis*
Feb 2nd	ERIC BURDON AND WAR	
Feb 7th	LEON RUSSELL	*Steamhammer; High Broom*
Feb 12th	JULIE FELIX (with Danny Thompson)	
Feb 15th	JOHNNY WINTER	*Formerly Fat Harry*
Feb 16th	THE SPINNERS	
Feb 20th	7 15pm- THE SWINGLE SINGERS 10pm –TOM PAXTON	
Feb 23rd	THEODOKARIS	
Feb 24th	RALPH McTELL	*Famous Jug Band*
Feb 26th	JACKSON HEIGHTS; EVERY WHICH WAY; AUDIENCE	
March 3rd	*FESTIVAL OF FOLK* with Magna Carta	*The Johnstons; The Pennine Folk*
March 5th	THE ROLLING STONES (two houses)	*Groundhogs*
March 6th	JUDITH DURHAM	
March 8th	JOHN MAYALL	*Randall's Island*
March 13th	QUINTESSENCE	*"Friends"*
March 22nd	EMERSON, LAKE AND PALMER	
March 29th	SOFT MACHINE	
March 30th	THE WHITE HEATHER SHOW	
April 3rd	GLENN MILLER ORCHESTRA with Buddy de Franco	
April 6th	YES	*Lancaster; Highly Inflammable*
April 19th	SHIRLEY BASSEY (two houses)	
April 20th	CARAVAN	*Barclay James Harvest; Gringo*

April 23rd	THE DUBLINERS	
April 25th	THE HOLLIES	*Labi Siffre*
April 26th	VAN DER GRAAF GENERATOR	*Genesis; Bell + Arc*
April 30th	THE STRAWBS	*Brake And Crane*
May 11th	THE BYRDS	*Rita Coolidge and The Dixie Flyers*
May 12th	THE MIGHTY SPARROW SHOW (two houses)	
May 14th	THE SPINNERS	
May 16th	T.REX	
May 18th	COUNT BASIE ORCHESTRA	
May 19th	RORY GALLAGHER	*Jellybread*
May 20th	ROD McKUEN with orchestra (conductor- Arthur Greenslade)	
May 25th	KING CRIMSON	*Roger Ruskin Spear's Giant Kinetic Wardrobe*
June 15th	GROUNDHOGS	*Savoy Brown*
June 16th	WISHBONE ASH	*Renaissance; Stackridge*
June 18th	LINDISFARNE	*Bell + Arc; Halfbreed; Maiden Law*
June 20th	CURVED AIR	*Mick Abrahams Band; Marc Ellington*
July 8th	SHA NA NA ; URIAH HEEP	*Paladin*
July 11th	JAMES TAYLOR; CAROLE KING (two houses)	*Jo Mama*
July 23rd	AUDIENCE; RENAISSANCE	*Gordon Giltrap*
August 26th	IF	*Steamhammer; James Litherland's Million*
Sept 1st	CREEDENCE CLEARWATER REVIVAL (two houses)	
Sept 8th	CAT STEVENS	*Sutherland Brothers Band*
Sept 22nd	DEEP PURPLE	*Bullet*

Sept 26th	TEN YEARS AFTER	*Supertramp; Keith Christmas*
Sept 29th	RAY CHARLES And His Orchestra with The Raelets (two houses)	
Oct 1st	YES	*Jonathan Swift*
Oct 4th	JOHN MAYALL	*Eggs Over Easy*
Oct 9th	HAWKWIND with the Freaky Kinetic Circus	*Paul Brett Sage; Anon Din*
Oct 10th	MAGNA CARTA	*Gillian McPherson*
Oct 12th	STEELEYE SPAN	*Andy Roberts*
Oct 15th	JACQUES LOUSSIER TRIO	
Oct 22nd	HARRY JAMES ORCHESTRA with Rita Graham	
Oct 25th	THE FACES	*Cochise*
Oct 27th	PACO PENA	
Oct 29th	INCREDIBLE STRING BAND	
Oct 30th	KING CRIMSON	*Keith Christmas*
Nov 1st	LUIS ALBERTO DEL PARANA Y LOS PARAGUAYOS	*Carmen de Santana*
Nov 3rd	TOM PAXTON	
Nov 5th	PENTANGLE	
Nov 6th	T.REX	*Bob Harris-DJ*
Nov 9th	ARGENT	*Climax Chicago; Duffy Power*
Nov 12th	RALPH McTELL	*Robin and Barry Dransfield*
Nov 17th	GROUNDHOGS	*Egg; Quicksand*
Nov 20th	FAIRPORT CONVENTION	
Nov 22nd	ELTON JOHN	*England Dan and John Ford Coley*
Nov 23rd	FAMILY	*America*
Nov 24th	LED ZEPPELIN	
Nov 25th	THEODOKARIS	

Nov 26th	SOFT MACHINE	*Loudon Wainwright III*
Nov 27th	BLASTER BATES	
Nov 30th	MANITAS DE PLATA	
Dec 7th	SYD LAWRENCE ORCHESTRA	*Kevin Kent & The Serenaders*
Dec 10th	EMERSON, LAKE AND PALMER (two houses)	*Michael Chapman*
Dec 11th	THE SPINNERS	
Dec 15th	WORLD'S GREATEST JAZZ BAND with Yank Lawson and Bob Haggart	
Dec 22nd	EAST OF EDEN	*Troggs; Gravy Train*

BLACK SABBATH MADE THEIR FIRST APPEARANCE AT THE Free Trade Hall in January as the last night of a ten-date tour. Their album, *Paranoid* (Vertigo 1970) had reached No.1 the previous October and the title track reached No. 8 in the singles charts. Black Sabbath hailed from the Midlands and are often credited as the British pioneers of heavy metal. Their first six albums all reached the Top 10.

The **Eric Burdon & War** gig is hard to verify; it was possibly cancelled as Burdon had a throat problem which led him to abandon the tour. The group War continued without him. Their second album, *Black Man's Burdon* (Liberty 1971) would reach No. 25 later this month. Eric Burdon parted company with the band later in the year.

The Charisma Package Tour was extraordinary good value: three bands - **Van Der Graaf Generator**, **Lindisfarne** and **Genesis** - for just six shillings (30p). In 'Not Dead Yet', Phil Collins says, "The tour is a raging success, establishing all three bands as major, hall-filling acts." According to *NME*, the Free Trade Hall "had crocodiles of long-haired youths surrounding it for the last remaining tickets."

Dave Jackson of Van Der Graaf Generator told Mick Dillingham in *Ptolemaic Terrascope* a different story: "We did the now legendary "six-bob tour". We topped the bill, Lindisfarne next and Genesis at the bottom. The tour really helped break Lindisfarne in this country, while ironically Van Der Graaf Generator with its less commercial sound were starting to ceiling out. We had to look to the Continent for support more and more." Van Der Graaf Generator had just released their third album, *H To He, Who Am The Only One* (Charisma 1971). The band returned to the Free Trade Hall in April, again with Genesis as support, along with fellow Charisma artists, Bell & Arc.

Collins quotes more of the *NME* review of Genesis: "In the demonic, black-clad figure of Peter Gabriel, Genesis have a vocal performer who has the precocious magnetism of which contemporary pop heroes are hewn. A macabre entrepreneur,

Peter introduces each selection with strange neo-fantasy monologues which at times border on the realms of insanity."

Leon Russell had made his name on Joe Cocker's Mad Dogs And Englishmen tour of the USA in 1970, the film of which was released in January 1971. Russell's first album, *Leon Russell* (Shelter 1970) had not charted in Britain. By the end of this year, Russell had performed with George Harrison et al at The Concert For Bangladesh and recorded with Bob Dylan.

Johnny Winter was another artist in the CBS Sounds Of The 70's promotion who had played the Royal Albert Hall in April 1970. Winter was signed to Columbia in the USA for reportedly the highest advance in recording history at $600,000. His third album, *Johnny Winter And Live* (CBS 1971) would soon reach No. 20 in Britain, his highest ever placing. This long-haired albino blues performer was an extraordinary sight at the time. When Winter played live, he would often opt for crowd-pleasing rock 'n' roll numbers.

Theodokaris, the Greek songwriter and composer appeared twice this year. Imprisoned after the right wing coup in Greece in the 1960's, Theodokaris's case was championed by the likes of Leonard Bernstein and Arthur Miller. Once released from prison, he was exiled from his home country and performed at hundreds of concerts throughout Europe. Theodokaris is most famous for his theme to the *Zorba The Greek* film soundtrack.

Ralph McTell made his first appearance at the Free Trade Hall in February, the first of nine concerts over the next decade. One of Britain's leading folk singer-songwriters, McTell had left Transatlantic Records and was promoting his new album *You Well Meaning Brought Me Here* (Famous 1971).

Magna Carta headlined a Festival Of Folk in March and reappeared in October on their first major tour. The group had charted briefly with their second album, *Seasons* (Vertigo 1970). Multi-instrumentalist Davey Johnstone had played on *Seasons* as a session musician and then joined the group full time. Johnstone's sole studio album with Magna Carta was *Songs From Wasties Orchard* (Vertigo 1971).

The Rolling Stones made their only Free Trade Hall appearance in March on their Goodbye Britain tour, before they became tax exiles in France. This was their first British tour in over four years; the Stones had played the ABC Ardwick in 1966. The Free Trade Hall date was the second of ten dates, eight of which saw the group playing two houses. The Stones' Leeds gig was recorded and appeared as a second disc in the deluxe reissue/ remaster of *Sticky Fingers* (Rolling Stones 1971). Luckily, the Free Trade Hall night was extensively photographed and the pictures have been widely published, notably in Bill Wyman's *Rolling With The Stones* book. The Stones were joined by Nicky Hopkins on keyboards, Bobby Keyes on saxophones and Jim Price on trumpet. Tickets for the concert started at 50p and went up to £1!

Free Trade Hall diary: "Whilst concerts went well, second house attracted Hells Angels. Some 60/70 hung around outside throughout. 20/25 police on duty- one stabbed with bayonet (in leg) after concert was over."

When tickets went on sale, fans queued overnight leaving an extraordinary amount of litter, discarded bedding and tarpaulin outside the venue. This was photographed and published by the press.

Groundhogs supported the Rolling Stones, apparently at Mick Jagger's request. Tony McPhee, "we were selling out venues everywhere. We did a 10 day tour with the Stones, and went straight from that to headlining our own gigs. I remember playing to a full house in Glasgow with the Stones, and going back there 3 months later on our own and playing to a full house again. A hell of a buzz. It went on like that for 2 or 3 years..." It must have been similar in Manchester. The Groundhogs played the Free Trade Hall three times in 1971; after supporting the Stones in March they headlined in both June and November. Their fourth album, *Split* (Liberty 1971) had been released in March and peaked at No. 5 in a 27-week chart run.

Judith Durham was the voice and face of The Seekers throughout the 1960's. Australian Judith had returned to her homeland and tried hard to reinvent herself as a singer of a wider repertoire than the commercial folk of her old group. Her third solo album, *Climb Ev'ry Mountain* (A&M) 1971) had been recorded in London. I think that we can safely assume that - however hard she tried with her new songs - some Seekers hits would have been expected, performed and appreciated during the concert.

Quintessence were a multi-racial band who hailed from Notting Hill in London. Fascinating footage can be seen on YouTube, including a short documentary about the band. Their third album, *Dive Deep* (Island 1971) had just been released and peaked at No. 43. Their concert in March cost only 60p a ticket.

Yes made their Free Trade Hall debut as headliners in April this year, just as *The Yes Album* (Atlantic 1971) hit the Top 10. They returned in October on their first tour with their new keyboard player, Rick Wakeman who would later have his own tales to tell about the Free Trade Hall.

Caravan were part of the Canterbury Scene that had also spawned Soft Machine. In May the band would release their fourth album, *In The Land Of Grey And Pink* (Deram 1971) which had a 22 minute-long track, 'Nine Feet Underground.' Tickets for their first Free Trade Hall appearance were priced at just 40p.

The Hollies appeared in Manchester for the first time in three years, playing - according to the review in *NME* - to a "packed audience." In June the group released *Distant Light* (Parlophone 1971), their final album on that label. The group would lose lead singer Allan Clarke at the end of the year. But Clarke was soon back in the group and the Hollies returned to the Free Trade Hall with him in 1974.

The Calypso Carnival Package saw a return of **The Mighty Sparrow** (who had previously appeared in 1962); this was a twelve-date tour with a quarter of these gigs in the London area.

T.Rex appeared twice – in May and November- at the height of their British success. Their audience was now very different to their acoustic Tyrannosaurus Rex days. The band's first single as T. Rex, 'Ride A White Swan' had reached No. 2 and their next two singles, 'Hot Love' and 'Get It On' both reached No.1. Both concerts this year– firmly aimed at teenage fans – were priced at only 60p a ticket. The second T.Rex album, *Electric Warrior* (Fly 1971) would reach No. 1 in December and stay there for six weeks. It became the best-selling album in Britain in 1971.

Rory Gallagher, now a solo act after the split of Taste, became a stalwart of the Free Trade Hall with the first of eight appearances. His first two solo albums only reached the Top 40, but his third album, *Live In Europe* (Polydor 1972) was a lot more successful and peaked at No. 9. Gallagher's concerts were legendary for the artist's incredible technique, energy and passion.

Cheap three, sometimes four, band packages continued after the success of the Charisma one in January. There was another Charisma package in February with the two off-shoot bands led by former Nice members, **Every Which Way** (Brian Davidson) and **Jackson Heights** (Lee Jackson). **Audience** were perhaps a more interesting band with a subtle mixture of acoustic guitar and saxophone. Their singer, Howard Werth, was even invited to join the Doors after Jim Morrison died. This gig also cost only 30p. Audience returned in July alongside Renaissance and Gordon Giltrap for 40p again!

Rod McKuen was a one-off; a poet, singer-songwriter, composer and actor. He translated songs by Jacques Brel which became known as 'Seasons In The Sun' and 'If You Go Away'. McKuen's output was phenomenal: albums of poetry with mood music backing from Anita Kerr & The San Sebastian Strings; dozens of solo albums, thirty books of poetry and umpteen concerts around the world. Critics hated McKuen but the public - for a time - loved him. His third and final appearance at the Free Trade Hall in 1975 was poorly attended.

Wishbone Ash had a twin guitar sound and their second album, *Pilgrimage* (MCA 1971) reached No. 14 this year. The group's breakthrough came the following year with the best selling album, *Argus* (MCA 1972). Wishbone Ash would return to the Free Trade Hall four more times. Their first Free Trade Hall appearance had tickets for just 50p.

By June **Lindisfarne** were headlining their own concerts - with no less than three support acts. Their second album *Fog On The Tyne* (Charisma 1971) would enter the charts in October this year and eventually reach No. 1.

Curved Air had supported Black Sabbath in January and headlined for the first time in June. The group's unique selling points were their female lead singer - Sonja Kristina - (very unusual in British rock bands) and an electric violinist, Darryl Way. Way had studied at the Royal College of Music and his treatment of Vivaldi's music was something of a crowd pleaser. Keyboard player, Francis Monkman was also classically trained, at the Royal Academy of Music. Curved Air's sole hit single

'Backstreet Luv' reached No. 4 in August and gave them national exposure on *Top Of The Pops*. Their eponymous second album (Warner Bros 1971) peaked at No. 11.

The Byrds made their only appearance in Manchester (on their 1965 British tour the nearest that they had played was the Lancashire mill town of Nelson). By now the band had an excellent reputation for playing live - as the live half of their album, *Untitled* (CBS 1970) demonstrated. Manchester was the penultimate date on their seven-night British tour. Their album, *Byrdmaniax* (CBS 1971) was released in August in Britain, two months after its American release.

Sha Na Na were an American rock 'n' roll revival group who famously performed 'At the Hop' in the film of the Woodstock Festival in 1969. Their gold lame jackets and slicked back hair contrasted with the tie-dye T-shirts and long hair of the festival audience. On record the group were less impressive and less successful. Later in the 1970's the group had their own syndicated television show in the USA and appeared in the film *Grease*.

Uriah Heep were co-headlining with Sha Na Na; this was not the most obvious or compatible pairing. The concert was billed as *Bronze Records Summer Outing*. This British heavy rock band were to make seven appearances at the Free Trade Hall during the next decade, surviving several line-up changes including the departure of their lead singer David Byron in 1976.

Demand for **James Taylor** and **Carole King** was so high that a second (earlier) show was quickly arranged for the same day. Taylor had already broken through in Britain with his albums, *Sweet Baby James* (Warner Bros 1970) and *Mud Slide Slim* (Warner Bros 1971), while King's album, *Tapestry* album (A&M 1971) had only just been released. *Tapestry* went on to become one of the biggest sellers of the decade, staying in the British album charts for 90 weeks. King returned to the Free Trade Hall only once, in 1982.

If were a jazz rock band, often seen as Britain's equivalent to America's Blood, Sweat & Tears or Chicago. Their album titles were numbered rather than named : *If*, *If 2*, *If 3* and *If 4*, following Chicago's example, perhaps. If were signed first to Island and then United Artists. The Free Trade Hall concert was part of the band's ten-date tour, promoting their album, *If 3* (United Artists 1971). **Steamhammer** were yet another British blues-rock band; their first album featured Martin Quittenton who went on to co-write Rod Stewart's first hit singles. By 1971 the band had a different line-up and co-headlined with If.

Creedence Clearwater Revival were now a three-piece as rhythm guitarist Tom Fogerty had left the band earlier in the year. Their Free Trade Hall concert was the band's only northern appearance; their only other British concerts were two nights at the Royal Albert Hall in London. Creedence's album, *Live In Europe* (Fantasy 1973) was recorded on this tour.

Cat Stevens had signed to Island in 1970 and had reinvented himself as a serious singer-songwriter, in complete contrast to his pop star image in the 1960's. He appeared at the Free Trade Hall just before the release of *Teaser And The Firecat* (Island 1971) which would reach No. 3 in an incredible 93 week chart run. This was his only Free Trade Hall appearance, part of a six-date British tour.

Deep Purple were scheduled to appear at the Free Trade Hall on February 19th, but were banned from the venue and the concert was switched to Kings Hall, Belle Vue. However, the ban was lifted by September when they did play the Free Trade Hall. This was the same week that Deep Purple's album, *Fireball* (Harvest 1971) reached No. 1 in Britain.

Hawkwind made the first of four appearances at the Free Trade Hall. Their second album, *In Search Of Space* (United Artists 1971) had reached No. 18 this year. In summer 1972 their single 'Silver Machine' reached No. 2, bringing them crossover success and enough money to launch the *Space Ritual* tour. In the next two years Hawkwind visited Manchester five times; three more at the Free Trade Hall and two gigs at the Hardrock Concert Theatre.

Jazz fans had only two concerts to enjoy: **Count Basie** and **World's Greatest Jazz Band,** but there was a swing band revival represented by the Glenn Miller, Harry James and Syd Lawrence orchestras.

Steeleye Span had formed in the winter of 1969/1970 after Ashley Hutchings left Fairport Convention. The group's second line-up had supported Jethro Tull on a ten-date British tour earlier in 1971, but did not play Manchester. October's concert was the first of an incredible eleven appearances by Steeleye Span at the Free Trade Hall over the next decade. Singers Maddy Prior and Tim Hart were the only constant group members during this time. Tickets were only 50p for this first appearance. Steeleye Span were always a popular act at the Free Trade Hall even before their commercial peak in the mid-1970's.

The Faces appeared at the Free Trade Hall just as their lead singer, Rod Stewart, had the No. 1 single and album in the UK and USA simultaneously with 'Maggie May' and *Every Picture Tells A Story* (Mercury 1971). When Stewart appeared on *Top Of The Pops*, he used The Faces to mime the backing track to "Maggie May". But only Ronnie Wood of The Faces actually played on the original record; the other musicians were co-writer Martin Quittenton (acoustic guitar), Micky Waller (drums), Pete Sears (keyboards) and Ray Jackson of Lindisfarne (mandolin). Stewart had a solo contract with Mercury while The Faces were signed to Warners. The Faces would reach the singles charts later in the year with 'Stay With Me'. Their third album, *A Nod's As Good As A Wink To A Blind Horse* (Warner Bros 1971) would enter the charts in Christmas week, eventually reaching No. 2.

King Crimson were touring for the first time in nearly eighteen months and had - apart from Robert Fripp and Pete Sinfield - a completely new line-up. Their third album, *Lizard* (Island 1971) was a lot less successful than its two predecessors. **Ten Years Afte**r were also touring the UK for the first time in eighteen months. This clearly had a negative effect as TYA's new album, *A Space In Time* (Chrysalis 1971) only reached No. 36 in Britain, after the band had had four Top 10 albums in a row.

Argent made the first of five appearances at the Free Trade Hall; the group was led by Rod Argent, former keyboard player of The Zombies. Their breakthrough came the following year with hit single 'Hold Your Head Up'. Argent were on a lengthy tour of 32-dates.

Elton John only ever played twice at the Free Trade Hall. In November he was touring to promote his album, *Madman Across The Water* (DJM 1971) which did not repeat the success of his two previous releases in Britain. This was the second night of his thirteen-date British tour.

Led Zeppelin made their second - and final appearance - at the Free Trade Hall. The venue's diary states "No Thank You" for this concert, an assessment on which the reader can draw their own conclusions. Six days later, the group appeared again in Manchester at Kings Hall, Belle Vue, reflecting the incredible demand for tickets. Their fourth album, *Four Symbols* (Atlantic 1971) reached No. 1 at the beginning of December.

Blaster Bates was a raconteur who used his experiences as a demolition and explosives expert to comic effect. He recorded eight albums of this material and the first three, *Laughter With A Bang* , *1001 Gelignites* and *TNT For Two* were especially popular.

Other events at the Free Trade Hall

May 7th – Scottish Concert
September 4th – Wrestling
October 16th – Vienna Boys Choir

Elsewhere (Headliners Only):

Belle Vue (King's Hall): Johnny Cash, Deep Purple, Ken Dodd, Led Zeppelin, Merle Travis.

Odeon : Chairmen Of The Board, Crosby And Nash, Manitas De Plata, Sacha Distel, The Four Tops, Engelbert Humperdinck, Tom Jones, The Moody Blues, Gene Pitney, Martha Reeves And The Vandellas, The Supremes, Frankie Valli And The Four Seasons, The Who, Stevie Wonder.

Palace Theatre : Johnny Mathis, Buffy Sainte-Marie, Dorothy Squires, Slim Whitman.

1972		
Jan 14th	CURVED AIR	
Jan 22nd	PROCOL HARUM	*Amazing Blondel*
Jan 31st	YES	*Curved Air*
Feb 4th	BLACK SABBATH	*Wild Turkey*
Feb 5th	WISHBONE ASH	*Glencoe*
Feb 8th	MOUNTAIN	*The Jimmy McCulloch Band*
Feb 11th	PINK FLOYD	
Feb 12th	THE STRAWBS	*Jonathan Kelly; Tony Crerar*
Feb 14th	MOTT THE HOOPLE	*Mike Harrison's Junkyard Angel*
Feb 28th	ROY HARPER	
Feb 29th	OSIBISA	*Ashton, Gardner and Dyke*
March 5th	QUINTESSENCE	
March 11th	STONE THE CROWS	*Van Der Graaf Generator*
March 14th	*IRISH NATIONAL CONCERT* with Kevin Hilton, Cathie Harrop; Michael O'Dea; Bill McMahon; Noel Smith; Dan Armstrong; The Byrom Singers	
March 17th	HAWKWIND	*Status Quo*
March 24th	HEAD, HANDS AND FEET	*Patto; Claire Hamill*
March 25th	RORY GALLAGHER	*Byzantium*
March 28th	JETHRO TULL	*Tir Na Nog*
March 29th	PINK FLOYD	
March 30th	PINK FLOYD	
April 1st	CAPTAIN BEEFHEART AND HIS MAGIC BAND	*Karen Bernhard; The Fantastic Farina (dancers)*
April 2nd	BARCLAY JAMES HARVEST	*Trees; Matthew Ellis*
April 4th	EDGAR BROUGHTON BAND	
April 8th	STEELEYE SPAN	

April 9th	CURVED AIR	*Nick Pickett*
April 14th	THE TEMPTATIONS (two houses)	*Carla Thomas*
April 15th	THE NEW SEEKERS	
April 17th	ARGENT	*Gallagher and Lyle*
April 18th	THE DUBLINERS	
April 21st	DAVID BOWIE	*JSD Band*
April 22nd	JOHNNY NASH PERCY SLEDGE	*Monica Day*
April 26th	JOHN MAYALL	*Matching Mole (didn't play)*
May 2nd	JERRY LEE LEWIS (two houses)	*James Royal; Country Fever; Liz Christian*
May 5th	NANA MOUSKOURI AND THE ATHENIANS	
May 6th	THE SPINNERS	
May 9th	ELECTRIC LIGHT ORCHESTRA	*Colin Blunstone; F, F & Z*
May 10th	KRIS KRISTOFFERSON and The Band Of Thieves	*Rita Coolidge*
May 11th	ROD McKUEN	
May 30th	SLADE	*Status Quo*
June 18th	THE FACES	
June 19th	URIAH HEEP	*Mike Maran*
June 22nd	JOHN WILLIAMS	
June 26th	THE KINKS (War On Want benefit)	*Steve Goodman*
Sept 1st	ELTON JOHN	*Linda Lewis*
Sept 16th	MOTT THE HOOPLE	*Home*
Sept 20th	THE EVERLY BROTHERS	*Dave Loggins*
Sept 21st	HAWKWIND	*Magic Muscle*
Sept 23rd	THE SPINNERS	
Sept 25th	DEEP PURPLE	*Glencoe*

Sept 26th	STONE THE CROWS	
Oct 1st	VICTOR BORGE	*Marylyn Mulvey; Sahan Arzruni*
Oct 2nd	JACKSON HEIGHTS	*Magna Carta; Jefferson*
Oct 9th	RALPH McTELL	*Natural Acoustic Band*
Oct 10th	LINDISFARNE	*Genesis; Rab Noakes*
Oct 13th	STEELEYE SPAN	*Amazing Blondel*
Oct 16th	THE KINKS	*Blackfoot Sue*
Oct 18th	TOM PAXTON	
Oct 25th	BB KING	
Oct 27th	SOFT MACHINE	*Mick Greenwood*
Oct 31st	HUMBLE PIE	*Frampton's Camel*
Nov 6th	THE OSMONDS	
Nov 10th	BARCLAY JAMES HARVEST and Symphony Orchestra	*Camel*
Nov 11th	JIMMY CLIFF	*Mona Richardson; Mighty Explosion*
Nov 13th	EMERSON, LAKE AND PALMER	*Jimmy Stevens*
Nov 15th	SLADE	*Thin Lizzy; Suzi Quatro*
Nov 18th	AL STEWART	*Planxty*
Nov 24th	PENTANGLE	*C.O.B; Wizz Jones*
Nov 27th	ARGENT	*Bronco*
Dec 1st	GROUNDHOGS	*Gentle Giant; Stray*
Dec 4th	WISHBONE ASH	*Curtiss Maldoon*
Dec 5th	FAMILY	*Linda Lewis*
Dec 8th	SYD LAWRENCE ORCHESTRA	*Roy Marsden; The Serenaders*
Dec 9th	THE SPINNERS	
Dec 23rd	THE FACES	*Vigrass and Osborne; Stumble*

SEPTEMBER OF THIS YEAR SAW THE OPENING OF A SERIOUS rival to the Free Trade Hall's dominance of popular music concerts. The Hardrock Concert Theatre opened in Stretford and immediately attracted several big names. Decades later it was described by Joyce Woolridge in *Mojo* magazine as a "converted bowling alley, sprayed black, with the acoustics of a biscuit tin" but when the venue first opened hopes were high; *NME* reported: "Britain's first purpose-built rock venue has a dual-purpose facility and can convert from a 3000 capacity concert hall to a 1500 capacity disco. Also incorporated are a revolving stage, fully-fitted quadraphonic sound and a 24-channel mixer."

NME's Tony Stewart interviewed Mike O'Shea of the Hardrock's management team and asked him if the new venue will take artists away from Belle Vue and The Free Trade Hall. Mike O'Shea: "I don't think that these two venues are really worried about popular music ... They've plenty of bookings from the Hallé Band Orchestral (sic) evenings. I don't think what we take from them will cause any concern at all."

The Hardrock's opening night was David Bowie, setting the bar high for a new venue. Bowie appeared four times at this venue before the end of the year.

Nevertheless the Free Trade Hall had a busy year with over fifty rock nights from Argent to Yes and other shows with pop, blues and folk. Jazz had totally disappeared save for Syd Lawrence's tribute to Glenn Miller.

Mountain's song 'Nantucket Sleighride' was used as the theme to ITV's political show *Weekend World*. The group disbanded after this eleven-date British tour as bass player Felix Pappalardi was suffering from deafness and tiredness. A live album, *The Road Goes Ever On* (Island 1972) reached No. 21 in July.

Pink Floyd's February concert suffered a power failure. Glenn Povey: "About 25 minutes into the show during 'Careful With That Axe, Eugene', there was a power cut and, despite cries of 'Acoustic!' from the audience, the concert was abandoned." Floyd returned to the Free Trade Hall for two concerts six weeks later, having just toured Japan and Australia. Their album, *Meddle* (Harvest 1971) had been released the previous November, reaching No. 3 and staying in the charts for 82 weeks.

Mott The Hoople appeared twice this year. In February their fourth album, *Brain Capers* (Island 1971) had flopped but later in the year David Bowie persuaded the band to stay together and cover his composition, 'All The Young Dudes' which reached No. 3 in the late summer. This was also the title track for Mott The Hoople's fifth album (CBS 1972) which reached No. 21. The band had, effectively, reinvented itself and went on to have a string of hit singles and albums. As Charles Shaar Murray said, "He (Bowie) got Mott The Hoople out of the dumper. Mott had been a hugely popular live band who'd never quite figured how to make records which would sell outside their hardcore fanbase." (Sinker 2018)

Steven Morrissey was a Mott The Hoople fan; in his *Autobiography* he recalls a "young and patronising.. local priest" asking him what he liked in life. Morrissey's reply was "Mott The Hoople". Later in the book, Morrissey writes, "In this year (1972) I also see Mott The Hoople and Lou Reed live, and my senses never return." Mott were at the Free Trade Hall on September 16th and Reed appeared at the

Hardrock – close to Morrissey's Stretford home - on October 22nd.

Osibisa was an Afro-beat group who have been overlooked in many histories of rock. Their first two albums - famous for their Roger Dean illustrations of flying elephants on the front covers - both reached No. 11 in the charts. Art Garfunkel covered the title track of their second album, *Wowaya* (MCA 1972).

Stone The Crows featured the voice of Maggie Bell and were well regarded as a live act. Tragically, their guitarist Les Harvey was electrocuted on stage on May 3rd at the Top Rank, Swansea when he touched an unearthed microphone. This was just two months after the band's Free Trade Hall appearance. Harvey's replacement was Jimmy McCulloch. The band toured in the autumn to promote their fourth album, *Ontinuous Performance* (Polydor 1972) which reached No. 33 later in the year. Stone The Crows would split up in 1973.

Head, Hands & Feet appeared as part of another cheap package, alongside fellow Island artists Patto and Claire Hamill. Tickets were just 40p! Head, Hands & Feet was a British country rock group and featured a pre-Cockney Chas Hodges and guitar wizard, Albert Lee. Both would reappear at the Free Trade Hall in future years: Hodges as half of Chas & Dave and Lee in Emmylou Harris's Hot Band.

Captain Beefheart made his first appearance at the Free Trade Hall. His album, *Lick My Decals Off Baby* (Straight 1970) had reached No. 20 in the British charts. Beefheart had played in Manchester in 1968 but this was his first major British concert tour. He would return to the Free Trade Hall on three more occasions.

The Edgar Broughton Band was prominent in the counter-culture with their "Out Demons Out!" chant. Originally a blues band - like so many progressive acts - Broughton signed to Harvest in 1968. Many people thought that his voice sounded like a mix of Howlin' Wolf and Captain Beefheart. After two Top 30 albums, the band's fourth offering, *In Side Out* (Harvest 1972) was less successful.

The New Seekers were originally formed by Keith Potger who was one of the original Seekers. Potger soon dropped out and the group became regulars on *Top Of The Pops* and other television music shows. Their adaptation of a Coke commercial, 'I'd Like To Teach The World To Sing' had reached No.1 in January. The group went on to represent Britain in the Eurovision Song Contest with 'Beg, Steal Or Borrow'.

David Bowie headlined at the FTH for the first time in April with an early date on his Ziggy Stardust tour. According to Haslam (2005) , "there were 300 there at most." This appearance was a week before the release of the single 'Starman' and two months before it entered the charts. Bowie's famous *Top Of The Pops* appearance, performing the single was not until July 6th. The album, *The Rise And Fall Of Ziggy Stardust And The Spiders From Mars* (RCA Victor 1972) was released on June 16th and entered the charts two weeks later.

Texan-born **Johnny Nash** had reached the Top 10 three times in the late 1960's. His cover of Bob Marley's 'Stir It Up' had entered the British charts at the beginning of

April and would reach No. 13. This was the first Marley composition to enter the charts. Nash's follow-up single, 'I Can See Clearly Now' was self-penned and would reach No. 5.

At the **John Mayall** concert in April support band Matching Mole - featuring ex-Soft Machine drummer/ vocalist Robert Wyatt -failed to appear as their equipment had been mislaid! Mayall's band went on stage around 9pm, by which time some of the audience had given up and gone home. The line-up - apart from Mayall and drummer Keef Hartley - were all American jazz musicians. Most of them would feature on his next albums, *Jazz Blues Fusion* (Polydor 1972) and *Moving On* (Polydor 1973). This tour consisted of eight dates.

Jerry Lee Lewis made his only Free Trade Hall appearance this year. Lewis had spent over a decade making country albums, but had returned to rock 'n' roll recently and would have a minor hit in Britain with his own version of 'Chantilly Lace', his first chart showing since 1963. He clearly still had a wild reputation as the Free Trade Hall diary says: "our piano not to be made available; remove steps, watch stage alcoves."

The Electric Light Orchestra (ELO) was scheduled to tour in March but this was cancelled because the group had been unable to find the necessary extra string-playing musicians. Eventually the tour started on April 16th in Croydon where there were sound problems. Three weeks later, the tour reached the Free Trade Hall. Roy Wood, having developed a wilder and wilder image in the last years of The Move, now sported a long white wig and sunglasses! Within three months Wood had left ELO, leaving Jeff Lynne in charge. Wood's new band, Wizzard, was more successful in the short term but ELO's eventual success was global.

Kris Kristofferson was touring to promote his third album, *Border Land* (CBS 1972). He played the Royal Albert Hall five days later on this short tour. Kristofferson's wife Rita Coolidge was also on the bill, having appeared a year earlier as a support act on The Byrds tour.

Slade played twice this year: in May it was their first major headlining tour. Their new album *Slade Alive* (Polydor 1971) had entered the charts in April and would eventually reach No. 2. Slade played about 170 gigs this year, along with recording sessions and umpteen television appearances. In between they had two more No. 1 singles with 'Take Me Bak 'Ome' and 'Mama Weer All Crazee Now'. Slade's autumn tour consisted of twenty dates with future stars, Thin Lizzy and Suzi Quatro as support acts.

Suzi Quatro told *Shindig* magazine: "That (the Slade/ Thin Lizzy tour) was great! I had twenty minutes at the beginning of the show and did all original material. Noddy would always say that Slade fans did not like support acts, but they loved me! That's nice. We were all close."

The Kinks appeared at the Free Trade Hall twice this year. They were touring in the autumn after the release of *Everybody's In Showbiz, Everybody's A Star* (RCA 1972), a double album featuring one disc of new songs and one live disc of the band's Carnegie Hall concert. The Kinks were now an impressive live act, enhanced by a horn section from The Mike Cotton Sound and female backing singers.

Elton John appeared for the second time at the Free Trade Hall in September. He was now playing in a quartet with Davey Johnstone who had joined in February. The Free Trade Hall concert was the second date of a short eight-date British tour before John returned to the USA. This was a breakthrough year for Elton John; both his single, 'Rocket Man' and album, *Honky Chateau* (DJM 1972) reached No. 2 in Britain, while success in the USA was even bigger. The Free Trade Hall diary states "Do not make our piano available," clearly thinking that Elton would copy Jerry Lee Lewis!

The Everly Brothers were touring to promote their country rock album, *Stories We Could Tell* (RCA 1972) which contained songs by John Sebastian, Kris Kristofferson and Jesse Winchester. Their Free Trade Hall concert was the first of an eleven-date tour. The Everlys would not tour Britain again as a duo for twelve years.

Deep Purple had played in Japan where they recorded their famous live album, *Made In Japan* (Purple 1972) and the USA. They were now over halfway through a seventeen-date British tour.

Ralph McTell was promoting his new album, *Not Til Tomorrow* (Reprise 1972) with a 34-date tour. This album was produced by Tony Visconti and was the first chart entry for McTell.

Lindisfarne headlined in October, supported by Genesis as part of a twenty-date tour. This was the peak of the group's career. They had hit singles with 'Meet Me On The Corner' and a reissue of 'Lady Eleanor'. Lindisfarne's album, *Fog On The Tyne* (Charisma 1971) reached No.1 in March and became the best-selling album of the year.

Steeleye Span appeared twice this year. In October the band were on a seventeen-date autumn tour with new members Bob Johnson (guitar) and Rick Kemp (bass guitar) having replaced Martin Carthy and Ashley Hutchings. They were promoting their new album, *Below The Salt* (Chrysalis 1972).

Humble Pie were on an eight-date tour with their former guitarist, Peter Frampton, as the support act. *Smokin'* (A&M 1972) was Pie's first album without Frampton.

The Osmonds played the Free Trade Hall in November, one of four British dates. This was a very successful year for the Mormon family act; Donny had hit No.1 in the summer with 'Puppy Love' and nine-year-old Jimmy would do the same at Christmas with 'Long Haired Lover From Liverpool'. In between, the Osmonds group were about to chart with 'Crazy Horses'.

Barclay James Harvest was on their *Outlandish* tour, promoting their latest album, *Baby James Harvest* (Harvest 1972). The Free Trade Hall was one of just five dates on the tour where the band was accompanied by a symphony orchestra. The 35-piece orchestra included fifteen members of the Hallé. Reviews mention a "capacity crowd."

Jimmy Cliff had had two Top 10 singles in 1969 and 1970. Originally signed to Trojan, Cliff had moved to the Island label and covered Cat Stevens' song, 'Wild World.' He had also appeared in the film, *The Harder They Come* and contributed to the soundtrack. Cliff left Island and signed to EMI, but this was not a successful move. It appears that his Free Trade Hall concert in November was also problematic.

Free Trade Hall Diary: "No money to pay J.C. 1 song then cancelled."

Emerson, Lake And Palmer were on a fifteen-date tour. Their third studio album, *Trilogy* (Island 1972) was still in the charts, four months after its release. This was ELP's last appearance at the Free Trade Hall.

Al Stewart returned to the Free Trade Hall after a gap of four years. He had released his fourth album, *Orange* (CBS 1972) at the beginning of the year. Stewart was a very popular live performer with his perfect annunciation, interesting lyrics and expert guitar playing. He returned twice the following year.

Groundhogs were halfway through a 26-date tour when they played the Free Trade Hall in December. They were promoting their latest album, *Hogwash* (United Artists 1972) which failed to chart.

Family were on a sixteen-date tour, promoting their latest album, *Bandstand* (Reprise 1972). They had just had a Top 20 hit with their single 'Burlesque'.

Other events at the Free Trade Hall

January 24th - 25th – Faraday Lectures
March 10th – NCH Festival Of Queens
May 12th – Scottish Concert
November 11th – Youth Christian Rally
December 11th – RSPB Film Show

Elsewhere (Headliners Only)

Belle Vue (King's Hall): Shirley Bassey, The Beach Boys, Joe Cocker, Leonard Cohen, The Flamin' Groovies, Benny Goodman, Richie Havens, The Jackson Five, Sha Na Na, T.Rex, Andy Williams, Yes.

Hardrock Concert Theatre– David Bowie, Curved Air, Electric Light Orchestra, Emerson, Lake And Palmer, Fanny, Genesis, Hawkwind, Incredible String Band, King Crimson, Led Zeppelin, Melanie, Pink Fairies, Billy Preston, Lou Reed, Roxy Music, Santana, Stephen Stills and Manassas, Status Quo, Three Dog Night, Ten Years After, Ike And Tina Turner, Wizzard, Yes.

Odeon: Neil Diamond, Sacha Distel, The Four Tops, Gladys Knight And The Pips, Don McLean, Joni Mitchell, Gilbert O'Sullivan, Cliff Richard, Stevie Wonder.

Opera House: Cat Stevens.

Palace Theatre: Tony Bennett, Cilla Black, Des O'Connor.

1973		
Jan 14th	JACK JONES (two houses)	*Ronnie Scott And His Orchestra; Jerry Stevens*
Jan 16th	URIAH HEEP	*Curtiss Maldoon*
Jan 17th	ROBERTA FLACK And Her Musicians	
Jan 26th	FAMILY	*Linda Lewis*
Jan 27th	DARRYL WAY'S WOLF	*Gnidrolog*
Feb 2nd	AL STEWART	
Feb 6th	GROUNDHOGS	*Greasy Bear*
Feb 13th	COLIN BLUNSTONE	*Stealers Wheel*
Feb 16th	RORY GALLAGHER	*Greenslade*
Feb 19th	DEEP PURPLE	*Nazareth*
Feb 24th	GENESIS	*String Driven Thing*
March 2nd	FARON YOUNG	*Connie Smith*
March 6th	SLIM WHITMAN (two houses)	
March 7th	THE SPINNERS	
March 8th	JOSE FELICIANO with The New Philharmonia Orchestra	
March 10th	STEELEYE SPAN	*Planxty*
March 12th	STATUS QUO	*Byzantium*
March 16th	MARTY ROBBINS	
March 17th	HUMBLE PIE	
March 19th	ELECTRIC LIGHT ORCHESTRA	*Steve Gibbons Band*
March 20th	YAMINI KRISHNAMURTHI with Ashid Khan (sarod)	
March 23rd	KING CRIMSON	*Claire Hamill*
March 27th	PETULA CLARK and The Concert Orchestra	
March 28th	GEORGE MELLY WITH ALEX WELSH AND HIS BAND	*Smoky City with Sheila Collier*

March 31st	THE STRAWBS	*Wheels*
April 3rd	CURVED AIR	*The Wag's Band*
April 5th	CAPTAIN BEEFHEART AND HIS MAGIC BAND	
April 14th	THE DUBLINERS	
April 21st	BERT JANSCH	*Gasworks*
April 22nd	WEST, BRUCE AND LAING	*Jimmy Stevens*
April 24th	ARTHUR BROWN'S KINGDOM COME	*Kala; Ange*
April 27th	THE NEW SEEKERS	*Ofarim And Winter*
May 8th	NANA MOUSKOURI AND THE ATHENIANS	
May 16th	RALPH McTELL	*Hunter Muskett*
May 18th	CHARISMA ON THE ROAD with Capability Brown; Jo'burg Hawk; Darien Spirit	
May 21st	FANNY	*Moonstone*
May 23th	BARCLAY JAMES HARVEST	*Bridget St John*
May 27th	GORDON LIGHTFOOT	
May 28th	SHA NA NA	*Esperanto*
May 31st	FLEETWOOD MAC	
June 1st	CLEO LAINE WITH JOHN DANKWORTH QUARTET	
June 2nd	THE FIVEPENNY PIECE	
June 6th	FAUST	*Gong*
June 7th	DAVID BOWIE (two houses)	
June 8th	LOUDON WAINWRIGHT III	*Longdancer; Jaki Whitren*
June 9th	THE SWEET	*Sun Chariot*
June 17th	MAHAVISHNU ORCHESTRA	*Jaki Whitren*
June 24th	THE SPINNERS	
July 1st	JACK BENNY	*Susan Maughan and The New Faces*

July 26th	VAN MORRISON and the Caledonia Soul Orchestra	
Aug 31st	STEELEYE SPAN	
Sept 3rd	JOHNNY CASH	*June Carter; Carl Perkins; The Tennessee Three*
Sept 4th	FAMILY	*Philip Goodhand-Tait*
Sept 5th	JOHNNY MATHIS	
Sept 16th	WIZZARD	*Raymond Froggatt*
Sept 18th	SERGIO MENDEZ AND BRASIL '77	*The Fourmost*
Sept 28th	ARGENT	*Glencoe*
Sept 29th	THE SPINNERS	
Oct 1st	RAY CONNIFF AND ORCHESTRA	
Oct 3rd	TEN YEARS AFTER	*Bloodstone*
Oct 5th	STATUS QUO	*Savoy Brown*
Oct 8th	THE MOODY BLUES	*Nicky James Band*
Oct 10th	LINDISFARNE	*Capability Brown; Darien Spirit*
Oct 19th	STEFAN GROSSMAN	*Planxty; Mike Harding; Canton Trig*
Oct 20th	JACQUES LOUSSIER TRIO	
Oct 22nd	NAZARETH	*Silverhead*
Oct 24th	THE FIVEPENNY PIECE	
Oct 28th	ROXY MUSIC	*Leo Sayer*
Oct 30th	VICTOR BORGE	*Marylyn Mulvey*
Oct 31st	DARRYL WAY'S WOLF	*Hemlock*
Nov 1st	LABI SIFFRE	
Nov 5th	INCREDIBLE STRING BAND	*McGuinness Flint*
Nov 7th	ROY HARPER	*Theatre Nightshade*
Nov 9th	SHIRLEY BASSEY with Arthur Greenslade (conductor) (two houses)	*The Majestics*

Nov 16th	TOM PAXTON	
Nov 20th	RAVI SHANKAR	*Alla Rakha*
Nov 25th	GREENSLADE	*Lucas & McCulloch*
Nov 26th	AL STEWART	
Nov 27th	RORY GALLAGHER (two houses)	*Strider*
Nov 28th	YES	
Nov 29th	YES	
Dec 1st	THE SPINNERS	
Dec 3rd	GROUNDHOGS	*Jonesey*
Dec 5th	FAIRPORT CONVENTION	*Amazing Blondel*
Dec 10th	HAWKWIND	*Andy Dunkerley*
Dec 11th	THE FACES	*John Baldry*
Dec 17th	GOLDEN EARRING	*Ducks Deluxe*

THIS YEAR, DESPITE EVEN STRONGER COMPETITION FROM the Hardrock Concert Theatre (see below), the Free Trade Hall had its busiest year ever. Some groups such as Groundhogs, Status Quo, Steeleye Span and Yes – even appeared twice.

Jack Jones had been making records since 1959; his biggest pop hit was 'Wives And Lovers' in 1963. Jones moved to a more to middle of the road sound. He had recently recorded an album of Michel Legrand songs. The two performances at the Free Trade Hall were in aid of charity.

Uriah Heep were on a seventeen-date tour, promoting their new album, *The Magician's Birthday* (Bronze 1972).

Roberta Flack played the Free Trade Hall on the first night of a four-date British tour; this was the very first time that she had played outside London. Flack reached No. 14 in Britain later in 1972 with her cover of Ewan MacColl's 'The First Time Ever I Saw Your Face'. Its parent album, *First Take* (Atlantic 1969) scraped into the Top 50 for just two weeks. In contrast, both the single and album reached No. 1 in the USA.

Darryl Way had been the electric violinist in Curved Air but left the group in 1972 to form his own band, **Wolf.** The group released two albums this year, *Canis Lupus* (Deram 1973) and *Saturation Point* (Deram 1973). Tickets for their January concert were priced at just 65p. They appeared again at the Free Trade Hall in October as part of a twenty-date tour with tickets now an exorbitant 66p! A third album followed in

1974, but Way soon rejoined Curved Air.

Colin Blunstone had been lead singer with The Zombies and his distinctive voice gained him a loyal following. His version of Denny Laine's 'Say You Don't Mind' had reached No. 15 in 1972, but follow-ups did not do as well. Blunstone made a series of well-received albums on Epic. He later recorded with David A. Stewart and The Alan Parsons Project and both collaborations brought Blunstone back into the charts.

The **Genesis** concert in February was sold out. The concert was recorded and one song ('Return Of The Giant Hogweed') appears on the mid-price stop-gap album, *Genesis Live* (Charisma 1973) released between *Foxtrot* (Charisma 1972) and *Selling England By The Pound* (Charisma 1973). The other tracks on the live album were recorded in Leicester on the following night of this tour.

It was a year for vintage country stars: **Faron Young** had had a surprise No. 3 hit single in Britain with 'It's Four In The Morning' in 1972, while **Slim Whitman** had not been in the charts since the late 1950's. Whitman was undertaking a 25th Anniversary tour; his concert at the Liverpool Empire, two days earlier, was recorded for a live album. Later in the month, **Marty Robbins** appeared at the Free Trade Hall; his last hit single in Britain had been in 1963.

Humble Pie made just two British appearances in March; the Free Trade Hall and the London Palladium. They were promoting their latest album, *Eat It* (A&M 1973), their last to chart in Britain.

Jose Feliciano had made his first appearance at the Free Trade Hall. Puerto Rican by birth, Feliciano had a big hit in 1968 with his striking cover version of 'Light My Fire'. Most subsequent versions of this song tend to copy Feliciano's treatment, rather than the original Doors performance. Feliciano's combination of a soulful voice and an extraordinary guitar technique was, to coin that much misused word, unique. This Free Trade Hall appearance was part of a six-date tour which had started at the Royal Albert Hall. The tour was sponsored by Peter Stuyvesant cigarettes!

Status Quo played at the Free Trade Hall twice this year; their March gig was the fifth date on the band's *Piledriver* tour. This was definitely Quo's most successful year to date. They had recorded a session for John Peel in January and a Radio One *In Concert* programme in March. The band played to great acclaim at the Reading Festival and they returned to the Free Trade Hall in October promoting their next album, *Hello* (Vertigo 1973) which entered the charts at No. 1 later that month.

Yamini Krishnamurthi was an Indian classical dancer who performed on her own, accompanied by a sarod player. She specialised in the Bharatanatyam and Kuchipudi styles.

Petula Clark made her only appearance at the Free Trade Hall. Clark had a varied career, singing songs in air raid shelters in the Second World War, French language songs in the 1950's and the Tony Hatch songbook in the 1960's. From 1972 to 1974 she hosted a musical variety series on BBC television. Clark had recently left Pye

Records and her first album on Polydor was released this year.

George Melly returned to the Free Trade Hall after a gap of eleven years. In the intervening years Melly had worked, among other things, as an arts critic for *The Observer*. Melly was now signed to Warner Brothers and had made two well-received albums, *Nuts* and *Son Of Nuts*. Soon Melly would join up with John Chilton's Footwarmers who would work together for the next 30 years.

West, Bruce and Laing were a power trio with guitarist Leslie West and drummer Corky Laing from Mountain and former Cream bassist and singer, Jack Bruce. They were on a short tour to promote their first album, *Why Dontcha* (CBS 1972). This was Bruce's first appearance at the Free Trade Hall; he would return in 1975.

Arthur Brown's Kingdom Come's concert charged just 80p a ticket for all seats. Brown had come to fame in 1968 with his previous band, The Crazy World Of Arthur Brown who had a No. 1 hit with 'Fire' while the band's eponymous album reached No. 2. His new band's third album was *Journey* (Polydor 1973). By now Brown had dispensed with a drummer and fronted one of the first bands to have a drum machine.

There was yet another Charisma package tour; this one consisted of nine dates. **Capability Brown** was a six-piece group of multi-instrumentalists formed from members of Harmony Grass. **Jo'burg Hawk** were exiles from South Africa. **Darien Spirit** made an album, *Elegy To Marilyn* (Charisma 1973) which had an eye-catching front cover of the Hollywood star's face. Their bass player was former Bonzo, Dennis Cowan. Tickets were priced at just 50p.

Fanny was one of the first all-female rock bands and recorded on the Reprise label. Fronted by sisters June and Jean Millington, the band's first three albums were produced by Richard Perry. Despite their fine musicianship and television appearances, Fanny did not enter the British charts. Their fourth album, *Mother's Pride* (Reprise 1973) was produced by Todd Rundgren. This was an eighteen-date tour.

Canadian singer-songwriter **Gordon Lightfoot** was best known for his much covered song, 'Early Morning Rain'. Lightfoot's sole Free Trade Hall appearance was part of a short tour of just five dates to promote his latest album, *Old Dan's Records* (Reprise 1973).

This was **Sha Na Na's** first full British tour which consisted of eight dates. The band had hardly changed their act since the Woodstock Festival.

Fleetwood Mac made a return visit and were now fronted by Christine McVie, Bob Welch and Dave Walker with only the rhythm section of Mick Fleetwood and John McVie remaining from the 1969 line-up. They were touring to promote a new album, *Penguin* (Reprise 1973) which did not chart in Britain. The band would soon relocate to the USA where they still had a following. Within eighteen months, Fleetwood Mac would rise again, when they met Lindsey Buckingham and Stevie

Nicks in a recording studio.

Cleo Laine's thirteen-date tour with her husband, **John Dankworth** and his quartet marked her first album with a new record label, *I Am A Song* (RCA 1973).

American singer-songwriter, **Loudon Wainwright III** was introduced to British audiences - like so many other artists over the years - by Radio One's John Peel. Peel often played Wainwright's songs such as 'Be Careful There's A Baby In The House' and 'Motel Blues.' This was part of a short, six-date tour. He released his fourth album this year, *Attempted Moustache* (CBS 1973).

The Sweet appeared once at the Free Trade Hall. The glam rock band was at its commercial peak in 1973 with a No. 1 single, 'Blockbuster' at the start of the year and two No. 2 placings for the follow-ups. The Sweet's hits were written by Nicky Chinn and Mike Chapman who also wrote for Suzi Quatro and Mud. The band's outrageously camp *Top Of The Pops* appearances did not help any 'we are serious musicians' claims. Behind all this, The Sweet had a good live act, the result of years on the road.

The Mahavishnu Orchestra were touring to promote their second album, *Birds Of Fire* (CBS 1973). This jazz rock group received wide coverage in the music press; they were all virtuosos on their own instruments. Even their equipment was heralded - Billy Cobham's see-through drum kit; Jerry Goodman's electric violin and so on - in the pages of *Melody Maker*. Guitarist John McLaughlin would reappear at the Free Trade Hall with a different line-up of the group and subsequently with Shakti and in a duo with Katie Labeque.

Faust were a German band whose recordings were licensed to Virgin Records. Their album, *The Faust Tapes* (Virgin 1973), a collection of private recordings put together by a British fan, was sold for just 49p and, unsurprisingly, sold in vast quantities. Most purchasers - including radio presenter, Simon Mayo - found the listening experience challenging!

David Bowie, having played four nights at the Hardrock in 1972, returned to the Free Trade Hall in June. He had just released his album *Aladdin Sane* (RCA 1973). Bowie had recently played the vast Earls Court arena in London and, within another month, would publicly "retire" from touring on the stage of the Hammersmith Odeon in London. The Free Trade Hall concert must have been memorable as the venue's diary states "decline further booking"! A fourteen-year-old Steven Morrissey was in the audience with his friend, Mick Foley. Both had visited a hairdresser to try and replicate Bowie's haircut. Foley told biographer Johnny Rogan, "We got all painted up and the old lady had a bloody fit."

Jack Benny was an American comedian, comic actor and violinist. A master of comic timing, Benny was a pioneer of radio and television comedy, but returned to stand-up in the 1960's. 1973 saw his health failing and Benny passed away at the end of 1974.

Van Morrison was touring Britain for the first time since the days of Them and played just six concerts. His current album was *Hard Nose The Highway* (Warner Bros 1973) which briefly charted in August. Morrison was touring with his eleven-piece Soul Orchestra. Critic Johnny Rogan has said that "Morrison was in the midst of what was arguably his greatest phase as a performer."

Johnny Cash returned to the Free Trade Hall after a gap of five years. He had recently reached the British Top 10 with a single and album, both called *A Thing Called Love* (CBS 1972). The titles of Cash's releases this year speak for themselves: *The Gospel Road* (CBS 1973) and *Johnny Cash And His Woman* (CBS 1973). Neither album reached the British charts.

Family were on their farewell British tour which consisted of sixteen dates. They were promoting their album, *It's Only A Movie* (Raft 1973) which just scraped into the Top 30. Singer Roger Chapman and guitarist Charlie Whitney would return to the Free Trade Hall with their new band, Streetwalkers.

Johnny Mathis was on a six-date British tour which started at the London Palladium. He was promoting his latest album, *I'm Coming Home* (CBS 1973) which was a collaboration with writers Thom Bell and Linda Creed. A single from the album, 'I'm Stone In Love With You' had already been a Top 10 hit for Bell with The Stylistics in Britain. Mathis's version did not enter the British charts until March 1975, but also reached the Top 10. The album reached the Top 20. This was Mathis's greatest success in Britain for fifteen years.

Wizzard had previously appeared in Manchester at the Hardrock and Manchester University; their September concert at the Free Trade Hall was cancelled at the interval because Roy Wood had lost his voice! The group appeared six months later at Kings Hall, Belle Vue. Wizzard had two No. 1 singles this year, 'See My Baby Jive' and 'Angel Fingers'.

Sergio Mendes & Brasil '77 played just two dates in Britain; three days after the Free Trade Hall concert, they appeared at the Royal Festival Hall in London. Mendes had changed his group's name from Brasil '66 at the start of the 1970's. His blend of bossa nova and easy listening was still very popular.

This year **The Moody Blues** made their sole appearance at the Free Trade Hall as part of a ten-date tour to promote their new album, *Seventh Sojourn* (Threshold 1972). The band would soon have a lengthy sabbatical, allowing all members to make solo albums.

Ragtime guitarist **Stefan Grossman** had previously appeared as a support act at the Free Trade Hall but was now headlining a mixed evening of folk music. Brooklyn-born Grossman was a protege of Rev. Gary Davis and studied with him for several years. Grossman had signed to Transatlantic in Britain in 1970 and had released his fifth album on that label, *Memphis Jellyroll- A New Selection Of Guitar Instrumentals* (Transatlantic 1973).

Nazareth were having a very successful year; having supported Deep Purple in February, they were on their second headlining British tour in one year! The writer saw the band at Liverpool Stadium in the summer of 1973 and can testify to their incredible live power in those days. Nazareth were promoting their latest album, *Loud 'N' Proud* (Mooncrest 1973) which reached No. 10.

The Fivepenny Piece hailed from Tameside and sang a commercial brand of folk music that focussed on nostalgia and humour. They made two appearances in June and October, going on to be Free Trade Hall regulars. The group had won ITV's *New Faces* earlier in the decade and were frequently seen on television. Their second album, *Making Tracks* (Columbia 1973) reached the Top 40 this year.

1973 had been an incredibly busy year for **Roxy Music** with the release of two albums and Bryan Ferry's first solo album, along with two British tours. Their third album, *Stranded* (Island 1973), the first without Eno in the line-up, reached No. 1 in December.

Labi Siffre's headlining appearance this year attracted a very small audience. This Nigerian-English singer songwriter is most famous for writing 'It Must Be Love' which Madness covered in 1981. In the early 1970's Siffre was a regular presence on television, appearing on *The Cliff Richard Show* and *Top Of The Pops*.

Incredible String Band were on a lengthy 35-date British tour. This was the band's final Free Trade Hall appearance – the last of eight concerts at the venue. Within a year the Incredibles would split. By now the band had a full rhythm section and had lost much of their unique appeal.

Roy Harper's appearance on November 7th was recorded by EMI. His latest album was *Lifemask* (Harvest 1973) which included a twenty-minute track entitled 'The Lord's Prayer'.

Yes were touring to promote *Tales From Topographic Oceans* (Atlantic 1973). One of their two Free Trade Hall performances in November is now legendary because of the Rick Wakeman curry incident. Wakeman was standing behind his "great big analogue keyboard set-up" and his roadie (or "keyboard tech") was lying underneath the Hammond organ, ready to do running repairs, if necessary. The two men discussed Wakeman's plans for an after-show curry but the roadie misunderstood and thought that the famed keyboard player wanted a curry there and then. Within half an hour the roadie had ordered and collected "chicken vindaloo, pilau rice, half a dozen poppadums, bhindi bhajii, Bombay aloo and a stuffed paratha". These items - all in foil containers - were passed up to Wakeman who laid them out on the top of his various keyboards. The smell of curry wafted over the stage catching singer Jon Anderson's attention! Wakeman: "The rest of the band weren't too impressed at the time, although in later years they did laugh about it. And I tell you what... It was a bloody nice curry.." Subsequent re-tellings of this incident needlessly elaborate; it stands by itself in Free Trade Hall lore. Within six months Wakeman had left Yes to concentrate on his solo career.

The Faces made their final Free Trade Hall appearance two weeks before Christmas, just as their penultimate single, 'Pool Hall Richard' entered the charts.

Golden Earring hailed from Holland and had supported The Who on their 1972 European tour. This led to the band being signed to The Who's label, Track. Golden Earring's sole British hit single, 'Radar Love', was in the charts as they toured. When the band performed this song live there was a lengthy solo by their drummer which ended by him jumping over his drum kit!

Other events at the Free Trade Hall

January 22nd & 23rd – Faraday Lectures
January 31st – Mountaineering Lecture
March 5th – RSPB Film Show
June 10th – Erich von Däniken - lecture

Elsewhere (Headliners Only)

Belle Vue (Kings Hall) – Glen Campbell, David Cassidy, Gary Glitter, Elton John, James Last, The Rolling Stones, The Who.

Hardrock Concert Theatre – Beck, Bogart & Appice, Chuck Berry, Birtha, Black Sabbath, Colin Blunstone, James Brown, Fats Domino, The Dubliners, The Faces, Fairport Convention, Focus, Gary Glitter, Al Green, Richie Havens, Hawkwind, Isaac Hayes, Humble Pie, Elton John, Don McLean, Medicine Head, Roxy Music , Santana, Slade, 10cc, Traffic, Uriah Heep, Wings.

Odeon: Gilbert O'Sullivan, The Supremes, The Temptations.

Palace Theatre - The Beach Boys, Lulu, Slim Whitman.

1974		
Jan 7th	STOMU YAMASHTA'S EAST WIND	*Sun Treader*
Jan 11th	BECK, BOGART AND APPICE	*Up*
Jan 25th	THE BOB HOPE SHOW	
Jan 26th	T.REX	*Chilli Willi And The Red Hot Peppers*
Feb 4th	GEORGE MELLY AND THE FEETWARMERS	*Peter Skellern*
Feb 11th	*AMERICAN BLUES LEGENDS* Big John Wrencher; Cousin Joe Pleasant; George G.P. Jackson; Doctor Ross; Eddie "Playboy" Taylor	
Feb 12th	RALPH McTELL	*Prelude*
Feb 15th	ARGENT	*John Verity Band*
Feb 16th	THE SPINNERS	
Feb 18th	ELECTRIC LIGHT ORCHESTRA	*Raymond Froggatt*
Feb 19th	CARPENTERS (two houses)	*Skiles And Henderson*
Feb 22nd	THE KINGS SINGERS	
Feb 23rd	MANITAS de PLATA	*Los Baliardos*
March 9th	BLASTER BATES	
March 11th	GENTLE GIANT	*String Driven Thing*
March 14th	THE WOLFETONES	*Sean Dunphy; Gemma Hassan; Paddy Riley*
March 19th	THE DUBLINERS	
April 9th	MUD	*Light Fantastic*
April 11th	MICK RONSON	
April 19th	JOSE FELICIANO (two houses)	*Shepstone and Dibbens*

April 22nd	TEN YEARS AFTER	*Wild Turkey*
April 23rd	GONG; HATFIELD AND THE NORTH	*Tubular Bells on film*
April 29th	JUNIOR WALKER AND THE ALL-STARS	*Edwin Starr*
April 30th	CLEO LAINE AND JOHNNY DANKWORTH QUINTET	
May 3rd	THE STYLISTICS	*Jimmy James & The Vagabonds*
May 4th	ALVIN STARDUST	*Fable*
May 9th	JOSHUA RIFKIN PLAYS SCOTT JOPLIN	
May 12th	STEELEYE SPAN	*Gryphon*
May 13th	TRAFFIC	*Sour Grapes (Richard and Linda Thompson)*
May 18th	LIONEL HAMPTON ORCHESTRA	
May 20th	THE HOLLIES	*James Griffin*
May 21st	NAZARETH	*Heavy Metal Kids*
May 22nd	THE FIVEPENNY PIECE	
May 23rd	DANNY KAYE WITH THE HALLÉ ORCHESTRA	
May 24th	BLACK SABBATH	*Black Oak Arkansas*
May 25th	NANA MOUSKOURI AND THE ATHENIANS	
May 26th	NANA MOUSKOURI AND THE ATHENIANS	
May 27th	ALAN STIVELL	
May 28th	SENSATIONAL ALEX HARVEY BAND	*Strider*
May 29th	LOVE	*Casablanca*
May 31st	LOU REED	*Ducks Deluxe*
June 8th	CAPTAIN BEEFHEART AND THE MAGIC BAND	*Henry Cow*
June 10th	HOT CHOCOLATE	*Linda Kendricks*
June 11th	MAGMA	*No support*

June 12th	HENRY MANCINI (two houses)	*Labi Siffre*
June 15th	BARCLAY JAMES HARVEST	*Rare Bird*
June 16th	STRIFE	
June 24th	REFUGEE	*String Driven Thing*
July 14th	SHOWADDYWADDY	*Hector*
Sept 7th	THE SPINNERS	
Sept 12th	LEONARD COHEN	
Sept 14th	10CC	*Julian Brook; Andy Peebles (compère)*
Sept 15th	GREENSLADE	*Aj Webber*
Sept 16th	PROCOL HARUM	*Strife*
Sept 18th	GONG	*Isotope*
Sept 20th	BLACK OAK ARKANSAS	*Medicine Head*
Oct 5th	MAGGIE BELL	*Pretty Things*
Oct 14th	URIAH HEEP	*Peter Frampton*
Oct 18th	WISHBONE ASH	*The Winkies*
Oct 21st	GROUNDHOGS	*Stray*
Oct 30th	SLIM WHITMAN (two houses)	*Springfield Revival*
Nov 3rd	LINDISFARNE	*Wally*
Nov 4th	TANGERINE DREAM	
Nov 8th	DEMIS ROUSSOS	
Nov 9th	DAVID ESSEX	*Merlin; Batti Mazelle*
Nov 13th	RALPH McTELL	*Jack The Lad*
Nov 15th	KEVIN AYERS	*John Baldry's Barracudas*
Nov 18th	TOM PAXTON	
Nov 20th	HUMBLE PIE	*McGuinness Flint*
Nov 21st	STEELEYE SPAN	*Richard Digance*

Nov 22nd	SPARKS	*Pilot*
Nov 27th	GOLDEN EARRING	*Lynyrd Skynyrd*
Nov 29th	BERT JANSCH	*Decameron*
Dec 3rd	GEORGE McCRAE AND THE GM EXPRESS	*Gonzalez*
Dec 11th	CLIFF RICHARD and The Concert Orchestra	
Dec 13th	THE OLDHAM TINKERS	*The Fairey Band; Henry Livings (compère)*
Dec 17th	ANDY WILLIAMS WITH MICHEL LEGRAND	*Rolf Harris; Elaine Delmar*
Dec 19th	RORY GALLAGHER	*Jackie Lynton's Grande*
Dec 21st	THE SPINNERS	
Dec 22nd	*KINGS OF JAZZ* with Pee Wee Irwin; Bernie Previn; Johnny Mince; Kenny Daverne; Cliff Leeman; Ed Hubbe; Dick Hyman; Major Holby	

S**TOMU YAMASHTA** WAS BORN IN KYOTO IN JAPAN AND LATER studied at Juilliard. He worked with Peter Maxwell Davies. This Japanese percussionist and composer had recorded his first album for Island Records in 1973 with Isotope's Hugh Hopper and Gary Boyle. Yamashta's successful collaboration with Steve Winwood and other rock and jazz musicians on the *Go* album was some years off.

Beck, Bogart & Appice were a supergroup featuring British guitarist Jeff Beck with the rhythm section from Vanilla Fudge/Cactus. Their first album was released in Britain in April 1973 and the band had spent most of that year touring. Their Free Trade Hall appearance in January was one of sixteen dates on what would become their final tour. By May BBA had split.

Bob Hope was a British-born comedian and actor. His career included the 'Road' films with Bing Crosby, countless radio and television series and his work entertaining American troops. Hope's career lasted an extraordinary eighty years.

T.Rex were on a six-date tour, promoting their album, *Zinc Alloy And The Hidden Riders Of Tomorrow* (EMI 1974). The band's sales were gradually declining and the album only reached No. 12. However, the concert was nearly sold out. The damage bill was an incredible £935!

George Melly And The Feetwarmers played the Free Trade Hall in February as part of 'Melly Mania '74', a tour co-promoted by *Melody Maker*.

This year's **American Blues Legends** were not perhaps as 'legendary' as some previous blues acts who played the Free Trade Hall. The artists were unfortunately not "big" names. The box office receipts suggest that the venue was less than half full.

The Carpenters' hits compilation album *The Singles 1969- 1973* (A&M 1973) had entered the British charts in January and stayed there for over two years. This was their first British tour. The group performed once more in Manchester at the ABC Ardwick in 1976. In the 1970's the Carpenters' squeaky clean image and beaming smiles on their album covers tended to make them patronised and under-appreciated by critics. Time has shown that the combination of Karen's faultless contralto voice and Richard's arrangements and compositions (with John Bettis) was pop music of the highest quality.

The King's Singers were a British acapella vocal sextet who originally were all choral scholars at King's College, Cambridge. They performed many different types of music and frequently appeared on television and radio. The group still exists with a different line-up.

Gentle Giant made the first of three Free Trade Hall appearances in March. Formed from members of Simon Dupree And The Big Sound, the group released four albums on Vertigo, before moving to WWA. Their current album was *In A Glass House* (WWA 1973).

The Wolfetones were an Irish folk group from Dublin with unashamed rebel views. They had formed in the early 1960's and have been performing ever since. This appearance, appropriately, was three days before St. Patrick's Day.

Mud had their first chart-topper, 'Tiger Feet', at the start of the year and would later have 1974's Christmas No.1. The group had formed in the late 1960's and were an experienced live act. The Free Trade Hall concert was part of their first major tour which consisted of 30 dates. The Free Trade Hall was an unlikely venue for such a danceable chart act as the group usually played ballrooms on the Top Rank circuit. Ticket sales were disappointing.

Mick Ronson was now a solo act in his own right, following David Bowie's dissolution of the Spiders From Mars. Ronson's first solo album, *Slaughter On 10th Avenue* (RCA Victor 1974) was released in February and reached No. 9. After two lavish concerts at London's Rainbow, he went on a thirteen-date British tour. A second solo album, *Play Don't Worry* (RCA Victor 1975) was less successful and Ronson joined Mott The Hoople. He then teamed up with their lead singer, Ian Hunter after the group splintered.

Mick Rossi of Slaughter And The Dogs told Weird and Gilly in their biography of Mick Ronson :"..the first time I saw Mick perform was in Manchester, at the Free Trade Hall on the Slaughter On 10th Avenue tour. I bunked off school to go and get the tickets for that. I got caught but it was worth it. We rushed the stage when he was doing 'Only After Dark' and I shouted out 'Ronno!' and he made eye contact with me and put his thumb up. That was so cool."

Jose Feliciano was on a five-date tour, promoting his latest album, *For My Love-Mother Music* (RCA 1974).

Ten Years After's popularity in Britain continued to decline. The Free Trade Hall concert was part of their final British tour which was only five dates long. A final album, *Recorded Live* (Chrysalis 1974) reached No. 36 later in the year.

Gong and **Hatfield & The North** were both on the Virgin label and they appeared on the same night as a screening of the *Tubular Bells* film featuring their more successful label mate, Mike Oldfield. This ten-date tour was billed as 'Crisis Concerts' and the two groups alternated as the headlining act - all for just 44p! Hatfield & The North - named after the famous road sign - were part of the Canterbury scene and formed of ex-members of Delivery. They were touring to promote their eponymous first album (Virgin 1974). Gong had released the second part of their Radio Gnome Invisible Trilogy, *Angel's Egg* (Virgin 1973), at the end of the previous year.

Junior Walker And the All-Stars were one of the very few soul acts who played the Free Trade Hall, no doubt because of the formal seating of the venue. Walker was having something of a chart renaissance with singles 'Walk In The Night' and 'Take Me Girl I'm Ready'.

Strife's tickets for their June appearance were priced at just 35p, but takings were £192.15 thus around 500 tickets were sold.

The Stylistics appeared at the Free Trade Hall three times. Their debut concert this year was not well attended even though the group had had a Top 10 hit earlier in the year with 'Rockin' Roll Baby'. In the summer their follow-up, 'You Make Me Feel Brand New' reached No. 2. A compilation album, *Best Of The Stylistics* (Avco 1975) hit the top spot and stayed in the charts for over 60 weeks.

Alvin Stardust was enjoying great success in 1974 on the Magnet label. He had one week at No. 1 with the single, 'Jealous Mind' and even his album, *The Untouchable* (Magnet 1974) reached No. 4. The Free Trade Hall appearance was part of a 36-date national tour. This was the peak of Stardust's career; just over a year later, another Free Trade Hall concert was reportedly cancelled after poor ticket sales.

This writer attended the **Traffic** concert in May and remembers an appreciative crowd. This was the first time Traffic played the Free Trade Hall on what was to be their final tour. They were promoting their new album, *When The Eagle Flies* (Island 1974). There was a heckle incident, not as significant as one in 1966; someone requested 'Hole In My Shoe', the title of Traffic's untypical No. 2 hit single from 1967! This remark was followed by someone else shouting "hole in my arse" (sic) displaying that unique Mancunian wit. Steve Winwood said that he had forgotten that he was in Manchester and there were grumblings and mumblings from the audience. Traffic were now a quartet as percussion player Reebop Kwaku Baah had recently left the band. They were on dazzling form. Jim Capaldi was back on drums and new bassist, Rosko Gee, was effective. Winwood's guitar playing was as skilful as Eric Clapton's, but he also had about the best white soul voice in Britain and phenomenal keyboard skills. History forgets that there was often heckling and shouting out at the Free Trade Hall. The name, 'Wally' was frequently heard and support acts were not always given sufficient respect or attention by the audience.

Lionel Hampton had worked in the swing era with Benny Goodman in the 1930's and went on to form his own orchestra. Hampton played the vibes, drums and piano as well as singing. His orchestra was the longest established one in jazz history. Attendance at their sole Free Trade Hall concert was disappointing.

Danny Kaye performed with the Hallé Orchestra and James Loughran. The proceeds of the concert were in aid of the Charities of the Variety Club of Great Britain's 'Heart Fund' for under-privileged children, along with the Hallé Trust Fund. Tickets were priced £1, £2, £4 and £5. The concert programe gives some details of the running order. The National Anthem was to be followed by the Overture of Strauss's 'Die Fledermaus' with guest conductor, Danny Kaye. Then there is large question mark with the footnote 'The Hallé Concerts Society and the Variety Club of Great Britain accept no responsibility for this part of the programme.' On the same day there was a gala banquet at the Piccadilly Hotel. Kaye appeared as guest conductor for many of the world's leading orchestras, even though he could not read music. He had worked tirelessly for charities,notably as a UNICEF ambassador for many years.

Alan Stivell had been playing the Breton harp since he was nine years old. He went on to also learn the bombarde (a double reeded oboe) and Scottish bagpipes. Stivell's album *Renaissance Of The Celtic Harp* (Fontana 1971) received wide acclaim. He had been named *Melody Maker* Folk Artist Of 1973. Ticket sales for his only Free Trade Hall appearance, however, were disappointing.

Sensational Alex Harvey Band made their Free Trade Hall debut this year. Harvey was a veteran of the Scottish music scene and had also played in the pit band for the London production of *Hair.* He teamed up with the band Tear Gas to form an extraordinary live attraction. Their Free Trade Hall appearance was part of a 23-date tour, but not well attended. The band's first successful album, *The Impossible Dream* (Vertigo 1974) would enter the charts later in the year.

Love did not play outside the USA until 1970 and came to Manchester Polytechnic in February of that year with a different line-up to the *Forever Changes* group. Four years later, Love returned to the UK for a twenty-date tour. Their Free Trade Hall appearance in May was badly attended with actual takings being only a quarter of the possible gross. It took many years for leader Arthur Lee to realise that what audiences really wanted to hear was the classic *Forever Changes* album, sounding as near as possible to the studio sound. In the 1990's and 2000's, Lee did exactly that - using a sympathetic backing band. Unsurprisingly people loved it. The author saw one of these performances at Manchester Academy where a delighted crowd sang 'Arthur Lee' to the tune of 'Here We Go!'

Lou Reed's career was given a huge boost by David Bowie and Mick Ronson who produced his second solo album, *Transformer* (RCA 1973). The first single taken from the album, 'Walk On The Side' had been an unlikely hit in 1973. Reed was on a ten-date British tour promoting his new live album, *Rock 'N' Roll Animal* (RCA 1974).

Bernard Sumner: *"One place we could get into was the Free Trade Hall,and one of the first gigs I remember is seeing Lou Reed there in 1974. I was a big fan; I loved his solo stuff. I got into Transformer, his live album, Rock 'N' Roll Animal and Berlin before I'd even heard the Velvet Underground. I think this was the Sally Can't Dance tour, and I was really looking forward to seeing him live. The band came on and started playing 'Sweet Jane' and I was thinking about how great it was going to be when Lou himself finally came on. Then this short-arse guy with blond hair started singing, and I thought, that can't be Lou Reed, can it? But it was.*

" He was off his chump - really off his chump; he kept smashing microphones one after the other - but it was a fantastic concert, and the audience was really up for it. I guess in a way this was my first punk gig, but I didn't know it. They finished their set with a storming 'Goodnight Ladies' and trooped off. Everyone expected them to come out for an encore, but the stage remained resolutely empty and the crowd began to grow restless. I was near this guy who looked like a Rod Stewart clone and he lobbed this beer bottle from about five hundred yards, with phenomenal accuracy, straight through the skin of the bass drum. And that was it. Pandemonium; people were swarming on to the stage, getting into fights with the roadies and security, everything. Lou Reed never came back to Manchester after that, all because one bloke with a dodgy haircut and incredible aim..."

Mick Middles offers a slightly different account: "On this night a vastly disparate audience came to the Free Trade Hall. Not only would the Bowie freaks mix uneasily with straggly-haired rockists, they would be forced, also, to mingle with straight-faced disco trendies, twenty-something couples gazing adoringly into each other's eyes and menacing pockets of clean-jeaned car mechanics, fitters and turners."

Hot Chocolate was a highly successful singles act with an unrivalled string of hits for every year of the 1970s. 1974, however, was not a vintage year for them; 'Emma' had reached No. 3 in the spring, but its follow-up 'Changing World' failed to chart. The next release - 'Cheri Babe' - only reached No. 31 in the autumn. Similarly, the Hot Chocolate concert in June had a tiny audience.

German band **Magma** (a favourite, apparently, of snooker star Steve Davis!) played the Free Trade Hall in June as part of a thirteen-date tour. They were promoting their album, *Kohntarkosz* (A&M 1974). Unfortunately, barely £200 worth of tickets were sold!

Refugee consisted of The Nice's rhythm section Lee Jackson and Brian Davidson, along with Swiss keyboard player Patrick Moraz. Both Jackson and Davidson had had their own bands with limited success. They made one album, *Refugee* (Charisma 1974) and toured once before Moraz was asked to join Yes. Another date on their tour, Newcastle City Hall, was recorded but not released until 2007. Less than half of the Free Trade Hall's seats were occupied for Refugee's appearance.

Showaddywaddy hailed from Coventry and were winners of ITV's *New Faces* talent show. Their rock 'n' roll revival act has had enduring popularity. Showaddywaddy's first hits were self-penned, but they soon changed reviving classic old rock 'n' roll songs and had even greater success.

Leonard Cohen was on a ten-date tour promoting his fourth studio album, *New Skin For The Old Ceremony* (CBS 1974). This album was a lot less successful than Cohen's first three albums, but he was still a popular live act.

10cc was formed of the three ex-members of Hotlegs plus hit songwriter Graham Gouldman. They based themselves at their own Strawberry Studios in Stockport. 10cc were signed to Jonathan King's UK label and reached No.1 with their 'Rubber Bullets' single. September saw 10cc touring Britain while their second album, *Sheet Music* (UK 1974) was in the charts. This was the first of five appearances at the Free Trade Hall. *NME* reported that the "audience nearly brought down (the) balcony!"

Greenslade were formed in 1972 by ex-Colosseum keyboardist Dave Greenslade and bassist Tony Reeves; they were joined by another keyboard player, Dave Lawson, and drummer Andrew McCulloch. Another former Colosseum player, guitarist Dave Clempson, joined for their third album, *Spyglass Guest* (Warner Bros 1974) which the band were promoting. Despite a £1 ticket price for all areas, less than 800 people attended their September concert. A return visit the following May also only charged £1 for a ticket, but still fewer than 1000 were sold!

Black Oak Arkansas appeared twice at the Free Trade Hall and both concerts had disappointing ticket sales. The band really was from Arkansas and featured lead singer Jim Dandy whose stage antics were briefly notorious. On this tour they were promoting a new album, *Street Party* (Atco 1974).

Maggie Bell had been lead singer with Stone The Crows. After the tragic death of their guitarist, Les Harvey, the group made one more album and then split up. Despite being managed by Peter Grant (also manager of Led Zeppelin) and having Jerry Wexler produce her first album, *Queen Of The Night* (Swan Song 1974), Bell's solo career did not really take off. Ticket sales for this Free Trade Hall appearance on her first British solo tour were similarly disappointing.

Slim Whitman returned to the Free Trade Hall this year. By now he had re-entered the British charts with an album, *Happy Anniversary* (United Artists 1974) which reached No. 44. The title track was released as a single and reached No.14

Lindisfarne's split in 1973 had a devastating effect on their career. Three of the band formed Jack The Lad, leaving Alan Hull and Ray Jackson from the original line-up; the latter recruited four new members. After three Top 10 albums, the new line-up's two albums - *Roll On Ruby* (Charisma 1973) and *Happy Daze* (Charisma 1974) failed to chart. Similarly, box office receipts for their concert this year were disappointing.

Tangerine Dream were on their first British tour. Earlier in the year their album, *Phaedra* (Virgin 1974) was the band's first chart entry, reaching No. 15.

Demis Roussos, as his 1976 No.1 hit E.P. would later be called, was a "phenomenon". An unlikely star with his kaftans, high pitched voice and unkempt appearance, Roussos was another Greek export, following Nana Mouskouri and Theodokaris into British hearts. This year Roussos had a No. 2 album with *Forever And Ever* (Philips 1974) which stayed in the charts for an extraordinary 68 weeks. This was his first British tour consisting of just four dates.

David Essex was on his first solo tour, promoting his eponymous album (CBS 1974) which included the No. 1 hit single, 'Gonna Make You A Star.' The tour consisted of 22 provincial dates followed by six nights at London's New Victoria Theatre.

Sparks relocated to Britain in 1973 where they signed with Island Records and hired a British rhythm section. A *Top Of The Pops* appearance transformed their career and 'This Town Ain't Big Enough For The Both Of Us' reached No. 2 while its parent album, *Kimono My House* (Island 1974) went to No. 4. This 25-date tour was promoting their follow-up album, *Propaganda* (Island 1974). The group earned a blunt "No Thank You" in the Free Trade Hall diary; did Ron Mael, the keyboard player, smile perhaps?

George McCrae had a huge hit with 'Rock Your Baby' which topped the charts in both Britain and America. Born and based in Florida, McCrae's effortless vocals were backed by members of KC And The Sunshine Band who also wrote and produced the record.

Cliff Richard first appeared at the Free Trade Hall in 1958 and returned three times the following year. He returned – after a gap of fifteen years – in 1974 which was something of a chart desert for him. The 'Peter Pan of Pop' had one hit single in the spring, '(You Keep Me) Hangin' On', but his studio album, *The 31st Of February* (EMI 1974) was a flop. Despite all this, Cliff's Free Trade Hall concert in December was sold out!

The Oldham Tinkers were formed by John Howarth and brothers Gerry and Larry Kearns in 1965. They appeared on the *Deep Lancashire* and *Owdham Edge* albums alongside other local folk acts, as well as recording their own albums such as *Best O' T' Bunch* (Topic 1974). The Tinkers were popular on the local folk club scene, but low box office receipts at the Free Trade Hall suggests that they should have played smaller venues. In January 1975 they had a session for Radio One's John Peel programme broadcast.

The threat of the Hardrock appeared to be over as there were only a handful of gigs compared to the previous two years. Meanwhile, The Palace Theatre was increasing its number of rock and pop concerts.

Other events at the Free Trade Hall

March 4th – RSPB Film Show
October 24th – Segovia concert
November 1st – Thai Boxing

Elsewhere (Headliners Only):

Belle Vue (Kings Hall): Bay City Rollers, Ray Conniff, Deep Purple, David Essex, The Faces, Gary Glitter, The Jackson Five, James Last, Roxy Music, Slade, Status Quo, Andy Williams, Wizzard.

Hardrock Concert Theatre - Argent, Bad Company, Blue, Cockney Rebel, Focus.

Opera House – The Four Tops, Gallagher And Lyle, Neil Sedaka, Jethro Tull.

Palace Theatre-- Herb Alpert, Kevin Ayers, Genesis, Herbie Hancock, Man, Roger McGuinn, Mud, Pink Floyd, Queen, Leo Sayer, Sensational Alex Harvey Band, Steely Dan, Ike And Tina Turner.

An artist's impression of the new Large Hall taken from the 1951 Commemorative Brochure

The side walls of the ground floor are lined with limed oak panelling and the rear wall with walnut, whilst the wall behind the platform, faced with decorative panelling, is a combination of teak, sycamore and walnut with the City coat of arms, carved in obeche and in full colours, as its central feature.

Above the Side Circles the main walls of the Hall embody decorative pilastered features which also provide acoustically diffusing and absorbent surfaces. The upper panels display coats of arms in full colours of bodies prominent in the city and of neighbouring local authorities. They include the arms of the See of Manchester, the Manchester Chamber of Commerce, the Manchester Ship Canal Company, the City of Salford, the County Boroughs of Stockport, Bolton, Oldham, Rochdale and Bury, and the Boroughs of Stretford, Sale and Ashton-under-Lyne. For acoustic reasons, the splayed side walls to the Circle and Balcony and at the rear of the ground floor are broken into a series of vertical planes at right angles to each other and the lofty ceiling over the body of the Hall is deeply coffered.

Overlooking Peter Street at the first floor level, and easily accessible from all parts of the Hall, is a promenade Lounge containing the Refreshment Bar. Above this Lounge is the Lesser Hall with seats for 417 people, 95 of which are in the balcony. The seating on the main floor is removable to permit dancing, small exhibitions and other functions requiring a cleared floor space. The small stage is fully equipped to suit amateur theatrical productions and a suite of dressing rooms and a Green Room are provided. The Lesser Hall is insulated structurally from the Large Hall so that there can be no sound transmission between the two.

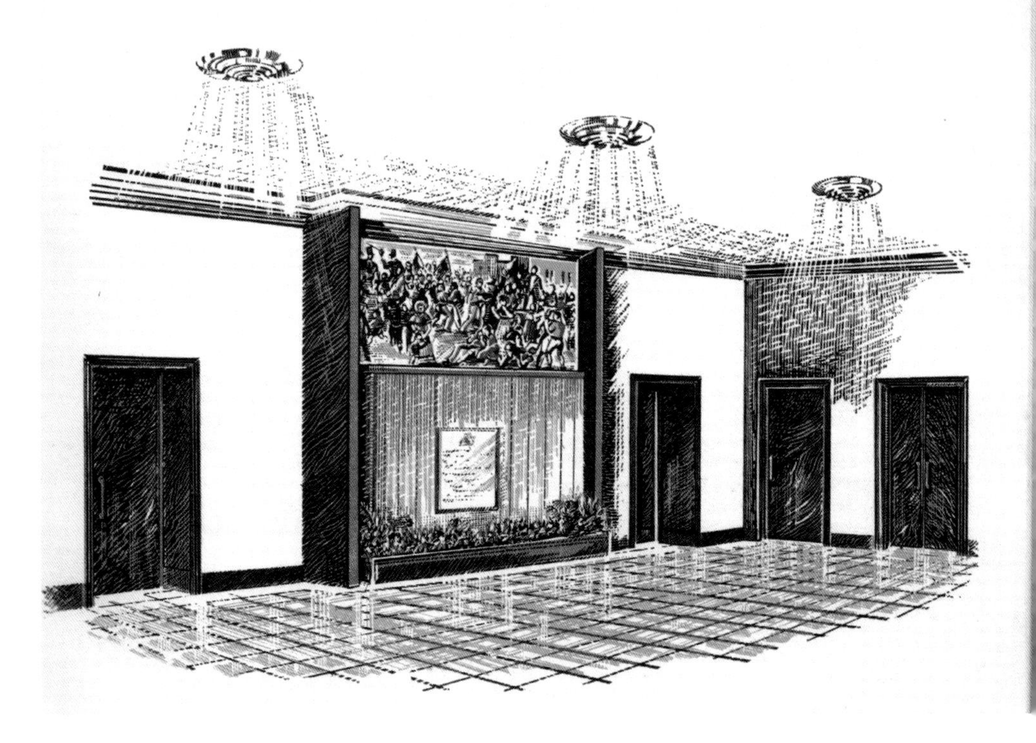

An artist's impression of the new Rear Foyer taken from the 1951 Commemorative Brochure

Manchester Corporation in association with the Hallé Concerts Society and the Arts Council of Great Britain

FREE  TRADE

HALL

INAUGURAL FESTIVAL OF CONCERTS

NINTH CONCERT

SUNDAY, NOVEMBER 25th, 1951

at 7 p.m.

HALLÉ ORCHESTRA

Leader: LAURANCE TURNER

CONDUCTOR

SIR JOHN BARBIROLLI

SOLOISTS

ISOBEL BAILLIE (*Soprano*)

RICHARD LEWIS (*Tenor*)

MARJORIE THOMAS (*Contralto*)

NORMAN WALKER (*Bass*)

HALLÉ CHOIR

(*Chorus Master*: HERBERT BARDGETT)

Programme and Notes - Sixpence

Poster for the ninth concert in the Inaugural Festival Of Concerts November 25th 1951

A cinema projection suite is located above the rear of the Balcony and all electrical services are provided to suit the future installation of projection equipment.

The building is equipped throughout with automatic fire detectors with an indicator at a central point to show the location of any outbreak. Alarm is given by means of a fire bell and by a direct telephone line to the Central Fire Station.

Reconstruction of the Free Trade Hall under prevailing conditions has been achieved only by the close and enthusiastic co-operation of the professional staff of the City Architect's Department, the general contractors and sub-contractors, specialist firms and the suppliers of materials, and by the strenuous efforts of the operatives on the site and in the workshops. All concerned have taken pride in their association with the restoration of the great public building which has played such a prominent part in Manchester life for almost a hundred years, and which can now look forward to another century of service to the city.

GROUND FLOOR PLAN

Ground Floor Plan for the Large Hall taken from the Commemorative Brochure.

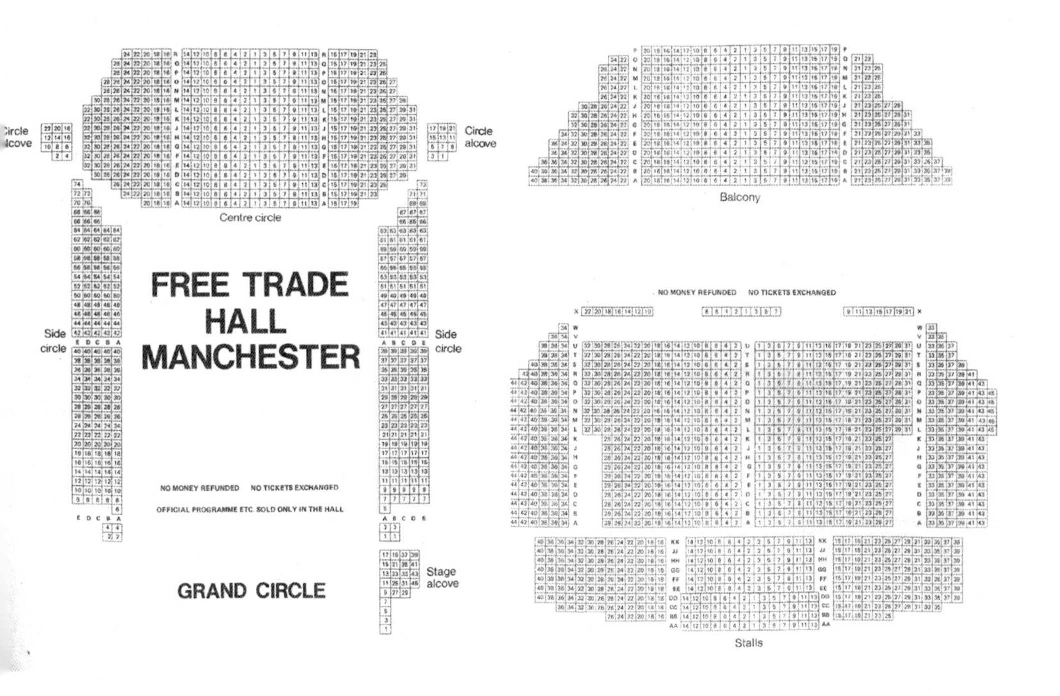

Seating plans for the Grand Circle, Stalls and Balcony

Arthur Howes presents
Oh Boy! It's CLIFF RICHARD
The Cliff Richard Show
Souvenir Programme

Paddy McKiernan's
'JAZZ UNLIMITED'
presents
CHRIS BARBER AND HIS BAND
free trade hall : manchester : monday, april 20, 1959

THE CARMEN McRAE SHOW

THE DAVE BRUBECK QUARTET

Shirley Bassey and Ted Heath and his Music
MANCHESTER FREE TRADE HALL
FRIDAY, DECEMBER 9, 1960
THE FABULOUS MISS
Souvenir Programme and Photograph

Mr ACKER BILK
(THE PHENOMENON OF THE AGE)
and Her Majesty's Servants the
Paramount Jazz Band
SOUVENIR PROGRAMME

ANNA RUSSELL
The Maddest Minx in the Business

ALL-NIGHT SWINGER
Souvenir Dance Card
Programme and
Running Order

FOLK DIRECTIONS
presents
FOLK SONGS
ANCIENT
AND MODERN
FREE TRADE HALL · MANCHESTER
Monday, 14th February, 1966

Sunday, 26th February, 1961 at 7.30 p.m.
Free Trade Hall - - - Manchester

HAROLD DAVISON
DAVE BRUBECK
QUARTET
PAUL DESMOND

NORMAN GRANZ
JAZZ AT THE PHILHARMONIC

FITZGERALD & DUKE ELLINGTON
SOUVENIR BROCHURE TWO SHILLINGS & SIXPENCE

ROBERT PATERSON and HAROLD DAVISON
present
Exclusive appearance of
swingle
singers

THE
STAN GETZ
QUARTET

PRESENTED BY THE
CATACOMBS
CLUB MANCHESTER
SATURDAY
MAY 28th. 1966
FREE TRADE HALL
MANCHESTER
Gospel Rhythm Festival
7·30 pm
PROGRAMME
3d.

WOODY
HERMAN

Free Trade Hall
Manchester
Thursday
9 March 1967

Basil Douglas Ltd present
RAVI SHANKAR
sitar
ALLA RAKHA
tabla
Programme Two Shillings

THE JOHNNY CASH SHOW
OFFICIAL PROGRAM

The early years of the New Free Trade Hall saw a mixture of popular entertainers, Jazz, Folk and Country singers and a brief flirtation with Rock 'n' Roll until a non-appearance by Billy Fury caused a riot!

Blues fans (including members of Manfred Mann and the Rolling Stones) travelled from all over the UK to Manchester for the American Folk Blues Festival held on October 21st 1962. (Top) T-Bone Walker and (bottom) Sonny Terry & Brownie McGhee thrill the cognoscenti.

Photographs by Brian Smith

AMERICAN FOLK BLUES FESTIVAL OCTOBER 22ND 1964
The Free Trade Hall had firmly established itself as the northern Mecca for Jazz and Blues and this trend continued with performances by Sonny Boy Williamson II (top) and Howlin' Wolf (below). The subsequent Blues explosion in British popular music can be traced to these seminal concerts.

Photographs by Brian Smith

BRIAN SMITH always maintains that he was just a "fan with a camera" yet his photographs of American rhythm and blues musicians on English stages are highly regarded around the world.

At the age of 19 Brian was given free rein to take photographs of the historic American Folk Blues Festival at the Free Trade Hall in 1962. Two years later, he photographed the 1964 Festival.

Now retired and living in rural Cheshire, Brian's book "Boom Boom Boom Boom - American Rhythm & Blues In England 1962-1966" will be published by Easy On The Eye Books in 2021.

AMERICAN FOLK BLUES FESTIVAL OCTOBER 22ND 1964
Lightnin' Hopkins (left) and Willie Dixon (below)

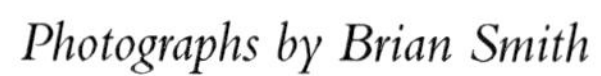

Photographs by Brian Smith

AMERICAN FOLK BLUES FESTIVAL OCTOBER 22ND 1964
Mississippi Fred McDowell (top) and Sunnyland Slim (bottom).
Photographs by Brian Smith

Chrysalis
presents
TEN YEARS AFTER
BLODWYN PIG
STONE THE CROWS

IN CONCERT
WISHBONE ASH
RENAISSANCE
STACKRIDGE
10p

ROY HARPER
SPECIAL GUESTS THE STRAWBS
FREE TRADE HALL MANCHESTER
7.45 — THURSDAY, 11th JUNE — 7.45
ONE PERFORMANCE ONLY
ONE NIGHT ONLY
PRICES: 15/- 10/- 8/- 6/-
From Hime & Addison Ltd., 37 John Dalton Street, Manchester 2
and Lewis's Ltd., Market Street.
HIME & ADDISON / LEWIS'S LTD.
POSTAL BOOKING FORM
"ROY HARPER" Date
Please forward ....SEATS 15/-, 10/-, 8/-, 6/-.
for the 7.45 performance on Thursday, 11th June, 1970.
I enclose stamped addressed envelope & P.O. / Cheque value

Chrysalis presents
Jethro Tull
Ten Years After
Clouds
Introduced by PETE DRUMMOND
(in Bristol - JOHN PEEL)
There will be Two short intermissions between groups

Ray Charles

FREE TRADE HALL
MANCHESTER
WEDNESDAY, 1st SEPT.
at 6.30 & 9.00 p.m.
CREEDENCE
CLEARWATER
REVIVAL
ONLY NORTHERN APPEARANCE
TICKETS NOW ON SALE
£1.00 90p 80p 65p 55p
PLUS BOOKING FEE

Frederick Bannister
Presents
'In Concert'
Captain Beefheart
and his
Magic Band

GROUNDHOGS

Lindisfarne
GENESIS

Polydor Records Present
ON TOUR
TASTE
STONE THE CROWS
JAKE HOLMES
SEP. 6 · CROYDON · Fairfield Hall
SEP. 7 · BRISTOL · Colston Hall
SEP. 9 · MANCHESTER · Free Trade Hall
SEP. 10 · GLASGOW · City Hall
SEP. 11 · LIVERPOOL · Philharmonic Hall
SEP. 12 · ABERDEEN · Music Hall
SEP. 13 · EDINBURGH · Caley Cinema
SEP. 14 · LEICESTER · De Monfort Hall
SEP. 30 · BIRMINGHAM · Town Hall
OCT. 1 · SOUTHAMPTON · Guild Hall
OCT. 4 · LONDON · Lyceum
OCT. 5 · GUILDFORD · Civic Hall

MAN
FREE TRADE HALL
MANCHESTER
PETER ST. MANCHESTER 2
THURSDAY 18TH MARCH
AT 7·30PM

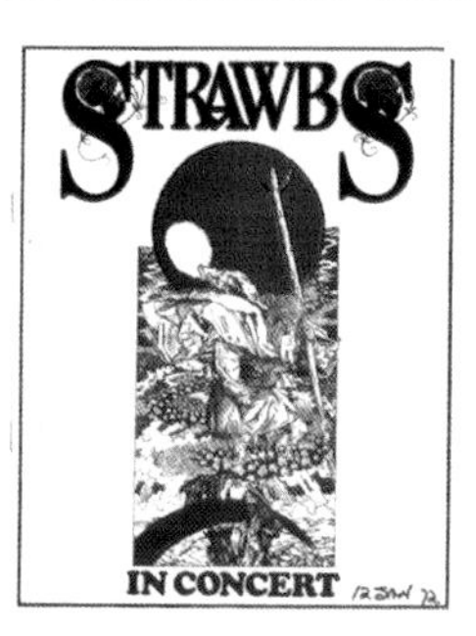
STRAWBS
IN CONCERT

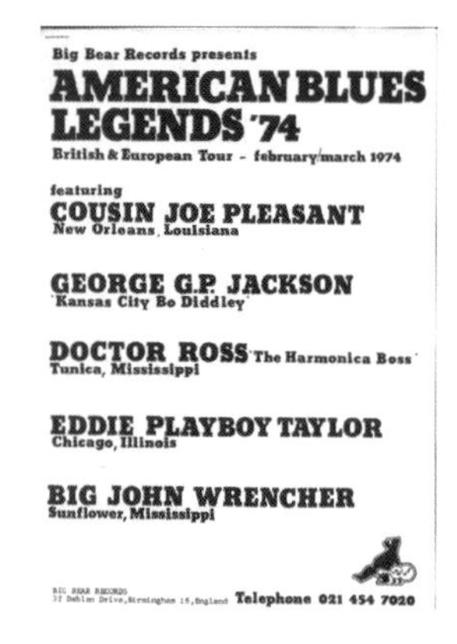

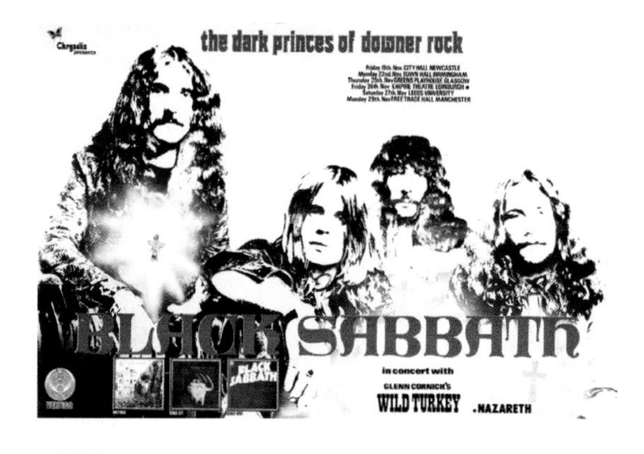

The musical revolution, started in part by the Blues concerts hosted a decade earlier, meant that a seemingly endless streams of British Blues-inspired bands played the venue during the late 60s early 70s alongside Progressive Rock acts, entertainers and comedians.

Straight Music Presents
TED NUGENT
IF IT'S TOO LOUD YOU'RE TOO OLD
UK TOUR
Ted Nugent EPC 81196
Free For All EPC 81397
Ted Nugent on Records & Tapes

GOOD EARTH PRESENTS
KOOL & THE GANG
+ FBI
ON TOUR:
Wed. 15 Sept. TOP RANK, CARDIFF
Fri. 17 Sept. ODEON, HAMMERSMITH
Sat. 18 Sept. VILLAGE BOWL, BOURNEMOUTH
Sun. 19 Sept. TOP RANK, SOUTHAMPTON
Tues. 21 Sept. BAILEYS, BRISTOL
Wed. 22 Sept. TOP RANK, BRIGHTON
Fri. 24 Sept. EMPIRE THEATRE, LIVERPOOL
Sat. 25 Sept. CALIFORNIA, DUNSTABLE
Sun. 26 Sept. TOP RANK, READING
Tues. 28 Sept. BAILEYS, DERBY
Wed. 29 Sept. BAILEYS, STOKE
Fri. 1 Oct. FREE TRADE HALL, MANCHESTER
Sat. 2 Oct. ODEON, BIRMINGHAM

SEX PISTOLS
MANCHESTER
LESSER FREE TRADE HALL
FRIDAY
JUNE 4
7.30.pm.
TICKETS ON SALE AT-
Free Trade Hall Office
Virgin Records
& Black Sedan
Price 50p

THE J. GEILS BAND
LIVE
JUNE 1st LONDON LYCEUM
JUNE 2nd MANCHESTER FREE TRADE HALL
JUNE 3rd BIRMINGHAM TOP RANK

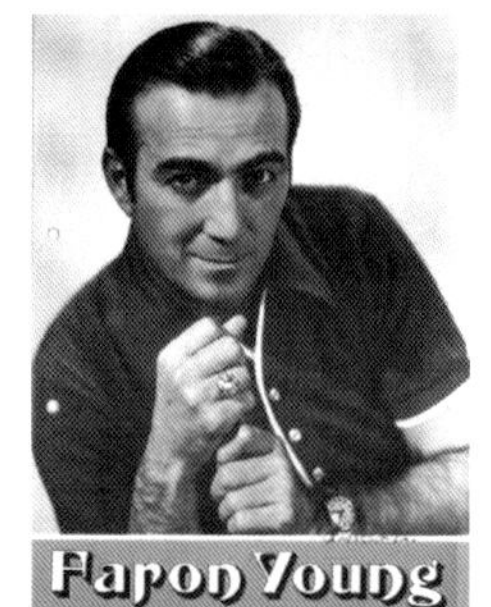
Faron Young

LESSER FREE TRADE HALL
MANCHESTER
SLAUGHTER & THE DOGS
PRESENTED BY R. & B.
THE SEX PISTOLS
PRESENTED BY MALCOLM McLAREN
PLUS SUPPORT
TUES. 20th JULY 1976
from 7.30 p.m.

STRAIGHT MUSIC PRESENTS
B.B.KING
& HIS BAND
WITH GUESTS
SON SEALS BAND
BIRMINGHAM ODEON
FRIDAY 13th OCTOBER at 7·30
HAMMERSMITH ODEON
SAT/SUN - 14th/15th OCT. at 7·30
FREE TRADE HALL
MONDAY 16th OCTOBER at 7·30

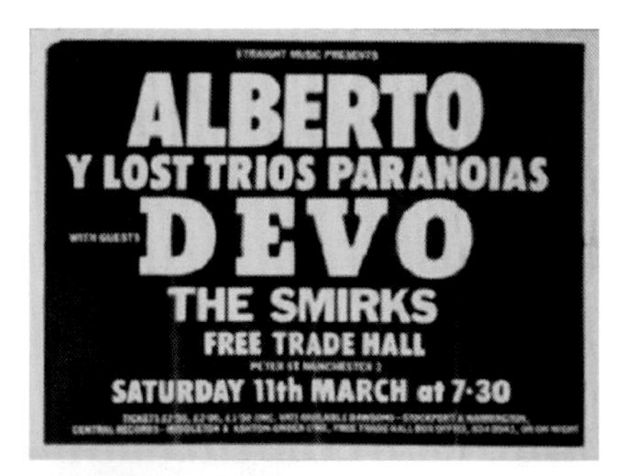

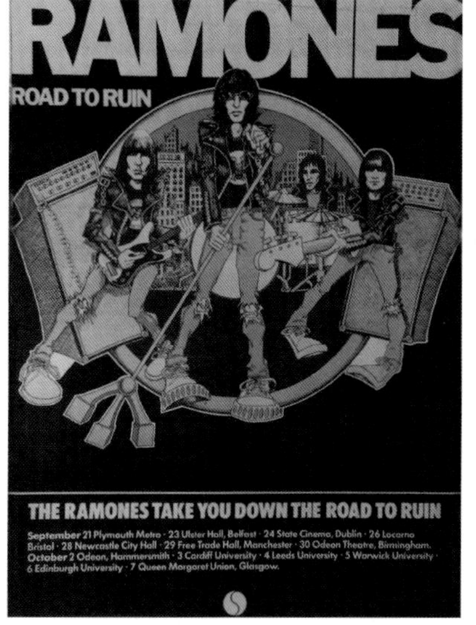

The concert put on in the Lesser Free Trade Hall on 4th June 1976 has been well-documented as inspiring the re-birth of Manchester popular music and subsequent years would see the bands inspired by the Sex Pistols performance take the stage in the main hall alongside Irish country artists, American Glam and Heavy Rock artistes.

(PAGE OVER) The 1980s saw the continued rise of the Mancunian music scene as its most prominent bands played the city's most respected music venue.

TALKING HEADS
Manchester Free Trade Hall
December 1st 1979
this ain't no party this ain't no disco

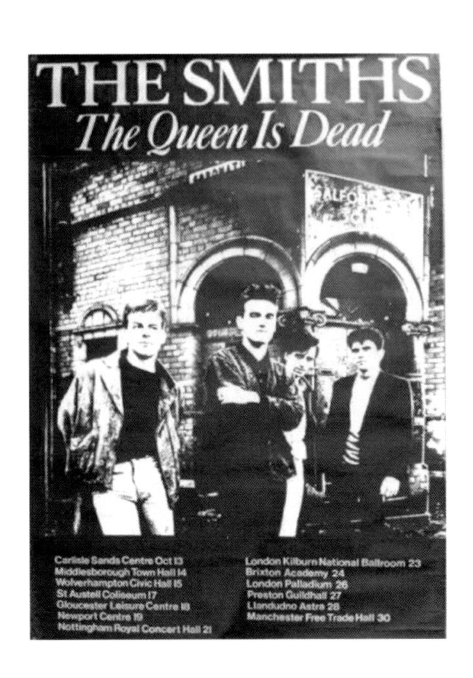
THE SMITHS
The Queen Is Dead
Carlisle Sands Centre Oct 13
Middlesborough Town Hall 14
Wolverhampton Civic Hall 15
St Austell Coliseum 17
Gloucester Leisure Centre 18
Newport Centre 19
Nottingham Royal Concert Hall 21
London Kilburn National Ballroom 23
Brixton Academy 24
London Palladium 26
Preston Guildhall 27
Llandudno Astra 28
Manchester Free Trade Hall 30

live
happy
MONDAYS
plus special guests
STEREO MC'S
DJ's JAM MC'S
OCTOBER
10 LEICESTER DE MONTFORD HALL
tickets available from box office tel: 0533 544444
11 MANCHESTER FREE TRADE HALL
tickets available from library box office tel: 061 236 7110, piccadilly records tel: 061 839 0858
13 NEWCASTLE CITY HALL
tickets available from box office tel: 091 261 2606
14 GLASGOW BARROWLANDS
tickets avaible from virgin records, union st glasgow, virgin records, edinburgh and all tocta agents
16 NEWPORT CENTRE
tickets available from box office tel: 0633 841522
17 BRIXTON ACADEMY
tickets available from box office tel: 071 326 1022, credit card hotline: 071 287 0932 and usual agents
18 KILBURN NATIONAL BALLROOM
tickets available from box office tel: 071 328 3141 and usual agents
20 SHEFFIELD CITY HALL
tickets available from box office tel: 0742 735295/6 and usual agents
21 HANLEY VICTORIA HALL
tickets available from mim, newcastle tel: 0782 21464 and usual agents
22 PRESTON GUILDHALL
tickets available from box office tel: 0772 58858
tickets available from box office tel: 0902 312030 and usual agents
tickets available from box office tel: 0223 357851
tickets available from box office tel: 0705 824355

TUESDAY 11TH JUNE
MANCHESTER FREE TRADE HALL
THURSDAY 13TH JUNE
CORNWALL COLISEUM ST AUSTELL
SATURDAY 15TH JUNE
ROYAL ALBERT HALL LONDON
SOLD OUT
MONDAY 17TH JUNE
WOLVERHAMPTON CIVIC HALL
SJM CONCERTS PRESENT
TUESDAY 18TH JUNE
BRIDLINGTON SPA
plus
CATHERINE WHEEL
AT MANCHESTER + WOLVERHAMPTON
the charlatans
plus NEW FAST AUTOMATIC DAFFODILS & SOUL FAMILY SENSATION
AT LONDON, BRIDLINGTON + ST.AUSTELL.

Echo & The Bunnymen
THE PRIMITIVES
BIRMINGHAM NEC ARENA
THURSDAY 7th JANUARY 8.00 pm
MANCHESTER FREE TRADE HALL
LIVERPOOL EMPIRE THEATRE
MONDAY 11th JANUARY 7.30 pm
BRADFORD ST. GEORGES HALL
TUESDAY 12th JANUARY 7.30 pm
NEWCASTLE CITY HALL
WEDNESDAY 13th JANUARY 7.30 pm
ALL ORIGINAL TICKETS STILL VALID

SJM CONCERTS PRESENTS
James
PLUS INSPIRAL CARPETS
NEWCASTLE UNIVERSITY
TUESDAY 14th MARCH 8pm
TICKETS £4.50 adv
STUDENTS UNION 091 2328402 R.P.M. RECORDS * OLD HITS
SHEFFIELD UNIVERSITY
WEDNESDAY 15th MARCH 7.30pm
TICKETS £4.50 adv — STUDENTS UNION
(0742 724076) HMV RECORDS. FON * RECORD COLLECTOR
HULL UNIVERSITY
THURSDAY 16th MARCH 8pm
TICKETS £4.50 adv — STUDENTS UNION (0482 466264)
* SYDNEY SCARBOROUGHS (UNDER CITY HALL)
MANCHESTER, FREE TRADE HALL
SATURDAY 18th MARCH 7.30pm
TICKETS £5.50 * £5 — THE TICKET SHOP (061 4340943) *
PICCADILLY RECORDS

1975		
Jan 10th	BILLY CONNOLLY	
Jan 15th	LITTLE FEAT	*Montrose; Tower Of Power*
Jan 16th	THE DOOBIE BROTHERS	*Graham Central Station. Bonaroo*
Jan 18th	CLIFF RICHARD - Gospel Concert	*Choralerna*
Jan 25th	JOHN McLAUGHLIN and The New Mahavishnu Orchestra	
Jan 29th	SUPERTRAMP	*Gallagher and Lyle; Chris de Burgh*
Jan 30th	*NAUGHTY RHYTHMS TOUR* with Dr Feelgood; Kokomo; Chilli Willi And The Red Hot Peppers	
Feb 1st	THE FIVEPENNY PIECE	
Feb 2nd	THE LARRY CUNNINGHAM SHOW	*Margo; Joe Lynch; Dermot Hegarty; Dermot O'Brien*
Feb 3rd	BARCLAY JAMES HARVEST	*Julian Brook*
Feb 10th	ROBIN TROWER	*Mandalaband*
Feb 14th	BAKER GURVITZ ARMY	*Strife*
Feb 15th	THE SPINNERS	
Feb 17th	PLANXTY	*Steve Ashley*
Feb 18th	BLACK OAK ARKANSAS	*Sassafras*
Feb 22nd	CHUCK BERRY	*Maxim; Bob Stewart (compère)*
Feb 24th	CURVED AIR	*Trace*
Feb 28th	THE KIKI DEE BAND	*Sailor*
March 1st	NEIL SEDAKA	*Philip and Vanessa*
March 8th	10CC	*Fancy*
March 11th	RICHARD AND LINDA THOMPSON	*Hedgehog Pie*

March 21st	IAN HUNTER AND MICK RONSON	*Jet*
March 22nd	JACQUES LOUSSIER TRIO	
March 23rd	SOFT MACHINE	*Zzebra*
March 26th	RALPH McTELL	*Gay and Terry Woods*
March 29th	ANDY FRASER BAND	*Mike Heron's Reputation*
April 1st	10CC	*Fancy*
April 4th	PERRY COMO with The Tony Mansell Singers (two houses)	*The Wedgewoods; Ted Rogers*
April 18th	THE GLITTER BAND	
April 23rd	GONG	*Global Village Trucking Company*
April 28th	PILOT	*Smokey*
May 2nd	BACHMAN TURNER OVERDRIVE	*Thin Lizzy*
May 4th	THE OLDHAM TINKERS	*Bernard Cribbins*
May 6th	LOVE WITH ARTHUR LEE	*Dog Soldier*
May 12th	SENSATIONAL ALEX HARVEY BAND	*Skyband*
May 16th	GREENSLADE	*Rab Noakes*
May 17th	PAUL KOSSOFF AND BACK STREET CRAWLER	*Out To Lunch*
May 18th	ROD McKUEN	
May 20th	MAN with John Cipollina	*A Band Called "O"; The Flying Aces*
May 30th	PFM	*Wally*
June 1st	JACK BRUCE BAND featuring Carla Bley and Mick Taylor	
June 4th	ROY HARPER	*Headstone*

June 5th	CLIFF RICHARD (Charity concert for the Williams and Rodgers Fund, promoted by Piccadilly Radio)	*The Fivepenny Piece; Tony Maiden; The Greater Manchester Police Military Band; Roger Day; Dave Eastwood; Pete Reeves; Tony Emmerson*
June 6th	DONOVAN	
June 7th	LOUDON WAINWRIGHT III	*Nicol and Marsh's Easy Street*
June 9th	BE-BOP DELUXE	
June 26th	THE SPINNERS	
June 30th	CAMEL	*The Mike Storey Band*
July 27th	THE STYLISTICS (two houses)	*Wigan's Ovation*
Sept 6th	THE SPINNERS	
Sept 7th	HAMILTON BOHANNON And His All American Band	
Sept 8th	HANK LOCKLIN	*Ray Lynam; Philomena Begley; The Hillbillies; Pat Campbell (compère)*
Sept 10th	BUDGIE	*Hobo*
Sept 12th	PAUL McCARTNEY AND WINGS	
Sept 13th	THE FIVEPENNY PIECE	
Sept 14th	KRAFTWERK	*Aj Webber*
Sept 18th	AMERICA	*Poco*
Sept 29th	JOHN MAYALL	*Moonrider*
Oct 7th	BARCLAY JAMES HARVEST	*Café Society*
Oct 8th	THIN LIZZY	*String Driven Thing; City Boy*
Oct 10th	BILLY CONNOLLY	
Oct 11th	THE TEMPTATIONS (two houses)	*FBI*
Oct 17th	BAKER GURVITZ ARMY	*Strife; Tea*

Oct 22nd	DIANE SOLOMON	*Pete Winslow, His Orchestra And Singers*
Oct 31st	LINDA LEWIS	*Labi Siffre*
Nov 1st	STEELEYE SPAN	*Richard Digance*
Nov 3rd	SYD LAWRENCE ORCHESTRA	
Nov 7th	DR FEELGOOD	*GT Moore with the Reggae Guitars*
Nov 14th	BLACK SABBATH	*Bandy Legs*
Nov 15th	CAPTAIN BEEFHEART AND HIS MAGIC BAND	*Secret Oyster*
Nov 17th	*GRAND CHARITY CONCERT* in aid of the Little Sisters Of The Poor with Millican and Nesbitt; The TV All Stars; Tiny Ted, Kathleen Lewis	
Nov 21st	BLUE OYSTER CULT	*Birth Control*
Nov 24th	NAZARETH	*Snafu*
Nov 26th	QUEEN	*Mr Big*
Nov 27th	JOHN CALE	*Nasty Pop*
Dec 1st	MOIRA ANDERSON	
Dec 2nd	CARAVAN	*Michael Chapman*
Dec 6th	THE OLDHAM TINKERS	
Dec 8th	URIAH HEEP	*Tim Rose*
Dec 9th	GENTLE GIANT	*Michael Moore*
Dec 16th	RORY GALLAGHER	*Frankie Miller Band*
Dec 20th	THE SPINNERS	

The *MELODY MAKER* (NOVEMBER 22ND 1975) ANNOUNCED "Jays Open Major Venue", saying "Rock music returned to the Manchester ABC this week when the Blue Jays played at the cinema - a significant addition to the city's rock venues." This turned out to be the beginning of the end for the Free Trade Hall once Ardwick ABC rebranded itself as the Apollo.

Within just two years, the former cinema in Ardwick Green became the main rock venue in Manchester. A spokesman said, "We had such success with late night boxing relays like the Ali-Frazier fight, that we thought we'd try it again as a live venue."

Unlike most large cinemas at the time, the ABC Ardwick had luckily not been sub-divided into smaller auditoriums. The Blue Jays (Moody Blues members Justin Hayward and John Lodge) were the first rock act to play this venue in nearly a decade.

The year started with **Billy Connolly** appearing at the Free Trade Hall. This would be the year that changed his life and career. The first of many guest spots on the *Parkinson* chat show on BBC-1 gave Connolly a new, larger audience outside his native Scotland. The programme was repeated in October and had the highest ratings for a *Parkinson* show. His January Free Trade Hall appearance was about half full, but by October Connolly had virtually sold out the venue. During 1975 Connolly had three chart albums and a No. 1 single with his parody of Tammy Wynette's 'D.I.V.O.R.C.E."

The Warner Brothers *Looney Tunes* package tours were headlined by **Little Feat** and **The Doobie Brothers** on two consecutive nights. The tour was heavily promoted at the time with full page advertisements in the music press and the release of a special sampler album. Manchester was one of nine European cities that were visited. Barry Coleman in *The Guardian* enjoyed Little Feat saying that they were, "rich and refreshingly tight". Little Feat had recently released their most successful album so far, *Feats Don't Fail Me Now* (Warner Bros 1974), while The Doobies were just about to release their fifth album, *Stampede* (Warner Bros 1975).

Cliff Richard was on a short gospel tour in January, appearing with Choralerna, a Swedish Christian choir.

John McLaughlin was now leading the **New Mahavishnu Orchestra** with Jean Luc Ponty on violin and Narada Michael Walden on drums. This line-up's second album, *Visions Of the Emerald Beyond* (CBS 1975) was about to be released. This was part of a ten-date tour.

Supertramp's concert had a £1 admission charge and over 2000 fans attended. This was the band's first headlining British tour. *Crime Of The Century* (A&M 1974) was already in the album charts and the single 'Dreamer' would reach No. 13 later in the spring.

The Naughty Rhythms Tour showcased three pub-rock acts - **Chilli Willi & The Red Hot Peppers, Dr Feelgood** and **Kokomo** -for just 75p admission. The tour posters stated, 'All the turns are playing sets of equal time but the playing order will change nightly.' This tour took place before Dr Feelgood broke through and attendance was poor with barely 400 people in the audience. It was clear throughout the tour which act was most popular.

In *No Sleep Till Canvey Island,* Will Birch writes: "*Dr Feelgood emerged as the stars of the Naughty Rhythms Tour and were poised to become a national attraction in their own right, but for Chilli Willi, this last-ditch attempt at national acceptance had failed and the group never recovered from the ignominy of being upstaged nightly by the Feelgoods.*"

The Feelgoods' first album, *Down By The Jetty* (United Artists 1975) was released this month. Later in the year, Dr Feelgood played UMIST as part of a spring tour. The writer saw the Liverpool University date of this tour and remembers the band being on incendiary form. There was simply no other band like them at the time. Their November Free Trade Hall appearance on their *Malpractice* tour was sold out and just under £100 worth of damage was committed! The Feelgoods returned to the Free Trade Hall in June 1976 and the damage bill rose to nearly £650.

Barclay James Harvest were on a 21-date tour in the spring, promoting their latest album, *Live* (Polydor 1974), their first to chart in Britain. They returned to the Free Trade Hall in October as part of a 30-date tour promoting *Time Honoured Ghosts* (Polydor 1975).

Robin Trower had played guitar with Procol Harum and was now fronting a power trio. He was touring to support his third solo album, *For Earth Below* (Chrysalis 1975), his first to chart in Britain. Trower was more successful in the USA where the album went Top 10.

The Baker Gurvitz Army appeared twice this year, the first appearance being part of the tour to promote their second album, *Elysian Encounter* (Vertigo 1975). Former Cream drummer Ginger Baker had teamed up with Paul and Adrian Gurvitz who had been in The Gun and Three Man Army. Their second appearance in October was part of a twenty-date tour but had a smaller audience.

Irish band **Planxty** were on a fifteen-date tour. Their album, *Cold Blow And The Rainy Night* (Label 1974) had been *Melody Maker* Folk Album Of 1974.

Black Oak Arkansas were on an eleven-date tour. Tickets were priced at only £1, but fewer than 800 people attended.

The Free Trade Hall diary entry for the **Chuck Berry** concert states: "Audience only given nineteen minutes, members of audience then turned on fire hose in balcony and pulled No. 2 stair lights off the wall. CB conducted himself badly all through the tour. Not prepared to accept again!"

Kiki Dee had been making records since 1963 and was the first white British artist to be signed to Tamla Motown in 1970. It was only when she signed to Elton John's Rocket Record Company that hit singles such as 'Amoureuse' and 'I've Got The Music In Me' happened. The following year saw Dee reach No. 1 with her duet with Elton John on 'Don't Go Breaking My Heart'.

Neil Sedaka had been enjoying a second run of success since he had used 10cc as session musicians for his comeback album in 1972. Sedaka went on to have Top 20 albums and sold out concerts at the Royal Albert Hall and Royal Festival Hall. He was touring to promote his new album, *Overnight Success* (Polydor 1975).

10cc were on a twenty-date tour and played the Free Trade Hall on two nights, three weeks apart. They were promoting their new album on a new label, *The Original Soundtrack* (Mercury 1975).

Richard And Linda Thompson were on a twelve-date tour, promoting their second album, *Hokey Pokey* (Island 1975). Tickets were just 80p!

Ian Hunter and **Mick Ronson** stayed together after the split of Mott The Hoople. Hunter's eponymous first solo album (CBS 1975) reached No. 21 and contained his only solo hit single, 'Once Bitten Twice Shy.' Ronson both played on the album and co-produced it. Ronson's own second album, *Play, Don't Worry* (RCA 1975) was also a new release but would only reach No. 29. Morrissey biographer Johnny Rogan: "The spring of 1975 brought Mott The Hoople descendants Hunter/Ronson to Manchester, and Morrissey, (Mike) Ellis and Chris Power religiously attended the gig, sneaking in a camera to take some pictures."

Two former members of Free appeared with their own bands; the **Andy Fraser Band** in March and **Paul Kossoff and Back Street Crawler** in May. Neither concert was successful.

Perry Como had been having hit singles and albums since the 1950's. He made something of a comeback in the early 1970's with several Top 10 singles in Britain including covers of songs by Don McLean and Kris Kristofferson. This was Como's first British concert tour. He was touring to promote his album, *Memories Are Made Of Hits* (RCA Victor 1975).

The Glitter Band had, of course, backed their leader (Gary) but went on to have a parallel career with their own recordings. They had seven Top 20 singles including 'The Tears I Cried' which was in the charts at the time of the band's Free Trade Hall appearance. Their second album, *Rock 'N' Roll Dudes* (Bell 1975) reached No. 17 the following month. Ticket sales, however, were disappointing. This often seemed to happen to pop acts at the Free Trade Hall; despite appealing to teenagers, the gigs did not always generate large ticket sales.

Pilot had had a No.1 hit single earlier in the year with 'January'. Great things were predicted for this Scottish band who were signed to EMI and produced by Alan Parsons, but their follow-up records failed to even reach the Top 30. The musicians in Pilot were later to be heard on Kate Bush's first album and several Alan Parsons Project releases.

Bachman Turner Overdrive were from Canada. Their single 'You Ain't Seen Nothing Yet' reached No.2 in Britain and was in the grand tradition of stuttering records. An album, *Not Fragile* (Mercury 1974) peaked at No. 12. Both single and album reached the top spot in the USA.

Sensational Alex Harvey Band were on an eighteen-date tour, promoting their album, *Tomorrow Belongs To Me* (Vertigo 1975). Later in the summer their cover of Tom Jones' 'Delilah' would reach No. 7 in the singles chart.

Welsh band **Man** was often described as Britain's answer to the Grateful Dead, sharing the latter's liking for lengthy jams. They had found a safe haven at United Artists alongside Hawkwind, Groundhogs and others. Man was touring with their guitar hero, John Cipollina of Quicksilver Messenger Service. The London Roundhouse date of the tour was recorded and released as the album, *Maximum Darkness* (United Artists 1975). Man appeared again at the Free Trade Hall the following March; neither concert was full.

PFM (Premiata Formeria Marconi) was an Italian band. Their sixth album, *Chocolate Kings* (Manticore 1975) featured new lead vocalist Bernardo Lanzetti. Just over 1100 people attended their May concert, even though tickets were priced at only £1.

Former Cream bassist **Jack Bruce** was on a four-date tour with jazz pianist Carla Bley and ex-Rolling Stones guitarist Mick Taylor. Bruce had previously played the Free Trade Hall as part of West, Bruce & Laing, while Taylor had appeared with both John Mayall and the Stones. A highlight of Bruce's set was a twelve-minute version of Cream's 'Sunshine Of Your Love.' This concert was recorded and eventually released as *The Jack Bruce Band Live '75* (Polydor 2003).

Cliff Richard returned to the Free Trade Hall in June to headline a special charity concert, promoted by Piccadilly Radio with all proceeds going to the dependants of two Manchester policemen who died on duty, Sgt Williams and PC Rodgers. Sgt Williams had died outside Granada TV's studios. This was a tragic incident when Bay City Rollers fans thought that their heroes were in a police van. The van actually contained Cliff Richard who had just appeared as a guest on the Rollers' television show, *Shang-A-Lang.* The fans had surged forward and knocked Sgt Williams over. He was taken to hospital but was pronounced dead on arrival, having suffered a fatal heart attack. PC Rodgers was fatally injured when hit by a train at Brinnington whilst he was checking for children trespassing on the railway.

Be-Bop Deluxe played to a tiny audience when they appeared for the first time in June as part of a 27-date tour. They were touring to promote their second album, *Futurama* (Harvest 1975) which failed to chart. Subsequent appearances in 1976 and 1977 were better attended.

Camel had supported Barclay James Harvest in 1972, but headlined their first Free Trade Hall concert in June. *The Snow Goose* (Gama 1975) was Camel's first album to chart and was "inspired" by Paul Gallico's children's novel. A recording exists of this concert. Camel returned to the Free Trade Hall four more times in the late 1970's.

Hamilton Bohannon had led The Motown Sound backing group who played on tours with acts such as The Four Tops, Stevie Wonder and the Temptations. When the Motown organisation moved to California, Bohannon stayed in Detroit and formed his own band. His second hit in Britain, 'Disco Stomp', reached No. 6 earlier in the year. Bohannon's appearance at the Free Trade Hall was poorly attended with box office receipts barely a sixth of the possible gross. Disco - and often, pop - acts did not really 'work' at the Free Trade Hall.

Hank Locklin was an American country singer and songwriter who had six Number Ones in the Billboard country chart in the USA. He was very popular in Europe, especially Ireland. Locklin's biggest hit in Britain was 'Please Help Me I'm

Falling' which reached No. 6 in 1960.

Paul McCartney was the only former Beatle to play the Free Trade Hall; this concert was in the first leg of a thirteen-month tour of ten countries with his band **Wings**. Their album, *Venus & Mars* (Apple 1975) had reached No.1 in June in Britain.

German electronic pioneers **Kraftwerk** had had a Top 20 hit single in Britain with an edited version of the title track of their album, *Autobahn* (Vertigo 1974). The album had reached No. 4. Surprisingly, their appearance at the Free Trade Hall in September was not well-attended.

America had supported Family at the Free Trade Hall back in 1971. Their fifth album, *Hearts* (Warner Bros 1975) did not chart in Britain, despite being produced by George Martin and containing a US No. 1 single, 'Sister Golden Hair.'

Thin Lizzy had supported both Slade and Bachman Turner Overdrive at the Free Trade Hall but headlined for the first time in October. They were touring to promote their first chart album, *Fighting* (Vertigo 1975) which just scraped into the Top 60 for one week. This appearance was not well attended. Thin Lizzy's breakthrough came with the single 'The Boys Are Back In Town' which reached No. 8 in July 1976.

Diane Solomon was an American singer and songwriter who had moved to Britain. She was spotted by a BBC executive and this led to Solomon having her own television programme, *The Diane Solomon Show*. Her second album, *Take Two,* (Philips 1975) had reached No. 26 and included songs by Donovan, John Denver and Randy Edelman.

Linda Lewis had been a support act at the Free Trade Hall on three occasions but, at last, she was headlining. Lewis had replaced Marsha Hunt in The Ferris Wheel before embarking on a solo career. 1975 saw her cover of 'It's In His Kiss' reaching No. 6 and an album, *Not A Little Girl Anymore* (Arista 1975) which just scraped into the Top 40.

Steeleye Span were on a 24-date tour, promoting their album, *All Around My Hat* (Chrysalis 1975) which was their biggest seller, benefiting from the production skills of Womble-meister, Mike Batt. The title track would reach No. 5 in the singles charts.

Queen were about to top the British singles chart with 'Bohemian Rhapsody' and, soon after, the album charts with *A Night At The Opera* (EMI 1975). They were in the middle of a 25-date UK tour which would culminate in a televised concert at the Hammersmith Odeon on Christmas Eve. For the rest of their career, Queen rarely came to Manchester; they appeared for two nights at the Apollo in 1979 and at an open air show at Maine Road Football Ground in July 1986. This Free Trade Hall appearance was sold out.

John Cale had been a member of The Velvet Underground alongside Lou Reed., before going solo. 1975 saw the release of his album, *Helen Of Troy* (Island 1975) and Cale was on a twelve-date British tour. His Free Trade Hall appearance was poorly attended.

Moira Anderson was a Scottish singer who had attended the Royal Scottish Academy of Music and Drama. She appeared several times in television's *The White Heather Club* and in her own series, *Moira Anderson Sings*. Anderson's sole chart album was *These Are My Songs* (Decca 1970) which stayed in the Top 50 for a solitary week.

The Hardrock Concert Theatre continued to decline and only about half a dozen big names played there. Meanwhile, The Palace Theatre continued to increase its number of concerts.

Other events at the Free Trade Hall

February 11th – British Mountaineering Club Lecture
March 10th – Julian Bream and John Williams concert
April 11th – Anti-Common Market Meeting
September 23rd – Marks & Spencer Charity Fashion Show

Elsewhere: (Headliners Only)

ABC Ardwick - The Blue Jays.

Belle Vue (Kings Hall) – David Essex, Melanie, Demis Roussos, Roxy Music, Slade, Status Quo, The Who.

Hardrock Concert Theatre – Edgar Broughton Band, The Chi-Lites, Bob Marley And The Wailers, Don McLean, Rufus, Alvin Stardust, Tangerine Dream.

Opera House – Captain Beefheart, Detroit Spinners, The Four Tops, George Hamilton IV, Tom Paxton, Showaddywaddy, Peter Skellern, Van Der Graaf Generator.

Palace Theatre – Chris Barber Jazz Band, The Chieftains, Duane Eddy And The Rebelettes, Jose Feliciano, David Gates, Genesis, Steve Harley And Cockney Rebel, Mott, Alan Price, Santana, Leo Sayer, Paul Simon, Sparks, Supertramp, The Supremes, Dionne Warwick, Yes.

1976		
Jan 16th	BUCK OWENS AND THE BUCKAROOS	*Frank Jennings Syndicate; Susan Page*
Jan 17th	ELECTRIC LIGHT ORCHESTRA	*Fast Buck*
Jan 22nd	RONNIE LANE'S SLIM CHANCE	*Rab Noakes*
Jan 24th	MIKE HARDING	
Jan 26th	COMMANDER CODY AND THE LOST PLANET AIRMEN	*Barry Melton*
Jan 31st	BLASTER BATES	*Joyce Robinson*
Feb 3rd	10CC	*Chas and Dave*
Feb 4th	10CC	*Chas and Dave*
Feb 6th	GALLAGHER AND LYLE	*Brian Cookson Esq*
Feb 11th	LYNYRD SKYNYRD	*Steve Gibbons Band*
Feb 14th	BE-BOP DELUXE	*Doctors Of Madness*
Feb 16th	STEVE HARLEY AND COCKNEY REBEL	
Feb 19th	EMMYLOU HARRIS AND THE HOT BAND	
Feb 20th	ROBIN TROWER	*John Miles*
Feb 21st	ROBIN TROWER	*John Miles*
Feb 24th	T. REX	*Lennie Macdonald Band*
Feb 27th	MAX BYGRAVES	
Feb 28th	THE SPINNERS	
March 13th	THE DRIFTERS (two houses)	*The Dooley Family*
March 15th	TOOTS & THE MAYTALS	*The Heptones*
March 18th	MAN	*Glenn Cardier*
March 19th	THIN LIZZY	*Graham Parker and the Rumour*
March 20th	THE FIVEPENNY PIECE	

March 26th	GONG	*Wigwam*
March 28th	TOMITA	*Isotope*
April 9th	CAMEL	*Hazzard and Barnes*
April 10th	FRANKIE VALLI AND THE FOUR SEASONS	*R and J Stone*
April 13th	THE MIRACLES	*Madame*
April 17th	THE STYLISTICS	*Brook Benton*
April 19th	NOOR JEHAN - Queen of Melody	
April 20th	NAZARETH	*Widowmaker*
April 26th	PFM	*Back Door*
April 30th	CARAVAN	*Stars*
May 3rd	RICK WAKEMAN and the English Rock Ensemble	
May 4th	ROGER WHITTAKER	*Saffron; Quinny Lawrence*
May 7th	NILS LOFGREN	*Unicorn*
May 9th	SENSATIONAL ALEX HARVEY BAND	*Pat Travers Band*
May 10th	SENSATIONAL ALEX HARVEY BAND	*Pat Travers Band*
May 11th	SHIRLEY BASSEY	*Sparrow*
May 12th	GENTLE GIANT	*Solution*
May 13th	KISS	*Stray*
May 19th	LEONARD COHEN	
May 20th	HALL AND OATES	*The Chanter Sisters*
May 21st	BUDGIE	*Hobo*
May 25th	JASPER CARROTT	*Joanna Carlin*
June 9th	DR HOOK	*Unicorn*
June 14th	DR FEELGOOD	*George Hatcher Band*
June 15th	WAR	*Moon*
June 17th	CHAPMAN WHITNEY STREETWALKERS	*Dirty Tricks*

June 19th	ELECTRIC LIGHT ORCHESTRA	*Steve Gibbons Band*
June 20th	THE OHIO PLAYERS	*Muscles*
June 27th	THE SPINNERS	
July 11th	THE FIVEPENNY PIECE	
July 15th	SWINGLE II	
Sept 5th	RITCHIE BLACKMORE'S RAINBOW	*Stretch*
Sept 17th	CROSBY AND NASH	
Sept 19th	MANFRED MANN'S EARTH BAND	*Racing Cars*
Sept 20th	FLYING BURRITO BROTHERS	*Barbara Dickson*
Sept 29th	THE STRAWBS	*Philip Goodhand-Tait*
Oct 1st	KOOL & THE GANG	*FBI*
Oct 2nd	THE FIVEPENNY PIECE	
Oct 8th	THE CHIEFTAINS	
Oct 9th	BARCLAY JAMES HARVEST	*Easy Street*
Oct 29th	THIN LIZZY	*Clover*
Nov 2nd	JACK THE LAD	*Split Enz*
Nov 3rd	CLIFF RICHARD	*The Brian Bennett Band*
Nov 5th	TANGERINE DREAM	
Nov 6th	MIKE HARDING	
Nov 13th	WISHBONE ASH	*Supercharge*
Nov 15th	LARRY CORYELL AND THE ELEVENTH HOUR	*Brand X featuring Phil Collins*
Nov 19th	STEELEYE SPAN	*Martin Simpson*
Nov 20th	THE OLDHAM TINKERS	
Nov 22nd	VAN DER GRAAF GENERATOR	
Nov 29th	VICTOR BORGE	*Marilyn Mulvey*

Dec 7th	EDDIE AND THE HOT RODS	*Aswad*
Dec 14th	ANDY WILLIAMS	*Brotherhood Of Man; Ray Fell (compère); Vic Lezal's Professionals*
Dec 18th	THE SPINNERS	
Dec 21st	THE KING'S SINGERS	

THIS WAS A VERY BUSY YEAR WITH OVER 70 MAJOR concerts ranging from rock and pop to folk and country. There were first time appearances by Kiss; Hall & Oates, Dr Hook, several black acts and Crosby and Nash.

Buck Owens was born in Texas and developed the 'Bakersfield Sound', an alternative to the dominant influence of Nashville in country music. His first No. 1 hit was 'Act Naturally', later covered by The Beatles on their album, *Help*. The loss of Buckaroos guitarist Don Rich in a road accident in 1974 had a big effect on Owens.

Ronnie Lane had played at the Free Trade Hall with The Faces but left the group in 1973 and formed Slim Chance. After one hit single, 'How Come', Lane created the Passing Show, an over ambitious tour involving a circus big top, but this was a financial disaster. He came to the Free Trade Hall with a new Slim Chance line-up, promoting the new album, *One For The Road* (Island 1976).

Commander Cody & The Lost Planet Airmen were a cult American act specialising in Western swing and country. After four albums on the Paramount label, the group signed to Warner Brothers who wanted to make them more commercial. This resulted in better-produced but duller albums which did not sell either!

10cc's two consecutive dates in February were both sold out. These were their last Free Trade Hall appearances. The band had just released their final album as a quartet, *How Dare You!* (Mercury 1976) which reached No. 5. This tour consisted of 29 dates.

Gallagher & Lyle were signed to Apple Publishing in 1968 and later joined McGuinness Flint. After providing the group with two hit singles, they left in 1971 and formed a duo. After one album with Capitol, they signed with A&M and made three more unsuccessful albums. Later in 1976 Gallagher & Lyle would have hit singles with 'I Wanna Stay With You' and 'Heart On My Sleeve' and their parent album, *Breakaway* (A&M 1976) also charted. This Free Trade Hall concert appearance was a few weeks before the duo's first hit single and was poorly attended, despite its £1 ticket price.

Lynyrd Skynyrd peaked creatively early with their first two albums and such songs as 'Freebird' and 'Sweet Home Alabama'. The band were now promoting their fourth album, *Gimme Back My Bullets* (MCA 1976) with a short British tour. In October

1977 tragedy struck the band when three members of the band and their personal manager were killed in a plane crash.

Be-Bop DeLuxe were on a 28-date tour promoting their third album, *Sunburst Finish* (Harvest 1976). This was the band's first album to chart, reaching No. 17. A single from the album, 'Ships In The Night' entered the charts a week after the band's Free Trade Hall appearance. It peaked at No. 23.

Steve Harley and Cockney Rebel came to the Free Trade Hall in February as part of a tour to promote their album, *Timeless Flight* (EMI 1976). The group had peaked the previous year with a No. 1 single ('Come Up And See Me, Make Me Smile') and an accompanying album *The Best Years Of Our Lives* (EMI 1975) that reached No. 4.

After releasing two well-received albums in 1975, **Emmylou Harris** was touring Europe with her Hot Band which included former members of Elvis Presley's backing group. Her second album, *Elite Hotel* (Reprise 1975) reached No. 17 in March 1976.

T.Rex were on their first full scale British tour for two years, promoting their latest album, *Futuristic Dragon* (EMI 1976). The album just scraped into the Top 50. The band's Free Trade Hall concert was not a good night for the band; ticket sales were disappointing and over £1000 worth of damage was reported in the venue's official diary.

Max Bygraves was a household name; his Singalonga albums on the Pye label sold in huge numbers in the 1970's. His album, *100 Golden Greats* (Ronco 1976) would enter the charts in November of this year and reach No. 3.

The Drifters signed with the British office of Bell Records in 1973 and worked with British songwriters such as Roger Cook and Roger Greenaway. They had a series of hits on Bell with new songs, while their previous record company would undermine this with the release of *24 Original Hits* (Atlantic 1975) which reached No. 2. The Drifters were promoting their new album, *There Goes My First Love* (Bell 1976) with eight concert dates before appearing in cabaret.

Toots Hibbert had led a vocal trio since the early 1960's. His group, **Toots & The Maytals,** signed to Island Records in 1971 and went on to have international hits with 'Funky Kingston' and 'Reggae Got Soul'. They were one of the very few reggae acts to play the Free Trade Hall.

Thin Lizzy's breakthrough came this year with the single 'The Boys Are Back In Town' which reached No. 8 in July and its parent album *Jailbreak* (Vertigo 1976) which reached No. 10 in September. The group toured twice this year and the Free Trade Hall box office receipts reflected the group's fortunes. Thin Lizzy's March concert ticket sales were about half of the possible gross, whereas in October the Free Trade Hall was virtually sold out. In November 1977 the group sold out two consecutive nights at the Free Trade Hall on their *Bad Reputation* tour.

Tomita was a Japanese keyboard wizard and a pioneer of electronic music. His album, *Snowflakes Are Dancing* (RCA Red Seal 1975) of Debussy pieces was heard everywhere this year, especially on commercial radio. The album was a worldwide success and Tomita went on to take a similar approach to works by Holst, Mussorgsky and Stravinsky. Tomita only played two British concerts – at the Free Trade Hall and London's Hammersmith Odeon.

Camel were on a seventeen-date tour promoting their latest release, *Moonmadness* (Gama 1976). This was their highest charting album, reaching No. 15.

Frankie Valli And The Four Seasons - as the new title suggested -were now a five piece band with a joint lead singer, Gerry Polci who also played drums. Polci sang lead on the verses of 'December '63 (Oh What A Night)' which reached No. 1 in the British charts in February. The spring tour consisted of eleven dates, finishing at Batley Variety Club, the latter usually seen as a low point in a pop band's career. This was not the case for Valli's band who were having Top 10 singles and albums. Within a year they played a week at the London Palladium.

The Miracles were now recording and touring with a new lead singer- Billy Griffin. Despite a No. 3 hit single in Britain earlier in the year with 'Love Machine', their Free Trade Hall appearance was poorly attended.

Caravan were touring to promote their album, *Blind Dog At St Dunstans* (BTM 1976) which appeared in the Top 75 for just one week.

Noor Jehan – the Queen of Melody – was a Pakistani playback singer and actress who worked first in British India and then in Pakistan. She started singing and acting in Punjabi films in 1935. Later in life, Noor Jehan gave up acting completely and concentrated exclusively on playback singing.

Less than three years after the curry incident with Yes, **Rick Wakeman** returned to the Free Trade Hall with his English Rock Ensemble touring to promote his fourth solo album *No Earthly Connection* (A&M 1976). The concert was sold out.

Roger Whittaker's easy-going mixture of folk songs and cover versions, along with his extraordinary whistling, had made him an international star. In 1975 his single 'The Last Farewell' was a hit in the USA and sold over eleven million copies worldwide. The song reached No. 2 in Britain and a compilation album, *The Very Best Of Roger Whittaker* (Columbia 1975) reached No. 5.

Nils Lofgren had led his own band Grin, as well as working with Crazy Horse, backing Neil Young. His second solo album, *Cry Tough* (A&M 1976) was a surprise hit in Britain, reaching No. 8. This was part of a ten-date British tour.

Sensational Alex Harvey Band played two consecutive nights in May, promoting their album, *The Penthouse Tapes* (Vertigo 1976). The album consisted mainly of cover versions, including such crowd-pleasers as 'Crazy Horses', 'School's Out' and 'Runaway'.

Gentle Giant were promoting their album, *Interview* (Chrysalis 1976) on a thirteen-date tour.

Kiss were notorious for their make-up, outrageous costumes and stage effects. They did not chart in Britain until their fourth studio album, *Destroyer* (Casablanca 1976) which reached No. 22 following their short British tour. Their Free Trade Hall concert was sold out.

Hall & Oates had left Atlantic Records and were now signed to RCA. They were on an eight-date tour of Britain to promote their eponymous 'Silver Album' (RCA Victor 1976). Later in the year, the album reached only No. 56 in Britain, but was a huge seller in the USA. Hall & Oates would have to wait until 1982 for real chart success in Britain.

Welsh band **Budgie** were on a lengthy tour promoting their first album on a new label, *If I Were Brittania I'd Waive The Rules* (A&M 1976). Despite all this, the album did not follow its two predecessors into the charts.

Jasper Carrott had run a folk club in Birmingham for many years. His single 'Funky Moped' reached No. 5 in 1975, principally because of its notorious B-side, 'Magic Roundabout' monologue. Carrott's album, *Rabbitts On And On* (DJM 1975) had reached No.10. This was a fifteen-date tour.

The **Sex Pistols** made their first appearance at the Lesser Free Trade Hall on June 4th. I mention this event here to put it into context among the concerts happening in the main auditorium. The gig was promoted by future Buzzcocks, Howard Devoto and Pete Shelley. Whole books have been written about this night, notably David Nolan's *I Swear I Was There*; both Heylin (2016) and Robb (2010) are also vital reading.

The Lesser Free Trade Hall had mostly been used for amateur theatre groups and the occasional folk concert had been held there. Devoto and Shelley hired the venue for just £32. Tickets were 50p each. The FTH's financial records state that takings were just £14. A young Steven Morrissey wrote an enthusiastic letter to *NME* about the gig.

A great deal has been written and said about who was in the audience, a topic that both Nolan and Robb cover in their fascinating oral histories. Just six weeks later, on July 20th, The Sex Pistols appeared again at the Lesser Hall. Two local bands, Slaughter & The Dogs and Buzzcocks, played support.

Dr Hook (now without the Medicine Show) had left CBS and signed to Capitol. Their second album on their new label, *A Little Bit More* (Capitol 1976) was full of commercial country ballads and reached No. 5 in the British charts. The album stayed in the charts for 42 weeks.

War, now without Eric Burdon, were signed to a distribution deal with Island Records. Their single, 'Low Rider' had reached No. 12 earlier in the year.

Chapman Whitney Streetwalkers were formed by Roger Chapman and Charlie Whitney, both former members of Family. Their album, *Red Card* (Vertigo 1976) reached No. 16 this year.

The Electric Light Orchestra were apparently "exhausted" after a 70-date American tour (who wouldn't be?) and played only nine dates on this British tour. The band's real commercial breakthrough in Britain came at the end of 1976 with *A New World Record* (Jet 1976) which would peak at No 6 and stay in the album charts for nearly two years. Provincial appearances for ELO would soon become a thing of the past. In 1978 the band played eight consecutive nights at Wembley Arena.

American funk act, the **Ohio Players** had only one minor hit single in Britain - 'Who'd She Coo' reached No. 43 - but were huge in the USA. Their albums were notorious for their sexually risque front covers, reflecting such titles as *Pain, Pleasure* and *Ecstasy*. The band were on a short British tour promoting their new album, *Contradiction* (Mercury 1976).

Ritchie Blackmore's Rainbow were promoting their second album, *Rainbow Rising*. (Polydor 1976) with their first British concert tour. Blackmore had, of course, played the Free Trade Hall with his previous band, Deep Purple. Rainbow would have ever-changing personnel with Blackmore seemingly restless in his quest for the perfect band. This 1976 line-up included Ronnie James Dio (vocals) and Cozy Powell (drums).

David Crosby and Graham Nash had played Manchester Odeon in December 1971 and returned to the city nearly five years later. The duo had just released their third album together, *Whistling Down The Wire* (Polydor 1976) and their sole Free Trade Hall appearance was nearly sold out.

Manfred Mann's Earth Band were promoting their seventh album, *The Roaring Silence* (Bronze 1976) which reached No. 10 in Britain. The cause of this success was the band's cover of Bruce Springsteen's 'Blinded By the Light' which reached No. 6. A year later, the single hit the top of the American charts.

The writer saw the **Flying Burrito Brothers** gig in September; but only "Sneaky" Pete Kleinow was left from the original line-up who had recorded the classic album, *The Gilded Palace Of Sin* (A&M 1969). Despite the presence of ex-Byrd, Skip Battin, the performance was unmemorable. The band later became Sierra, possibly realising that they had no moral right to use the Burritos name. This was my first country rock gig and I was surprised at the number of Stetsons, bootlace ties and fringed jackets worn by members of the audience!

This was the final time that **The Strawbs** played at the Free Trade Hall, after appearing at the venue on four previous occasions. The band were promoting their latest album, *Deep Cuts* (Oyster 1976). The Strawbs' British tour was just ten dates long, a far cry from the lengthy tours of previous years.

Kool & The Gang's commercial peak came in the 1980's in Britain, but the title track from their album, *Open Sesame* (De-Lite 1976) was included on the film soundtrack album, *Saturday Night Fever* (RSO 1977). Their sole appearance at the

Free Trade Hall would be controversial.

On the front page of the following week's *Melody Maker* the headline read *'MANCHESTER BAN ON BLACK MUSIC'*, continuing: *Black music has been banned from Manchester's Free Trade Hall following crowd violence during a recent Kool & The Gang show.* The article links this with incidents at concerts in London by Bob Marley And The Wailers and The Mighty Diamonds.

Free Trade Hall Manager, Ron O'Neill is quoted, "We had a rough time with Kool & The Gang. The knives were out and we had the front door smashed by people trying to get in." The following week's *Melody Maker* elaborates: *Free Trade Hall manager Ron O'Neill has reacted swiftly and sharply. Reggae and soul is out until, he claims, the audiences 'prove they can mend their ways'*. O'Neill said, "*But my action was not based on one concert alone. We had problems all last year. The attitude of these people is terrible. Security at these sorts of concerts is the greatest problem. You can't blame the artists, but I often think they could do something to help. They could talk to the audience, ask them to go back to their seats.*"

The promoter, Bob England, claimed that the Free Trade Hall had over-reacted over the incidents. 'No-one was hurt and there were only six or seven seats done in. Later the front of the stage was rushed and Kool led the group off; It was the only thing to do... A couple of microphones were stolen and a roadie saw one in the possession of one in the crowd. He went in to get it and the kid drew a knife. And that was that.'

The *Manchester Evening News* reported on the concert a full three weeks after the event. Ron O'Neill (aged 57 at the time): "*About 80 kids got in without paying when they rushed the doors... later youngsters made their way round a side balcony and dropped eleven feet on to the stage. When I tried to stop them, I was threatened with sharpened drumsticks. The kids collect broken drumsticks as souvenirs but they must have brought these with them... The music does seem to get the kids worked up. It also seems to attract undesirable elements. I don't like the idea of banning any particular type of music but there is no alternative.*"

O'Neill added that rock music had been banned from the Free Trade Hall "some years ago" (I assume that he is referring to the temporary ban of Deep Purple in 1971; I can find no other example.) The article goes on to say that after O'Neill took over, he "successfully pleaded that only groups that brought trouble should be kept away".

There is no suggestion in either *Melody Maker* or the *Manchester Evening News* that a ban on reggae and soul could be construed as racist in relation to either artists or audience. It is highly likely that a lot of reggae and soul fans would have been black. Very few black groups played at the Free Trade Hall over the next two decades and any that did tended to be Motown/ Philadelphia soul acts, rather than funk or disco ones.

The following night after Kool & The Gang, in complete contrast, Tameside folk group **The Fivepenny Piece** appeared at the Free Trade Hall, just eleven weeks after their previous concert at the venue. This year saw the group's fifth album, *King Cotton* (EMI 1976) reach No. 9 in the charts.

The Chieftains were formed in 1962 but remained semi-professional until the mid-1970's. The group were renowned for their skilful versions of traditional Irish music. The Chieftains were brought to the mainstream American public's attention with their contribution to the soundtrack of Stanley Kubrick's *Barry Lyndon* film. Their Free Trade Hall concert was the first night of an eighteen-date tour.

Barclay James Harvest were on a 24-date tour promoting their album, *Octoberon* (Polydor 1976) which became their highest charting studio album in Britain, reaching No. 19.

Thin Lizzy's October appearance at the Free Trade Hall was sold out. The band were on a 25-date tour promoting their album, *Johnny The Fox* (Vertigo 1976).

Jack The Lad was originally formed from former members of Lindisfarne and Hedgehog Pie. They were promoting their new album, *Jackpot* (United Artists 1976). The Free Trade Hall concert was the final night of a 25-date tour.

Cliff Richard appeared at the Free Trade Hall in November, still basking in the success of his album, *I'm Nearly Famous* (EMI 1976). This was Cliff's first collection of new material to reach the Top 10 in a decade, containing the hits, 'Miss You Nights' and 'Devil Woman'.

Tangerine Dream were on a nine-date tour promoting their album, *Stratosfear* (Virgin 1976) which entered the charts a week after their Free Trade Hall concert.

Wishbone Ash made their fifth and final appearance at the Free Trade Hall with a virtually sold out concert. The band were on a 22-date tour to promote their latest album, *New England* (MCA 1976). Although the band's late 1970's albums did not sell as well as their classic, *Argus* (MCA 1972), they were still a strong live attraction, playing King's Hall, Belle Vue in 1977.

Larry Coryell was an American jazz guitarist and known as the "Godfather of Fusion". He had played with Gary Burton in the late 1960's and formed Eleventh House in 1973. 1976 saw Coryell in a duo with Philip Catherine.

Steeleye Span followed their hit album, *All Around My Hat* (Chrysalis 1975) with *Rocket Cottage* (Chrysalis 1976), another Mike Batt production. However the results were disappointing both artistically and commercially. Despite this, the band's November concert this year was nearly sold out.

Van Der Graaf Generator were on a thirteen-date tour promoting their album, *World Record* (Charisma 1976). The band's November concert was their final appearance at the Free Trade Hall. This was the last tour of the band's classic line-up of Peter Hammill, Dave Jackson, Hugh Banton and Guy Evans.

Eddie And The Hot Rods were a pub rock act from Southend who had a tremendous live reputation. They were caught up in the hype of punk rock this year. During the summer the Rods had broken house records at the Marquee Club in London where they recorded a live EP which contained covers of Bob Seger's 'Get Out Of Denver' and Question Mark & The Mysterons' '96 Tears.' The band were on a twenty-date *Christmas Dancing Party* tour.

Andy Williams appeared at the Free Trade Hall in December, the day after his Royal Gala performance at Talk Of the Town.

Unfortunately, the Free Trade Hall's dominance of popular music concerts was under serious threat. The Palace Theatre – about ten minutes walk from the Free Trade Hall – played host to dozens of gigs from a huge range of artists. To make matters worse, in December the Ardwick ABC was rebranded as a live venue as Manchester Apollo Theatre. The Apollo has dominated Manchester popular music ever since.

Other events at the Free Trade Hall

January 19th – Everest Lecture
February 7th – Kung Fu/ Karate Tournament
March 1st – RSPB Films
March 12th – NCH Festival Of Queens

Elsewhere (Headliners Only)

ABC Ardwick – The Carpenters, John Denver, The Fatback Band, Marvin Gaye, Johnny Mathis, Our Kid, Sherbert.

Belle Vue (Kings Hall)- Bay City Rollers, Eric Clapton, Fatback Band, Peter Frampton, Elton John, James Last, Bob Marley And The Wailers, Gilbert O'Sullivan, Demis Roussos, Santana, Rod Stewart.

Palace Theatre - Albertos Y Los Trios Paranoias, Joan Armatrading, Average White Band, Jim Bailey, Tony Bennett, Jackson Browne, Eric Burdon Band, Donald Byrd, Petula Clark, Kiki Dee, Sydney Devine, Dr Feelgood, Randy Edelman, David Essex, Gallagher And Lyle, Hawkwind, Steve Hillage, Hinge And Brackett, Hot Chocolate, Gladys Knight And The Pips, Little Feat, John Miles, Osibisa, Poco, Noel Redding, Diana Ross, Sailor, Leo Sayer, Neil Sedaka, Slik, Freddie Starr, Sutherland Brothers & Quiver, Tangerine Dream, Trammps, Marshall Tucker Band, Loudon Wainwright III, Bob Williamson.

1977		
Jan 3rd	ANDRAE CROUCH AND THE DISCIPLES	*Choralerna*
Jan 10th	GENESIS	
Jan 11th	GENESIS	
Jan 17th	RORY GALLAGHER	*Joe O'Donnell*
Jan 21st	BE-BOP DELUXE	*Steve Gibbons Band*
Jan 27th	RY COODER and his Chicken Skin Band	*Meal Ticket*
Jan 28th	CHICAGO	
Jan 29th	CHICAGO	
Feb 4th	LYNYRD SKYNRD	*Clover*
Feb 6th	MIKE AND BERNIE WINTERS	*Stan Boardman; Rainbow Cottage; Greater Manchester Police Band*
Feb 11th	ABBA	
Feb 12th	THE SPINNERS	
Feb 19th	MIKE WESTBROOK *(Communist Party promotion)*	
Feb 23rd	TED NUGENT	*Steve Gibbons Band*
March 4th	URIAH HEEP	*Woody Woodmansey's U-Boat*
March 5th	BOB WILLIAMSON	*"Friends"*
March 14th	BRENDAN SHINE	
March 25th	FRANKIE MILLER'S FULL HOUSE	*George Hatcher Band; Andy Dunkerley*
March 26th	AZANIAN SINGERS & DANCERS PRESENT *SOUNDS OF SOWETO*	
April 7th	RAY LYNAM AND THE HILLBILLIES	
April 9th	MAX BOYCE	
April 22nd	JOHN CALE	*The Boys; Count Bishops*

April 25th	ELLA FITZGERALD; COUNT BASIE ORCHESTRA	
April 29th	ROY HARPER and Black Sheep	*Chips; Albion Dance Band*
May 2nd	ROGER McGUINN'S THUNDERBYRD	*Gene Clarke; Chris Hillman Band*
May 3rd	JAKE THACKERAY	
May 6th	JOHNNY MATHIS	
May 7th	SLADE	*Liar*
May 15th	SHAKTI WITH JOHN McLAUGHLIN	*Kevin Coyne*
May 21st	RALPH McTELL	*Magna Carta*
May 23rd	DORY PREVIN	*Illusion*
May 26th	TELEVISION	*Blondie; Andy Dunkerley*
June 1st	STEPHANE GRAPPELLI WITH THE DIZ DISLEY TRIO	
June 2nd	RUSH	*Stray*
June 8th	IAN HUNTER'S OVERNIGHT ANGELS	*The Vibrators*
June 9th	HEAVY METAL KIDS	*The Motors*
June 11th	UFO	
June 26th	THE SPINNERS	
June 27th	BILLY CONNOLLY	*Albion Dance Band*
July 10th	THE FIVEPENNY PIECE	
July 11th	BOXER; CRAWLER; MOON	
July 14th	RAVI SHANKAR with Alla Rakha	
July 29th	LITTLE FEAT	
Sept 15th	JONATHAN RICHMAN AND THE MODERN LOVERS	*Andy Dunkerley*
Sept 23rd	CAMEL	*Andy Desmond*
Sept 27th	CARAVAN	*Nova*
Oct 1st	THE SPINNERS	

Oct 6th	DR FEELGOOD	*Mink DeVille*
Oct 8th	DENIECE WILLIAMS	*Lenny Williams*
Oct 10th	LONE STAR	
Oct 14th	CLIFF RICHARD (Gospel Concert)	
Oct 22nd	TOM PAXTON	
Oct 24th	AC/DC	
Oct 25th	ROY HARPER and Black Sheep	*Spriguns*
Nov 7th	THE TUBES	*Wire*
Nov 12th	THE RUNAWAYS	*999*
Nov 14th	THE CHIEFTAINS	
Nov 19th	STEVE GIBBONS BAND	*Bethnal*
Nov 25th	THIN LIZZY	*Radiators From Space*
Nov 26th	THIN LIZZY	*Radiators From Space*
Nov 29th	ALAN PRICE	*Gonzalez*
Dec 2nd	MAHOGANY RUSH	*Lone Star*
Dec 17th	THE SPINNERS	

DESPITE THE RISE OF THE APOLLO (WHICH PRESENTED about 70 concerts this year), the Free Trade Hall still played host to an impressive range of acts from rock, folk, jazz and pop.

Andrae Crouch was known as the 'father of modern gospel music'. He later worked with such big names as Madonna and Michael Jackson. This was Crouch's first British tour which consisted of five dates. His latest album was *This Is Another Day* (Light 1977).

Genesis played two nights in January, promoting their new album, *Wind And Wuthering* (Charisma 1977). The band were now a quartet with American session drummer, Chester Thompson joining them on live dates. These were Genesis's final appearances at the Free Trade Hall.

Ry Cooder was something of a cult artist in Britain whose eclectic albums did not reach the charts until 1979. His Chicken Skin Band took their name from his album, *Chicken Skin Music* (Reprise 1976) which included both Tex-Mex and Hawaiian music. His Free Trade Hall appearance was part of a five-date British tour.

Chicago performed for two nights this month as part of a seven-date tour. Their recent No.1 single in Britain, the ballad 'If You Leave Me Now', was something of a change of style for this jazz rock band and clearly a commercially sound one. Their album, *Chicago X* (CBS 1976) had reached No. 21 in Britain. Chicago had no support act and promised a two-and-a-half hour set.

Abba visited Manchester on a four-date British tour; they also played Birmingham, Glasgow and London. Pre-orders for the group's two London performances at the Royal Albert Hall exceeded three million! This was Abba's only ever appearance in Manchester. In 1979 Abba only played Wembley Arena, Glasgow and Bingley Hall in Stafford. This was part of a growing pattern where the world's largest acts did not bother to play Manchester, expecting fans to travel the 60 odd miles to Stafford. Between the closure of Belle Vue's Kings Hall and the opening of G-Mex and, subsequently, the arena, Manchester lacked a large indoor venue.

Mike Westbrook was a British jazz pianist, composer, arranger and bandleader. Westbrook had been leading jazz bands since the early 1960's and formed a Concert Band in 1967 to play his own long compositions. He had recently moved from RCA to the Transatlantic label. Later in the year, Westbrook's Brass Band would team up with Henry Cow and Frankie Armstrong to form The Orckestra.

Hard rock guitar hero **Ted Nugent's** first two solo albums had charted in Britain, but both failed to reach the Top 30. His third album *Cat Scratch Fever* (Epic 1977) reached No. 28 later in the year. In the USA Nugent enjoyed multi-platinum success. His Free Trade Hall appearance was part of a nine-date tour.

Bolton born **Bob Williamson** was very much in the tradition of other folk/comedy performers such as Max Boyce, Billy Connolly and Mike Harding. He frequently appeared on regional television and radio. Williamson's song parodies - such as 'Kippers For Tea' - were much enjoyed at the time.

Brendan Shine was an Irish folk and country singer, television presenter and accordion player from Athlone. He had had several No. 1 singles in Ireland and frequently appeared on television. Shine went on to perform ten times at the Free Trade Hall, many of them in the month leading up to Christmas or – as in this case- just before St Patrick's Day.

Frankie Miller, a Scottish singer-songwriter, had supported Rory Gallagher in 1975 but headlined in March with his Full House band. Later in the year he had a hit single with 'Be Good To Yourself'.

Welsh comedian and vocalist **Max Boyce** had worked in a colliery and taken a mining engineering degree. He started performing in folk clubs in 1970 and his performances became more humorous and focussed on both Welsh life and rugby union. Boyce's third live album, *We All Had Doctors' Papers* (EMI 1975) was recorded at Pontarddulais Rugby Club and unexpectedly reached No. 1 in the British charts in November 1975.

Ella Fitzgerald and **Count Basie** returned to the Free Trade Hall after a gap of many years, both making their final appearances there. Basie had appeared no less than eleven times over nearly two decades, while Fitzgerald made a dozen appearances. By now Basie was in his early seventies and Fitzgerald was sixty years old.

Roy Harper had just released *Bullinamingvase* (Harvest 1977) which was his most successful album, reaching No. 25. His backing band, **Black Sheep** had played on the album and included Andy Roberts and Henry McCullough on guitars, Dave Lawson on keyboards, John Halsey on drums and Dave Cochran on bass.

Roger McGuinn had appeared at the Free Trade Hall in 1971 as leader of The Byrds, but in May had a new band, **Thunderbyrd** which was also the title of his new album (CBS 1977). He was supported by two other former members of The Byrds - Gene Clark and Chris Hillman- with their own bands. Inevitably, all three would reunite for encores on this tour. This later led to the formation of the group, McGuinn, Hillman and Clark.

Jake Thackeray was a highly individual and humorous singer songwriter. Teaching in France and Algeria had exposed him to the French chansonnier tradition. Thackeray even translated a Georg Brasson song 'Le Gorille' into English as 'Brother Gorilla'. Appearances on British radio and television unfortunately did not translate into record sales.

Slade were slowly making a comeback after two years in the USA and disappointing chart positions in Britain. Their album, *Whatever Happened To Slade ?* (Barn 1977) took its title from some apt graffiti the band had seen in London. The band's final appearance at the Free Trade Hall was part of an eleven-date British tour.

Shakti was John McLaughlin's new group which featured his acoustic guitar within an Indian classical music group. McLaughlin had already appeared at the Free Trade Hall with two different line-ups of his Mahavishnu Orchestra. Shakti were touring after the release of their second album, *A Handful Of Beauty* (CBS 1976).

Dory Previn had been a lyricist for her then husband, Andre Previn and later became a singer-songwriter in her own right. She had released a series of albums on three different record labels. This was her first British concert tour and consisted of ten dates. A compilation album, *One A.M. Phone Calls* (United Artists 1977) brought together Previn's most popular songs such as 'Lady With The Braid' and 'Mythical Kings And Iguanas.'

Television have a lot to thank *NME* writer Nick Kent for after he gave their debut album *Marquee Moon* (Elektra 1977) an incredibly positive review calling it "a 24 carat inspired work of pop genius". The album became an unexpected success in Britain, reaching No. 28 in the charts. Although Television were branded as punk, their music was far more complex than most of their peers.

Jazz violinist **Stephane Grappelli** had trained at the Paris Conservatoire before playing in the famous Hot Club de France with Django Reinhardt. Grappelli's revival began in 1973 when Jasper Carrott was persuaded by guitarist Diz Disley to book the violinist at Carrott's folk club the Boggery. As Carrott explains in *Singing From The Floor*, "..this was the first time that he'd played with a guitar-based quartet in twenty-five years...That's what kicked off Stephane Grappelli's resurgence." In the same year Grappelli appeared at the Cambridge Folk Festival with Diz Disley and Denny Wright. The violinist continued to tour the world for the next 25 years.

Rush, the Canadian heavy rock trio, were on their first British tour; the Free Trade Hall was a sold out date and reviewed in *NME* by Paul Morley. Morley was intrigued how a relatively unknown band could attract such dedicated fans. Later in the year Rush's first chart album, *A Farewell To Kings* (Mercury 1977) reached No. 22. The trio returned to Manchester the following February to play two nights at the Apollo on their second sell out British tour.

Ian Hunter's Overnight Angels took their name from his third solo album, *Overnight Angels* (CBS 1977). The album failed to chart in Britain and led to Hunter signing to the Chrysalis label. This was a short tour of just eight dates.

The Heavy Metal Kids' name was rather misleading for this not particularly "heavy" band. The band were first spotted, signed and produced by Dave Dee who was A&R man for Atlantic Records. The Kids moved labels and their third album, *Kitsch* (RAK 1976) was produced by Mickie Most. The band's lead singer Gary Holton later appeared in the first *Auf Wiedersehn, Pet* television series, but died in 1985.

UFO made the first of three appearances at the Free Trade Hall. Their sixth album, *Lights Out* (Chrysalis 1977) included a cover version of Love's 'Alone Again Or' which received some radio airplay. Guitarist Michael Schenker appeared on the album. UFO's Free Trade Hall appearance was part of a nine-date tour.

A cheap twenty-date package tour called 'Heat On The Street' featured **Boxer**, **Crawler** and **Moon** just for £1! Boxer featured Mike Patto (ex Timebox; Patto); Crawler were the remnants of the late Paul Kossoff's band, Back Street Crawler; while Moon were a seven-piece British funk band. All three bands had new albums to promote: Boxer with *Absolutely* (Epic 1977); Crawler's eponymous album (Epic 1977) and Moon's *Turning The Tide* (Epic 1977).

Jonathan Richman And The Modern Lovers had emerged as a cult act just before punk and their albums were only available as expensive imports. Fortunately, their record label, Beserkley, set up a British arm and 'Roadrunner' had reached No. 11 earlier in the summer. Richman's new album, *Rock 'n' Roll With The Modern Lovers* (Beserkley 1977) was something of a misnomer with its acoustic sound, containing the novelty hit 'Egyptian Reggae.' His tour was advertised as "the most fun you can have with your clothes on" and visited the Free Trade Hall, Birmingham and London.

Camel started their fourteen-date tour at the Free Trade Hall. They were promoting their new album, *Rain Dances* (Decca 1977) which reached No. 20.

Caravan were on a nine-date tour advertised as their "first ever major headlining tour" (sic) when they were promoting their new album, *Better By Far* (Arista 1977). Tickets were priced at just £1.

Dr Feelgood were touring for the first time without guitarist Wilko Johnson who had left the band to go solo. They were promoting their second studio album of the year, *Be Seeing You* (United Artists 1977) with a 25-date tour.

Deneice Williams had been a backing vocalist for Stevie Wonder on four of his classic albums. Her single 'Free' had been top of the British charts for two weeks in May and its follow-up, 'That's What Friends Are For' reached No. 8.

Lone Star were a Welsh rock band, often cited as the "new" Led Zeppelin. They had supported Ted Nugent on a British tour and were now headlining to promote their second album, *Firing On All Six* (CBS 1977) which reached No. 36.

Cliff Richard was on a two-week gospel tour of Britain. Cliff's Free Trade Hall appearance coincided with his 37th birthday.

AC/DC came from Australia and featured two brothers, Malcolm and Angus Young. The latter was the one who adopted a schoolboy's uniform. The band had already played the Electric Circus in March of this year. Their fourth album, *Let There Be Rock* (Atlantic 1977) was released in July and featured AC/DC's timeless 'Whole Lotta Rosie'. This was part of a fourteen-date tour.

The Tubes were fronted by the outrageous Fee Waybill and the group's mixture of rock music, satirical lyrics and theatre was popular for a while. Their single, 'White Punks On Dope' was a hit in Britain two years after its original release. Manchester punk chronicler, Martin Ryan was there: "The Tubes' big band sound attracted an early roar of approval as it blended into 'Young And Rich' before the inevitable series of musical sketches that provided a perceptibly literal interpretation of the songs such as Fee Waybill and Re Styles performing pseudo sex during 'Don't Touch Me There'." Earlier, Ryan describes the negative reception given to the support band, Wire.

The Runaways had made their British debut at the Roundhouse in London in October 1976. This all-female rock band had been formed by pop legend Kim Fowley. A year later lead singer Cherie Currie left the band and Joan Jett took over vocals. The Runaways were on a short tour to promote their third album, *Waitin' For The Night*. (Mercury 1977).

The Chieftains released two albums this year: *Chieftains 7* (CBS 1977) and *Chieftains Live* (CBS 1977). They were on a twenty-date tour.

After years of playing pubs and clubs the **Steve Gibbons Band** were signed by The Who's management which gave the band useful support slots. Their single 'Tulane', taken from their second album, *Rollin' On* (Polydor 1977) reached No. 12.

Thin Lizzy returned to the Free Trade Hall for two consecutive nights promoting their latest album, *Bad Reputation* (Vertigo 1977). These were the final appearances of the band at the Free Trade Hall.

Alan Price left The Animals in 1965 and formed his own group, The Alan Price Set who had a series of hits in the late 1960's. Later, Price worked with Georgie Fame and film-maker Lindsay Anderson. After a hit single and album on Warner Bros in 1974, Price was now promoting his eponymous album (Jet 1977) with a sixteen-date tour. He had a minor hit single, 'Just For You' in 1978.

Mahogany Rush were a Canadian rock band led by Frank Marino. The group formed in 1969 and are still making records. Marino's guitar style has often been compared to Hendrix. The band were promoting their fifth album, *World Anthem* (CBS 1977) with a short tour.

Other events at the Free Trade Hall

January 13th – Julian Bream and John Williams – concert
March 7th – RSPB Films
June 30th – Paco Pena
September 11th - Wurlitzer Organ Inaugural Concert
December 28th – Atarah's Band

Elsewhere (Headliners Only):

Apollo – Jan Akkerman, Alessi, Pam Ayres, Joan Baez, Chuck Berry, Boney M, Brass Construction, Brothers Johnson, Burning Spear, Glen Campbell, Captain & Tennille, Harry Chapin, Cher & Greg Allman, The Clash, The Commodores, Paul Daniels, Detroit Spinners, Barbara Dickson, Eddie and The Hot Rods, Randy Edelman, Duke Ellington Orchestra, David Essex, Fleetwood Mac, Bruce Forsyth, The Four Tops, Peter Gabriel, Ian Gillan Band, Gary Glitter, Hall & Oates, Steve Hillage, Hot Chocolate, The Jam, Jethro Tull, Hank Locklin, Nils Lofgren, Jacques Loussier Trio, The Manhattans, Harold Melvin And The Bluenotes, John Miles, Nazareth, Iggy Pop, Procol Harum, Rainbow, The Ramones, The Real Thing, Cliff Richard, Smokey Robinson, Rose Royce, Leo Sayer, Sensational Alex Harvey Band, The Shadows, Slik, Small Faces, Smokie, David Soul, Chris Spedding, Status Quo, Jo-Ann Steele, Stiff Tour, The Stranglers, The Stylistics, Donna Summer, Sutherland Brothers & Quiver, Tavares, 10cc, T.Rex, Frankie Valli And The Four Seasons, Barry White, Faron Young.

Belle Vue (Kings Hall) – Joan Armatrading, Eric Clapton, Bing Crosby, Dr Hook, James Last, Jerry Lee Lewis, Demis Roussos, Supertramp, 10cc, Andy Williams, Wishbone Ash.

Opera House – Kate & Anna McGarrigle, Roy Orbison, Streetwalkers.

Palace Theatre– Barclay James Harvest, Buster, Sandy Denny, Gallagher And Lyle, Hawkwind, Horslips, Manhattan Transfer, Graham Parker And The Rumour, Twiggy, Uriah Heep, Barry White.

1978		
Feb 6th	JUDAS PRIEST	*English Assassins*
Feb 7th	STEELEYE SPAN	*Tannahill Weavers*
Feb 10th	MARY O'HARA	
Feb 11th	EMMYLOU HARRIS AND THE HOT BAND	
Feb 27th	GIL EVANS ORCHESTRA	*Stan Tracey Octet*
March 11th	ALBERTO Y LOS TRIOS PARANOIAS	*Devo; The Smirks*
March 14th	GORDON GILTRAP	*John Glover*
March 31st	MANITAS de PLATA with Los Baliardos	
April 1st	THE SPINNERS	
April 3rd	SHIRLEY BASSEY (two houses)	*The New Seekers*
April 4th	SHIRLEY BASSEY (two houses)	*The New Seekers*
April 19th	THE FIVEPENNY PIECE	
April 21st	THE COMMODORES	*3 Ounces Of Love*
April 28th	BLUE OYSTER CULT	*Japan*
April 30th	GHULAN FARID SABRI AND BROTHERS	
May 1st	ELKIE BROOKS	
May 6th	AC/DC	*British Lions*
May 25th	DARTS	*The Late Show*
May 26th	FIVE HAND REEL	
May 28th - afternoon	*FESTIVAL FOR RACIAL EQUALITY* Trevor Hyett; Bob Williamson; John Cooper Clarke; Peggy Seeger and Ewan MacColl; Mike Harding; Exodus	
May 31st	IAN DURY AND THE BLOCKHEADS	*Whirlwind; Matumbi*
June 12th	DON McLEAN	*Bowles Brothers*
June 16th	JONATHAN RICHMAN AND THE MODERN LOVERS	

June 17th	UFO	
July 9th	THE FIVEPENNY PIECE	
Sept 2nd	ROBINSON CLEAVER	
Sept 14th	BLONDIE	*The Boyfriends*
Sept 15th	BRENDAN GRACE	
Sept 16th	CAMEL	*Michael Chapman*
Sept 29th	THE RAMONES	*Snips*
Oct 3rd	DR FEELGOOD	*Ray Campi and His Rockabilly Rebels*
Oct 14th	THE SPINNERS	
Oct 16th	BB KING	*Johnny Mars and No Mystery*
Oct 18th	TOM PAXTON	
Oct 31st	ISAAC HAYES AND HIS ORCHESTRA	*Edwin Starr*
Nov 3rd	MOTORHEAD	*Johnny Moped*
Nov 4th	CHUCK GIRARD	
Nov 11th	THE OLDHAM TINKERS VERSUS BRIGHOUSE AND RASTRICK BAND;	
Nov 15th	LINDISFARNE	*Chris Rea*
Dec 4th	DEVO	*Doll By Doll*
Dec 16th	THE SPINNERS	

SOUL BANDS RETURNED TO THE FREE TRADE HALL THIS YEAR with appearances from The Commodores and Isaac Hayes, suggesting that the ban on "black music" was over.

British heavy metal band **Judas Priest** made their sole appearance at the Free Trade Hall in February. They were on a 21-date tour to promote the release of their fourth studio album *Stained Class* (CBS 1978).

Steeleye Span were on a 31-date tour with a new line-up. Martin Carthy had returned to the band and brought with him his colleague, John Kirkpatrick on concertina. Unfortunately, this line-up's album, *Storm Force Ten* (Chrysalis 1977) did not chart and the band split up in May.

Mary O'Hara was an Irish soprano and harpist from County Sligo who had made records in the 1950's. She had appeared on the Edinburgh Fringe and the Ed Sullivan

Show in the USA, as well as starring in her own BBC television series. From 1962 to 1974 O'Hara was a Benedictine nun at Stanbrook Abbey, but left the order for health reasons. She returned to performing and recording, becoming a huge international success story. Her album, *Mary O'Hara At The Royal Festival Hall* (Chrysalis 1977) charted later in 1978. The Free Trade Hall concert was part of O'Hara's first national tour.

The Gil Evans Orchestra made just one appearance at the Free Trade Hall. Evans was a Canadian jazz pianist, composer and bandleader who had worked with Miles Davis. Two days before his Free Trade Hall concert, Evans recorded a live album at the Royal Festival Hall (RCA Victor 1979). Evans led a thirteen-piece orchestra which also played in Birmingham. This was the final night of a six-date tour.

Emmylou Harris was on a short British tour, promoting her fourth album, *Quarter Moon In A Ten Cent Town* (Warner Bros 1978) which just scraped into the Top 40.

The extraordinary story of **Alberto y Los Trios Paranoias** is best told by the late C.P. Lee in his book *When We Were Thin*. The group's ability to satirise popular music put them in a small premier league alongside Tom Lehrer and The Bonzos. The songs on the Albertos' *Snuff Rock* E.P. (Stiff 1977) were better than most of the punk rock they ridiculed. The Albertos' album *Skite* (Logo 1978) included arguably the best ever Abba parody, 'Juan Lopez (The Lonely Goatherd)' co-written and produced by Chaz Jankel of The Blockheads. Later in the year the group's Status Quo parody, 'Heads Down No Nonsense Mindless Boogie' reached No. 37 in the singles charts. C.P. Lee had appeared at the Free Trade Hall with his earlier group, Greasy Bear.

Gordon Giltrap had started as a singer-songwriter, but later found fame as an expert guitarist. He was touring to promote *Perilous Journey*, (Electric 1977) an all-instrumental album. Giltrap's 'Heartsong' single reached No. 21 at the beginning of the year, no doubt helped by its use as the theme tune to the BBC *Holiday* series.

Shirley Bassey's concerts were part of 25 performances at thirteen venues to celebrate her 25 years in showbusiness. This was billed as her "last major British tour" (sic). Bassey's *25th Anniversary Album* (United Artists 1978) was a lavish double set with an insert booklet. It reached No. 3 in Britain and was awarded a Platinum Disc.

The Commodores, led by Lionel Richie, were an American funk and soul band, signed to Tamla Motown. The band were now showing a softer sound after their funk beginnings. Later in the year the band's single, 'Three Times A Lady' reached No. 1. Their album *Natural High* (Motown 1978) reached No. 8.

Ghulan Farid Sabri was a Pakistani qawwali singer and leading member of the Sabri Brothers, the first exponents of Qawwali to perform to Western audiences. The group appeared at such prestige venues as New York's Carnegie Hall. This concert prompted a complaint about the level of stewarding at the Free Trade Hall. Ticket sales were just under the 400 mark, but it was claimed that between 700 and 800 people were present!

Elkie Brooks was born in Salford and started recording in 1964. She worked with Robert Palmer in Vinegar Joe before both of them embarked on solo careers. Brooks' first hit 'Pearl's A Singer' reached No. 8 in 1977, while its parent album *Two Days Away* (A&M 1977) reached No. 16. She was at the Free Trade Hall on the second night of a sold out 29-date tour which included a week at the London Palladium.

Darts were a doo-wop revival band formed from the remnants of Rocky Sharpe And The Razors. They just missed the top spot with two No. 2 hits, 'Come Back My Love' and 'The Boy From New York City'. The band were on a 31-date tour to promote their second album, *Everybody Plays Darts* (Magnet 1978) which reached No. 12. Darts had a strong visual element with four singers sharing lead vocals.

Five Hand Reel was a Celtic folk rock band which had former Boy Of The Lough Dick Gaughan in their line-up. The band's third album was *Earl O'Moray* (RCA 1978) which had been produced by Fairport Convention's Simon Nicol. Later in the year, Gaughan left the band following the injury of his daughter in a road accident.

In May The Festival For Racial Equality continued the hall's proud tradition of radical events. **Trevor Hyett** was a popular presenter and journalist on Granada TV, as well as being a singer and writer. **Peggy Seeger** and **Ewan MacColl** were central figures in the folk revival with a huge influence.

John Cooper Clarke was relatively unknown when he appeared at this event. The 'Bard of Salford's' breakneck speed poetry had become popular on the Manchester punk scene. Later in the year Clarke would release *Disguise In Love* (CBS 1978).

Exodus were a Manchester reggae band hailing from Hulme and Moss Side. They formed in 1975. Later they changed their name to X-O-Dus to avoid confusion with a London band of the same name. X-O-Dus went on to record a single, 'English Black Boys' on Factory Records which was produced by Dennis Bovell.

Ian Dury And The Blockheads had been together since October of the previous year. Their first hit, 'What A Waste', had been released just before their tour started. Dury's first album, *New Boots And Panties* (Stiff 1977) had reached No. 5 and was a steady seller, staying in the charts for 90 weeks. 1979 would bring a No. 1 single, 'Hit Me With Your Rhythm Stick', but follow-up albums would be less successful.

Jonathan Richman's tour had been cut back to just nine dates after what *Melody Maker* described as "underwhelming sales."

This year saw the first of **Don McLean's** six appearances at the Free Trade Hall. After the success of 'American Pie' and 'Vincent', his career had quietened down a little, but McLean continued to release albums; *Prime Tree* (Arista 1977) and *Chain Lightning* (EMI 1978). This concert was the last night of a fifteen-date tour.

Cinema organist **H. Robinson Cleaver** was the stage name of Harold Robinson. He took the name "Cleaver" from the Manchester department store Robinson & Cleaver! Born in Derbyshire in 1906, Cleaver gained his ARCO qualification at Manchester. He played on various cinema circuits as well as doing summer seasons.

Blondie had supported Television in 1977 at the Free Trade Hall, but were now signed to Chrysalis and selling huge quantities of singles and albums. Blondie's third album, *Parallel Lines* (Chrysalis 1978) was released during the seven-date tour. The Free Trade Hall concert was sold out.

Kris Needs of *Zigzag* accompanied the band on the tour and reported: *"Manchester erupts as the group start their instrumental theme before Debbie (Harry) appears, yells 'Surf's Up!' and they're off with 'In The Sun', followed in rapid succession by 'X Offender' and songs from all three albums, energy levels stoked by the rabid crowd climbing on shoulders, throwing gifts ranging from sweets to the odd item of underwear. 'Fade Away' is the big set-piece, Clem (Burke) and Jimmy (Destri) starting the cliff-hanging intro with the lights down, until Debbie returns in a mirrored gown and shades, sending blinding white light beams at the crowd to stunning effect. She drops the gown for the home stretch rock-out, which powers through 'Pretty Baby', 'Youth Nabbed As Sniper', 'I'm On E', 'One Way Or Another', 'A Shark In Jet's Clothing', (wherein the band are individually introduced) and 'Kung Fu Girls'... 'Denis' brings the house down, while tonight's encores are 'Rip Her To Shreds' , 'Attack Of the Giant Ants', T.Rex's 'Get It On' and 'Jet Boy' for their New York roots."*

Camel were on a 28-date tour promoting their album, *Breathless* (Gama 1978). This was the band's last tour with founder member and keyboard player, Peter Bardens. Bardens joined Van Morrison's band soon after.

Brendan Grace was an Irish comedian and singer who had had the original hit with 'Combine Harvester' in Ireland.

The Ramones had appeared at London's Roundhouse in 1976 supporting Sire label mates The Flamin' Groovies. The Ramones had a huge influence on British punk bands who tried to emulate their sheer simplicity. The band's fourth album, *Road To Ruin* (Sire 1978) reached No. 32.

Dr Feelgood were on a lengthy tour promoting *Private Practice* (United Artists 1978). Although the album only reached No. 41, a track taken from it, 'Milk And Alcohol' would become the band's biggest selling single early in 1979 reaching No. 9.

B.B. King returned to the Free Trade Hall in October on one of four British dates. He was promoting his latest album, *Midnight Believer* (Anchor 1978).

Seven years after his Oscar-winning hit with 'Theme from Shaft', **Isaac Hayes and his Orchestra** appeared at the Free Trade Hall on his first British tour since 1973. Following a Top 10 hit single with 'Disco Connection' in 1976, Hayes had been made bankrupt before releasing a new album, *For The Sake Of Love* (Polydor 1978)

Motörhead's singer and bassist, Lemmy, had already performed at the Free Trade Hall with his former band Hawkwind, but this was the first of two appearances with his own band, just five months apart. In 1978 their cover of 'Louie Louie' was a minor hit but it gave Motörhead their first *Top Of The Pops* appearance. This led to a longer contract with the Bronze label and the release of their second album, *Overkill* (Bronze 1979), the following spring.

Chuck Girard was born in Los Angeles and had been a member of a surf band called The Hondells. Girard played Christian rock and his fourth album was *Take It Easy* (Good News Records 1978).

Lindisfarne returned to the Free Trade Hall after an absence of four years with a reunion of the classic line-up of Clements, Cowe, Hull, Jackson and Laidlaw from the early 1970's. At 40 dates, this was Lindisfarne's longest ever tour. Their single 'Run For Home' reached the Top 10 and its parent album, *Back & Fourth* (Mercury 1978) reached No. 22 - their best chart positions for six years.

Devo had supported the Albertos earlier in the year but headlined in December. The group's robotic/electronic/ironic approach was briefly in vogue. Their album, *Q:Are We Not Men ? A: We Are Devo* (Virgin 1978) had reached No. 12 in Britain.

Other events at the Free Trade Hall

February 17th – Darts Contest
April 25th – Everest 25th Anniversary Lecture
May 15th – Mothers Union Rally
June 13th – Henna Hair Health Show
November 6th – British K2 Expedition Lecture with Chris Bonington

Elsewhere (Headliners Only)

Apollo – AC/DC, Angel, Barclay James Harvest, Be-Bop Deluxe, George Benson, Black Sabbath, Boney M, Boomtown Rats, Bootsy's Rubber Band, Max Boyce, Brand X, Budgie, Buzzcocks, Jasper Carrott, Harry Chapin, The Chieftains, Child, Eric Clapton, The Clash, Crusaders, Dire Straits, Sacha Distel, Rory Gallagher, David Gates & Bread, Steve Gibbons Band, Gordon Giltrap, Steve Hackett, Mike Harding, Richie Havens, Hawkwind, Heatwave, Hot Chocolate, Millie Jackson, The Jam, Jethro Tull, Jack Jones, Journey, Judas Priest, Kansas, The Kinks, Kris Kristofferson & Rita Coolidge, James Last, Manhattan Transfer, Marshall Hain, Meat Loaf, John Miles, Randy Newman, Olivia Newton-John, Maddy Prior, Gerry Rafferty, Revillos, Cliff Richard, Tom Robinson Band, Demis Roussos, Rose Royce, Rush, Sad Café, Santana, Leo Sayer, The Shadows, Showaddywaddy, Patti Smith, Smokie, Steel Pulse, Al Stewart, The Stranglers, Styx, Tangerine Dream, Tavares, Television, 10cc, Bonnie Tyler, UK, Van Halen, Weather Report, Whitesnake, Wishbone Ash, X Ray Spex.

Belle Vue (Kings Hall) – Gallagher And Lyle, Parliament/ Funkadelic, Rod Stewart, Thin Lizzy, Wishbone Ash.

Palace Theatre - Manfred Mann's Earth Band.

1979		
Jan 8th	ELVIS COSTELLO AND THE ATTRACTIONS	*Richard Hell And The Voidoids; John Cooper Clarke*
Feb 12th	UFO	*Liar*
Feb 13th	HERBIE HANCOCK	
Feb 23rd	STEVE HILLAGE	*Telephone*
March 13th	THE BOTHY BAND	*Jimmy Crowley*
March 23rd	NANA MOUSKOURI	
April 4th	KLAUS WUNDERLICH	
April 11th	MOTORHEAD	*Girlschool*
May 9th	*BENEFIT FOR GOLBORNE MINERS FUND* with Mike Harding; Peter Skellern	*The Grimethorpe Colliery Band; Turnpike*
May 13th	*LANKY SPOKEN 'ERE* with Dave Dutton; The Fivepenny Piece; Bernard Wrigley	
May 18th	SCORPIONS	*Terra Nova*
May 20th	BURL IVES; THE SPINNERS	
June 1st	TALEET MAHMOOD	
June 8th	THE POLICE	*The Cramps; Bobby Henry*
June 13th	ROCKPILE WITH DAVE EDMUNDS AND NICK LOWE	*Lew Lewis Reformer*
June 15th	GERARD KENNY	
June 18th	THE REAL THING	
June 25th	JOHN COOPER CLARKE	*Fashion; Joy Division*
July 3rd	JOY DIVISION	
Sept 2nd	MARIA KUMAGAI	

Sept 5th	RICKIE LEE JONES	*Uncle Sam*
Sept 13th	LOUDON WAINWRIGHT III	
Sept 14th	SAMMY HAGAR	*Def Leppard*
Oct 4th	SKY	
Nov 6th	STEVE HILLAGE	*Trevor Rabin*
Nov 9th	THE ENID	*Jon Benns*
Nov 28th	THE HOUGHTON WEAVERS	
Dec 1st	TALKING HEADS	*A Certain Ratio*
Dec 15th	THE SPINNERS	
Dec 19th	IRISH CHRISTMAS CONCERT	
Dec 28th	BLONDIE	*The Boyfriends*

ELVIS COSTELLO AND THE ATTRACTIONS WERE PROMOTING his third album *Armed Forces* (Radar 1979). The album - and the single, 'Oliver's Army' - both reached No. 2. The writer saw this tour at Southampton Gaumont where Costello was now a very powerful live performer.

American jazz pianist and composer **Herbie Hancock** had worked with Donald Byrd and Miles Davis. He also crossed over into disco music and had had a No.15 hit in Britain with 'I Thought It Was You' the previous year.

Steve Hillage had played the Free Trade Hall with his former band Gong, but went solo in 1976 . Hillage appeared twice this year; in February he was on an eleven-date tour to promote his album *Live Herald* (Virgin 1979) which only reached No. 54. This was followed by an ambient album, *Rainbow Dome Music* (Virgin 1979) with Miquette Giraudy. In the autumn Hillage was touring again to promote his next album, *Open* (Virgin 1979) which proved to be his least successful release so far.

The Bothy Band were an Irish traditional folk group, formed by former Planxty member, Donal Lunny. They made three studio albums and recorded a live album in Paris. The band would split later in the year and some members would go on to re-form Planxty.

Nana Mouskouri was on a seventeen-date British tour, her first for two years. She was promoting her latest album, *Roses And Sunshine* (Philips 1979).

German organ virtuoso, **Klaus Wunderlich** was touring Britain for the second time and playing nineteen dates.

On March 18th there was a mining disaster at Golborne Colliery near Wigan; ten miners lost their lives and, less than two months later, a benefit concert was held for their dependants. **Mike Harding** and Peter Skellern joined forces along with the **Grimethorpe Colliery Band. Peter Skellern** was a singer-songwriter-pianist from nearby Bury. His single 'You're A Lady' reached No. 3 in 1972 and became a modern standard. Later in the year Skellern would release *Astaire* (Mercury 1979) which featured songs made famous by Fred Astaire in RKO film musicals. This album reached No. 23 and featured the Grimethorpe Colliery Band.

Actor and writer **Dave Dutton** was from the Lancashire town of Atherton and contributed to a Lancashire evening alongside **The Fivepenny Piece** and **Bernard Wrigley**. Singer and actor Wrigley, sometimes referred to as the "Bolton Bullfrog", appeared in both folk clubs and television dramas. He has a naturally comic face along with an unmistakeable voice. Wrigley had released records since 1971 on both the Topic and Transatlantic labels.

Scorpions are a German rock band who had originally formed in the 1960's. They had a new guitarist, Matthias Jabs, and a new album, *Lovedrive* (Harvest 1979) which had a tasteless front cover featuring a man pulling bubblegum off a woman's bare breast. The band were touring Britain after a two-year absence.

Burl Ives was an American folk singer and actor who had appeared in Manchester back in the 1950's. On this occasion he shared a bill with Free Trade Hall regulars The Spinners. Born in 1909, Ives was something of a renaissance man in his ability to perform in plays on Broadway, host radio programmes, appear in films and sing folk and country music.

Talat Mahmood was born in Utter Pradesh and was a notable Indian Ghazal singer. He specialised in non-classical and semi-classical singing and playback recordings for films. Mahmood was said to have had the softest voice on the Indian sub-continent.

The Police made their only Free Trade Hall appearance this year. This was one of fourteen British dates on their *Outlandos D'Amour* tour. They had appeared at the Russell Club in Manchester in 1978. The band had a very successful year with two No.1 singles - 'Message In A Bottle' and 'Walking On The Moon' - in the autumn and a No.1 album with *Reggatta De Blanc* (A&M 1979).

Rockpile featured **Dave Edmunds** and **Nick Lowe**. Between them they had five hit singles this year, notably Edmunds' cover of Elvis Costello's 'Girls Talk' and Lowe's own song 'Cruel To Be Kind'. Each played on the other's recordings. A Rockpile album proper, *Seconds Of Pleasure* (F-Beat 1980) was less successful.

American singer-songwriter **Gerard Kenny** celebrated his city of birth in 'New York New York (So Good They Named It Twice)' which reached No. 48 after receiving wide airplay. His album, *Made It Through The Rain* (RCA Victor 1979) was more successful and made the Top 20 during the summer.

The Real Thing hailed from Toxteth in Liverpool and had a No.1 hit in 1976 with 'You To Me Are Everything' and continued to have hits. Their single 'Can You Feel The Force?' had reached No. 5 earlier in the year, while its parent album of the same name (Pye 1979) scraped in to No. 73.

John Cooper Clarke was having a successful year. He reached a huge, new audience when he was a support act on Elvis Costello's tour at the beginning of the year and was now a headlining act. Clarke even had a minor hit single when 'Gimmix! Play Loud' reached the Top 40.

Charles Shaar Murray: *"John Cooper Clarke is bounding on stage at Manchester Free Trade Hall, a cavernous building steeped in musty Victorian municipality, a room dusted with hard work and religion. It is Manchester's principal venue, a hall which has played host to the likes of 10cc and Black Sabbath and David Bowie in its time, and now the headlining attraction is a man whose job it is to stand on stages armed with nothing but a microphone, a jug of vodka and orange juice and two plastic carrier bags stuffed with notebooks and scrawled sheets of paper…*

"He operates in a nebulous territory bounded by four corners : the points of his compass are poet, comic, musician and author. You could say he is an entertainer, and certainly none of the people filling between half and three-quarters of the Free Trade Hall's seating would gainsay you. Laugh? Thought they'd wet themselves."

Murray briefly refers to one of the two support bands; "..while, onstage, Joy Division ram dark slabs of organised noise at the audience while a scarecrow singer moves like James Brown in hell.." Clarke's set is delayed because he has left one of his carrier bags of poetry at Martin Hannett's house in Didsbury. A taxi is sent to collect the bag.

Charles Shaar Murray: *"John Cooper Clarke appears in a cold oval of light, stage centre. The effect is comic. The stage has been built for choirs and brass bands, political meetings and rock shows, and across the vast acreage stalks a skinny streak like some elongated insect on its hind legs, carrier bags stuffed with plunder, a mutant centipede who's just looted 1966."*

In 1979, Clarke's look appeared to be very much modelled on Bob Dylan's 1966 image – the hair, the dark glasses, even the suits. I wonder if Murray realised that Dylan had appeared, sporting that look, on that very same stage thirteen years earlier!

Two of **Joy Division's** members were from Macclesfield and the other two from the Salford area. Their first recording, 'An Ideal For Living', led to a John Peel session in early 1979 and soon the band signed to Manchester's Factory Records. Joy Division's first album, *Unknown Pleasures* (Factory 1979) had been released in June to wide acclaim and brisk sales. Later in the year the band would play the Apollo as support to Buzzcocks.

Maria Kumagai was a Japanese organist who moved to the USA in 1969. She played both classical and theatre organs and toured Europe and Australia. Kumagai's appearance at the Free Trade Hall saw her playing the venue's famous Rodgers organ.

Rickie Lee Jones's eponymous first album (Warner Bros 1979) and the single, 'Chuck E's In Love' both reached No. 18 in their respective charts. Jones' easy jazz style was very popular; *Time* magazine called her "The Duchess Of Coolsville."

Sammy Hagar was a former member of Montrose who had embarked on a solo career. He was touring to promote his fifth album, *Street Machine* (Capitol 1979) which reached No. 38. Hagar's Free Trade Hall appearance was one of only four British dates. In the mid-1980's he would replace David Lee Roth as lead singer of Van Halen.

Sky were a five-piece instrumental group featuring classical guitarist John Williams; Tristan Fry (a classical percussionist) and three rock musicians: Herbie Flowers (bass); Francis Monkman (keyboards) and Kevin Peek (guitar). Their music reflected this fusion of styles and was extremely popular. Their eponymous first album (Ariola 1979) reached the Top 10 and stayed in the charts for over a year.

The Enid were an old school progressive rock band who had somehow survived punk. They mixed long instrumental pieces with excerpts from 'Dambusters March' and 'The Skye Boat Song'. The band were on a short tour to promote their fourth album, *Six Pieces* (Pye 1979). Keyboardist Robert John Godfrey had previously conducted the Barclay James Harvest Orchestra and had worked as an arranger. Radio One DJ Tommy Vance was a keen supporter of the band.

Talking Heads were on a nine-date tour promoting their third album, *Fear Of Music* (Sire 1979). The band would appear later in December on ITV's *South Bank Show*. The band had previously played at the Electric Circus in 1977 and at Manchester University in early 1978.

A concert by punk band, **Penetration** was booked for March of this year, but it was cancelled. A letter was sent to the promoter stating, "As you know, Punk Rock is not acceptable to the Free Trade Hall."

This was the last year that pop concerts were held at Belle Vue's Kings Hall; brass band contests continued until 1982 which was soon followed by the venue's demolition.

Other events at the Free Trade Hall

February 3rd – An Evening of Rodgers & Hammerstein music
May 5th – Handbell Ringing Rally & Concert
July 5th – Marian Montgomery and Richard Rodney Bennett – Hallé Prom
November 23rd – National Trust Lecture & Film Show

Elsewhere (Headliners Only)

Apollo: AC/DC, Joan Armatrading, Average White Band, Roy Ayers, Bad Company, Shirley Bassey, Blue Oyster Cult, Boney M, Boomtown Rats, Elkie Brooks, Dennis Brown, Jean-Jacques Burnel, Kate Bush, Buzzcocks, Camel, Johnny Cash, Harry Chapin, Chic, Leonard Cohen, Billy Connolly, Andrae Crouch, Crown Heights Affair, The Crusaders, Culture, The Damned, Darts, Chris de Burgh, John Denver, Dire Straits, Dr Feelgood, Ian Dury And The Blockheads, The Enid, David Essex, Gallagher And Lyle, Gloria Gaynor, Steve Hackett, Mike Harding, Hawkwind, Hi-Tension, Horslips, Hot Chocolate, Engelbert Humperdinck, Joe Jackson Band, The Jacksons, The Jam, J.Geils Band, Billy Joel, Elton John, Journey, Judas Priest, The Kinks, Gladys Knight And The Pips, James Last, Lindisfarne, Nils Lofgren, Magazine,

Manfred Mann's Earth Band, Manhattan Transfer, John Miles, Van Morrison, Motorhead, Nazareth, Bill Nelson's Red Noise, Gary Numan, Graham Parker And The Rumour, Planxty, Queen, The Ramones, Lou Rawls, Helen Reddy, Renaissance, Cliff Richard, Roxy Music, Rush, Sad Café, Leo Sayer, The Shadows, Sham 69, Siouxsie And The Banshees, Sister Sledge, The Skids, Sky, The Specials, Squeeze, Status Quo, Stiff Little Fingers, The Stranglers, Thin Lizzy, The Three Degrees, Peter Tosh, The Tubes, Tina Turner, The Undertones, Uriah Heep, Van Halen, Whitesnake, Andy Williams, Wings, XTC, Frank Zappa.

Belle Vue (Kings Hall) – Mike Oldfield, Don Williams.

The Eighties

Performances by the rising stars of Manchester music but a declining number of gigs

1980		
Jan 12th	*GOSPEL CONCERT* – British Youth For Christ	
Feb 2nd	THE DUBLINERS	
Feb 9th	IRISH TRADITIONAL CONCERT	
Feb 22nd	THE CHIEFTAINS	
March 7th	THE KING'S SINGERS	
March 28th	THE SPINNERS	
April 11th	SECRET AFFAIR	
April 18th	B.A. ROBERTSON	
April 26th	THE HOUGHTON WEAVERS	
April 29th	THE UNDERTONES	*The Moondogs*
May 10th	CLEO LAINE WITH JOHN DANKWORTH	
May 18th	INDIAN VARIETY CONCERT	
May 23rd	*GOSPEL CONCERT* WITH BILL GAITHER TRIO	
June 2nd	THE J. GEILS BAND	*Q Tips*
Sept 6th	MEHFIL E QAWWALI	
Sept 9th	INDIAN RELIGIOUS CULTURAL SHOW	
Sept 12th	MARTY WILDE AND THE WILDCATS	*Larry Walker; Tony Rivers; Toni Rose; Rondevu*
Sept 15th	DON McLEAN	*Prelude*
Oct 4th	BRENDAN SHINE	
Oct 13th	SHEENA EASTON; GERARD KENNY; DENNIS WATERMAN	*Leeson and Vale*
Oct 24th	LOUDON WAINWRIGHT III	*Beverley Martyn*
Oct 28th	GLADYS KNIGHT AND THE PIPS (two houses)	
Oct 31st	RALPH McTELL	*Pasadena Roof Orchestra*
Nov 3rd	CHINESE ACROBATS	

Nov 4	BARBARA DICKSON	
Nov 7th	DON WILLIAMS (two houses)	*Raymond Froggatt; Diane Pfeifer*
Nov 15th	URIAH HEEP	*Samson*
Nov 19th	JESSY DIXON	*Choralerna*
Nov 25th	ALL PRIESTS HOLY ROAD SHOW	
Nov 28th	GIRLSCHOOL	*Angel Witch; Tank*
Dec 9th	*CHARITY CONCERT for Manchester Taxi Drivers Organisation For Handicapped Children* WITH MIKE HARDING	*The Dobcross Band; Therapy*
Dec 12th	GOSPEL CONCERT	
Dec 17th	THE SPINNERS	
Dec 19th	*IRISH CHRISTMAS CONCERT* with Johnny McEvoy	

The Chieftains were on their *Boil The Breakfast Early Tour* which consisted of nineteen dates.

Secret Affair were part of the mod revival and their first album *Glory Boys* (I-Spy 1979) had been a minor hit; their singles were more successful with two Top 20 hits with 'Time For Action' and 'My World'.

B.A. Robertson seemed to come from nowhere to emerge as an omnipresent television personality. He had been releasing records since 1973 and had co-written hits for Cliff Richard. Robertson's first hit, 'Bang Bang' reached No. 2 in 1979; but this was the peak of his own performances. He was promoting his album, *Instant Success* (Asylum 1980).

Irish punks **The Undertones** hailed from Derry and were championed by John Peel and signed to Sire Records. Their Free Trade Hall appearance coincided with their biggest hit 'My Perfect Cousin' and was part of their 26-date *Humming* tour. The band's second album, *Hypnotised* (Sire 1980) would reach No. 6.

This year saw **Cleo Laine's** first concert tour for six years, accompanied by her husband, **John Dankworth** and his quartet. The tour consisted of thirteen provincial dates.

The J. Geils Band had been together since the late 1960's but had had more commercial success in the USA with their album *Love Stinks* (EMI 1980). This year they only played two concerts in Britain; London and the Free Trade Hall. A date in Birmingham was cancelled at the last minute. The band would have to wait another two years for a British hit single with 'Centerfold' and album, *Freeze Frame* (EMI 1981).

Marty Wilde made his second appearance at the Free Trade Hall after a gap of 21 years. During this time he had written hits for Status Quo, The Casuals and Lulu, as well as appearing in films. Within a year, Wilde would be writing hits for his daughter, Kim.

Don McLean had topped the charts for three weeks in the summer with his slowed down version of Roy Orbison's 'Crying.' Its parent album, *Chain Lightning* (EMI International 1980) reached No. 19. McLean was on a lengthy British tour while a compilation, *The Very Best Of Don McLean* (United Artists 1980) would soon reach No. 4.

Sheena Easton had appeared on one of the first reality TV programmes, *The Big Time,* trying to become a pop star. This actually happened and she achieved two Top 10 single hits earlier in the year. **Gerard Kenny** returned to the Free Trade Hall, alongside actor **Dennis Waterman** who had recorded Kenny's composition 'I Could Be So Good For You' as the theme song for ITV's *Minder* series. Waterman's single reached No. 3. This package played other major venues including London's Dominion Theatre.

Gladys Knight And The Pips had had greater success on the Buddah label than their earlier stint on Tamla Motown. In 1980 the group had moved to CBS where their singles were less successful.

Barbara Dickson had appeared as the support to the Flying Burrito Brothers in 1976, but now was headlining her own 30-date tour. *The Barbara Dickson Album* (Epic 1980) included the hit single 'January February', one of several songs on the album by Alan Tarney who also acted as producer.

Don Williams was from Texas and had had huge success in the American country charts. He had reached No. 2 in Britain with his album, *Images* (K-Tel 1978) which clearly benefitted from the marketing skills of that record label. Williams was touring to promote his latest album *I Believe In You* (MCA 1980) which reached No. 36.

Uriah Heep were on their first tour with new vocalist John Sloman. This was the band's final Free Trade Hall appearance, the last of seven concerts in a decade.

Jessy Dixon was an American gospel singer, songwriter and pianist from Texas. He had appeared on two Paul Simon albums and toured with Simon for eight years.

Girlschool were something of a novelty in Britain - an all female rock band following the American tradition of Fanny and Birtha. This was their first tour as headliners consisting of twenty dates.

Other events at the Free Trade Hall

January 12th – Gospel Concert – British Youth For Christ
March 3rd – RSPB Films
December 1st-2nd – Faraday Lectures

Elsewhere (Headliners Only):

Apollo: AC/DC, Adam And The Ants, Allman Brothers Band, Jon Anderson, April Wine, Joan Armatrading, Average White Band, Barclay James Harvest, Shirley Bassey, Black Sabbath, Blizzard Of Oz, Blood, Sweat & Tears, Max Boyce, Elkie Brooks, Brothers Johnson, Buzzcocks, Captain Beefheart, Caravan, Jasper Carrott, Ry Cooder, John Cooper Clarke, The Clash, The Crusaders, The Damned, Def Leppard, The Detroit Spinners, Devo, Dexy's Midnight Runners, Dire Straits, Dr Hook, The Dooleys, Ian Dury & The Blockheads, David Essex, Peter Gabriel, Rory Gallagher, David Gates, Marvin Gaye, Genesis, Gillan, Sammy Hagar, Hall & Oates, George Hamilton IV, Hawkwind, Hot Chocolate, Iron Maiden, Joe Jackson Band, Jethro Tull, Jack Jones, Judas Priest, Bert Kaempfert Orchestra, BB King, The Kinks, Kool & The Gang, Krokus, James Last, Jerry Lee Lewis, Madness, Johnny Mathis, Motorhead, Pauline Murray & The Invisible Girls, Ted Nugent, Gary Numan, Hazel O'Connor's Megahype, Mike Oldfield, Roy Orbison, OMD, The Osmonds, Tom Petty And The Heartbreakers, Iggy Pop, The Pretenders, The Psychedelic Furs, Suzi Quatro, Gerry Rafferty, Rainbow, The Ramones, Helen Reddy, Roxy Music, Rush, Sad Café, Saxon, Michael Schenker Group, Scorpions, Secret Affair, Selecter, The Shadows, Sham 69, Siouxsie And The Banshees, Sky, David Soul, The Specials, Spyrogyra, Steeleye Span, Stiff Little Fingers, Tangerine Dream, 10cc, Thin Lizzy, The Tourists, Pat Travers Band, Triumph, Robin Trower, Judie Tzuke, UFO, Ultravox, The Undertones, Uriah Heep, Frankie Valli & The Four Seasons, Van Halen, Rick Wakeman, Weather Report, Whitesnake, Wishbone Ash, XTC, Yellow Magic Orchestra, Yes, Frank Zappa.

Belle Vue (Kings Hall) – Andrae Crouch And His Disciples.

1981		
Feb 14th	THE HOUGHTON WEAVERS	
Feb 27th	*VARIETY CONCERT* in aid of Italian earthquake victims	
March 6th	GAMMA FEATURING RONNIE MONTROSE	*Praying Mantis*
March 24th	PLANXTY	*Hamish Imlach; Steve & Les Chilcott*
April 3rd	NANA MOUSKOURI	
April 4th	STEELEYE SPAN	
April 21st	SIAMSA TIRE (National Folk Theatre Of Ireland)	
April 24th	GIRLSCHOOL	*A II Z*
May 2nd	*BOND US TOGETHER* – Religious Musical	
May 15th	LARRY NORMAN GOSPEL CONCERT "FRIENDS ON TOUR"	*Alwyn Hall; Barratt Band*
May 23rd	INDIAN VARIETY CONCERT	
May 28th	ANDRAE CROUCH	*Van Shipley; Enoch Daniels; Paradise*
June 2nd	LIGHT OF THE WORLD FEATURING BEGGAR & CO.	*The Inversions*
June 7th	CHINESE CONCERT	
June 15th	KRAFTWERK	
June 16th	JUDIE TZUKE	*Woolly Wolstenholme*
June 19th	THE TUBES	
June 20th	SPIRIT	*Inner City Unit*
June 28th	DIAMOND HEAD	*Silverwing*

July 6th	*CHARITY CONCERT* The Dooleys, Houghton Weavers; Fogwell Flax; Angie Gold	*Dave Ward (compère)*
Sept 13th	KEN DODD AND COMPANY	
Sept 26th	LARRY CUNNINGHAM WITH HIS COUNTY BLUE BOYS	*Mary O'Connor; Foster and Allen; Just Four; Celene Wilson; Country Cousins*
Sept 30th	DAVID ESSEX	*Top Secret*
Oct 3rd	*IRISH VARIETY CONCERT* with Johnny McEvoy; Margo & Brendan Blake	
Oct 16th	RANDY EDELMAN	*Labi Siffre*
Oct 23rd	JOHN MARTYN	*Bumble And The Beez*
Oct 27th	THE NOLANS	
Oct 30th	MARY O'HARA	
Nov 2nd	TOM PAXTON	
Nov 23rd	PETER SKELLERN	
Nov 24th	THE ALL PRIESTS HOLY ROAD SHOW	*Nashville Express; Mary Walsh Dancers; St Wilfrid's Ceili Band*
Nov 25th	GARY "US" BONDS	*The Jets*
Nov 26th	HOT GOSSIP ROAD SHOW	*The Berlin Blondes*
Dec 12th	THE SPINNERS	
Dec 16th	GOSPEL CONCERT	
Dec 18th	BRENDAN SHINE	*Joe Cuddy; Anna McGoldrich; Fr Michael Cleary*
Dec 27th	ATARAH'S BAND	

WHILE THE APOLLO PRESENTED OVER 80 CONCERTS OF major artists, the Free Trade Hall's programme for 1981 had only half a dozen rock concerts. There were folk, reggae, funk, gospel, Asian, Irish and comedy performances.

Gamma were formed by Ronnie Montrose in 1979 after leading the band Montrose previously. Montrose had often been called America's answer to Led Zeppelin and originally had Sammy Hagar on vocals. Gamma's album, *Gamma 2* (Elektra 1980) had been released the previous August. This was the band's debut British tour where they performed at just five concerts.

Planxty were on a seven-date tour promoting their album, *The Woman I Loved So Well* (Tara 1980).

Steeleye Span had now reformed with the successful line-up from the mid-1970's. They had released an album, *Sails Of Silver* (Chrysalis 1980) and were on a 22-date tour.

Siamsa Tire were the National Folk Theatre of Ireland. As far back as the 1960's, efforts were made to preserve Irish traditions of music and dance before they disappeared. Folk academies were established in different parts of rural Ireland including Tralee where there is now a permanent base.

Girlschool were on a sixteen-date tour promoting their new album, *Hit 'N' Run* (Bronze 1981) which reached No. 5 in the charts. The title track reached only No. 32 when released as a single.

Paul Morley reviewed the gig in *NME*: "*For Girlschool the audience seem no different – in attitude, uniform, politeness and ultimate total submission – to audiences ten years ago, half lost and resenting any glimmer of glamour. The bar isn't very full - most of the audience have yet to start drinking. The only change in HM (heavy metal) audiences is that they get younger. I count a dozen girls on my travels around the hall. Kim (McAuliffe – guitarist in Girlschool) registers disgust and disbelief when I tell her...*"

Light Of The World were a British jazz-funk band and their offshoot band **Beggar & Co** had a Top 20 hit with '(Somebody) Help Me Out'. Later in the year Beggar & Co were featured on Spandau Ballet's 'Chant #1 (We Don't Need This Pressure On)' hit single. This was the band's first headlining tour consisting of twelve dates.

Kraftwerk were on an eighteen-date tour promoting their new album, *Computer World* (EMI 1981) which reached No. 15. Later in the year, a single from the album, 'Computer Love' was a hit once DJ's emphasised its B-side, 'The Model', a three year old track from *The Man-Machine* (EMI 1978). This combination would eventually reach No. 1 in February 1982.

Judie Tzuke was signed to Elton John's Rocket Records; her evergreen classic 'Stay With Me Till Dawn' reached No. 16 in 1979 and she had a Top 10 album with *Sports Car* (Rocket 1980). Tzuke was touring to promote her third album, *I Am Phoenix* (Rocket 1981). Later she would sign to Chrysalis.

Spirit had been a cult band for years, lionised in fanzines and by certain journalists. They rarely appeared in Britain, but recorded a live album at London's Rainbow in 1978, before splitting up. The band later reunited and 1981 saw some mainstream success with appearances on *The Old Grey Whistle Test* and at Hammersmith Odeon. Spirit played a short British tour promoting their current album, *Potatoland* (Beggars Banquet 1981) which briefly charted.

Diamond Head were an English heavy metal band. Their first album, *Borrowed Time* (MCA 1982) would reach the Top 30.

David Essex returned to the Free Trade Hall after a gap of seven years. He was on a 24-date tour promoting his album, *Be-Bop The Future* (Mercury 1981). The album was the first of Essex's not to chart, but he was more successful the following year with a Christmas hit single and two charting albums.

The Dooleys were a family band from Ilford in Essex who had seven Top 30 hit singles. Their album, *Best Of The Dooleys* (GTO 1979) had reached No. 6. They were the largest family act ever featured on a hit single.

Randy Edelman had had hits in the 1970's with 'Concrete And Clay' and 'Uptown Uptempo Woman' on the 20th Century label. Later, Edelman signed to Elton John's Rocket Records but his records were less successful.

John Martyn opened his tour at the Free Trade Hall, promoting *Glorious Fool* (WEA 1981) which was produced by Phil Collins of Genesis. This was Martyn's most successful album to date, reaching No. 25.

Tom Paxton made his final appearance at the Free Trade Hall, the last of thirteen concerts that started back in 1966.

Gary 'U.S.' Bonds had had hits in the early 1960's and twenty years later he teamed up with Bruce Springsteen and the E. Street Band. Bonds went on to have minor hits in Britain with 'It's Only Love' and 'Jole Blon', the latter a duet with Springsteen. His album *Dedication* (EMI America 1981) charted briefly in Britain.

Hot Gossip had danced on Kenny Everett's ITV programmes with outrageous movements and costumes. Their choreographer was Arlene Phillips who publicly defended their act when it was criticised by the likes of Mary Whitehouse. By now Sarah Brightman had left the troupe to pursue a solo vocal career. Hot Gossip released an album, *Geisha Boys And Temple Girls* (Dindisc 1981) which was masterminded and produced by Ian Craig Marsh and Martyn Ware of Heaven 17.

Other events at the Free Trade Hall

January 26th – Fashion Show
March 2nd – Vidal Sassoon Hair Show
March 13th – NCH Festival Of Queens
April 11th – Crusade For World Revival

Elsewhere (Headliners Only):

Apollo – AC/DC, Adam And The Ants, Joan Armatrading, Rowan Atkinson, Bad Manners, Barclay James Harvest, The Beat, Jeff Beck, The Boomtown Rats, Burning Spear, Camel, Glen Campbell, Johnny Cash, Harry Chapin, The Clash, Billy Connolly, Rita Coolidge, Elvis Costello And The Attractions, The Cure, Def Leppard, Diamond Head, Barbara Dickson, Dr Hook, Duran Duran, Sheena Easton, Echo And The Bunnymen, Marvin Gaye, Gillan, Steve Hackett, Mike Harding, Emmylou Harris, Hawkwind, The Human League, Janis Ian, Iron Maiden, Japan, The Kinks, Kool & The Gang, Krokus, James Last, Linx, Nils Lofgren, Madness, Manhattan Transfer, Johnny Mathis, The Moody Blues, Hazel O'Connor's Megahype, OMD, Robert Palmer, The Pointer Sisters, Iggy Pop, The Pretenders, Rainbow, Cliff Richard, Rose Royce, Roxy Music, Sad Café, Leo Sayer, Michael Schenker Group, Neil Sedaka, The Shadows, Simple Minds, Siouxsie And The Banshees, Sky, Slade, Billie Jo Spears, Split Enz, Bruce Springsteen, Squeeze, Status Quo, Tommy Steele, Shakin' Stevens, Stiff Little Fingers, The Stranglers, Tangerine Dream, Teardrop Explodes, Thin Lizzy, Toyah, UB40, UFO, Ultravox, The Undertones, Frankie Valli & The Four Seasons, Tom Waits, Rick Wakeman, The Who.

Belle Vue (Kings Hall) – Country Music Festival starring Boxcar Willie.

Palace Theatre - (reopened in March 1981):10cc.

1982		
Feb 13th	THE HOUGHTON WEAVERS	
Feb 19th	ISLA ST CLAIR WITH HER BAND	*Nigel Ogdon*
Feb 22nd	HERB MILLER ORCHESTRA	
March 1st	TONY BENNETT	
March 13th	*ST PATRICK'S VARIETY CONCERT* with Frank Carson	*Dermot Hegarty; Dermot O'Brien; FR. Michael Cleary;*
March 15th	*ST PATRICK'S CONCERT* with Philomena Begley and the Rambling Men	*Sean O'Se; Pascal Spellman; The Borderline Showband*
March 26th	DIAMOND HEAD	*Fire Clown*
March 29th	MOSCOW BALALAIKAN ORCHESTRA	
April 9th	CAROLE KING	
April 28th	DON McLEAN	*Jenny Peters*
May 18th	JUDIE TZUKE	*The Bloomsbury Set*
June 5th	MAHESH KUMAR AND COMPANY	
June 18th	THE WOLFETONES	*MacMurrough; The Downbeats*
Sept 20th	JOHN MARTYN	*Durutti Column*
Oct 2nd	THE BACHELORS	
Oct 30th	THE WOLFETONES	
Nov 6th	KEITH JARRETT	
Nov 13th	THE SPINNERS	
Nov 19th	CHAS AND DAVE	*Diz And The Doormen*
Nov 22nd	THE CHIEFTAINS	
Dec 17th	BRENDAN SHINE CHRISTMAS CONCERT	

THE FREE TRADE HALL'S POPULAR CONCERTS HAD diminished to a scale unseen since the 1950's. Only one rock group -Diamond Head – appeared, alongside a mixture of folk, jazz, singer songwriters and Irish acts. The Irish element accounted for about a third of the concerts and was a trend that continued.

Isla St Clair was a Scottish folk singer who recorded her first album in 1971 after years of singing in folk clubs. In 1978 her life was transformed when she became hostess on BBC-1's *The Generation Game* alongside Larry Grayson. St Clair was soon offered her own television series, *The Song And The Story.*

Tony Bennett made his final appearance to the Free Trade Hall this year, returning after a gap of twelve years. Bennett had experienced both financial and health problems, and had not released new material for several years. Later in the decade he would re-sign with Columbia and reunite with his long-time accompanist, Ralph Sharon.

Diamond Head were on a fourteen-date tour promoting their E.P, *Four Cuts* (MCA 1982).

Carole King returned to the Free Trade Hall after a gap of eleven years. This was one of her first concerts in Britain for seven years. King was touring to promote her album, *One To One* (Atlantic 1982), her first release for that label.

Don McLean was on a 21-date tour, his first in Britain for two years. He had a minor hit single this year with a re-recording of 'Castles In The Air', a song that had originally appeared on his first album, *Tapestry* (United Artists 1972) and in its re-recorded form on *Believers* (EMI 1981).

Judie Tzuke was touring to promote her latest album, *Shoot The Moon* (Chrysalis 1982) which reached No. 19.

John Martyn was on his longest tour to date, promoting his album, *Well Kept Secret* (WEA 1982) which was his highest chart placing, reaching No. 20.

The Bachelors had had great success outside their native Ireland in the 1960's with several Top 10 singles in the British charts and a chart-topper with 'Diane'. Like a lot of 1960's pop acts, they later found a career in cabaret.

Keith Jarrett was an American jazz pianist and composer who had been touring as solo pianist for nearly a decade.

Chas & Dave were veterans of British rock and pop, but broke through as a Cockney duo in 1979 with 'Gertcha' and supported Led Zeppelin at Knebworth in the same year. Chas Hodges had previously appeared at the Free Trade Hall a decade earlier as a member of Heads, Hands And Feet.

Other events at the Free Trade Hall

March 29th – Moscow Balalaika Concert
May 4th – Littlewoods Fashion Show
October 1st – Divine Light Mission Conference

Elsewhere (Headliners Only):

Apollo- ABC, AC/DC, Adam And The Ants, Altered Images, Shirley Bassey, Boomtown Rats, Elkie Brooks, Budgie, Chris de Burgh, Camel, Ry Cooder, Alice Cooper, Elvis Costello And The Attractions, Kid Creole & The Coconuts, The Cure, The Damned, John Denver, Depeche Mode, Sydney Devine, Diamond Head, Dire Straits, Dr Hook, Duran Duran, Echo And The Bunnymen, Fashion, Rory Gallagher, Gillan, Girlschool, Sammy Hagar, Hall & Oates, Mike Harding, Hawkwind, Julio Iglesias, Imagination, Iron Maiden, Joe Jackson, The Jam, Japan, Joan Jett And The Blackhearts, Elton John, Kool & The Gang, Krokus, Lindisfarne, Barry Manilow, Freddie McGregor, Steve Miller Band, Mike Oldfield, Graham Parker And The Rumour, Teddy Pendergrass, Tom Petty And The Heartbreakers, Graham Parker, Todd Rundgren, Sad Café, Saxon, Michael Schenker Group, Scorpions, Neil Sedaka, The Shadows, Shakatak, Simple Minds, Siouxsie And The Banshees, Shakin' Stevens, Shalamar, Steeleye Span, Stiff Little Fingers, Talk Talk, Tangerine Dream, Teardrop Explodes, 10cc, Thin Lizzy, Third World, Toyah, Tygers Of Pan Tang, UB40, UFO, Ultravox, U2, Whitesnake, Kim Wilde.

Palace Theatre - Van Morrison, Yazoo.

1983		
Feb 12th	THE DUBLINERS	
March 12th	*ST PATRICK'S IRISH VARIETY CONCERT* Johnny McEvoy; Dermot Hegarty; Mary O'Hara	*Fr. Michael Cleary; Vince Miller*
March 26th	MARI WILSON AND THE WILSATIONS featuring The Marines and The Marionettes	*Vince Bereley*
April 30th	THE WOLFETONES	*The St. Chad's Irish Dancers; The Lomax Irish Dancers; St Brendan's Junior Ceilidhe Band; Manchester Junior Comhaltas Musicians*
May 15th	*ELVISLY YOURS CONVENTION* with The Joe Esposito Show	*David Hamilton; Heathcliffe*
May 22nd	INDIAN VARIETY CONCERT	
May 28th	FOSTER AND ALLEN	*Ann Breen*
June 23rd	JOHN WILLIAMS AND FRIENDS	
Sept 24th	GHULAM ALI	
Oct 5th	THE SPINNERS	
Oct 14th	THE FUREYS AND DAVEY ARTHUR	
Nov 25th	DONOVAN	
Dec 16th	BRENDAN SHINE	*Paddy Reilly; Bridie Gallagher; Brendan Blake; Vince Miller (compère)*
Dec 30th	NUSRAT FATEH ALI KHAN	

THE FREE TRADE HALL WAS STILL BEING USED FOR LECTURES, film shows, religious and political meetings, as well as school speech days, but the number of pop and folk concerts had considerably diminished.

Mari Wilson's retro-style pop was briefly popular and she had two Top 30 singles and a Top 30 album, *Showpeople* (Compact 1983). Her Free Trade Hall appearance was followed by a prestige concert at the London Palladium.

Joe "Diamond Joe" Esposito had served in the U.S. Army with Elvis Presley and subsequently became his road manager and friend. After Presley's death, Esposito worked as a consultant on various Elvis-related projects. Elvisly Yours was the largest and oldest Presley fan club and also a memorabilia company. The event was a fan club convention on a Sunday afternoon, with – according to *NME* - "..over 1000 people.." Home movies were screened, as well as the 1971 documentary, *That's The Way It Is*. Radio 1 disc jockey David Hamilton hosted an Elvis dancing competition in the evening.

Foster And Allen were an ever-popular Irish folk duo who had had a crossover hit in 1982 with 'A Bunch Of Thyme' which reached No. 18. Two albums scraped into the Top 75 this year.

Ghulam Ali was a Pakistani ghazal and playback singer.

The Fureys & Davy Arthur were an Irish folk band who had a worldwide hit in 1981 with the standard 'When You Were Sweet Sixteen.' The single reached No. 14 in Britain and the band even appeared on *Top Of The Pops*.

Nusrat Fateh Ali Khan was a Pakistani singer known as the "Emperor of Qawwali", introducing this music to international audiences.

Other events at the Free Trade Hall

March 6th – Brass Band Championship
April 19th – Institute of Sales & Marketing Management Roadshow
June 7th -8th – World Evangelism Society

Elsewhere (Headliners Only):

Apollo: The Animals, Joan Armatrading, Bauhaus, Belle Stars, Big Country, Elkie Brooks, Bucks Fizz, Cannon & Ball, Eric Clapton, Billy Connolly, Culture Club, Def Leppard, Depeche Mode, Diamond Head, Dio, Duran Duran, Echo And The Bunnymen, Eurythmics, Flock Of Seagulls, Fun Boy Three, Peter Gabriel, Eddie Grant, Steve Hackett, Mike Harding, Nick Heyward, Imagination, Iron Maiden, Tom Jones, Judas Priest, Kajagoogoo, Kid Creole And The Coconuts, Kids From Fame, Level 42, Lindisfarne, Madness, Marillion, Johnny Mathis, Maze, Meat Loaf, Mezzaforte, Van Morrison, Motorhead, Gary Numan, OMD, Robert Plant, Public Image Ltd, Cliff Richard, Leo Sayer, Michael Schenker Group, The Shadows, Shakin' Stevens, The Stranglers, Tears For Fears, 10cc, Thin Lizzy, Thompson Twins, Toyah, Judi Tzuke, UB40, UFO, U2, Dionne Warwick, Wham! Whitesnake, Don Williams, Steve Winwood, Y&T, Paul Young, ZZ Top.

Palace Theatre : Stuart Burrows, Richard Clayderman, David Essex, The Houghton Weavers, Modern Jazz Quartet, Peter, Paul And Mary, Sky, Spandau Ballet, Freddie Starr, Tears For Fears, Weather Report.

1984		
March 2nd	KLAUS WUNDERLICH	
March 10th	*ANNUAL ST PATRICK'S VARIETY CONCERT* with Johnny McEvoy	*Margo; Vince Miller; Fr. Michael Cleary; Pat Phoenix*
March 13th	THE SMITHS	*Red Guitars*
April 9th	AN EVENING WITH DORIS STOKES	
May 8th	DON McLEAN	*Netty Brook with Guitar George*
May 22nd	SYD LAWRENCE ORCHESTRA	
June 3rd	ASIAN VARIETY CONCERT	
Sept 14th	CLEO LAINE; JOHNNY DANKWORTH	
Oct 12th	ROBERT WHITE	
Oct 13th	AZTEC CAMERA	*The Go-Betweens*
Oct 20th	NANCY WILSON; BUDDY GRECO; ASTRUD GILBERTO	
Oct 22nd	INTI ILLIMANI	
Oct 28th	SIAMSA TIRE (National Folk Theatre of Ireland)	
Nov 12th	HOLLY NEAR	
Nov 13th	JOHN MARTYN	
Nov 21st	AN EVENING WITH DORIS STOKES	
Nov 27th	*ST ANDREW'S SHOW* with Kenneth McKellar and Andy Stewart	
Dec 1st	ASIAN VARIETY CONCERT	
Dec 15th	BRENDAN SHINE	*Niall Toibin; Anna McGoldrick; Vince Miller*

THE SMITHS WERE ON THEIR first major British tour, promoting their eponymous first album (Rough Trade 1984). The 32-date tour was a huge success with sold out concerts. Their rider requested "£50 selection of flowers to include gladioli - NO ROSES"! A year later, The Smiths played the Palace Theatre but returned to the Free Trade Hall in autumn 1986 on what was to become their final tour.

Doris Stokes was a British spiritualist and professional medium. She wrote several best-selling books, the first of which was *Voices In My Ear.*

Don McLean was on a nineteen-date tour which would finish at London's Royal Festival Hall. He would not release a new studio album until 1987.

Robert White was an American singer who specialised in the "Irish tenor" style of John McCormack.

Aztec Camera's "main man" was Roddy Frame. The band's early singles on the Postcard label impressed both John Peel and the music press. Their first album, *High Land, Hard Rain* (Rough Trade 1983) had reached No. 22. Manchester was the twelfth stop on a fifteen-date British tour to promote the second album, *Knife* (WEA 1984) which was produced by Mark Knopfler of Dire Straits.

October 20th's concert saw the first appearances at the Free Trade Hall of Nancy Wilson and Astrud Gilberto, both singers and icons from the 1960's. **Buddy Greco** had appeared previously with Cleo Laine in 1962. **Nancy Wilson** was an America jazz singer who had worked with Cannonball Adderley. She had crossover success in the 1960's with, most notably, "How Glad I Am." **Astrud Glberto** was the singer of 'Girl From Ipanema' which she had recorded with Stan Getz and Joao Gilberto in 1963. The single went on to be a million seller. Gilberto later toured with Getz but then went solo. Gilberto saw her career revive in 1984 when 'Girl From Ipanema' was reissued and re-entered the British charts.

Inti Illimani were a Chilean folk music group who were working abroad at the time of General Pinochet's coup in 1973. The group stayed abroad in exile and continued to record and tour. In 1983 the group charted with their soundtrack album, *The Flight Of The Condor* (BBC 1983) for the television documentary series.

Holly Near was a singer/songwriter from California who often focussed on social and political issues. She formed her own Redwood record label and worked with such radical singers as Ronnie Gilbert and Pete Seeger. Her current releases were both collaborations: *Watch Out* (Redwood 1984), with John McCutcheon and Trapezoid and *Sing To Me The Dream* (Redwood 1984) with Inti Illimani.

John Martyn was on a twelve-date tour promoting his new album, *Sapphire* (Island 1984) which saw him returning to his original record label after being with WEA.

Kenneth McKellar had last appeared at the Free Trade Hall in 1960, but teamed up with fellow Scotsman **Andy Stewart** for a St Andrew's Show in November.

Other events at the Free Trade Hall

February 25th – Anti-Trident Convention
March 18th – International Dance Festival
May 20th – Arts For Labour
September 25th – Marks & Spencer Charity Fashion Show
November 9th – Alpine Extravaganza – folk groups from Austria, Italy, Switzerland and Yugoslavia

Elsewhere (Headliners Only):

Apollo: Accept, Barclay James Harvest, Shirley Bassey, Big Country, Blancmange, Blue Oyster Cult, Elkie Brooks, Bucks Fizz, Chris de Burgh, Camel, The Clash, Elvis Costello And The Attractions, The Crusaders, The Cure, Depeche Mode, Dio, Joe Dolan, Dr Hook, The Enid, David Essex, The Everly Brothers, Roberta Flack, Foster And Allen, The Grumbleweeds, Herbie Hancock, Hawkwind, Iron Maiden, Joe Jackson, Al Jarreau, Jethro Tull, Howard Jones, Kajagoogoo, Nik Kershaw, The Kinks, Kool And The Gang, James Last, Level 42, Lindisfarne, ManO'War, Marillion, Meatloaf, Metallica, The Moody Blues, Gary Moore, Motorhead, Alison Moyet, Nena, Gary Numan, OMD, Pallas, Pretenders, Charley Pride, Psychedelic Furs, Quiet Riot, Chris Rea, The Rods, Sade, Saga, Saxon, Leo Sayer, Scorpions, Simple Minds, Siouxsie And The Banshees, Status Quo, Style Council, Thompson Twins, Tina Turner, Twelfth Night, UFO, Ultravox, U2, Dionne Warwick, Whitesnake, Slim Whitman, Roger Whittaker, Don Williams, Bobby Womack,

Palace Theatre– The Commodores, Barbara Dickson, The Flying Pickets, Juan Martin, Van Morrison, Tom Robinson, Sky,

1985		
Jan 12th	GOSPEL CONCERT	
Feb 9th	*COME ALIVE FOR '85* - CND EXTRAVAGANZA	
March 9th	*ST PATRICK'S IRISH VARIETY CONCERT* Johnny McEvoy; Bridie Gallagher; Charlie Daze; Daniel O'Donnell; Father Michael Funge; Vince Miller (compère)	
March 15th	*ST PATRICK'S CONCERT* WITH JOE DOLAN & THE DRIFTERS	*Leo McCaffrey; Donna Duffin*
May 10th	MANCHESTER SCOTS NIGHT	
May 16th	THE ENID	*Glen Baker*
Sept 13th	THE CHAMELEONS	*Frank Sidebottom; The Membranes; Alternative TV*
Sept 20th	KODO DRUMMERS	
Nov 11th	JOHN MARTYN	
Nov 12th	THE FUREYS & DAVEY ARTHUR	
Nov 20th	ARMENIAN FOLK SONG AND DANCE ENSEMBLE	
Nov 25th	SIMPLY RED	*Live For The Weekend*
Dec 9th	AN EVENING WITH DORIS STOKES WITH *VOICES IN MY EAR*	
Dec 14th	BRENDAN SHINE CHRISTMAS SHOW	*Hal Roach; Anne Breen*

"COME ALIVE FOR 85 - MANCHESTER FESTIVAL FOR Peace" proclaimed the advertisement for the **CND Extravaganza** in February, held at the "Nuclear Free Trade Hall" (sic). The free event started at 6 pm and promised Bruce Kent, Chair of CND, E.P.Thompson, Petra Kelly, bands, an entertainers bar, stalls, side shows and videos.

The Enid returned to the Free Trade Hall as part of a seven-date tour promoting their new album, *The Spell* (Not On Label 1985).

The Chameleons hailed from Middleton in north Manchester. They were about to release their second album, *What Does Anything Mean ? Basically* (Statik 1985). The band used their Manchester Festival showcase to feature two local acts and one of their punk influences, Alternative TV, led by former *Sniffin' Glue* editor Mark Perry.

The Chameleons' rehearsal for this gig has been released as *Tripping Dogs* (Glass Pyramid 1990) and *Free Trade Hall Rehearsal* (Imaginary 1993).

The Kodo Drummers were a taiko drumming troupe based on Sado Island in Japan. The troupe had performed for thirteen nights at Queen Elizabeth Hall, London earlier in the year.

The Fureys & Davey Arthur returned to the Free Trade Hall this year. They were promoting another compilation album, *At The End Of The Day* (K-Tel 1985) which did not match the success of its predecessor, *Golden Days* (K-Tel 1984).

Simply Red were a Manchester band led by Mick Hucknall. The band were on a fourteen-date tour, promoting their album, *Picture Book* (Elektra 1985) which stayed in the charts for over two years. The album included the classic, 'Holding Back The Years' which was a No. 2 hit single on its reissue in 1986.

It was around this time that serious discussion was happening about replacing the Free Trade Hall with a new purpose-built venue for the Hallé Orchestra. There were three possible options: acquiring the adjacent Theatre Royal building and extending the Free Trade Hall onto its neighbour's site; building a new auditorium inside the Refuge Insurance building on Oxford Road (now, of course, a hotel) or a new build on derelict land on Lower Mosley Street alongside the G-Mex (now Manchester Central). Bob Scott, famous for his work in reviving both the Palace Theatre and Opera House in Manchester was keen on the Refuge building option. The council, however, preferred Lower Mosley Street which went ahead as the Bridgewater Hall. Beale (2000) explains how complicated the relationship was between the Hallé Orchestra and its venues. On July 4th The *Stage & Television Today* announced that "plans that Manchester's Free Trade Hall might be renamed after the Peterloo Massacre have been shelved." The article went on to describe this decision as "good news" - something of an understatement.

The International Club (later International One) opened on April 23rd this year in Anson Road, Longsight with Flaco Jimenez. With a wide variety of acts booked by Manchester legend Roger Eagle, the venue soon became central to the Manchester live scene. There is a listing of gigs at The International in Sykes (2012).

Other events at the Free Trade Hall

January 30th – Ukrainian Rally
September 7th – British Open Brass Band Championship
October 12th – British Federation Of Body Building Championships
December 26th -28th – Faraday Lectures

Elsewhere (Headliners Only)

Apollo: Bryan Adams, The Alarm, Adam Ant, Joan Armatrading, Billy, Frank & Hank, Blancmange, Blue Oyster Cult, Bon Jovi, Boomtown Rats, Bucks Fizz, Cameo, David Cassidy, China Crisis, Stanley Clarke and George Duke, Leonard Cohen, Lloyd Cole And The Commotions, The Commodores, Phil Collins, Billy

Connolly, Kid Creole And The Coconuts, The Cult, The Cure, The Damned, Dead Or Alive, Dexy's Midnight Runners, Bo Diddley, Al Di Meola Project, Dire Straits, Dr Hook, David Essex, The Everly Brothers, Foster & Allen, Frankie Goes To Hollywood, Gary Glitter, Go West, Mike Harding, Hawkwind, Millie Jackson, Elton John, Howard Jones, Chaka Khan, Killing Joke, King, The Kinks, James Last, Level 42, Lindisfarne, Nils Lofgren, Madness, Magnum, Marillion, Rik Mayall & Ben Elton, Maze, Meatloaf, Pat Metheney Group, , Gary Moore, Van Morrison, Rick Nelson, Gary Numan, OMD, Chris Rea, REO Speedwagon, Cliff Richard, Uli Roth, Sade, Saxon, Shalamar, Del Shannon, Siouxsie And The Banshees, Sister Sledge, Sky, Spear Of Destiny, Squeeze, The Stranglers, Style Council, Tears For Fears, Thin Lizzy, Thompson Twins, Tina Turner, Judie Tzuke, UFO, Midge Ure, Uriah Heep, Bobby Vee, Venom.

Opera House –Dave Brubeck Quartet, Carmel, Clannad, Lenny Henry, Kelly Montieth, Al Stewart.

Palace Theatre– Chas & Dave, The Hollies, BB King, Skellern & Stilgoe, The Smiths, Marti Webb.

1986		
Feb 8th	*BLACK AND WHITE FOR CHRIST* Gospel Choir Evening	
Feb 18th	FOSTER AND ALLEN	*Don Leather and Cindy; Manuel Bagorro*
March 7th	*FR. FULLEN MEMORIAL CONCERT* with Dermot Hegarty; Brendan Blake; Leo McAfferty; Chris Ball; Father Cotter & The Holy Road Show; Tony Howley; Paddy And The Wild Country	
March 15th	*ST PATRICK'S IRISH VARIETY CONCERT* with Johnny McEvoy; The All Priests Holy Road Show; Eileen Donaghy; Fr Michael Cleary	*The Mary Walsh and Francesca Lomax Irish Dancers*
June 4th	THE ALL PRIESTS HOLY ROAD SHOW	*St Malachy's Ceili Band*
June 14th	ALAAP	
Sept 26th	ASIAN FOLK EVENING	
Sept 30th	KLAUS WUNDERLICH	
Oct 2nd	ARMENIAN STATE CHOIR	
Oct 10th	NANA MOUSKOURI	
Oct 30th	THE SMITHS	*Raymonde*
Nov 3rd	*INDIAN MUSICAL EVENING* 'BOMBAY FEVER'	
Nov 4th	THE FUREYS & DAVEY ARTHUR	
Dec 13th	BRENDAN SHINE CHRISTMAS CONCERT	*Ann Breen; Shaun Connors; Vince Miller (compère)*
Dec 22nd 2 pm - 1030 pm	*THE FESTIVAL OF THE MILLIONS* WITH THE FALL	*A Certain Ratio; Courtney Pine; Jazz Defektors; The Supernatrals; Inner Sense Percussion*

ALAAP WERE PIONEERS OF UK BHANGRA, LED BY THEIR singer and producer, Channi Singh. Founded in the late 1970's, Alaap combined Western and Punjabi instruments to produce a modern Punjabi style which later became known as UK Bhangra.

Klaus Wunderlich's concert was advertised as starring "the world's greatest organist". The German keyboard maestro was about to release his new album, *From New York To Yokohama* (Conifer 1986).

Nana Mouskouri returned to the Free Trade Hall after an absence of five years. Earlier in the year her album, *Alone* (Philips 1986) reached No. 19 in the charts, her first hit album in a decade. She had had a surprise hit single with 'Only Love', the theme to the TV series, *Mistral's Daughter*, reaching No. 2 in Britain. The song was a worldwide hit that Mouskouri also sang in French, German and Spanish.

The Smiths made their second appearance at the Free Trade Hall this year on what was to be their final British tour. The band were now touring as a five-piece with Craig Gannon as second guitarist. Their album, *The Queen Is Dead* (Rough Trade 1986) was still in the charts. A week before the Smiths' Free Trade Hall appearance, their Kilburn National Ballroom appearance was transmitted by BBC Radio One and later released as the contractual obligation album, *Rank* (Rough Trade 1988).

The tour was notorious for its Preston Guild Hall date when Morrissey was struck by a missile from the audience and the band left the stage after only one number.

Johnny Rogan: "The violence in Preston led to a cancellation of the following night's show in Llandudno, but there was no way The Smiths were going to miss their hometown grand finale at Manchester's Free Trade Hall on 30 October. This was the eve of Johnny Marr's 23rd birthday..."

Tony Fletcher: "The tour's original schedule (before the cancelled shows were tacked back on to the end of it) called for it to conclude with two triumphant statements. One was a headliner at the Free Trade Hall, the seat of so much cultural and political history in Manchester, not least those shows with the Sex Pistols and Buzzcocks."

The Fall were having their most successful year so far in chart terms; their album, *Bend Sinister* (Beggar's Banquet 1986) reached No. 36 and their Free Trade Hall appearance coincided with their new single, 'Hey Luciani' which just scraped into the Top 60.

Other events at the Free Trade Hall

March 10th – RSPB Films
April 15th – The Bertil Fox Golden Body Builder Awards
September 25th – Anatoly Natan Sharansky – public meeting

Elsewhere (Headliners Only):

Apollo – Accept, AC/DC, Joan Armatrading, Shirley Bassey, Big Audio Dynamite,

Big Country, Black Sabbath, Bon Jovi, Billy Bragg, Bronski Beat, Bucks Fizz, Chris de Burgh, Cameo, Glen Campbell, Cheap Trick, Communards, Alice Cooper, The Cramps, Randy Crawford, The Damned, John Denver, Depeche Mode, Everything But The Girl, Five Star, Gary Glitter, Go West, GTR, Hawkwind, INXS, Iron Maiden, Joe Jackson, Al Jarreau, Killing Joke, Huey Lewis And The News, Lindisfarne, Magnum, Marillion, John Martyn, Metallica, Liza Minelli, The Moody Blues, Christy Moore, Motley Crue, Motorhead, Alison Moyet, Sinead O'Connor, OMD, Ozzy Osbourne, Owen Paul, P.I.L, Psychedelic Furs, The Ramones, Ratt, Red Wedge, Jennifer Rush, Sad Café, Saxon, Leo Sayer, The Shadows, Feargal Sharkey, Simply Red, Sting, The Stranglers, Tangerine Dream, James Taylor, Richard Thompson, Twisted Sister, Stevie Ray Vaughan, Suzanne Vega, Sheila Walsh and Alvin Stardust, WASP.

G-Mex – Festival Of The Tenth Summer (Smiths, New Order etc), Spandau Ballet.

Opera House - Clannad.

Palace Theatre - Rowan Atkinson, Barbara Dickson, Hinge & Bracket, Incantation, BB King, Syd Lawrence Orchestra, Van Morrison, Smith & Jones, The Spinners, Freddie Starr, Steeleye Span, Shakin' Stevens, Victoria Wood.

1987		
March 3rd	INCANTATION	
March 6th	*IRISH VARIETY – ST PATRICK'S DAY CONCERT.* Johnny McEvoy; The Holy Road Show	
March 22nd	*NORTHERN CARNIVAL AGAINST APARTHEID* MATINEE- Potato 5 and Laurel Aitken; The Railway Children; Frank Chickens; Ray Ramone; Simon Fanshawe EVENING – Microdisney; The Bhundu Boys; Damian; Tippa Irie (compère); Distant Cousins	
March 27th	BABLA KANCHAN	
April 11th	*MILLER MAGIC* Glenn Miller Band with Herb Miller and John Miller	
April 18th	*ASIAN CONCERT* with Mahesh Kumar and Party	
May 11th	SAWAI- KOTO ENSEMBLE	
June 10th	*SOLID SILVER 60'S SHOW* Gerry And The Pacemakers; The Searchers; Peter Sarstedt	
June 28th	DE DANAAN FEATURING DOLORES KEANE	
Sept 12th	HUMPHREY LYTTLETON; GEORGE MELLY AND THE FEETWARMERS; CHRIS BARBER'S JAZZ AND BLUES BAND	
Sept 16th	JOHN MARTYN	*Cry No More*
Sept 18th	VICTORIA WOOD	
Sept 19th	THE CHIEFTAINS	
Oct 11th	THE THREE DEGREES	*Brian and Stripe*
Oct 16th	*JAZZ 'N' JOPLIN* with The London Ragtime Orchestra	
Oct 31st	FOSTER AND ALLEN	
Nov 6th	BRENDAN SHINE	*Ann Breen; Charlie Daze*
Nov 14th	SHEILA WALSH	*Phil Keaggy*
Nov 16th	DON McLEAN	

ROCK ACTS HAD DISAPPEARED FROM THE FREE TRADE HALL apart from the bands that appeared at an anti-apartheid rally. September saw four concerts as part of the Manchester Festival.

Incantation played traditional South American music and formed to provide live backing music for a ballet called 'Ghost Dances.' The band comprised both European and Chilean musicians. They had a Top 10 album with *Cacharpaya (Panpipes Of The Andes)* (Beggars Banquet 1982) and a Top 20 hit single with the title track. The concert was advertised as "the haunting music of the Andes played on traditional panpipes, flutes, guitars and drums – by the musicians heard on the soundtrack of the film *The Mission*."

The Solid Silver 60's Show was advertised as a twenty-fifth anniversary celebration. **Peter Sarstedt** made his first return visit since 1969. This was alongside the first appearances at the Free Trade Hall of vintage Merseybeat groups **Gerry And The Pacemakers** and **The Searchers.** Gerry Marsden was the only original member from the chart-topping line-up from the 1960's and had a younger set of Pacemakers. The Searchers also had one original member - John McNally - following the departure of lead singer Mike Pender at the end of 1985. This type of nostalgia package has continued right up to the present day.

Three jazz veterans returned to the Free Trade Hall for the first time in many years; **Chris Barber** first appeared in 1956, while **Humphrey Lyttelton** and **George Melly** had both first appeared in 1952!

The Northern Carnival Against Apartheid started with a march in the morning from All Saints on Oxford Road before events at the Free Trade Hall in the afternoon and evening. The afternoon event featured speakers from the ANC and SWAPO and was compered by Lem Sissy (later better known as Lemn Sissay) and Glen Stevens.

Potato 5 were a ten-piece British ska group formed in 1983. They backed **Laurel Aitken,** "Godfather of Ska". Aitken had moved to Leicester in 1970 and had a minor hit with 'Rudi Got Married' during the ska revival in 1980. **Ray Ramone** was a guitarist from Moss Side. **The Railway Children** hailed from Wigan. Their current album was *Reunion Wilderness* (Factory 1987).

Microdisney were appropriate performers at the carnival; their second album was entitled *We Hate You South African Bastards* (Rough Trade 1984)! The band came from Cork in Ireland and were led by Cathal Coughlan and Sean O'Hagan. This year they released their fourth album, *Crooked Mile* (Virgin 1987). Microdisney's single, 'Town To Town', reached No. 55 this year. Coughlan went on to form Fatima Mansions while O'Hagan created The High Llamas.

The Bhundu Boys came from Zimbabwe and were incredibly popular in the mid-1980's, thanks to frequent radio play by John Peel and Andy Kershaw. Their album, *Tsvimbodzemoto* (Discafrique 1987) had been licensed from Shed Studios in Zimbabwe. Later in the year, the band would sign with Warners and even be a support act at Madonna's Wembley Stadium concerts. Unfortunately, the story of

The Bhundu Boys ended in tragedy.

Tippa Irie was a British reggae singer and DJ from Brixton. His biggest hit single was "Hello Darling" which reached No. 22 in 1986. Soul/pop band **Distant Cousins** came from Manchester and appeared frequently around the city at venues like The International Club. **Damian** was a popular drag act.

Babla and Kanchan were an Indian married couple musical duo whose brand of "chutney" music and desi made them popular, especially in the Caribbean.

De Danaan were an Irish folk group who formed in 1975. Dolores Keane was in the group's original line-up but left in 1976. She rejoined De Danaan in the mid-1980's to replace Mary Black. Their current album was *Ballroom* (De Danaan Music 1987).

Victoria Wood started to do solo stand-up comedy in 1983 and this Free Trade Hall appearance was one date on her one-woman show tour which included a sold out run at the London Palladium.

The Three Degrees' lead singer, Sheila Ferguson, had left the group in 1986, but the group carried on with original members Valerie Holiday and Helen Scott.

The London Ragtime Orchestra's concert was advertised as "recreating the authentic sound of orchestral ragtime and jazz from the turn of the century to the 1920's and featuring the works of Scott Joplin, Jelly Roll Morton and A.J. Piron."

Sheila Walsh was a Scottish born Christian singer/songwriter and appeared on television's *Rock Gospel Show*. Her seventh album was *Shadowlands* (Myrrh 1986).

Don McLean was on his 15th anniversary tour, a decade and a half since the success of 'American Pie'.

Other events at the Free Trade Hall

March 22nd – Anti-Apartheid Concert & Meeting
June 2nd – Asda Roadshow
September 25th – Spring Harvest 87 Celebration

Elsewhere (Headliners Only):

Apollo- A-ha, Anthrax, Atlantic Starr, Roy Ayers, Bad News, Barclay James Harvest, Beastie Boys, Blow Monkeys, Chris de Burgh, Cameo, Celtic Frost, Eric Clapton, Lloyd Cole and The Commotions, Elvis Costello And The Confederates, Randy Crawford, Robert Cray Band, The Cult, Terence Trent D'Arby, Def Leppard, Dio, Duran Duran, Europe, Five Star, the Gap Band, Bob Geldof, Gary Glitter, Go West, Guns N Roses, Helloween, The Hollies, The Human League, Engelbert Humperdinck, INXS, Freddie Jackson, Millie Jackson, Jethro Tull, Howard Jones, Tom Jones, Nik Kershaw, BB King, James Last, Lindisfarne, Little Steven, Magnum, Manowar, Johnny Mathis, Maze, Michael McDonald, Meat Loaf, Andrew Newton, Gary Numan, Sinead O'Connor, Daniel O'Donnell, Alexander O'Neal, P.I.L, Iggy Pop, The Pretenders, Psychedelic Furs, Chris Rea, Rose Marie, Run DMC, The Shadows, Simply Red, Slayer, Spear Of Destiny, Squeeze, Steeleye Span, Style Council, Donna Summer, Then Jericho, T'Pau, Suzanne Vega, Luther Vandross, Vow Wow, Wax, Wet Wet Wet, The Whispers.

G-Mex – Bryan Adams, Frankie Goes To Hollywood, Simply Red.

Palace Theatre - Kenny Ball, Acker Bilk, Cannon & Ball, Ben Elton, David Essex, Mike Harding, Ben E. King, Johnny Logan, Humphrey Lyttleton, Elaine Page, Courtney Pine Quartet, Pamela Stephenson, Marti Webb.

1988		
Jan 8th	ECHO AND THE BUNNYMEN	*The Primitives*
Jan 9th	ECHO AND THE BUNNYMEN	*The Primitives*
Feb 1st	*ASIAN CONCERT* with Nada Hussein	
Feb 27th	*ST PATRICK'S VARIETY CONCERT* with Johnny McEvoy	*Susan McCann; Father Michael Cleary; All Priests Holy Roadshow*
March 12th	THE SPINNERS	
March 19th	SIAMSA TIRE (National Folk Theatre of Ireland)	
March 25th	LOOSE TUBES; ANDY SHEPPARD QUINTET	
April 23rd	MIRIAM MAKEBA	
June 1st	SINEAD O'CONNOR	
July 10th	NUSRAT FATEH ALI KHAN	
July 15th	JOHN LEE HOOKER	*Big Town Playboys*
Sept 23rd	NATIONAL YOUTH JAZZ ORCHESTRA; KENNY BAKER	*Don Lusher; Danny Moss*
Sept 27th	THE PEKING ACROBATS	
Oct 1st	NANA MOUSKOURI	
Dec 10th	BRENDAN SHINE CHRISTMAS SHOW	*Mary O'Hara; Ann Breen; Charlie Daze*
Dec 30th	*ASIAN FAMILY CONCERT*	

BY NOW THE FREE TRADE HALL WAS BEING SQUEEZED FROM both sides; indie and world music at International One and Two and mainstream pop, rock and country music at the Apollo.

Liverpool band **Echo & The Bunnymen** were formed in 1978 and signed to the Zoo label. Their eponymous fifth album had been released in 1987 and reached No. 4. Later in 1988 lead singer Ian McCulloch left the band to go solo.

The Spinners were on their *Final Fling*; this was advertised as the only Manchester date on their National Farewell Tour. This was not their last appearance at the Free Trade Hall; see 1994!

Loose Tubes were a British jazz big band who formed in 1983 after a jazz workshop organised by Graham Collier. The band had twenty-one players and was run as a co-operative. Loose Tubes played the Proms in 1987. Their third album was *Open Letter* (Editions EG 1988). This was a double bill with the **Andy Sheppard Quintet.** Sheppard was an award-winning British jazz saxophonist who released his first solo album this year.

Miriam Makeba was a South African singer who was a strong critic of apartheid and became an exile. Mentored by Harry Belafonte, Makeba's career flourished in the USA until she married Stokely Carmichael, the leader of the Black Panther Party. She later toured with Paul Simon on his Graceland Tour. Her book, *Makeba - My Story* had just been published in paperback.

Sinead O'Connor grew up in suburban Dublin and had been singing in public since her mid-teens. She signed to Ensign Records and released her first single in October 1987. O'Connor's breakthrough single 'Mandinga' was released in January 1988 and reached No. 17, while her first album, *The Lion And The Cobra* (Ensign 1987) reached No. 27. O'Connor's only Free Trade Hall appearance was part of a mini-tour of Britain.

John Lee Hooker experienced a renaissance in the last decade or so of his life. His album *The Healer* (Silvertone 1989) had such famous guests as Keith Richards, Carlos Santana and Bonnie Raitt and became a best seller.

Hooker's Free Trade Hall gigs in July 1988 and July 1990 were both promoted by Manchester music legend Roger Eagle. Advance tickets for the first gig did not sell very well, but on the night things had changed. Brian Rae: "So I took (Roger Eagle) out for something to eat around tea-time, he was really worried by this time. But when we got back to the Free Trade Hall there was a queue half way round the building, people had got coaches from as far away as Newcastle and Carlisle without tickets, the place was absolutely packed." (Sykes 2012)

The National Youth Jazz Orchestra was founded in 1965, starting as the London Schools Jazz Orchestra and going on to become a national orchestra. Their alumni list is extraordinary including amongst its singers, Carol Kenyon, Julia Fordham and Amy Winehouse.

The Peking Acrobats were billed as "direct from The People's Republic Of China".

Nana Mouskouri returned to the Free Trade Hall promoting a new compilation album, *The Magic Of Nana Mouskouri* (Philips 1988). This was her tenth – and final - appearance at the Free Trade Hall.

Other events at the Free Trade Hall

January 30th – Alpha & Omega – evangelical musical
March 14th – RSPB Wildlife Films
March 26th – Ashton-on-Mersey Youth Showband
September 15th – Body & Soul – fashion and dance show
November 11th – Remembrance Evening concert
December 16th – *Manchester Evening News* OAP's Variety Show

Elsewhere (Headliners Only)

Apollo – The Adventurers, A-ha, The Alarm, All About Eve, Joan Armatrading, Aswad, Boy George, Elkie Brooks, Johnny Cash, The Christians, Cinderella, Clannad, Billy Connolly, Ry Cooder, Alice Cooper, Julian Cope, Robert Cray, Will Downing, Harry Enfield, Erasure, Everything But The Girl, Julia Fordham, Art Garfunkel, Gary Glitter, Nanci Griffith, Guns N Roses, Hawkwind, Helloween, Bruce Hornsby And The Range, Hothouse Flowers, The Icicle Works, Judas Priest, The Kinks, Magnum, Barry Manilow, Marillion, Maxi Priest, Meatloaf, Megadeth, Metallica, The Mission, Van Morrison, Andrew Newton, Ted Nugent, Gary Numan, Billy Ocean, Daniel O'Donnell, Alexander O'Neal, Jimmy Page, Robert Palmer, Ray Parker Jr, The Pasadenas, Robert Plant, The Pogues, Public Enemy, Run DMC, Salt 'N, Pepa, Saxon, Leo Sayer, Siouxsie And The Banshees, Slayer, Sweet Honey In The Rock, David Sylvian, James Taylor, The Temptations, T'Pau, Bonnie Tyler, Uriah Heep, Stevie Ray Vaughan, Barry White, Don Williams, Womack And Womack.

Odeon- (first live show in fifteen years) – John McLaughlin Trio.

Opera House – Billy Bragg, Rory Bremner, Steve Hackett, Hale & Pace, Barry Humphries, Tanita Tikaram.

Palace Theatre – Dave Allen, Shirley Bassey, Max Boyce, David Essex, Rory Gallagher, Lenny Henry, Cleo Laine & John Dankworth, Shakin' Stevens, Al Stewart.

1989		
March 1st	KLAUS WUNDERLICH	
March 11th	JOHNNY McEVOY	*All Priests Holy Roadshow; Bridie Gallagher; Sister Marie And Friends*
March 18th	JAMES	*Inspiral Carpets*
April 14th	FOSTER AND ALLEN	
May 14th	TED HEATH BAND featuring Lita Roza and Denis Lotis	
May 31st	10,000 MANIACS	*Kevin McDermott Orchestra*
June 14th	A CERTAIN RATIO	*808 State*
July 7th	IT BITES	
July 13th	THE FALL	*Man From Delmonte; The Sandmen*
Sept 6th	RAVI SHANKAR with Shubho Shankar and Kumar Bose	
Sept 12th	CHRIS BARBER'S JAZZ AND BLUES BAND with Paul Jones	
Oct 16th	CHRISTY MOORE	*Cindy Lee Berryhill*
Oct 17th	SUGARCUBES	
Oct 31st	CZECH ARMY CENTRAL BAND	
Nov 1st	JESUS AND MARY CHAIN	*Perfect Disaster*
Nov 4th	GLENN MILLER ORCHESTRA (UK)	*The Moonlight Serenaders; Uptown Hall Gang*
Nov 5th	LIONEL HAMPTON AND HIS ORCHESTRA	
Nov 18th	HAPPY MONDAYS	*Northside; MC Buzz B*
Dec 16th	BRENDAN SHINE'S CHRISTMAS SHOW	

VETERAN JAZZ ACTS CHRIS BARBER AND LIONEL HAMPTON made return appearances to the Free Trade Hall. World music and Irish acts were beginning to be a regular feature at the venue. Across town, the International 2 in Plymouth Grove closed down after five years.

James had formed in 1982 and had released their first EP on Factory. Their March appearance was the fourth of a short six-date British tour. Later in the year James played two nights at The Ritz and would play the Apollo in December. During the following year they would play Maine Road Stadium and G-Mex.

10,000 Maniacs were touring to promote their album, *Blind Man's Zoo* (Elektra 1989) which would reach No.18, their most successful release so far. They had previously played at The International in 1987.

A Certain Ratio were formed in 1977 and signed to Factory Records. The band later left Factory, signing with a major label. Their album, *Good Together* (A&M 1989) was released later in the year.

It Bites had their chart peak in 1986 when their second single, 'Calling All The Heroes' reached No. 6. 1989 saw the group move to a harder sound with *Eat Me In St Louis* (Virgin 1989) which was less successful. It Bites were still a popular live act.

Paul Jones was lead singer with Manfred Mann until 1966 and formed The Blues Band in the 1980's. His extraordinary harmonica playing still tends to be under-rated. This year he appeared as a guest with **Chris Barber**.

Irish singer and campaigner **Christy Moore** had previously been a member of Planxty and Moving Hearts before resuming his solo career. Moore was an extraordinary live performer. His current album was *Voyage* (WEA 1989).

Sugarcubes were that rarest of things, an Icelandic rock band. Even rarer was their international success with their first album, *Life's Too Good*. (One Little Indian 1988). The band had just released their second album, *Here, Today, Tomorrow, Next Week !* (One Little Indian 1989) Their lead singer, Bjork, would go on to even greater success as a solo artist.

Jesus & Mary Chain were from East Kilbride in Scotland and featured brothers Jim and William Reid. The group were touring to promote their fourth album, *Automatic* (Blanco y Negro 1989) which reached No. 11.

Happy Mondays were from Salford. Their EP *Madchester Rave On* (Factory 1989) had just been released and would reach No. 19. The band's breakthrough came the following year with two Top 5 singles and a Top 5 album when the Madchester boom took off. Tom Hingley, one time singer with Inspiral Carpets was at the gig:

"*When the Mondays came on stage; there was so much ganja smoke in the hall, mixed with dry ice, that you couldn't see any of the band- all you could see were vague shapes, eclipsed from behind by the frequent visual stab of the lights of the sequencers. It looked like the end of ET, when the aliens stand on the prow of the spaceship, blemished by a flood of light. It was the best concert I have ever seen...*"

Simon Spence: "*The Mondays' request to have the venue's seating removed had been denied and Shaun (Ryder) said before the gig that he hoped the audience would rip the seats out. At the start of the evening a large gang of lads rushed the door in a show of strength, forcing their way past the doormen, and there were fights out front between ticket touts, merchandisers and bootleggers. None of this was new to the Mondays, but it was on a different scale to what they had been accustomed to, and they revelled in the madness.*" This concert was filmed and was released as *One Louder* on VHS. Inevitably, excerpts can be seen on YouTube.

I suppose that you had to be there to appreciate the atmosphere.

Ted Heath had died in 1969 but his famous band reformed in 1976 with the full approval of his family. This year saw a reunion with two of the band's former vocalists. **Dennis Lotis** was from South Africa and had joined the Ted Heath Orchestra in the early 1950's singing alongside **Lita Roza,** a Liverpudlian. Roza had reached No. 1 in the singles charts in 1953 with 'How Much Is That Doggy In The Window?' and was voted Top British Female Singer in the *NME* Polls for five consecutive years in the early 1950's.

Other events at the Free Trade Hall

May 27th -28th – Yanomamo – Songs Of The Forest

Elsewhere (Headliners Only)

Apollo – All About Eve, Anthrax, The Bangles, Shirley Bassey, Big Country, Black, Black Sabbath, Blue Oyster Cult, Brother Beyond, Clannad, Elvis Costello, The Cult, Jim Davidson, Miles Davis, Deacon Blue, Duran Duran, David Essex, Europe, The Everly Brothers, Fairground Attraction, Fat Boys, Climie Fisher, Julia Fordham, Nanci Griffith, Gypsy Kings, Hawkwind, Hue & Cry, It Bites, Jethro Tull, Bert Kaempfert, Chaka Khan, BB King, Marillion, Maze, The Monkees, Van Morrison, Gary Numan, Sinead O'Connor, Daniel O'Donnell, REM, Scorpions, Neil Sedaka, The Shadows, Michelle Shocked, Simply Red, Skid Row, Spandau Ballet, The Stranglers, The Temptations, 10,000 Maniacs, The The, Then Jericho, Transvision Vamp, Judie Tzuke, WASP, Waterboys, Wishbone Ash, Womack And Womack, Yazz.

G-Mex – Erasure, Level 42, Alexander O'Neal.

Opera House – Julian Clary, Phil Cool, Barbara Dickson, Hale & Pace, Mike Harding, Don McLean, Jackie Mason, Shakin' Stevens.

Palace Theatre – Phil Cool, Ken Dodd, Ben Elton, French & Saunders, Inti-Illimani, Tammy Wynette.

The Nineties

The Final Years

1990		
March 9th	*ST PATRICK'S GALA CONCERT* with Susan McCann; Brendan Grace	
March 25th	*GALA CHARITY CONCERT* (tribute to Ernie Watson - trumpeter) Alan Randall; Denise Nolan; The Houghton Weavers; The Northern Dance Orchestra; Shades Of Kenton Orchestra	
April 21st	TED HEATH BAND with Lita Roza and Dennis Cotis	
May 19th	JULIAN CLARY	*Jungr and Parker; Russell Churney*
May 25th	MARTIN STEPHENSON AND THE DAINTEES	*Ruby Blue*
July 8th	JOHN LEE HOOKER and The Coast To Coast Blues Band	*Johnny Mars with The Brendan Gore Band*
Sept 13th	THE BLUE NILE	*Shawn Colvin*
Oct 6th	THE CHICK COREA ELEKTRIC BAND	
Oct 19th	COUNT BASIE ORCHESTRA; Special Guest: Nancy Wilson	
Oct 24th	THE MASSED BANDS OF THE ROYAL AIR FORCE	*The Beverley Sisters; Roy Castle (guest compère)*
Nov 18th	OSCAR PETERSON QUARTET	
Nov 19th	ROY HARPER	
Nov 26th	THE BEAUTIFUL SOUTH	*Mike Greaves & Lonesome Too*

SEVERAL JAZZ ACTS RETURNED TO THE FREE TRADE HALL after many decades of absence.

Julian Clary was originally billed as the Joan Collins Fan Club and had been seen on Channel Four's *Saturday Live*. His Free Trade Hall appearance was part of his *Mincing Machine Tour*. Clary's *Sticky Moments* show on Channel Four ran to ten episodes where his single-entendre humour could be seen.

Martin Stephenson And The Daintees hailed from the North East of England. Their fourth album, *Salutation Road* (Kitchenware 1990) reached No. 35. The band enjoyed much critical acclaim but record sales were disappointing.

The Blue Nile were from Glasgow and appeared at the Free Trade Hall as the opening night of their first British tour which consisted of only six dates. The band's second album, *Hats* (Linn 1989) had reached No. 12.

The Chick Corea Elektric Band played jazz fusion and had released their fourth album, *Inside Out* (GRP 1990). Corea had played with bassist Stanley Clarke in Return To Forever.

Count Basie himself had died in 1984 but an orchestra bearing his name (like Glenn Miller's and many others) continued to tour. The orchestra was now led by Frank Foster who had played tenor saxophone for Basie from 1953 to 1964. Carmen Bradford had joined the orchestra as singer in 1982, in her early twenties and remained with them after Basie's death. Special guest, **Nancy Wilson**, made a second appearance at the Free Trade Hall.

Oscar Peterson was now reunited with Herb Ellis and Ray Brown who had played with him in the 1950's.

Roy Harper had first appeared at the Free Trade Hall way back in 1970. In May he had released his sixteenth solo album, *Once* (Awareness 1990).

The Beautiful South had formed out of The Housemartins and this was their *Tonight I Fancy Myself Tour*, Manchester being the last of ten British dates. They had achieved a No. 1 single earlier in the autumn with 'A Little Time.' The band's second album, *Choke* (Go Discs 1990) reached No. 2.

Manchester University's Academy (generally known as Academy One) opened this year with a capacity of 2000 –usually standing -and attracted both students and the general public. This was yet another rival to the Free Trade Hall.

Other events at the Free Trade Hall

March 10th – Royal Air Force Spectacular
October 12th – The Band Of HM Royal Marines
October 24th - 50th Anniversary of the Battle Of Britain concert with Roy Castle and The Beverley Sisters

Elsewhere (Headliners Only) -

Apollo- Adeva, The Alarm, Joan Armatrading, Aztec Camera, Barclay James Harvest, The Barron Knights, Jeff Beck, Tony Bennett, Black Sabbath, Brother Beyond, Roy "Chubby" Brown, Belinda Carlisle, The Christians, Richard Clayderman, Lloyd Cole, Ry Cooder & David Lindley, The Cramps, Del Amitri, John Denver, Dio, Jason Donovan, Will Downing, Steve Earle, En Vogue, Everything But The Girl, Fish, Five Star, Guns N Roses, The Gypsy Kings, Hale & Pace, Hall And Oates, Hawkwind, Jeff Healey Band, The Hollies, Bruce Hornsby And The Range, Hothouse Flowers, Iron Maiden, It Bites, Peggy Lee, Jerry Lee Lewis, Michael McDonald, Magnum, Barry Manilow, The Mission, Gary Moore, Van Morrison, Neville Brothers, Andrew Newton, Gary Numan, Daniel O'Donnell, Pixies, Robert Plant, The Pogues, Prefab

Sprout, Public Enemy, Queensryche, Red Hot Chili Peppers, Reggae Philharmonic Orchestra, Runrig, Santana, Joe Satriani, The Shadows, Smokie, Spandau Ballet, Edwin Starr, The Stranglers, Tangerine Dream, Tears For Fears, Thunder, Tanita Tikaram, UB40, Suzanne Vega, Waterboys, Paul Weller, Barry White, White Lion, Paul Young.

G-Mex- Elkie Brooks, Erasure, Gary Glitter, Happy Mondays, Inspiral Carpets, INXS, James, Kenny Rogers, Simply Red, Soul II Soul, Status Quo.

Opera House – Eddie Fisher, Ted Heath Band, Engelbert Humperdinck, Alan King, Eartha Kitt, Courtney Pine, Charley Pride, Shakin' Stevens, Victoria Wood.

Palace Theatre– David Essex, Dizzy Gillespie And The United Nations Orchestra, *It's Only Rock 'n' Roll But We Like it Part 1*, Nana Mouskouri, Emo Philips, Victor Spinetti, Peter Ustinov.

1991		
March 9th	*ST PATRICK'S GALA CONCERT* – Johnny McEvoy	*The All Priests Holy Road Show; Margo*
March 16th	CLIFF RICHARD (Gospel Concert)	
March 30th	*SPIRITUALISM 1991*	
April 27th	ROMANIAN NATIONAL MUSIC & DANCE COMPANY	
May 24th	HARRY CONNICK JR & The Harry Connick Jr Orchestra	
May 27th	THE CHIPPENDALES	
June 11th	THE CHARLATANS	*Catherine Wheel*
Sept 4th	THE FAIRER SAX	
Sept 5th	BRANFORD MARSALIS	*Marcus Roberts*
Sept 16th	BEVERLEY CRAVEN	
Oct 18th	THE MASSED BANDS OF THE ROYAL AIR FORCE (compère Roy Castle)	
Oct 22nd	DON McLEAN	*Jamie Marshall Band*
Nov 22nd	BUDDY GUY BLUES BAND	*John Campbell Band*
Dec 6th	BONNIE RAITT	*Bela Fleck And The Flecktones*

THE HANDFUL OF CONCERTS THIS YEAR INCLUDED JAZZ, blues, gospel, Irish and even a male burlesque troupe.

Cliff Richard made his final Free Trade Hall appearance this year. Amazingly, his first Free Trade Hall show was 33 years previously in 1958! This was part of another gospel tour, the fourth of twelve dates.

Jazz singer and pianist, **Harry Connick Jr** had recently won a Grammy for Best Jazz Vocal Performance for his soundtrack for the film *When Harry Met Sally*. Connick also had an acting role in *Memphis Belle*. His only Free Trade Hall appearance was sold out.

The Charlatans hailed from the West Midlands and were based in Cheshire, but they were usually classed as a "Manchester band." The group's first album, *Some Friendly* (Situation Two 1990) entered the charts at No. 1. Their single 'The Only One I Know' reached No. 9.

The Fairer Sax were an American female saxophone group specialising in playing classical music, while fellow sax player **Branford Marsalis** worked with Sting for nearly fifteen years on various albums and tours. Marsalis had his own quartet and his album, *Crazy People Music* (CBS 1990) was the turning point in his career.

Beverley Craven's single 'Promise Me' had reached No. 3 in the charts in the spring. Her eponymous first album (Epic 1990) also reached that position and stayed in the charts for a whole year, achieving a Double Platinum disc. Craven won Best British Newcomer Award at the 1992 Brits.

Don McLean's concert in October was filmed and recorded and is still available on DVD. This was two decades after the phenomenal success of his singles 'American Pie' and 'Vincent'. It remains a fascinating record of what the Free Trade Hall looked like in the 1990's. McLean starts with one other guitarist and is later joined by his six-piece band.

Buddy Guy had last appeared at the Free Trade Hall over a quarter of a century earlier - in 1965. Guy was enjoying something of a career revival. His album, *Damn Right I Got The Blues* (Silvertone 1991) reached No. 43, his first to chart in Britain. Following the success of John Lee Hooker's *The Healer* album with its superstar guests, Silvertone did the same thing for Buddy Guy and guests included Mark Knopfler, Jeff Beck and Eric Clapton.

Bonnie Raitt's career had started showcasing her slide guitar and had been recording since the early 1970's. The 1990's saw Raitt develop a more popular, ballad style. 'I Can't Make You Love Me' only reached No. 50 in the British singles charts and its parent album *Nick Of Time* (Capitol 1990) did not even enter the Top 50, contrasting with its No. 1 status in the USA.

Other events at the Free Trade Hall

August 30th – Nigel Kennedy plays Vivaldi's The Four Seasons
October 7th – RSPB Wildlife Films

Elsewhere (Headliners Only)

Apollo- A-Ha, Allman Brothers Band, Chuck Berry, Big Country, The Black Crowes, Paul Brady Band, Elkie Brooks, Roy "Chubby" Brown, Cinderella, Clannad, Lloyd Cole, Color Me Badd, Robert Cray, Deacon Blue, Deep Purple, Cathy Dennis, John Denver, Will Downing, Duane Eddy, ELO Part 2, Joe Ely, The Everly Brothers, Fish, Gypsy Kings, Deborah Harry, Chesney Hawkes, Lenny Henry, The Hollies, Hue & Cry, Engelbert Humperdinck, Ice Cube, Joe Jackson, Jethro Tull, Judas Priest, Kraftwerk, Level 42, Shirley MacLaine, Magnum, Marillion, Maze, Megadeth, Kylie Minogue, The Moody Blues, Van Morrison, Motorhead, Gary Numan, OMD, Robert Palmer, Runrig, Salt 'N' Pepa, Seal, Slayer, Jimmy Sommerville, Squeeze, Sting, Tanita Tikaram, T'Pau, Transvision Vamp, Midge Ure, Vanilla Ice, Whispers, Tammy Wynette, Paul Young

G-Mex – The Beach Boys, Jose Carreras, The Cult, 808 State, Gary Glitter, New Kids On The Block, Pixies, Chris Rea, David Lee Roth, Status Quo, Rod Stewart, The Wonder Stuff.

Opera House – Duke Ellington Orchestra.

Palace Theatre – Johnny Cash & Family, Phil Cool, Barbara Dickson, Ken Dodd, David Essex, Kym Mazelle, Elaine Page, Courtney Pine, The Spinners, Rebecca Storm.

1992		
March 1st	JAN GARBAREK	*Eberhard Weber; Rainer Bruninghaus; Marilyn Mazur*
March 2nd	COWBOY JUNKIES	*Steve Forbert*
March 6th	KLAUS WUNDERLICH	
March 7th	*ST PATRICK'S VARIETY CONCERT*. Margo; Fr. Michael Cleary; John Kerr; Liam Harvey	*Bridie Gallagher*
March 20th	DIZZY GILLESPIE AND THE BEBOP BAND	
April 10th	TORI AMOS	*Boo Hewerdine*
April 25th	TED HEATH BAND with Lita Roza and Dennis Lotis	
April 28th	ORNETTE COLEMAN	*Prime Time*
May 5th	MARY BLACK	
June 6th	RICHARD THOMPSON	*Boo Hewerdine*
June 21st	JOAN ARMATRADING	*Martyn Joseph*
June 22nd	JOHN McLAUGHLIN TRIO AND KATIA LABEQUE	*Trilok Gurtu; Dominique Di Piazza*
July 16th	THE SPECTACULAR DRUMMERS OF BURUNDI	*Stella Chiweshe*
Sept 27th	CLAN ALBA FEATURING DICK GAUGHAN	
Sept 29th	K.D. LANG	
Oct 1st	JACQUES LOUSSIER AND THE PLAY BACH TRIO	
Oct 3rd	THE FALL	*The Sandmen*
Oct 11th	HAPPY MONDAYS	*Stereo MC's*
Oct 12th	DAVE BRUBECK QUARTET	
Dec 17th	JAMES	*The Spaceheads*

A FEW JAZZ ACTS RETURNED TO THE FREE TRADE HALL – Dizzy Gillespie; Jacques Loussier; Ornette Coleman; John McLaughlin and Dave Brubeck.

Jan Garbarek was a Norwegian jazz soprano and tenor saxophonist recording on the ECM label. He had begun his career in the 1960's and had worked with Keith Jarrett's Quartet. Gabarek later incorporated world music into his compositions.

The alternative country band **Cowboy Junkies** came to public attention with their second album, *The Trinity Sessions* (RCA 1988) which mixed original songs and country standards with Lou Reed's 'Sweet Jane'. The album had been recorded in the Church of Holy Trinity in Toronto, using the building's natural reverb. Their fourth album, *Black Eyed Man* (RCA 1992) reached No. 21 in the British charts.

Dizzy Glliespie was now 75 years old and celebrating his diamond jubilee of 60 years of playing jazz.

Tori Amos made the first of two appearances at the Free Trade Hall. Her breakthrough album, *Little Earthquakes* (East West 1992) reached No.14. Amos's follow-up, *Under The Pink* (East West 1994) entered the charts at No. 1.

The Ted Heath Band featured Kenny Baker and Jack Parnell, both of whom had played the Free Trade Hall in the past.

Irish folk singer **Mary Black** visited the Free Trade Hall as part of a sell-out tour which included the Royal Albert Hall. Her album, *Babes In The Wood* (Grapevine 1991) reached No.1 in Ireland, but failed to chart in Britain. Subsequent album releases did enter the British charts, the most successful being *Circus* (Grapevine 1995) which reached No. 16.

Richard Thompson had already appeared at the Free Trade Hall - with Fairport Convention; with Sour Grapes supporting Traffic in 1974 and with his then wife Linda in 1975. His sixth solo album, *Rumour And Sigh* (Capitol 1991) had reached No. 32 in Britain, his first Top 40 album.

Joan Armatrading made her sole Free Trade Hall appearance this year; she was touring to promote *Square The Circle* (A&M 1992), her final album on that label. The album only reached No. 34. Armatrading subsequently signed to RCA.

Guitarist **John McLaughlin** had previously appeared at the Free Trade Hall with two different line-ups of the Mahavishnu Orchestra and with Shakti. His 1992 appearance was with virtuoso pianist Katia Labeque. Labeque had played in a piano duo with her sister, Marielle. Their performance of Gershwin's *Rhapsody In Blue* had been a huge hit.

The Burundi Drummers from Africa had been touring the world since the 1960's. Several Western acts had used their music in different ways - Burundi Stephenson Black needlessly added "rock" backing in 1971; Joni Mitchell sampled the drums on her song, 'The Jungle Line' on the album *The Hissing Of Summer Lawns* (Asylum 1975) while both Bow Wow Wow and Adam & The Ants had hit singles with the unique Burundi drum sound. The drummers were an eighteen-strong all-male group whose act centred around the gigantic Inkiranya drum. A live concert must have been mesmerising.

Clan Alba was formed by Dick Gaughan along with seven fellow Scottish folk musicians. The group made their debut at the 1992 Edinburgh Folk Festival.

k.d. lang had been releasing records since the early 1980's. Her album *Ingenue* (Sire 1992) saw her widening her audience and was a million seller in the USA. It reached No. 3 in Britain and stayed in the charts for a whole year. This sole Free Trade Hall appearance was sold out.

Jacques Loussier returned to the Free Trade Hall in 1992 for the last time with his tenth appearance, after a gap of seventeen years. This was billed as "Back To Bach"! His first Free Trade Hall concert was back in 1966. Curiously, Loussier's only chart album in Britain was the compilation, *The Best Of Play Bach* (Start 1985).

The Fall appeared for the second time at the Free Trade Hall in October. Six months previously they had released the album, *Code, Selfish* (Cog Sinister 1992).

Happy Mondays were promoting their album, *...Yes Please !* (Factory 1992) which reached No. 14. The band's career had peaked in 1990 with their G-Mex concert and Top 5 album, *Pills 'N' Thrills And Bellyaches* (Factory 1990).

The Dave Brubeck Quartet played the Free Trade Hall for the final time in October of this year, after a gap of 25 years. Brubeck's first Free Trade Hall appearance was in 1958 and only he remained a constant feature in his quartet. Saxophone player Paul Desmond had died in 1977.

The Free Trade Hall was the last stop for **James** on a short tour of five acoustic shows with a 60 minute set which was sold out. Andy Spinoza reported in the *Manchester Evening News*: "...classic James songs like 'Sit Down', 'Poison', 'Johnny Yen' and 'Walking The Ghost' gained from being stripped down to bare essentials, though the quieter moments tended to be lost among the youthful audience, out for a pre-Christmas night of boisterous fun. The band, ranged in a line across the stage with the drummer far left, looked like a bunch of seasoned travellers returned home with stories to tell."

Other events at the Free Trade Hall

June 30th – July 11th – Hallé Proms
October 9th - Band Of HM Royal Marines

Elsewhere (Headliners Only)-

Apollo- Anthrax, Sandra Bernhard, The B52's, Mary Black, The Black Crowes, Black Sabbath, Bjorn Again, Blur, The Charlatans, Joe Cocker, Chick Corea, Randy Crawford, Crosby Stills And Nash, Crowded House, Del Amitri, ELP, Erasure (14 nights!), Europe, The Four Tops, Amy Grant, Hawkwind, Jesus And Mary Chain, Tom Jones, The Jordanaires, Gladys Knight, James Last, Megadeth, Morrissey, Gary Numan, Ozzy Osbourne, Public Enemy, Shakespear's Sister, Curtis Stigers, Take That, Thunder, Toss the Feathers, Toto, Verve, WASP, Paul Weller, Wet Wet Wet, Barry White.

G-Mex – The Cure, Extreme, Madness, Metallica, Lisa Stansfield, Status Quo, U2.

Opera House – Michael Ball, The Chippendales, Mike Harding, Jethro, Punt & Dennis, Freddie Starr, Ruby Wax.

Palace Theatre - Billy Connolly, Lou Reed.

1993		
March 1st	TASMIN ARCHER	*Dean Collinson*
March 20th	BEN ELTON	
April 5th	BEN ELTON	
April 17th	THE RED ARMY OF RUSSIA ENSEMBLE	
April 23rd	NORMAN WISDOM	
May 23rd	JOE LOSS ORCHESTRA with Todd Miller	*Joan Regan*
May 27th	BEN ELTON	
May 31st	VICTORIA WOOD	
June 1st	VICTORIA WOOD	
June 2nd	VICTORIA WOOD	
June 3rd	VICTORIA WOOD	
June 7th	VICTORIA WOOD	
June 8th	VICTORIA WOOD	
June 9th	VICTORIA WOOD	
June 10th	VICTORIA WOOD	
Sept 15th	*CURVES, CONTOURS & BODY HORNS - 40TH BIRTHDAY OF THE FENDER STRATOCASTER* with Rory Gallagher; Sonny Curtis; Debbie Davies and The Strat Band	*Sherman Robertson*
Sept 17th	*THE BRADSHAWS..AN' ALL THAT*	
Sept 18th	*THE BRADSHAWS..AN' ALL THAT*	
Sept 24th	JACK DEE	*Richard Morton*
Sept 25th	JACK DEE	*Richard Morton*
Oct 15th	LENNY HENRY	
Oct 29th	DON McLEAN	
Dec 23rd	THE CARE BEARS CHRISTMAS SHOW	

Tasmin Archer was from Bradford and had signed to EMI in 1990. Her first single 'Sleeping Satellite' reached No.1 and her album, *Great Expectations* (EMI 1992) reached No. 8. Follow-up releases were less successful.

This year saw something of a reinvention of the Free Trade Hall as a comedy venue. **Ben Elton** had started doing stand-up at the Comedy Store in 1981, as well as writing scripts for *The Young Ones*. His television programme, *Ben Elton: The Man From Auntie*, had its first series in 1990 and was about to be recommissioned. Elton made three appearances this year.

Victoria Wood broke records with no less than eight sold out appearances at the Free Trade Hall. She appeared from Monday to Thursday on two consecutive weeks. In the same year Wood sold out fifteen nights at the Royal Albert Hall in London.

Norman Wisdom was now in his late 70's enjoying a career revival after years of seclusion on the Isle Of Man. He was knighted in 2000.

The dance band leader, **Joe Loss** had passed away in 1990, but his orchestra continued to tour. When Loss was too ill to tour, he had entrusted his vocalist, Todd Miller, with musically directing the band. Singer **Joan Regan** had had an eventful life. Her biggest hit was 'If I Give My Heart To You', a cover of a Doris Day song. Later Regan moved to America. In 1984 she slipped in her shower and suffered a brain haemorrhage. Eventually, helped and encouraged by her former accompanist, Russ Conway, Regan returned to the stage in Britain.

This year saw **Rory Gallagher's** final appearance in Manchester. This was as part of a night celebrating the 40th birthday of the Fender Stratocaster guitar. Such big names as Nils Lofgren, Joe Walsh, Jeff Lynne and Robin Trower (all of whom had previously played at the Free Trade Hall) were advertised to appear at this event, but it is unclear if they actually did. Former Cricket, Sonny Curtis did turn up. Gallagher had been appearing at the Free Trade Hall since 1970. Sadly he died in 1995 aged only 47.

Jack Dee gained a reputation as a deadpan and sarcastic comedian at the Comedy Store and later on his Channel 4 programme. He won Best Stage Newcomer at the British Comedy Awards in 1991.

Lenny Henry was a ubiquitous figure on British television. The Free Trade Hall was the first night of a 28-date stand-up comedy tour.

The Bradshaws were a fictional comic Northern family created by Buzz Hawkins who also voiced all the parts such as Billy, Alf and Audrey. *The Bradshaws* first appeared on Piccadilly Radio and were incredibly popular in the north of England. Hawkins sold thousands of cassettes featuring the family.

The Care Bears held two children's shows on December 23rd: at 11.30 am and 2.30pm.

Other events at the Free Trade Hall

March 8th – *Birdscreen '93* RSPB Wildlife Films
May 21st – Manchester Scots Night
October 8th – HM Royal Marines Band

Elsewhere (Headliners Only)

Apollo- Michael Ball, Big Country, The B52's, Roy "Chubby" Brown, Dina Carroll, Clannad, Julian Clary, Shaun Colvin, Harry Connick Jr, Crowded House, Terence Trent D'Arby, Deacon Blue, Deep Purple, David Essex, The Everly Brothers, EBTG, Jan Garbareg Group, Deborah Harry, Go West, Buddy Guy, Jeff Healey Band, Hothouse Flowers, Chris Isaak, Jethro Tull, The Kinks, Little Angels, Lynyrd Skynyrd, Barry Manilow, Brian May, Pat Metheney, The Moody Blues, Van Morrison, Newman & Baddiel, Gary Numan, Poison, Gerry Rafferty, Runrig, Joe Satriani, Lily Savage, Squeeze, David Sylvian and Robert Fripp, Tears For Fears, 10cc, The The, Suzanne Vega, Paul Weller, Roy Wood.

G-Mex - The Beach Boys, Depeche Mode, Duran Duran, Gary Glitter, Go West, Iron Maiden, James, Madness, Meat Loaf, OMD, Chris Rea, Status Quo, Take That, Luther Vandross, Wet Wet Wet.

Opera House – Mary Chapin Carpenter, Nanci Griffith, Christy Moore, Daniel O'Donnell.

Palace Theatre– Aztec Camera, The Bootleg Beatles, Beverley Craven.

1994		
Feb 25th	M PEOPLE	*Sub Sub*
Feb 26th	M PEOPLE	*Sub Sub*
March 1st	TORI AMOS	
March 11th	BAND OF THE UNITED STATES AIR FORCE Tribute To Major Glenn Miller	
March 12th	SEAN HUGHES	
March 24th	ROSTAL AND SCHAEFER	
May 13th	MANCHESTER SCOTS NIGHT	
June 1st	CHRIS BARBER'S JAZZ AND BLUES BAND with Lonnie Donegan's Skiffle Group (40th Anniversary Tour)	
Sept 17th	PENGUIN CAFÉ ORCHESTRA	
Oct 28th	BAND OF THE UNITED STATES AIR FORCES AND THE RED ARMY BAND	
Oct 31st	SUEDE	
Nov 28th	THE FUREYS	
Dec 16th	THE SPINNERS	

In February the popular dance act **M People** played two sold out nights. M People formed in 1990 and were led and named after DJ Mike Pickering. Their breakthrough came with the album, *Elegant Slumming* (Deconstruction 1993) which provided the band with four Top 10 hit singles. The album also earned M People the Mercury Prize this year. *City Life* magazine commented, "a strange venue for a dance band – it's seated".

Sean Hughes was an English born Irish stand up comedian. Like so many others, he started at the Comedy Store. Hughes won the coveted Perrier Award at the Edinburgh Festival in 1990, the youngest comedian to do so.

Rostal And Schaefer were a classical piano duo who had gained fame with their *Beatles Concerto* (Parlophone 1979).

This year **Chris Barber** and **Lonnie Donegan** had a reunion to celebrate an incredible forty years since their first tours.

Chris Barber: "Then in 1994 we came to the inevitable 40th anniversary of the band, which involved what turned out to be the final set of reunions with Monty, Lonnie, Ron (Bowden) and Jim (Bray). The eight-piece band played a set, then we featured Lonnie's skiffle group and finally the 1954 line-up appeared."

Penguin Cafe Orchestra, led by multi-instrumentalist Simon Jeffes, had been releasing albums since 1976. Their breakthrough album was *Signs Of Life* (Edition EG 1986). The orchestra's mix of pop, classical, world music and ambient sounds was unique and could often be heard in advertisements and films.

Suede formed in 1989 and their success was instant. Their eponymous first album reached No. 1 and also won the Mercury Prize. This year saw the release of the band's second album, *Dog Man Star* (Nude 1994); their last record with guitarist Bernard Butler. Suede were now touring with their new guitarist, teenage prodigy Richard Oakes who replaced Butler.

The Spinners had been appearing at the Free Trade Hall since 1965 and hold the record for the most appearances at the venue with no less than 57 shows! Chris Barber is runner-up with 24 appearances. Both artists made their final appearances at the Free Trade Hall in 1994.

Mick Groves of The Spinners told me: *"There were so many great nights at the Free Trade Hall (I was) always able to see my brothers and sister and their families. But probably one story that sticks is the autographed wall. When we made our first appearances there, our attention was drawn to the wall of the room near the stage where they stored the bass travel cases. It was originally the last port of call for any conductor or 'stars' to check (their) clothing was on properly. On the wall next to the mirror were three autographs – Gracie Fields, Louis Armstrong and Yehudi Menuhin. After a while we began to tease the hallkeeper, Ron (O'Neill) about getting our names up there, but he always had a resolute 'no'.*

"Then, one year when we were appearing for the third time, he (O'Neill) came on stage just before the interval and presented each of us with a wooly cap with three Manchester enamel badges and told the audience why. Then, when we finally came off, he was standing there with a pen for us to sign the wall with those greats of music. This, he said, was because of our record number of shows at the Free Trade Hall and because we equalled the record audience numbers that those other three (Fields, Armstrong and Menuhin) had achieved, three times in one year. He also informed us that due to alterations in the choir seating, no other artistes would ever have an audience to beat our numbers. When they sold the Free Trade Hall, that wall was cut out and is now ensconced outside the upstairs bar in the Radisson Hotel."

Other events at the Free Trade Hall

May 13th – Manchester Scots Night

Elsewhere (Headliners Only)

Apollo - Michael Ball, Black Sabbath, The Bootleg Beatles, Brand New Heavies, Roy "Chubby" Brown, Jackson Browne, David Byrne, Eric Clapton, Harry Connick Junior, Crash Test Dummies, Deacon Blue, John Denver, D.Ream, East 17, Eternal, Vince Gill, Amy Grant, Nanci Griffith, Buddy Guy, Emmylou Harris, Freddie Jackson, Kool And The Gang, Level 42, Huey Lewis And The News, Joe Longthorne, Magnum, Marillion, Hank Marvin and Brian Bennett, Paul McKenna, Mirage, Van Morrison, Willie Nelson And Family, Robert Newman, Andrew Newton, Gary Numan, The Pretenders, Punt And Dennis, Queensryche, Reeves And Mortimer, David Lee Roth, Santana, Frank Skinner, Slayer, Spin Doctors, Squeeze, SWV, Whitesnake, The Wonder Stuff, Dwight Yoakam, Paul Young.

G-Mex – Phil Collins, Crowded House, Duran Duran, The Four Tops, The Temptations, UB40, Paul Weller.

Opera House – Larry Adler, Phil Cool, Elvis Costello & The Attractions, Frank Skinner, Victoria Wood.

Palace Theatre– The Chuckle Brothers, David Essex, Fascinating Aida, Julia Fordham, The Hollies, Billy Pearce, Bonnie Raitt, Solid Sixties Silver Show, Kevin "Bloody" Wilson.

1995		
Jan 14th	BLEEDING LIFE CELEBRATE JESUS	
Jan 28th	JOE JACKSON	*Paul Kelly*
Feb 11th	EDDIE IZZARD	
March 8th	*LAMB AND BEEF IN A STEW* An evening with Ian Botham and Allan Lamb	*Jerry Atkinson (Compere)*
March 10th	BAND OF THE UNITED STATES AIR FORCE 50TH ANNIVERSARY OF V.E. DAY	
May 5th	DANIEL O'DONNELL	*Mary Duff*
May 12th	MANCHESTER SCOTS NIGHT	
May 14th	THE CHIEFTAINS	
Oct 6th	BAND OF HM ROYAL MARINES, SCOTLAND	
Oct 22nd	MIKE SCOTT	
Oct 26th	BAND OF UNITED STATES AIR FORCES AND RUSSIAN ARMY BAND	
Dec 11th	THE BOOTLEG BEATLES	

Joe Jackson emerged in the post punk era as a contemporary of Elvis Costello. He had hit singles and albums in a variety of styles, most notably *Night And Day* (A&M 1982) which reached No. 3 and featured the Top 10 single, 'Steppin' Out'.' In 1984 Jackson moved to New York. Jackson was now touring to promote his most recent album, *Night Music* (Virgin 1994).

Eddie Izzard started performing stand up in the 1980's but rarely appeared on television, safeguarding his material from over exposure. His breakthrough came in 1991 when his Raised By Wolves sketch at the *Hysteria 3 AIDS* benefit was televised.

Ian Botham and **Allan Lamb** appeared in "an evening of cricketing anecdotes and funnies". These two retired international cricketers also lent their names for a meat advertising campaign.

The Chieftains made their final appearance at the Free Trade Hall. Their current album, *Long Black Veil* (RCA 1995) featured several famous guest vocalists and was their most successful album in Britain.

Mike Scott was founder member, lead singer, guitarist and songwriter of The Waterboys. The group stopped recording in the early 1990's and Scott ended up at the Findhorn Community in Scotland where he recorded his first solo album, *Bring 'Em All In* (Chrysalis 1995). Scott was touring to promote the album which reached No. 23 earlier in the autumn.

The Beatles, of course, never appeared at the Free Trade Hall, but their most successful tribute band - **The Bootleg Beatles** - did in December. Formed in 1980, the group are the longest running Beatles tribute act. In November the Bootleg Beatles had supported Oasis at Earls Court for two nights.

The Manchester Arena opened on July 25th this year and became Manchester's largest indoor venue, holding over 10,000 seats. It became the largest indoor live music venue in Britain. The venue was successively sponsored over the years by Nynex; the *Manchester Evening News* and Phones 4 Us.

Other events at the Free Trade Hall

May 12th – Manchester Scots Night

Elsewhere (Headliners Only)-

Apollo - Laurie Anderson, Joan Armatrading, Joan Baez, Anita Baker, Mary Black, The Black Crowes, Black Grape, Black Sabbath, Boyzone, Jo Brand, Roy "Chubby" Brown, Mary Chapin Carpenter, Charlatans, Billy Connolly, Ry Cooder & David Lindley, Robert Cray, Sheryl Crow, Terence Trent D'Arby, Deep Purple, Del Amitri, Celine Dion, D:Ream, Bob Dylan, EMF, The Everly Brothers, Extreme, Bryan Ferry, Green Day, Jeff Healey, Human League, Incognito, Iron Maiden, Jethro Tull, Ben E King, James Last, The Levellers, Machine Head, Marillion, Hank Marvin, Megadeth, Van Morrison, Motorhead, Alison Moyet, Jimmy Nail, The Orb, Ozzy Osbourne, PJ & Duncan, The Prodigy, Queensryche, Red Hot Chilli Peppers, Reeves & Mortimer, Runrig, Joe Satriani, Seal, Skid Row, Squeeze, The Stone Roses, Status Quo, Therapy? Thunder, Toto, Vixen, Paul Weller, Barry White.

Arena – David Bowie, Jackie Cheurg, Celine Dion, Gary Glitter, Morrissey, M People, Rod Stewart, Take That (10 nights), Wet Wet Wet.

G-Mex - Cranberries, Jimmy Nail, Prince, Simple Minds, Luther Vandross.

Opera House – Christy Moore, Tanita Tikaram.

Palace Theatre – The Bradshaws, The Chuckle Brothers, Juke Box Giants, Vanessa Mae, Glenn Miller Orchestra, Andrew Newton, Neil Sedaka.

1996		
March 8th	THE AMBASSADORS OF THE BAND OF THE UNITED STATES AIR FORCES IN EUROPE	*The Beverley Sisters; The Liberty Belles Sound Association*
April 20th	DANIEL O'DONNELL	*Mary Duff*
May 18th	LIVE CINEMA *Four Horsemen Of The Apocalypse*; Wurlitzer Organ- Jim Riggs	
May 23rd	LEE EVANS	
May 24th	LEE EVANS	
June 30th	*FAREWELL TO THE FREE TRADE HALL: MUSIC TO REMEMBER & A PARTY TO CELEBRATE* Hallé Orchestra & Choir; Kent Nagano; Michael Kennedy	
July 19th	DALAI LAMA - *COMPASSION* *The Basis For Human Happiness*	
July 21st	*A TRIBUTE TO THE LIFE AND MUSIC OF NORMAN GEORGE* with Bernie Wenton as Nat King Cole; Julian Gregory Jazz Trio; Bernard Wrigley (narrator); Northern Dance Orchestra	

This was the year that the Free Trade Hall closed its doors forever. There were a handful of events – Daniel O'Donnell; Lee Evans, a cinema event and, extraordinarily, the Dalai Lama. A sad, inauspicious end to a unique part of Manchester culture.

Films - usually of a factual nature - had been shown at the Free Trade Hall in the past, but May 18th saw a genuine attempt to widen the sort of performances in the venue. *Four Horsemen Of The Apocalypse* was a silent film from 1921 which turned unknown actor Rudolph Valentino into an international star. Inspiring a tango craze in the USA, the film was the top grossing release in that year.

Bristol comedian **Lee Evans** had won the Perrier Award in 1993. His physical style of humour reminded many people of Norman Wisdom. This Free Trade Hall appearance was part of his *Same World, Different Planet* tour.

June 30th saw the **Hallé Orchestra's** last ever concert at the Free Trade Hall. The programme included music by Delius, Elgar and Sibelius. Within three days, the orchestra began its Proms season at the Manchester Airport Big Top at Salford Quays.

His Holiness the **Dalai Lama** appeared on July 16th from 6 pm to 7.30 pm. He was speaking on "Compassion, the Basis for Human Happiness." The event was organised by The Tibet Society Of The United Kingdom.

Norman George had been a violinist with the Northern Dance Orchestra. There is a violin scholarship at the Royal Northern College Of Music in honour of his name.

Other events at the Free Trade Hall

March 27th – Mozart Festival Orchestra – The Four Seasons By Candlelight
May 9th – Hallé Orchestra – last Thursday concert at the Free Trade Hall
May 11th – Manchester Camerata – last concert at the Free Trade Hall
June 1st -Sarah Brightman with the Liverpool Philharmonic Orchestra

Elsewhere (Headliners Only)

Apollo - Tori Amos, Backstreet Boys, Michael Ball, Black Grape, Boy George, Boyzone, Roy "Chubby" Brown, Jackson Browne, Chris de Burgh, Clannad, Julian Clary, Deep Purple, Judith Durham, Steve Earle, 808 State, Ben Elton, Erasure, Eternal, Everything But The Girl, The Fugees, Garbage, Buddy Guy, Hootie And The Blowfish, Lee Hurst, Incognito, Jamiroquai, Mark Knopfler, Alison Krauss, k.d. lang, Lighthouse Family, Lightning Seeds, Joe Longthorne, Manic Street Preachers, Johnny Mathis, Megadog, Natalie Merchant, Mike And The Mechanics, Alanis Morissette, Andrew Newton, Gary Numan, Ocean Colour Scene, Ardal O'Hanlan, Orbital, Courtney Pine, PJ & Duncan, The Prodigy, Radiohead, Rage Against The Machine, Lou Reed, Reeves & Mortimer, Runrig, The Saw Doctors, Sepultra, Slade II, Sleeper, Patti Smith, Soundgarden, Bruce Springsteen, Squeeze, Suede, Suggs, Richard Thompson, Thunder, Toto, Ce Ce Winnans, Jah Wobble.

G-Mex– Bjork, Smash Hits Tour '96.

Arena - AC/DC, Shirley Bassey, Boyzone, Glen Campbell, Mary Chapin Carpenter, Ray Charles, Eric Clapton, The Cure, Def Leppard, The Eagles, East 17, Gary Glitter, R.Kelly, Kiss, Lyle Lovett, Barry Manilow, Meatloaf, Metallica, Van Morrison, Pulp, Kenny Rogers, Simply Red, Smashing Pumpkins, The Who, Tammy Wynette.

Opera House – The Blue Nile, Jools Holland And His Rhythm And Blues Orchestra.

Palace Theatre – Chris Barber's Jazz & Blues Band, Tony Bennett, David Essex, Neil And Tim Finn, The Hollies, Gary Wilmot, Victoria Wood.

Aftermath

The best account of the aftermath of the Free Trade Hall is in Parkinson-Bailey (2000) which makes genuinely painful reading. In his excellent architectural history of Manchester, he summarises the sad stages of the building's demise. The first scheme proposed was a "219 bedroom, five-star hotel to be erected within and rising" from the Free Trade Hall. There would be sixteen storeys "set in a rectangular block running at an angle of about 45 degrees across the top of the hall". Objections to this proposal came from English Heritage, the Civic Society and others.

New architects came back with a more "sensitive" plan, increasing the hotel's size by 50% with eight more storeys in a cylindrical building 270 ft tall. Objections this time came again from English Heritage and the Civic Society, but were joined by the Victorian Society and the Royal Fine Arts Commission. This resulted in a public enquiry which was set up on 21st April 1998. All five of Manchester's MPs backed the second scheme!

However, the then Deputy Prime Minister, John Prescott "determined against the scheme" and the Free Trade Hall went back on the market. Parkinson-Bailey lists the possible future uses for the building that were discussed. These included a public lecture hall, a museum of Manchester and a conference centre. The latter was particularly ironic with the proximity of the G-Mex conference venue, just yards away in the old Central Station. Many, many people felt that it was the historical significance of the Free Trade Hall that was being ignored. This was the building where Christabel Pankhurst and Annie Kenney campaigned for women's suffrage and such politicians as Churchill, Keir Hardy, Asquith and Lloyd George had all spoken. Unfortunately, Parkinson-Bailey's fine book finishes at this point and we have to use other sources for the conclusion.

In Clare Hartwell's *Manchester* (2001), John H.G. Archer wrote the section on the Free Trade Hall. He sums up the final part of the saga well and describes the scheme that was finally approved: "It will conserve only the main facade and the northern three bays of the E (east) elevation. A tower of fourteen storeys will extend along the S (south) boundary, the main entrance will remove most of the E (east) elevation, and part of the open arcade will be glazed." Inside the triangular glassed atrium of The Edwardian, Manchester visitors can see the 1950's statues by Arthur Sherwood Edwards, the framed wall plaster signed by such past performers as Gracie Fields and The Spinners and the mural. The hotel staff are happy to allow visitors to look round.

I cannot hope to improve on Archer's concluding sentences so allow me to quote them in full: "*It is extraordinary that a civic authority with such a wide range of needs and activities has chosen to sacrifice a building of such distinction that was provided originally by public subscription specifically to meet the social, spiritual and cultural needs of its citizens. Is this true regeneration or iconophobia?*"

Details Of Major Manchester Venues

VENUE	DATES ACTIVE	CAPACITY
ABC ARDWICK (known as Apollo 1938-1962), Stockport Road, Ardwick Green	1962 -1976	*2631*
APOLLO, Stockport Road, Ardwick Green	1977-present	*Seated events: stalls: 1707; circle: 986. Total 2693. Standing events: 2514 standing in stalls with 986 seated in circle. Total 3500*
ARENA, Hunts Bank	1995- present	*21000*
FREE TRADE HALL, Peter Street	1951-1996	*Stalls- 1194 Circle – 880 Balcony – 460 Total 2534 (in 1951); later reduced to 2529 .*
G-MEX (now Manchester Central)	1986-1997; 2006 -present	*9500 (end stage) ; 12500 (standing)*
HARDROCK Concert Theatre, Great Stone Street, Stretford	1972- 1975	*3000 (approximately)*
HIPPODROME, Ardwick Green	1935-1961	*3000 (approximately)*
KINGS HALL, Belle Vue	1910- 1979	*5000*
ODEON, Oxford Street	1930- 1973	*2919, reduced to 2737*
OPERA HOUSE, Quay Street	1920 – present (bingo 1979-1984)	*1920*
PALACE THEATRE, Oxford Street	1891- present (closed 1978-1980)	*3675, reduced to 1955*

The Lesser Free Trade Hall

The Lesser Hall – as distinct from the main or Large Hall- is now almost synonymous with the two Sex Pistols gigs in June and July 1976.The original aims for the smaller venue were a lot different.

The architect, Leonard C. Howitt, stated in the 1951 Commemorative Brochure, "*A new Lesser Hall was to be incorporated which would be suitable for a number of different purposes, so that the building would be of greatest possible value to citizens... Adjoining the (Peter Street) arcade is the Lesser Hall Entrance, from which stairs and a lift give access to the small hall on the second floor.*

"*Above (the promenade) Lounge is the Lesser Hall with seats for 417 people, 95 of which are in the balcony. The seating on the main floor is removable to permit dancing, small exhibitions and other functions requiring a cleared floor space. The small stage is equipped to suit amateur theatrical productions and a suite of dressing rooms and a Green Room are provided. The Lesser Hall is insulated structurally from the Large Hall so that there can be no sound transmission between the two.*"

So, despite its rather demeaning name, the Lesser Hall was about the size of a smallish school hall. Over the years the venue had been used for folk concerts, amateur, student and professional theatrical productions, as well as lectures and meetings. For example, the week before the first Sex Pistols gig saw the M.P.A. Players present The Good Old Bad Old Days, an "olde tyme music hall"!

The cost to Howard Devoto and Pete Shelley of hiring the Lesser Hall seems to vary from £26 to £32 depending on whose book one reads! Likewise, there are differing accounts about the two Sex Pistols appearances by the various people who were there in David Nolan's oral history, *I Swear I Was There – The Gig That Changed The World* (2006). The book is an enjoyable read and there are fascinating photographs by Paul Welsh and Peter Oldham. The first concert on June 4th 1976 had tickets costing 50p each and – according to the FTH's financial records – had takings of £14. This first concert is recreated at the beginning of Michael Winterbottom's film *24 Hour Party People* and makes entertaining viewing, even if Steve Coogan's portrayal of Tony Wilson is not much different to his Alan Partridge character! The second concert on July 20th 1976 had tickets costing £1 and the takings - again, according to the FTH's financial records- were £121. By now the word had spread about the Pistols and there were clearly far more people there. Footage from a short 8mm cine film of this July 20th gig is available, of course, on YouTube.

Among the other more notable performers over the years were: Pete Seeger – 1961; Paco Pena – 1973; Michael Chapman – 1973; Buzzcocks; Magazine – 1978; Richard and Linda Thompson with Simon Nicol –1981; Alexei Sayle – 1982; The Alternative Christmas Spectacular with The Fall –1982

There is some fascinating footage on YouTube of the 1978 concert featuring

Buzzcocks and Magazine. This gig took place exactly two years and a day after the second Pistols appearance. At least two cameras were used and there are full performances of Buzzcocks playing 'Ever Fallen In Love' and a cover version of the Troggs' 'I Can't Control Myself'. On the latter song, Howard Devoto rejoins his former colleagues on lead vocals. Despite being written over a decade earlier by Troggs singer, Reg Presley, the song sounds just like a Buzzcocks composition! There is a fair sized audience, mostly male with some pogoing in evidence.

The Mighty Wurlitzer at the Free Trade Hall

THE STORY OF THE WURLITZER ORGAN AT THE FREE TRADE Hall could be the subject of a "feel good" movie with a happy ending. The organ was an important part of the FTH for nearly two decades.

The organ was made by the Rudolph Wurlitzer Company in New York State in 1930 and arrived in Manchester to be installed at the new Paramount Theatre, Oxford Street. It was the only model of this type that was shipped to the United Kingdom. The organ was a huge concern with four manuals. The instrument had 20 units of pipes, placed in two chambers behind ornamental grilles on the two sides of the cinema auditorium. On 6th October 1930 Manchester audiences heard the Wurlitzer for the first time in a performance that preceded a screening of the film, *The Love Parade* which starred Maurice Chevalier and Jeanette MacDonald.

Between 1930 and 1973 the organ was continuously used at the cinema which had changed its name to the Odeon in April 1940. Over the 43 years there were no less than fourteen resident organists at the cinema. The Wurlitzer was featured on records, radio broadcasts and even television. In the late 1960's and early 1970's most major cinemas were converted into multi-screen complexes by being "twinned" or "tripled"; the ABC/ Apollo at Ardwick Green, of course, being one of the notable exceptions in the area. A group of cinema organ enthusiasts in the Manchester area saw the writing on the wall and formed The Lancastrian Theatre Organ Trust to ensure that the famous Wurlitzer organ should stay in Manchester. A series of fundraising Sunday morning concerts took place over six years at the Odeon.

The Free Trade Hall had the space for the Wurlitzer as a place had been provided for a replacement pipe organ for the one destroyed during the air raids on Manchester. The space was occupied by the cabinets of an electronic organ that had been installed at the FTH. Reports suggest that this electronic model was, after 20 or so years, nearing the end of its useful life.

In 1973 plans for converting the Odeon were announced and Rank Leisure Services – who ran the cinema - arranged for the freeholders of the building (who owned the organ) to donate the Wurlitzer to the Trust who then donated it to the city of Manchester. After a final concert on 8th July 1973, the slow dismantling of the huge instrument began. The removal of the organ's console was even reported in the press. Different parts of the Wurlitzer were safely stored around Manchester and the council started preparing space at the FTH for the new organ chambers. The installation and reassembly of the organ took several years as work could only take place at the FTH when it was not in use for events and rehearsals.

Finally, on 8th July 1977 – exactly four years to the day after the final concert at the Odeon - the Wurlitzer was played in the FTH for the first time. Two months later, on 11th September, the official opening ceremony took place in front of the Lord Mayor of Manchester. Over the next two decades the Wurlitzer was used for broadcasting, recordings, accompanying choirs and, of course, with the Hallé Orchestra. Readers are encouraged to seek out The Entertaining Organist by Nigel Ogden (OS Digital 1993) to hear the Wurlitzer in its prime.

Less than twenty years later, the Wurlitzer was on the move again! When the FTH closed in 1996 (see Aftermath), the organ needed yet another new home. The Wurlitzer was moved by the Lancastrian Theatre Organ Trust to the Great Hall at Stockport's Town Hall and has been in regular use since 1999. The Trust and Stockport Council hold regular recitals and dances. See www.ltot.org.uk for details. The Cinema Organ Society also have a useful website: www.cinema-organs.org.uk .

Discrepancies, Myths and Mistakes

WITH DUE CREDIT TO A FELLOW MUSIC RESEARCHER, I AM writing this section not to cover myself, but to admit that this study will not be 100% complete or accurate. The official Free Trade Hall diaries are not totally reliable. For example, some jazz events are listed as "folk concert" (sic!) and often the entries are written in pencil (just like my transcription notes in the Record Office search room!) and have faded. Many events are not listed or the details are vague or misleading. Financial records only exist for a fraction of all the popular music events at the Free Trade Hall so it is hard to know how many tickets were purchased for many concerts. Some concerts seemed to change their support acts more than once in the *Manchester Evening News* listings; some support acts simply did not turn up. Reading 45 years of microfilm copies of the *Manchester Evening News* does not entitle me to a gallantry medal, but it certainly benefited my optician! Some editions of newspapers are simply unreadable. In complete contrast, the *Melody Maker* archive at the Sydney Jones Library at the University of Liverpool is in immaculate condition with sharp images of that journal. Similarly, the length of some tours could be challenged. Sometimes dates were cancelled at the last minute or extra ones added. In those pre-Internet days, the main source of information was in the weekly music press - or from the box office or ticket agency.

The headline/support slot differentiation is challenging too. Some concerts were effectively festivals with up to a dozen "headliners"; some tours had all three acts rotating the headline slot; some printed tickets are simply wrong. Someone on eBay was selling Free Trade Hall tickets for the Allman Brothers Band (whose gig never happened at the Free Trade Hall!) so why have a souvenir of a non-event?

The "Elsewhere" sections are not intended to be complete or definitive, but merely to provide the reader with a wider sense of the popular music and entertainment scene in Manchester. Each venue deserves its own history and I would encourage readers to pursue such studies if they wish.

There could be a separate chapter of cancelled Free Trade Hall concerts which would include - besides The Allman Brothers - The Bee Gees, Laura Nyro, Bread, Eno & The Winkies, Free, Monty Python, Tim Hardin and many, many more.

The details for many concerts aimed at the Irish, Indian/ Pakistani, Chinese and Scots communities are often notoriously vague. The entry, for example, for "Indian Cultural Concert" is not meant to insult, but is copied straight from the Free Trade Hall archives or the *Manchester Evening News*. Any information on any gaps will be welcomed.

For Further Study

AS WELL AS THE IMPORTANCE OF THE HISTORY OF BLACK music at the Free Trade Hall, a history of women and music at the Free Trade Hall needs emphasising. It is noticeable that virtually all the commentators about the venue have been male. Women performers, however, have been central to the history of popular music at the Free Trade Hall from 1951 to 1996.

Again, these categories are just to save time and space. The list is not exhaustive.

All Female Bands: Birtha, The Fairer Sax, Fanny, Girlschool, The Nolans, Diana Ross And The Supremes, The Runaways, The Three Degrees

Blues, Gospel, Jazz and Skiffle : Marian Anderson, Beryl Bryden, June Christy, Sugar Pie DeSanto, Ella Fitzgerald, Astrud Gilberto, Karen Hagen, Billie Holiday, Cleo Laine, Carmen McRae, Otillie Patterson, Bonnie Raitt, Irene Reid, Annie Ross (Lambert, Hendricks & Ross), Jeri Southern, Sister Rosetta Tharpe, Big Mama Thornton, Sarah Vaughan, Sheila Walsh, Clara Ward, Nancy Whiskey, Nancy Wilson, Yana

Soul : Roberta Flack, Gladys Knight, Nina Simone, Deniece Williams

Country, Folk and Folk Rock : Joan Baez, Paddie Bell, Mary Black, Anne Briggs, Isla Cameron, Lorna Campbell (Ian Campbell Folk Group), June Carter, Judy Collins, Sandy Denny (Fotheringay), Julie Felix, The Grehan Sisters, Emmylou Harris, Jacqueline & Bridie, Adrienne Johnston (The Johnstons), Dolores Keane (De Danaan), Sandra Kerr, Licorice McKechnie (Incredible String Band), Jacqui McShee (Pentangle), Lynda Meeks (The Fivepenny Piece), Mary O'Hara, Maddy Prior (Steeleye Span), Buffy Sainte-Marie, Peggy Seeger, Rose Simpson (Incredible String Band), Hylda Sims, Isla St Clair, Lyn Taylor, Linda Thompson, Mary Travers (Peter, Paul & Mary), Lal and Norma Waterson (The Watersons)

Humorists : Joyce Grenfell, Anna Russell, Victoria Wood

Pop and M.O.R. : Shirley Bassey, Eve Boswell, Elkie Brooks, Karen Carpenter, Petula Clark, Rita Coolidge, Kiki Dee, Barbara Dickson, Diana Dors, Judith Durham, Sheena Easton, Agnetha Faltskog (Abba), Gracie Fields, Judy Garland, Annafrid Lyngstad (Abba), Nana Mouskouri, Nina (Nina & Frederick), Esther Ofarim, Suzi Quatro, Lita Roza, Mari Wilson

Singer Songwriters: Tori Amos, Tasmin Archer, Joan Armatrading, Beverley Craven, Claire Hammill, Rickie Lee Jones, Carole King, K.D. Lang, Linda Lewis, Holly Near, Sinead O'Connor, Dory Previn, Judie Tzuke

Women in bands : Maggie Bell (Stone The Crows), Bjork (Sugarcubes), Briana Corigan (Beautiful South), Debbie Harry (Blondie) Sonja Kristina (Curved Air),

Natalie Merchant (10,000 Maniacs), Margo Timmins (Cowboy Junkies), Tina Weymouth (Talking Heads)

SELECT BIBLIOGRAPHY

Bacon Tony, London Live Balafon Books 1999

Badman Keith, The Beach Boys Backbeat Books 2004

Barber Chris with Shipton Alan, Jazz Me Blues - The Autobiography Of Chris Barber Equinox Publishing 2014

Beale Robert, The Hallé - A British Orchestra in the 20th Century (Music, Money, Maestros & Management) Forsyth Brothers 2000

Bean JP, Singing From The Floor: A History Of British Folk Clubs Faber 2014

Birch Bill, Keeper Of The Flame – Modern Jazz In Manchester 1946-1972 Privately Published 2010

Blamey John, A Howling Wind- Pub Rock And The Birth Of New Wave Soundcheck Books 2011

Boyd Joe, White Bicycles : Making Music In The 1960's Serpents Tail 2005

Bragg Billy, Roots, Radicals, Rockers – How Skiffle Changed The World Faber & Faber 2017

Celmins Martin, Duster Bennett - Jumping At Shadows - The Authorised Biography Jet Martin Publishing 2007

Collins Phil, Not Dead Yet - The Autobiography Arrow 2016

Creasy Martin, Legends On Tour; The Pop Package Tours Of The 1960's Tempus Publishing 2007

Cummins Kevin, Looking For The Light Through The Pouring Rain Faber & Faber 2009

Eyles Allan, Odeon Cinemas 2: From J. Arthur Rank To The Multiplex CTA 2005

Fletcher Tony, A Light That Never Goes Out Heinemann 2012

Fordham John, The Knowledge : Jazz Quadrille 2015

Frame Pete, The Restless Generation Rogan House 2007

Garner Ken, In Session Tonight : The Complete Radio 1 Recordings BBC Books 1993

Godbolt Jim, A History Of Jazz In Britain 1950 - 70 Quartet 1989

Hartwell Clare, Hyde Matthew and Pevsner Nikolaus, The Buildings Of England Lancashire: Manchester And The South East Yale University Press 2004

Hartwell Clare, Manchester- Pevsner Architectural Guide Penguin 2001

Heylin Clinton, Anarchy In The Year Zero : The Sex Pistols, The Clash And The Class Of '76 Route 2016

Heylin Clinton, Behind The Shades The Biography – Take Two Penguin 2001

Heylin Clinton, Judas ! Route 2016

Heylin Clinton, Revolution In The Air : The Songs Of Bob Dylan Vol 1: 1957-73 Constable 2010

Heylin Clinton, Bob Dylan Stolen Moments : The Ultimate Reference Book Wanted Man 1988

Hingley Tom, Carpet Burns – My Life With Inspiral Carpets Route 2012

Hjort Christopher, Strange Brew: Eric Clapton & The British Blues Boom 1965-1970 Jawbone 2007

Houghton Richard, The Who - I Was There Red Planet Publishing 2017

Innes Brian, A Long Way From Pasadena Montgaillard 2001

Larkin Colin, The Virgin Encyclopedia Of Popular Music (Fourth Edition) Virgin Books 2002

Lee C.P., Like The Night: Bob Dylan And The Road To The Free Trade Hall Helter Skelter 1998

Lee C.P., Shake Rattle And Rain - Popular Music Making In Manchester 1955-1995 Hardinge Simpole 2002

Lee C.P., When We Were Thin Hotun Press 2007

Lewisohn Mark, The Complete Beatles Chronicle Chancellor Press 1996

Manning Toby, The Rough Guide To Pink Floyd Rough Guides 2006

Marr Johnny Set The Boy Free – The Autobiography Arrow Books 2016

Melly George, Owning Up: The Trilogy Penguin Books 2000

McDevitt Chas, Skiffle -The Definitive Inside Story Robson Books 1997

Middles Mick, From Joy Division To New Order: The Factory Story Virgin 1996

Middles Mick, Red Mick Headline Books 1993

Middles, Mick & Reade, Lindsay - The Life of Ian Curtis Torn Apart - Omnibus Press 2006

Morrissey, Autobiography Penguin Classics 2013

Moules Joan, Our Gracie – The Life Of Dame Gracie Fields Hale 1983

Nash Graham, Wild Tales: A Rock & Roll Life Penguin 2014

Nolan David, I Swear I Was There: The Gig That Changed The World 2006

Independent Music Press

Parkinson-Bailey John J, Manchester- An Architectural History Manchester University Press 2000

Paytress Mark, I Was There: Gigs That Changed The World Bounty Books 2012

Porter Dick & Needs Kris, Parallel Lives -Blondie Omnibus Press 2017

Rees Dafydd & Crampton Luke, Q Rock Stars Encyclopedia Dorling Kindersley 1999

Rice Tim, Rice Jo, Gambaccini Paul & Read Mike Guinness British Hit Albums Second Edition Guinness Books 1986

Robb John, The North Will Rise Again : Manchester Music City (1977-1996) Aurum 2010

Roberts David, McAleer Dave and others, British Hit Singles & Albums Guinness World Records Limited 2004

Rogan Johnny, Morrissey & Marr: The Severed Alliance Omnibus Press 2012

Ryan Martin, Friends Of Mine - Punk In Manchester 1976-1978 Empire Publications 2018

Sinker Mark (ed), A Hidden Landscape Once A Week Strange Attractor Press 2018

Strong Martin C, The Great Folk Discography Volume 1 Polygon 2010

Southall Derek J. The Golden Years Of Manchester Picture Houses The History Press 2012

Spence Simon, Happy Mondays: Excess All Areas, A Biography Aurum Press 2014

Sumner Bernard, Chapter & Verse Bantam Books 2014

Sykes Bill, Sit Down ! Listen To This! The Roger Eagle Story Empire Publications 2012

Turner Alwyn W, Halfway To Paradise: The Birth Of British Rock V&A Publishing 2008

Van Der Kiste John, Roy Wood. The Move, Wizzard And Beyond privately published 2014

Wakeman Rick, Grumpy Old Rock Star And Other Wondrous Stories Preface 2008

Wallis Ian, American Rock 'N' Roll : The UK Tours 1956 -72 Music Mentor Books 2003

Wallis Ian, More American Rock 'N' Roll : The UK Tours 1973-84 Music Mentor Books 2012

Walters Neal & Mansfield Brian (eds), Music Hound: Folk : The Essential Guide Visible Ink 1998

Weird & Gilly, Mick Ronson - The Spider With The Platinum Hair Music Press books 2017

Williams, David, The First Time We Met The Blues, Music Mentor Books 2009

Williamson Nigel, The Rough Guide To The Blues Rough Guides 2007

Woolf Kurt, The Rough Guide To Country Music Rough Guides 2000

Wyke Terry, A Hall For All Seasons Charles Hallé Foundation 1996

Wyman Bill, Rolling With The Stones Dorling Kindersley 2002

Official Documents

Free Trade Hall Archives – diaries 1951- 1988; financial records; correspondence; programmes; posters; flyers; ticket stubs

Manchester Free Trade Hall Commemorative Brochure Manchester City Council 1951

All quotes and statistics from the Free Trade Hall Archive Collection (GB127. M619/1/1) courtesy of Manchester Libraries, Information and Archives. Special thanks to Sarah Hobbs and her colleagues at Archives Plus Search Room.

Newspapers and Magazines

City Life; The Guardian; Manchester Evening News; Melody Maker; Mojo; Mole Express; New Manchester Review; New Musical Express; Ptolemaic Terrascope; Shindig; The Stage & Television Today; Zigzag

Websites

There are hundreds of websites which offer gigographies of varying accuracy. Everyone can make mistakes, but some people have turned this into an art form ! The following websites, however, have been especially useful:

www.bradfordtimeline.co.uk/music.htm

www.discogs.com

www.manchesterbeat.com

www.marmaladeskies.co.uk

www.songkick.com

www.theballadeers.com

www.45worlds.com

SELECTED DISCOGRAPHY

THE FOLLOWING WERE RECORDED AT THE FREE TRADE HALL and have been officially released. This is a brief guide and makes no attempt to be comprehensive. Lack of space has meant that I have not included bootlegs and radio broadcasts. The Discogs website is recommended for further information. I have not seen or heard all of these recordings so inclusion is not a recommendation. All are CD's.

Chris Barber's Jazz Band - *Chris Barber's Jazz Band With Special Guest Sister Rosetta Tharpe 1957* (Lake Records)

Dave Brubeck Quartet with Paul Desmond – *At The Free Trade Hall 1958* 2 CD set (Solar)

Jack Bruce Band – *Live '75* (Esoteric)

Ornette Coleman Trio – *Manchester Free Trade Hall 1966* 2 CD set (Hi Hat)

Rev Gary Davis – *Manchester Free Trade Hall 1964* (Document)

Miles Davis Quintet – *Manchester Concert Complete 1960* (Lone Hill Jazz)

Bob Dylan - *Live 1966 The Bootleg Series Vol.4* 2 CD set (Columbia)

Duke Ellington Orchestra – *Duke Ellington's 70th Birthday Concert* (Solid State)

Genesis – *Genesis Live* (Charisma) – one track "Return Of the Giant Hogweed"

Stan Kenton – *Kenton '63 Concert In England Featuring Cuban Fire* (Astral Jazz)

Kingdom Come with Arthur Brown – *Live 1973* (Gonzo Multimedia)

George Lewis with Ken Colyer's Jazzmen – *The Famous Manchester Free Trade Hall Concert – First Half* (504)

The George Lewis Ragtime Band – *In Concert 1959: Manchester Free Trade Hall Second Half* (504)

Shelly Manne And His Men -*West Coast Jazz In England* (Solar)

Don McLean with John Platania & The Jamie Marshall Band – *Live In Manchester* Special edition : 2 CD set with bonus DVD (Wienerworld)

Pete Seeger- *Pete Seeger In England* 2 CD set; Disc 2 – Free Trade Hall (Spiral Earth)

Jack Teagarden & Earl Hines – *All Stars In Concert, Manchester Free Trade Hall 1957* Volumes 1 & 2 (Upbeat)

Various Artists : *Chris Barber Presents The Lost And Found Series*

Volume 1 – Sister Rosetta Tharpe with Chris Barber Band (1957); Sonny Terry & Brownie McGhee (1958) (Classic Studio T)

Volume 2 – Muddy Waters with Otis Spann with Chris Barber Band (1958); also includes Sonny Terry & Brownie McGhee, Champion Jack Dupree and Louis Jordan, recorded elsewhere (Classic Studio T)

Volume 3 – Sonny Boy Williamson with Chris Barber Band (1964) ; also features

Jimmy Witherspoon, recorded elsewhere (Classic Studio T)

Various Artists : *American Folk Blues Festival Live In Manchester 1962* (Rhythm and Blues)

Many bootleg recordings are now,of course, on YouTube, thus cutting out the "middle man" and the need to attend record fairs and purchase such recordings on vinyl, cassette or compact disc. To give the reader a sample of what is available, I have come across live recordings of Tori Amos, The Blue Nile, The Byrds, Johnny Cash, Genesis, Judas Priest, Pink Floyd and Queen.

SELECTED VIDEOGRAPHY (all DVD unless stated)

The American Folk-Blues Festival The British Tours 1963-1966 (Reelin' In The Years)

Don't Look Back – 65 Tour Deluxe Edition (Sony/BMG)

Bob Dylan - No Direction Home (Apple)

Happy Mondays - One Louder (Wienerworld) VHS

Don McLean – Live In Manchester (MVD Visual)

There are tantalising glimpses of the Free Trade Hall interior on YouTube. From 1995 there is a performance of "Shenandoah" on the Wurlitzer organ on the PadsterDood channel. The camera briefly gives us a view of the empty auditorium right up to the Centre Circle and Balcony. If the reader does not mind thirty minutes of Richard Strauss's Lieder, there is excellent footage of a 1990 concert of Kiri Te Kanawa accompanied by George Solti. The Free Trade Hall stage is decorated with exotic plants. Minor members of the Royal Family are in the audience. Excerpts of the 1966 Bob Dylan concert ("Like A Rolling Stone") and the Happy Mondays "rave" are all over YouTube.

ACKNOWLEDGEMENTS

The following have helped and encouraged me in all sorts of ways with this project: Every effort has been made to contact the copyright holders.

Norman Bamforth; Gary Canning; George Dawes; Alan Duffy; Simon Frith; Marc Gleeson; Mick Groves; Clinton Heylin; Mark Hodkinson; Sue Lawson; Spencer Leigh, Sara Littler, Mick Middles; Geoff Read; Steve Shepherd: Andrew Willan. "I would like to thank the staff at the following places: the former Greater Manchester Record Office, The Manchester Room at the temporary City Library on Deansgate, Archives Plus in Manchester Central Library, Sydney Jones Library at Liverpool University and the British Library Reading Room, Boston Spa. Thanks to all at Empire Publications. All photographs by Brian Smith are copyright and used by his kind permission.

Illustrations reproduced with the kind permission of Manchester Libraries, Information And Archives.

Index of Headlining Acts

Budgie
10/9/75; 21/5/76
Papa Bue And His Viking Jazz Band
30/9/62
Eric Burdon And War
2/2/71
Brian Burn's Boogie Bouncers
19/4/52
The Buskers
21/5/69
Billy Butler Band/ Orchestra
25/3/52; 10/10/52; 9/10/53
Max Bygraves
27/2/76
The Byrds
11/5/ 71

John Cale
27/11/75; 22/4/77
Eddie Calvert
12/03/56
Camel
30/6/75; 9/4/76; 21/2/77; 23/9/77; 16/9/78
Isla Cameron
04/04/64
Alex Campbell
24/5/64; 4/12/64; 19/11/66; 30/11/68
Ian Campbell Folk Group
30/3/63; 4/4/64; 4/12/64; 27/11/65; 31/3/67; 5/5/67
Canned Heat
13/9/70
Freddy Cannon
10/5/60
Capability Brown
18/5/73
Captain Beefheart
1/4/72; 5/4/73; 8/6/74; 15/11/75
Caravan
20/4/71; 2/12/75; 30/4/76; 27/9/77;
The Care Bears Christmas Show
23/12/93
The Carpenters
19/2/74
Jasper Carrott
25/5/76
Frank Carson
13/3/82
Benny Carter
03/12/66
Sydney Carter
20/2/65
Martin Carthy & Dave Swarbrick
6/4/68; 21/12/68; 25/4/69
Johnny Cash
4/5/68; 3/9/73
Keith Chalkley Trio
28/9/64
The Chameleons
13/9/85
The Charlatans
11/06/91
Ray Charles And His Orchestra And The Raelets
18/5/63; 11/7/64; 21/4/67; 29/9/71
Chas And Dave
19/11/82
Chicago
28/1/77; 29/1/77
Chicago Blues All-Stars
31/10/70
The Chieftains
8/10/76; 14/11/77; 22/2/80; 22/11/82; 19/9/87;14/5/95;
Chilli Willi And The Red Hot Peppers
30/1/75
Chinese Acrobats
03/11/80
Chinese Concert
07/06/81
The Chippendales
27/5/91
Ian Christie Trio
11/10/59
June Christy
25/2/61
Gladys Church
25/3/52
Captain Peter Churchill And Mrs Peter Churchill Gc
08/04/52
Clan Alba Featuring Dick Gaughan
27/9/92
The Clancy Brothers And Tommy Makem
18/10/65; 5/1/70
John Cooper Clarke
28/5/78; 25/6/79
Petula Clarke
27/3/73
Clarke-Boland Big Band
15/2/69
Julian Clary
19/5/90
Buck Clayton
18/3/67
Buck Clayton All-Stars
26/09/59
Robinson Cleaver
02/09/78
Jimmy Cliff
11/11/72
Alan Clive
31/5/56
Commander Cody And His Lost Planet Airmen
26/1/76
Leonard Cohen
12/9/74; 19/5/76
Ornette Coleman Trio
14/5/66; 28/4/92
Colosseum
21/4/70
Ken Colyer
27/04/57
Come Alive For '85 – Cnd Extravaganza
09/02/85
The Commodores
21/4/78
Perry Como
04/04/75
Eddie Condon And His All-Star Jazzmen
1/2/57;
Harry Connick Junior
24/5/91
Ray Conniff And Orchestra
01/10/73
Billy Connolly
10/1/75; 10/10/75; 27/6/77
Construction Company
27/2/70
Russ Conway
01/04/60
Ry Cooder
27/1/77
Chick Corea Electrik Band
06/10/90

19/2/66; 10/2/67; 26/11/69
Jack Elliott
04/06/65
E.L.O.
9/5/72; 19/3/73; 18/2/74; 17/1/76; 19/6/76
El Sali And His Spanish Dance Company
06/01/70
Ben Elton
20/3/93; 5/4/93; 27/5/93
Elvisly Yours
15/5/83
Emerson, Lake And Palmer
7/12/70; 22/3/71; 10/12/71; 13/11/72
The Enid
9/11/79; 16/5/85
An Entertainment Of Rare, Comic And Curious Music
21/11/59
The Joe Esposito Show
15/5/83
David Essex
9/11/74; 30/9/81
Sleepy John Estes
22/10/64; 29/9/66
Gil Evans Orchestra
27/2/78
Lee Evans
23/5/96; 24/5/96
The Everly Brothers
22/4/60; 20/9/72
Every Which Way
26/2/71
Exodus
25/05/78

The Faces
25/10/71; 18/6/72; 23/12/72; 11/12/73
The Fairer Sax
04/09/91
Fairport Convention
6/2/70; 6/11/70; 20/11/71; 5/12/73
Adam Faith
19/2/60
The Fall
22/12/86; 13/7/89; 3/10/92
Georgie Fame
27/4/68
Family
21/9/68; 16/11/70; 23/11/71; 5/12/72; 26/1/73; 21/4/73
Fanny
21/5/73
Simon Fanshawe
22/3/87
Farewell To The Free Trade Hall
30/6/96
Faust
6/6/73
Jose Feliciano
8/3/73; 19/4/74
Julie Felix
4/6/65; 25/4/66; 4/6/67; 20/1/68; 5/11/68; 8/3/69; 30/1/70; 12/2/71
Pete Fenton Orchestra
25/11/52
Maynard Ferguson And His Anglo-American Orchestra
07/10/67
Kathleen Ferrier
16/11/51
Festival Flamenco Gitaro 1967
14/4/67
Festival Flamenco Gitaro 1968
08/05/68
Festival For Racial Equality
28/05/78
Festival Of Folk
03/03/71
Festival Of Folk Dancing
15/10/60
Festival Of The Millions
22/12/86
Gracie Fields
09/09/64
Ella Fitzgerald
17/5/58; 9/5/59;12/3/60; 11/3/61; 24/2/62; 2/3/63; 8/4/64; 13/4/65; 19/2/66; 10/2/67; 24/5/69; 25/4/77
Five Hand Reel
26/5/78
The Fivepenny Piece
2/6/73; 24/10/73; 22/5/74; 1/2/75; 20/3/76; 2/10/76; 10/7/77; 19/4/78; 13/5/79
Roberta Flack
17/1/73
Fogwell Flax
6/7/81
Fleetwood Mac
29/4/69; 31/5/73
The Flying Burrito Brothers
20/9/76
Folk/CND
04/12/64
Folk Dance Festival
10/10/59
Folk Explorations
21/12/68
Folk Explorations No 2
10/05/69
Folk Festival '68
09/02/68
Folk Hootenanny
19/11/66
Folk Meets Jazz
22/9/67
Folk Song Ancient And Modern
14/2/66
Folk Song '66
22/10/66
Folk Special
24/5/68
Clinton Ford
25/3/62; 26/12/62
Emile Ford And The Checkmates
30/1/60
John Forde
10/10/52
Foster And Allen
28/5/83; 18/2/86; 31/10/87; 14/4/89
Fotheringay
20/3/70; 21/11/70
Four Horsemen Of The Apocalyse – Live Cinema
18/5/96
Peter Frampton
14/10/74
Frank Chickens
22/03/87
Andy Fraser Band
29/3/75
The Four Folk
22/9/67
Bud Freeman
18/3/67
The Four Freshmen
24/3/62
Dean Friedman
8/4/82

Tubby Hayes
14/10/57; 24/11/58; 23/11/59; 3/9/60
Head, Hands And Feet
24/3/72
Ted Heath BandOrchestra
21/1/55; 7/5/55; 19/1/57; 13/9/58; 9/12/60; 17/2/62; 1/12/62; 14/5/89; 21/4/90; 25/4/92
Heavy Metal Kids
09/06/77
Hedva And David
07/05/69
Henry Cow
8/6/74
Lenny Henry
15/10/93
Woody Herman And His All Stars
18/04/59
Woody Herman Orchestra
14/3/66; 10/2/68; 16/5/69; 4/12/70
The High Level Ranters
13/2/70
Steve Hillage
23/2/79; 6/11/79
The Hi-Lo's
13/9/58
Earl Hines All Stars
5/10/57; 18/3/67
Billie Holiday
12/02/54
The Hollies
25/4/71; 20/5/74
John Lee Hooker
21/10/62; 15/10/65; 26/10/68; 15/2/69; 15/7/88; 8/7/90
Hoot'nanny
24/5/64
Bob Hope
27/10/62; 25/1/74
Lightnin' Hopkins
22/10/64
Hot Chocolate
10/6/74
Hot Gossip Road Show
26/11/81
The Houghton Weavers
28/11/79; 26/4/80; 14/2/81; 6/7/81; 13/2/82; 25/3/90
Howlin' Wolf
22/10/64; 6/12/64; 31/5/69
Sean Hughes
12/03/94
Hullabaloo
04/04/64
Humble Pie
31/10/72; 17/3/73; 20/11/74
Hunter And Ronson
21/3/75
Ian Hunter's Overnight Angels
8/6/77
Mississippi John Hurt
08/05/64
Nada Hussein
01/02/88
Trevor Hyett
28/05/78

If
26/8/71
Incantation
3/3/87
Incredible String Band
11/11/67; 2/3/68; 18/10/68; 31/10/69; 18/7/70; 24/10/70; 29/10/71; 5/11/73
Indian Variety Concert
18/5/80; 23/5/81; 22/5/83
International Folk Dance Festival
14/10/61
Inti Illimani
22/10/84
Tipper Irie
22/3/87
Irish Christmas Concert
19/12/79; 19/12/80
Irish National Concert
16/3/57; 14/3/67
Irish Traditional Concert
09/02/80
Irish Variety Concert
3/10/81; 15/3/82;
Irish Variety - St Patrick's Day Concert
06/03/87
It Bites
07/07/89
Burl Ives
20/5/79
Eddie Izzard
11/2/95;
George GP Jackson
11/02/74
Joe Jackson
28/1/95;
Jump Jackson
21/10/62
Oliver Jackson
18/3/67
Jackson Heights
26/2/71; 2/10/72
Jack The Lad
2/11/76
Jacqueline And Bridie
22/10/66; 04/11/67
James
18/3/89; 17/12/92
Harry James Orchestra
2/10/70; 22/10/71
Horace James
30/3/62
Jimmy James & The Vagabonds
3/5/74
Bert Jansch (See Also Pentangle)
13/2/67; 21/4/73; 29/11/74
Keith Jarrett
6/11/82
Jazz And Joplin Concert
16/10/87
Jazz At The Phil
24/2/62
Jazz At The Philharmonic
17/5/58; 9/5/59; 12/3/60; 3/12/66
Jazz Couriers
14/10/57
Jazz From A Swinging Era
18/3/67
Jazz From Carnegie Hall
20/9/58
Jazz From The Ronnie Scott Club
03/09/60
Jazz Matinee
06/04/57
Jazz Panorama
23/11/59
Jesus And Mary Chain
01/11/89
Jethro Tull
6/5/69; 2/10/69; 3/10/70; 28/3/72
The J. Geils Band
02/06/80

A.l. Lloyd
27/11/65
Henry Locke
10/10/52
Hank Locklin
8/9/75
Nils Lofgren
7/5/76
Laurie London
29/3/58
London Ragtime Orchestra
16/10/87
Lonesome Jimmy Lee
15/10/65
Lone Star
10/10/77
Loose Tubes
25/3/88
Los Paraguayos
21/2/69
Joe Loss Orchestra
23/5/93
Dennis Lotis
14/5/89; 21/4/90; 25/4/92
Jacques Loussier Trio
24/11/66; 10/10/67; 19/3/68; 8/10/68; 17/10/69; 21/10/70; 15/10/71; 20/10/73; 22/3/75; 1/10/92
Love
29/5/74; 6/5/75
Ray Lynam And The Hillbillies
07/04/77
Lynyrd Skynyrd
11/02/76
Humphrey Lyttelton
3/5/52; 16/9/56; 6/4/57; 28/9/57; 11/5/58; 24/12/63; 12/9/87

Ewan MacColl
28/05/78
Ken Mackintosh And His Orchestra
08/04/60; 27/8/61;
Madrid Flamenco
27/11/69
Magma
11/06/74
Magna Carta
3/3/71; 10/10/71
Mahavishnu Orchestra
17/06/73
Taleet Mahmood
01/06/79
Mahogany Rush
02/12/77
Miriam Makeba
23/4/88
Man
20/5/75; 18/3/76
Manchester's First Country And Western Festival
15/7/67
Manchester Folk Festival
27/11/65
Manchester Jazz Fair
11/10/59
Manchester Scots Night
10/05/85
Henry Mancini
12/06/74
Manfred Mann's Chapter Three
06/09/70
Manfred Mann's Earth Band
19/9/76
Mantovani
26/3/62
Margo
07/03/92
Branford Marsalis
5/9/91
John Martyn
23/10/81; 20/9/82; 13/11/84; 11/11/85; 16/9/87
The Massed Bands Of The Royal Air Force
24/10/90; 18/10/91
The Master Singers
25/3/52
Johnny Mathis
1/12/62; 5/9/73; 6/5/77
John Mayall
13/5/69; 10/11/69; 11/5/70; 8/3/71; 4/10/71; 26/4/72; 29/9/75
Dave McAdam
30/03/63
Paul McCartney And Wings
12/09/75
George McCrae
03/12/74
Chas McDevitt
29/3/58
Mississippi Fred McDowell
15/10/65
Johnny McEvoy
12/3/83; 10/3/84; 9/3/85; 6/3/87; 27/2/88; 11/3/89; 9/3/91
Rory McEwen
04/04/64
Matt McGinn
16/2/65; 22/10/66; 19/11/66
Peter McGovern
16/10/65
Roger McGuinn's Thunderbyrd
02/05/77
Kenneth McKellar
27/5/60; 27/11/84
Rod McKuen
20/5/71; 11/5/72; 18/5/75
John McLaughlin And Katia Labeque
22/6/92
John McLaughlin & The New Mahavishnu Orchestra
25/1/75
Don McLean
12/6/78; 28/4/82; 8/5/84; 16/11/87; 22/10/91; 29/10/93
The McPeake Family
22/10/66; 5/5/67
Carmen McRae
29/10/60
Ralph McTell
24/2/71; 12/11/71; 9/10/72; 16/5/73; 12/2/74; 13/11/74; 26/3/75; 21/5/77; 31/10/80
Melbourne New Orleans Jazz Band
10/12/61
George Melly
22/3/52; 12/3/56; 17/6/56; 17/2/57; 16/6/57; 11/10/59; 29/4/60; 28/5/60; 28/3/73; 4/2/74; 12/9/87
Memphis Slim
21/10/62
Sergio Mendes And Brasil 77
18/9/73
Microdisney
22/3/87
Midsummer Special
16/6/57
The Mighty Sparrow
30/3/62; 12/5/71
Eddie Miller
17/4/67

Jack Parnell And His Orchestra
31/12/53
Don Partridge
21/5/69
Ottilie Patterson
12/3/56; 26/11/56; 9/12/57; 7/3/58; 26/10/58; 5/12/58; 20/4/59; 14/12/59; 3/4/60; 8/6/60; 12/9/60; 29/1/61; 1/4/61; 12/11/61; 25/3/62; 9/9/62; 9/12/62; 3/3/63; 24/1/64; 31/5/64; 6/12/64
Robert Patterson Singers
31/10/70
Tom Paxton
14/2/66; 5/11/66; 9/10/67; 15/11/68; 20/5/70; 20/2/71; 3/11/71; 18/10/72; 16/11/73; 18/11/74; 22/10/77; 18/11/78; 2/11/81
The Peking Acrobats
27/9/88
Bill Pemberton
18/3/67
Paco Pena
27/10/71
Penguin Café Orchestra
17/9/94
The Pennine Folk
08/04/67
Pentangle
9/11/68; 18/10/69; 9/10/70; 5/11/71; 24/11/72
Peter, Paul And Mary
24/9/65
Oscar Peterson Quartet
17/5/58; 9/5/59; 2/3/63; 13/4/65; 30/9/68; 26/9/69; 18/11/90
PFM
30/5/75; 26/4/76
Sid Phillips And His Band
26/12/60
Pilot
28/4/75
Courtney Pine
22/12/86
Pink Floyd
22/6/69; 21/12/70; 11/2/72; 29/3/72; 30/3/72
Planxty
4/5/74; 17/2/75; 24/3/81

Manitas De Plata
27/2/68; 16/11/68; 3/12/69; 23/2/74; 31/3/78
The Platters
16/1/60
Cousin Joe Pleasant
08/05/64; 11/2/74
The Police
8/6/79
Potato 5 And Laurel Aitken
22/3/87
Dory Previn
23/5/77
Alan Price
29/11/77
Malcolm Price Trio
04/04/64
Procol Harum
22/1/72; 16/9/74

Mefhil E Qawwali
06/09/80
Queen
26/11/75
Quintessence
13/3/71

Mohammed Rafi
28/07/63
The Railway Children
22/3/87
Bonnie Raitt
06/12/91
The Ramones
29/9/78
Alan Randall
25/03/90
Lou Rawls
17/5/68
Johnnie Ray
12/04/58
Chris Rea
15/11/78
The Real Thing
18/6/79
The Red Army Of Russia Ensemble
17/4/93
The Red Army Band
28/10/94
Jimmy Reed
26/10/68

Lou Reed
31/5/74
Refugee
24/6/74
Renaissance
23/7/71
Don Rendell Jazz Six
26/11/57
Irene Reid
07/04/62
Rhythm With The Stars
12/3/56; 20/10/56; 24/4/57; 14/10/57
Buddy Rich Orchestra
7/4/67; 18/3/68; 28/9/68; 22/11/69; 11/11/70
Cliff Richard
10/1/59; 11/7/59; 14/11/59; 11/12/74; 18/1/75; 5/6/75; 3/11/76; 14/10/77; 16/3/91
Jonathan Richman And The Modern Lovers
15/9/77; 16/6/78
Joshua Rifkin
09/05/74
Wilf Rigby And His Orchestra
26/12/51
Ralph Rinzler
27/11/65
Marty Robbins
16/3/73
Bob Roberts
27/11/65
Paddy Roberts
22/10/60
B.a.robertson
18/4/80
Paul Robeson
4/10/58; 4/3/60
Rockpile
13/6/79
The Rolling Stones
05/03/71
Romanian National Music And Dance Company
27/4/91
Mick Ronson
11/04/74
Diana Ross And The Supremes
23/11/68
Doctor Ross
15/10/65; 11/02/74

Fritz Spiegel With The Liverpool Music Group And Peter Mountain String Quartet
21/11/59
The Spinners
27/11/65; 5/2/66; 3/6/66; 3/9/66; 9/12/66; 18/2/67; 12/5/67; 2/2/68; 26/4/68; 4/10/68; 8/2/69; 3/5/69; 27/9/69; 13/12/69; 28/2/70; 26/9/70; 19/12/70; 16/2/71; 14/5/71; 25/9/71; 11/12/71; 19/2/71; 6/5/72; 23/9/72; 9/12/72; 7/3/73; 24/6/73; 29/9/73; 1/12/73; 16/2/74; 7/9/74; 21/12/74; 15/2/75; 26/6/75; 6/9/75; 20/12/75; 28/2/76; 27/6/76; 18/12/76; 12/2/77; 26/6/77; 1/10/77; 17/12/77; 1/4/78; 14/10/78; 16/12/78; 28/3/79; 17/12/79; 15/12/80; 12/12/81; 13/11/82; 5/10/83; 12/3/88; 16/12/94
Spirit
20/6/81
Spiritualism 1991
30/3/91
St Andrew's Show
27/11/84
Cyril Stapleton And His Show Band
28/05/65
Status Quo
12/03/73
Isla St Clair
19/2/82
Steeleye Span
12/10/71; 8/4/72; 13/10/72; 10/3/73; 31/8/73; 12/5/74; 21/11/74; 1/11/75; 19/11/76; 7/2/78; 4/4/81
Martin Stephenson And The Daintees
25/5/90
Cat Stevens
3/9/71
Al Stewart
18/11/72; 2/2/73; 26/11/73; 2/6/74
Andy Stewart
27/11/84
Alan Stivell
25/05/74

Bridget St John
23/5/73
St Patrick's Concert
15/3/85
St Patrick's Gala Concert
09/03/90; 9/3/91
St Patrick's Irish Variety Concert
12/03/83; 9/3/85
St Patrick's Variety Concert
13/3/82; 27/2/88; 7/3/92
Doris Stokes
9/4/84; 21/11/84; 9/12/85
Lew Stone
01/01/59
Stone The Crows
13/7/72; 26/9/72
Strawbs
30/4/71; 12/2/72; 31/3/73; 29/9/76
Stray
1/12/72
Streetwalkers
17/6/76
Strife
16/6/74
The Stylistics
3/5/74; 27/7/75; 17/4/76
Suede
31/10/94
Sugarcubes
17/10/89
Hubert Sumlin
22/10/64; 6/12/64
Sunday Night On The Delta
19/7/59
Monty Sunshine
26/10/58; 5/12/58; 20/4/59; 8/6/60; 12/3/61; 9/7/61;
Supertramp
29/1/75
The Sweet
09/06/73
The Swingle Singers
6/3/67; 20/2/71
Swingle II
15/7/76
Roosevelt Sykes
15/10/65; 29/6/66

Taj Mahal
29/4/70
Talking Heads
1/12/79

Tangerine Dream
4/11/74; 5/11/76
Taste
15/5/70; 9/9/70
The Taverners
08/04/67
Cyril Tawney
4/12/64; 13/2/70
Eddie "Playboy" Taylor
11/02/74
James Taylor
11/07/71
Lyn Taylor
8/4/67
Jack Teagarden
05/10/57
Television
26/5/77
The Temperance Seven
2/7/61; 11/2/62
Nat Temple And His Orchestra
24/12/52; 24/12/53
The Temptations
14/4/72; 11/10/75
10CC
14/9/74; 8/3/75; 1/4/75; 3/2/76; 4/2/76
10,000 Maniacs
31/5/89
The Tenor Of Jazz
17/4/67
Ten Years After
6/5/69; 19/12/69; 25/5/70; 26/9/71; 3/10/73; 22/4/74;
Billy Ternent And His Orchestra
04/02/61
Clark Terry
03/12/66
Sonny Terry And Brownie McGhee
21/10/62; 8/5/64; 31/10/70
Jake Thackeray
3/5/77;
Sister Rosetta Tharpe
9/12/57; 5/4/58; 3/4/60; 8/5/64; 31/10/70
Miki Theodorakis
23/2/71; 25/11/71
Thin Lizzy
2/5/75; 8/10/75; 19/3/76; 29/10/76; 25/11/77; 26/11/77
Third World
1/10/81

Johnny Winter
15/2/71
Mike & Bernie Winters
06/02/77
Norman Wisdom
23/4/93
Wishbone Ash
16/6/71; 5/2/72; 4/12/72; 18/10/74; 13/11/76
Wizzard
16/09/73
The Wolfetones
14/3/74; 18/6/82; 30/10/82; 30/4/83
Donald Wolfit
22/09/60
Victoria Wood
18/8/87; 31/5/93; 1/6/93; 2/6/93; 3/6/93; 7/6/93; 8/6/93; 9/6/93; 10/6/93;
World's Greatest Jazz Band
15/12/71
Big John Wrencher
11/02/74
Bernard Wrigley
13/5/79; 21/7/96
Klaus Wunderlich
2/3/84; 30/9/86; 1/3/89; 6/3/92;

Xmas Eve Carnival
24/12/63

Stomu Yamashta And East Wind
07/01/74
Yana
24/4/57; 14/10/57; 24/11/58
Yes
1/10/71; 31/1/72; 28/11/73; 29/11/73
Faron Young
2/3/73
The Young Contemporaries
22/10/66
Yugoslav National Dancers And Singers
09/10/54

Frank Zappa And The Mothers Of Invention
27/11/70
The Zenith Six
17/6/56; 22/9/67